SOCIAL WELFARE

ADDRESSING POVERTY AND HOMELESSNESS

ISSN 1937-3295

SOCIAL WELFARE
ADDRESSING POVERTY AND HOMELESSNESS

Mark Lane

INFORMATION PLUS® REFERENCE SERIES
Formerly Published by Information Plus, Wylie, Texas

GALE
CENGAGE Learning·

Farmington Hills, Mich • San Francisco • New York • Waterville, Maine
Meriden, Conn • Mason, Ohio • Chicago

GALE
CENGAGE Learning®

Social Welfare: Addressing Poverty and Homelessness

Mark Lane

Kepos Media, Inc.: Steven Long and Janice Jorgensen, Series Editors

Project Editors: Laura Avery, Tracie Moy

Rights Acquisition and Management: Ashley Maynard, Amanda Kopczynski

Composition: Evi Abou-El-Seoud, Mary Beth Trimper

Manufacturing: Rita Wimberley

Product Design: Kristine Julien

For product information and technology assistance, contact us at
Gale Customer Support, 1-800-877-4253.
For permission to use material from this text or product,
submit all requests online at **www.cengage.com/permissions.**
Further permissions questions can be e-mailed to
permissionrequest@cengage.com

Cover photograph: © Halfpoint/Shutterstock.com.

Gale
27500 Drake Rd.
Farmington Hills, MI 48331-3535

ISBN-13: 978-0-7876-5103-9 (set)
ISBN-13: 978-1-57302-651-2

ISSN 1937-3295

This title is also available as an e-book.
ISBN-13: 978-1-57302-675-8 (set)
Contact your Gale sales representative for ordering information.

Printed in the United States of America
1 2 3 4 5   19 18 17 16 15

TABLE OF CONTENTS

PREFACE

Social Welfare: Addressing Poverty and Homelessness is part of the *Information Plus Reference Series*. The purpose of each volume of the series is to present the latest facts on a topic of pressing concern in modern American life. These topics include the most controversial and studied social issues of the 21st century: abortion, animal rights, capital punishment, care of senior citizens, crime, the environment, health care, immigration, national security, water, women, youth, and many more. Although this series is written especially for high school and undergraduate students, it is an excellent resource for anyone in need of factual information on current affairs.

By presenting the facts, it is the intention of Gale, Cengage Learning, to provide its readers with everything they need to reach an informed opinion on current issues. To that end, there is a particular emphasis in this series on the presentation of scientific studies, surveys, and statistics. These data are generally presented in the form of tables, charts, and other graphics placed within the text of each book. Every graphic is directly referred to and carefully explained in the text. The source of each graphic is presented within the graphic itself. The data used in these graphics are drawn from the most reputable and reliable sources, such as from the various branches of the U.S. government and from private organizations and associations. Every effort was made to secure the most recent information available. Readers should bear in mind that many major studies take years to conduct and that additional years often pass before the data from these studies are made available to the public. Therefore, in many cases the most recent information available in 2015 is dated from 2012 or 2013. Older statistics are sometimes presented as well, if they are landmark studies or of particular interest and no more-recent information exists.

Although statistics are a major focus of the *Information Plus Reference Series*, they are by no means its only content. Each book also presents the widely held positions and important ideas that shape how the book's subject is discussed in the United States. These positions are explained in detail and, where possible, in the words of their proponents. Some of the other material to be found in these books includes historical background, descriptions of major events related to the subject, relevant laws and court cases, and examples of how these issues play out in American life. Some books also feature primary documents or have pro and con debate sections that provide the words and opinions of prominent Americans on both sides of a controversial topic. All material is presented in an evenhanded and unbiased manner; readers will never be encouraged to accept one view of an issue over another.

HOW TO USE THIS BOOK

Aid for the poor has long been a controversial topic in the United States. Most Americans agree that society should help those who have fallen on hard times, but there are many different opinions as to how this is best accomplished. The 1990s were a time of particularly heavy debate about this issue, and with the Great Recession (which officially lasted from December 2007 to June 2009) and the passage of comprehensive health care reform in 2010, the second decade of the 21st century may be another period of debate and change in means-tested assistance. This volume also describes those who make use of the welfare system, why they use it, and what they get out of it.

Social Welfare: Addressing Poverty and Homelessness consists of eight chapters and three appendixes. Each chapter is devoted to a particular aspect of social welfare. For a summary of the information that is covered in each chapter, please see the synopses that are provided in the Table of Contents. Chapters generally begin with an overview of the basic facts and background information on the chapter's topic, then proceed to examine subtopics of particular interest. For example, Chapter 6,

The Housing Problem, begins with a discussion of the rising cost of housing in the United States and the degree to which this phenomenon contributes to homelessness. The chapter then provides information about the various forms of government housing assistance that attempt to address this problem, outlines the shortcomings in these assistance programs, and describes the living situations of those who have been forced into homelessness. Readers can find their way through each chapter by looking for the section and subsection headings, which are clearly set off from the text. They can also refer to the book's extensive Index if they already know what they are looking for.

Statistical Information

The tables and figures featured throughout *Social Welfare: Addressing Poverty and Homelessness* will be of particular use to readers in learning about this topic. These tables and figures represent an extensive collection of the most recent and valuable statistics on social welfare, as well as related issues—for example, graphics cover the amount of money spent each year for various government welfare programs, the demographics of poverty, child poverty rates in high-income countries, and the number of people without health insurance in the United States. Gale, Cengage Learning, believes that making this information available to readers is the most important way to fulfill the goal of this book: to help readers understand the issues and controversies surrounding social welfare and reach their own conclusions.

Each table or figure has a unique identifier appearing above it for ease of identification and reference. Titles for the tables and figures explain their purpose. At the end of each table or figure, the original source of the data is provided.

To help readers understand these often complicated statistics, all tables and figures are explained in the text. References in the text direct readers to the relevant statistics. Furthermore, the contents of all tables and figures are fully indexed. Please see the opening section of the Index at the back of this volume for a description of how to find tables and figures within it.

Appendixes

Besides the main body text and images, *Social Welfare: Addressing Poverty and Homelessness* has three appendixes. The first is the Important Names and Addresses directory. Here, readers will find contact information for a number of government and private organizations that can provide further information on aspects of social welfare. The second appendix is the Resources section, which can also assist readers in conducting their own research. In this section the author and editors of *Social Welfare: Addressing Poverty and Homelessness* describe some of the sources that were most useful during the compilation of this book. The final appendix is the Index. It has been greatly expanded from previous editions and should make it even easier to find specific topics in this book.

COMMENTS AND SUGGESTIONS

The editors of the *Information Plus Reference Series* welcome your feedback on *Social Welfare: Addressing Poverty and Homelessness*. Please direct all correspondence to:

Editors
Information Plus Reference Series
27500 Drake Rd.
Farmington Hills, MI 48331-3535

CHAPTER 1
POVERTY AND HOMELESSNESS IN THE UNITED STATES

The U.S. government, like the governments of other developed nations, administers a number of programs that are intended to provide for the basic needs of poor and disadvantaged citizens. These programs are collectively called social welfare programs and can take a variety of forms, including direct financial payments, assistance with food purchases, housing aid, and free health care. Compared with other developed nations, the social welfare system in the United States is modest in scope, with eligibility requirements that frequently exclude all but the poorest of citizens and time limits that are meant to keep individuals and families from becoming permanently dependent on government aid.

Modern social welfare policy has its roots in the so-called English Poor Laws, which were first implemented during the late 16th century and then codified by Queen Elizabeth I (1533–1603) in the Act for the Relief of the Poor in 1601, which made local government authorities responsible for aiding the indigent. During the colonial period in U.S. history, social welfare policy represented an extension of the English Poor Laws, with programs and institutions created at the colonial level and with large variations in benefits and management from colony to colony. After U.S. independence, there remained questions about the constitutionality of the federal government's involvement in social welfare. It was only with establishment of the Freedmen's Bureau, which was created in 1865 to aid newly liberated slaves after the Civil War (1861–1865), that a precedent was established for the federal management of social welfare programs in emergency situations.

During the Great Depression (1929–1939) the U.S. national unemployment rate rose as high as 25%, and public opinion shifted markedly in favor of a federal social welfare system that would operate permanently, rather than only in emergency situations. President Franklin D. Roosevelt (1882–1945) laid the groundwork for the modern U.S. welfare system with his New Deal, which consisted of a set of laws that were passed between 1933 and 1938 to stabilize the country's economy and provide relief to the poor and unemployed. Among the most prominent New Deal programs were the Works Progress Administration, which employed many of those who had lost their jobs during the Depression in a wide variety of public works projects, and the Social Security Act, which established a permanent system of retirement benefits, unemployment insurance, and aid to poor and handicapped children. This last feature of the act, which established the federal Aid to Dependent Children program, was expanded during the 1960s, and the program was renamed Aid to Families with Dependent Children (AFDC). Roosevelt also established the first national Food Stamp Program, which provided assistance with food purchases. This program was later discontinued before being revived during the 1960s, when the U.S. welfare system was expanded.

Besides the expansion of the AFDC and the reestablishment of a federal food assistance program, the 1960s saw the establishment of Medicare, which provides health care to retirees, and Medicaid, which provides health care to the poor and disabled. These were crucial parts of President Lyndon B. Johnson's (1908–1973) War on Poverty, which consisted of a set of legislative initiatives that grew out of the concern for social justice mobilized during the civil rights movement.

The poverty rate in the United States decreased substantially in the wake of Johnson's antipoverty initiatives, but public support for social programs waned in the decades that followed. Increasing opposition to social welfare programs culminated with the Personal Responsibility and Work Opportunity Act of 1996 (PRWORA), which was passed by the Republican-controlled U.S. House of Representatives and signed into law by the Democratic President Bill Clinton (1946–). The PRWORA replaced the

AFDC, which offered open-ended support to impoverished families, with Temporary Assistance for Needy Families (TANF), which was intended to incentivize job-seeking by limiting the amount of time a recipient can participate in the program. Although most of the funding for TANF comes from the federal government, as did the funding for the AFDC, states were granted wide latitude in deciding how to allocate benefits.

A major addition to the U.S. social welfare system came with the passage of the Patient Protection and Affordable Care Act (commonly known as the Affordable Care Act [ACA] or Obamacare), which was signed by President Barack Obama (1961–) in 2010. Besides attempting to reform the market for health insurance and to control rapidly rising health care costs, the ACA was intended to provide health insurance to those who could not afford it. The law's provisions began to go into effect soon after its passage, and total implementation of the health care overhaul was achieved by 2014. Although subject to harsh criticism and characterized as a catastrophe by many right-leaning pundits and politicians, the law had by late 2014 significantly increased low-income Americans' access to health care.

THE FEDERAL DEFINITION OF POVERTY

Decisions about how to determine who is poor and deserving of government aid have inspired controversy at least since the time of the English Poor Laws. Many of the U.S. government's social welfare initiatives hinge on the official definition of poverty, with both the size of an individual's benefits and the overall scope of the programs hanging in the balance.

The federal government began measuring poverty in 1959. During President Johnson's national War on Poverty, researchers realized that few statistical tools were available to measure the number of Americans who continued to live in poverty in one of the most affluent nations in the world. To fight this so-called war, it had to be determined who was poor and why.

During the early 1960s Mollie Orshansky (1915–2006) of the Social Security Administration suggested that the poverty income level be defined as the income sufficient to purchase a minimally adequate amount of goods and services. The necessary data for defining and pricing a full market basket of goods were not available then, nor are they available now. However, Orshansky noted that in 1955 the U.S. Department of Agriculture (USDA) had published the Household Food Consumption Survey, which showed that an average family of three or more people spent approximately one-third of its after-tax income on food. She multiplied the USDA's 1961 economy food plan (a no-frills food basket meeting the then-recommended dietary allowances) by three.

Basically, this defined a poor family as any family or person whose after-tax income was not sufficient to purchase a minimally adequate diet if one-third of the income was spent on food. Differences were allowed for size of family, gender of the head of the household, and whether it was a farm or nonfarm family. The threshold (the level at which poverty begins) for a farm family was set at 70% of a nonfarm household. (The difference between farm and nonfarm households was eliminated in 1982.)

The poverty thresholds set by the U.S. Census Bureau are still based on the theoretical food budget. These thresholds are updated each year to reflect inflation. People with incomes below the applicable threshold are classified as living below the poverty level.

The Census Bureau's poverty thresholds are used for statistical purposes, such as the calculation of the number of poor in the United States. The U.S. Department of Health and Human Services (HHS) uses a simplified version of the Census Bureau's thresholds to arrive at a separate measure of poverty each year. These HHS poverty guidelines are used for administrative purposes by many federal agencies. The HHS uses them to determine eligibility for TANF, Community Services Block Grants, Low-Income Home Energy Assistance Block Grants, and Head Start educational allotments. The guidelines are also the basis for funding the USDA's Supplemental Nutrition Assistance Program (previously called the Food Stamp Program), the National School Lunch Program, and the Special Supplemental Food Program for Women, Infants, and Children. The U.S. Department of Labor uses the guidelines to determine funding for the Job Corps and other employment and training programs under the Workforce Investment Act of 1998. Some state and local governments choose to use the federal poverty guidelines for some of their own programs, such as state health insurance programs and financial guidelines for child support enforcement.

The poverty guidelines vary by family size and composition. In 2014 a family of four living in the 48 contiguous states and the District of Columbia was considered impoverished if it earned $23,850 or less annually. (See Table 1.1.) A person living alone who earned less than $11,670 was considered poor, as was a family of eight members making less than $40,090. The poverty level is set higher for Alaska and Hawaii, in keeping with federal practices dating from the 1960s that reflect those states' higher cost of living relative to the 48 contiguous states and the District of Columbia. (See Table 1.2 and Table 1.3.)

THE HISTORICAL EFFORT TO REDUCE POVERTY

Since the late 1950s Americans have seen some successes and some failures in the battle against poverty. Table 1.4 provides historical data on those living below

TABLE 1.1

Poverty guidelines for the 48 contiguous states and the District of Columbia, 2014

Persons in family/household	Poverty guideline
1	$11,670
2	15,730
3	19,790
4	23,850
5	27,910
6	31,970
7	36,030
8	40,090

Note: For families/households with more than 8 persons, add $4,060 for each additional person.

SOURCE: "2014 Poverty Guidelines for the 48 Contiguous States and the District of Columbia," in "Annual Update of the HHS Poverty Guidelines," *Federal Register*, vol. 79, no. 14, January 22, 2014, http://www.gpo.gov/fdsys/pkg/FR-2014-01-22/pdf/2014-01303.pdf (accessed October 27, 2014)

TABLE 1.2

Poverty guidelines for Alaska, 2014

Persons in family/household	Poverty guideline
1	$14,580
2	19,660
3	24,740
4	29,820
5	34,900
6	39,980
7	45,060
8	50,140

Note: For families/households with more than 8 persons, add $5,080 for each additional person.

SOURCE: "2014 Poverty Guidelines for Alaska," in "Annual Update of the HHS Poverty Guidelines," *Federal Register*, vol. 79, no. 14, January 22, 2014, http://www.gpo.gov/fdsys/pkg/FR-2014-01-22/pdf/2014-01303.pdf (accessed October 27, 2014)

TABLE 1.3

Poverty guidelines for Hawaii, 2014

Persons in family/household	Poverty guideline
1	$13,420
2	18,090
3	22,760
4	27,430
5	32,100
6	36,770
7	41,440
8	46,110

Note: For families/households with more than 8 persons, add $4,670 for each additional person.

SOURCE: "2014 Poverty Guidelines for Hawaii," in "Annual Update of the HHS Poverty Guidelines," *Federal Register*, vol. 79, no. 14, January 22, 2014, http://www.gpo.gov/fdsys/pkg/FR-2014-01-22/pdf/2014-01303.pdf (accessed October 27, 2014)

the federally established poverty level, and Figure 1.1 provides a graphic representation of the changes in the poverty rate between 1959 and 2013. Of the total population of nearly 176.6 million in 1959, 22.4%, or 39.5 million people, lived below the poverty level. After an initial decline through the 1960s and 1970s, the poverty rate began to increase during the early 1980s, coinciding with a downturn in household and family incomes for all Americans. The poverty rate rose steadily until it reached a 17-year high of 15.2% in 1983, a year during which the country was climbing out of a serious economic recession.

The percentage of Americans living in poverty then began dropping, falling to 12.8% in 1989. (See Table 1.4.) After that, the percentage increased again, reaching 15.1% in 1993. Thereafter, it dropped to 11.3% in 2000 and then rose to 15.1% in 2010 in the wake of the so-called Great Recession, which officially lasted from December 2007 to June 2009, but which had negative effects on employment and incomes well into the

following decade. In 2013 the poverty rate, at 14.5%, remained above its prerecession level.

One of the key factors driving the poverty rate at all times is the availability of jobs. When the overall economy falters, as it did during the Great Recession, employers typically cut costs by reducing the number of their employees. The labor market at the height of the Great Recession (in 2009) was weaker than at any time since World War II (1939–1945). As Table 1.5 shows, the nationwide unemployment rate (the percentage of all people who are looking for jobs but cannot obtain them) peaked at 10% in late 2009. Although the unemployment rate slowly declined over the following years, it remained high by historical standards through 2013 and only began to approach prerecession levels in mid-2014.

Analysts believe the overall decline in poverty between 1959 and 2013 was due to both the growth in the economy and the success of some of the antipoverty programs that were instituted during the 1960s. However, not all demographic subcategories experienced the same level of change; in fact, for many people the poverty rate rose between 1970 and 2013. Carmen DeNavas-Walt and Bernadette D. Proctor of the Census Bureau note in *Income and Poverty in the United States: 2013* (September 2014, https://www.census.gov/content/dam/Census/library/publications/2014/demo/p60-249.pdf) that the poverty rate for those aged 65 years and older, who enjoy guaranteed income and health care benefits through the Social Security and Medicare programs, declined dramatically (from around 35% in 1959) and remained relatively low through 2013 (when the poverty rate for this group was 9.5%). (See Figure 1.2.) For children under 18 years of age and for adults aged 18 to 64 years, however, the situation was different. Although these groups also experienced a dramatic reduction in their poverty rate as the programs associated with the War on Poverty took effect between 1959 and 1970, the poverty rate for children and working-age adults fluctuated over the succeeding 43 years and showed an overall upward tendency. In 2013, 19.9% of

TABLE 1.4

Poverty status of people by family relationship, 1959–2013

	All people			All families			People in families — Families with female householder no husband present			Unrelated individuals		
		Below poverty level			Below poverty level			Below poverty level			Below poverty level	
Year	Total	Number	Percent	Total	Number	Percent	Total	Number	Percent	Total	Number	Percent
All races												
2013[a]	312,965	45,318	14.5	254,988	31,530	12.4	47,007	15,606	33.2	56,564	13,181	23.3
2012	310,648	46,496	15.0	252,863	33,198	13.1	47,085	15,957	33.9	56,185	12,558	22.4
2011	308,456	46,247	15.0	252,316	33,126	13.1	48,103	16,451	34.2	54,517	12,416	22.8
2010[b]	306,130	46,343	15.1	250,200	33,120	13.2	46,454	15,911	34.3	54,250	12,449	22.9
2010	305,688	46,180	15.1	249,855	33,007	13.2	46,422	15,895	34.2	54,183	12,422	22.9
2009	303,820	43,569	14.3	249,384	31,197	12.5	45,315	14,746	32.5	53,079	11,678	22.0
2008	301,041	39,829	13.2	248,301	28,564	11.5	44,027	13,812	31.4	51,534	10,710	20.8
2007	298,699	37,276	12.5	245,443	26,509	10.8	43,961	13,478	30.7	51,740	10,189	19.7
2006	296,450	36,460	12.3	245,199	25,915	10.6	43,223	13,199	30.5	49,884	9,977	20.0
2005	293,135	36,950	12.6	242,389	26,068	10.8	42,244	13,153	31.1	49,526	10,425	21.1
2004[c]	290,617	37,040	12.7	240,754	26,544	11.0	42,053	12,832	30.5	48,609	9,926	20.4
2003	287,699	35,861	12.5	238,903	25,684	10.8	41,311	12,413	30.0	47,594	9,713	20.4
2002	285,317	34,570	12.1	236,921	24,534	10.4	40,529	11,657	28.8	47,156	9,618	20.4
2001	281,475	32,907	11.7	233,911	23,215	9.9	39,261	11,223	28.6	46,392	9,226	19.9
2000[d]	278,944	31,581	11.3	231,909	22,347	9.6	38,375	10,926	28.5	45,624	8,653	19.0
1999[e]	276,208	32,791	11.9	230,789	23,830	10.3	38,580	11,764	30.5	43,977	8,400	19.1
1998	271,059	34,476	12.7	227,229	25,370	11.2	39,000	12,907	33.1	42,539	8,478	19.9
1997	268,480	35,574	13.3	225,369	26,217	11.6	38,412	13,494	35.1	41,672	8,687	20.8
1996	266,218	36,529	13.7	223,955	27,376	12.2	38,584	13,796	35.8	40,727	8,452	20.8
1995	263,733	36,425	13.8	222,792	27,501	12.3	38,908	14,205	36.5	39,484	8,247	20.9
1994	261,616	38,059	14.5	221,430	28,985	13.1	37,253	14,380	38.6	38,538	8,287	21.5
1993[f]	259,278	39,265	15.1	219,489	29,927	13.6	37,861	14,636	38.7	38,038	8,388	22.1
1992[g]	256,549	38,014	14.8	217,936	28,961	13.3	36,446	14,205	39.0	36,842	8,075	21.9
1991[h]	251,192	35,708	14.2	212,723	27,143	12.8	34,795	13,824	39.7	36,845	7,773	21.1
1990	248,644	33,585	13.5	210,967	25,232	12.0	33,795	12,578	37.2	36,056	7,446	20.7
1989	245,992	31,528	12.8	209,515	24,066	11.5	32,525	11,668	35.9	35,185	6,760	19.2
1988	243,530	31,745	13.0	208,056	24,048	11.6	32,164	11,972	37.2	34,340	7,070	20.6
1987[i]	240,982	32,221	13.4	206,877	24,725	12.0	31,893	12,148	38.1	32,992	6,857	20.8
1986	238,554	32,370	13.6	205,459	24,754	12.0	31,152	11,944	38.3	31,679	6,846	21.6
1985	236,594	33,064	14.0	203,963	25,729	12.6	30,878	11,600	37.6	31,351	6,725	21.5
1984	233,816	33,700	14.4	202,288	26,458	13.1	30,844	11,831	38.4	30,268	6,609	21.8
1983[j]	231,700	35,303	15.2	201,338	27,933	13.9	30,049	12,072	40.2	29,158	6,740	23.1
1982	229,412	34,398	15.0	200,385	27,349	13.6	28,834	11,701	40.6	27,908	6,458	23.1
1981[k]	227,157	31,822	14.0	198,541	24,850	12.5	28,587	11,051	38.7	27,714	6,490	23.4
1980	225,027	29,272	13.0	196,963	22,601	11.5	27,565	10,120	36.7	27,133	6,227	22.9
1979[l]	222,903	26,072	11.7	195,860	19,964	10.2	26,927	9,400	34.9	26,170	5,743	21.9
1978	215,656	24,497	11.4	191,071	19,062	10.0	26,032	9,269	35.6	24,585	5,435	22.1
1977	213,867	24,720	11.6	190,757	19,505	10.2	25,404	9,205	36.2	23,110	5,216	22.6
1976	212,303	24,975	11.8	190,844	19,632	10.3	24,204	9,029	37.3	21,459	5,344	24.9
1975	210,864	25,877	12.3	190,630	20,789	10.9	23,580	8,846	37.5	20,234	5,088	25.1
1974[m]	209,362	23,370	11.2	190,436	18,817	9.9	23,165	8,462	36.5	18,926	4,553	24.1
1973	207,621	22,973	11.1	189,361	18,299	9.7	21,823	8,178	37.5	18,260	4,674	25.6
1972	206,004	24,460	11.9	189,193	19,577	10.3	21,264	8,114	38.2	16,811	4,883	29.0
1971[n]	204,554	25,559	12.5	188,242	20,405	10.8	20,153	7,797	38.7	16,311	5,154	31.6
1970	202,183	25,420	12.6	186,692	20,330	10.9	19,673	7,503	38.1	15,491	5,090	32.9
1969	199,517	24,147	12.1	184,891	19,175	10.4	17,995	6,879	38.2	14,626	4,972	34.0
1968	197,628	25,389	12.8	183,825	20,695	11.3	18,048	6,990	38.7	13,803	4,694	34.0
1967[o]	195,672	27,769	14.2	182,558	22,771	12.5	17,788	6,898	38.8	13,114	4,998	38.1
1966	193,388	28,510	14.7	181,117	23,809	13.1	17,240	6,861	39.8	12,271	4,701	38.3
1965	191,413	33,185	17.3	179,281	28,358	15.8	16,371	7,524	46.0	12,132	4,827	39.8
1964	189,710	36,055	19.0	177,653	30,912	17.4	(NA)	7,297	44.4	12,057	5,143	42.7
1963	187,258	36,436	19.5	176,076	31,498	17.9	(NA)	7,646	47.7	11,182	4,938	44.2
1962	184,276	38,625	21.0	173,263	33,623	19.4	(NA)	7,781	50.3	11,013	5,002	45.4
1961	181,277	39,628	21.9	170,131	34,509	20.3	(NA)	7,252	48.1	11,146	5,119	45.9
1960	179,503	39,851	22.2	168,615	34,925	20.7	(NA)	7,247	48.9	10,888	4,926	45.2
1959	176,557	39,490	22.4	165,858	34,562	20.8	(NA)	7,014	49.4	10,699	4,928	46.1

children and 13.6% of working-age adults lived in poverty, which was up substantially from the 1970 levels.

RATIO OF INCOME TO POVERTY LEVELS

For purposes of analysis, the Census Bureau uses income-to-poverty ratios that are calculated by dividing income by the respective poverty threshold for each family size. The resulting number is then tabulated on a scale that includes three categories: poor, near-poor, and nonpoor. Poor people have a poverty ratio below 1.00. People above the poverty level are divided into two groups: the near-poor and the nonpoor. The near-poor have a poverty ratio between 1.00 and 1.24 (100% to

TABLE 1.4

Poverty status of people by family relationship, 1959–2013 [CONTINUED]

NA—Not available.

[a]Data are based on the CPS ASEC (Current Population Survey, Annual Social and Economic Supplement) sample of 68,000 addresses. The 2014 CPS ASEC included redesigned questions for income and health insurance coverage. All of the approximately 98,000 addresses were eligible to receive the redesigned set of health insurance coverage questions. The redesigned income questions were implemented to a subsample of these 98,000 addresses using a probability split panel design. Approximately 68,000 addresses were eligible to receive a set of income questions similar to those used in the 2013 CPS ASEC and the remaining 30,000 addresses were eligible to receive the redesigned income questions. The source of the 2013 data for this table is the portion of the CPS ASEC sample which received the income questions consistent with the 2013 CPS ASEC, approximately 68,000 addresses.
[b]Implementation of Census 2010-based population controls.
[c]The 2004 data have been revised to reflect a correction to the weights in the 2005 ASEC.
[d]Implementation of Census 2000 based population controls and sample expanded by 28,000 households.
[e]Implementation of Census 2000 based population controls.
[f]Data collection method changed from paper and pencil to computer-assisted interviewing. In addition, the March 1994 income supplement was revised to allow for the coding of different income amounts on selected questionnaire items. Limits either increased or decreased in the following categories: earnings increased to $999,999; Social Security increased to $49,999; Supplemental Security Income and Public Assistance increased to $24,999; Veterans' Benefits increased to $99,999; Child Support and Alimony decreased to $49,999.
[g]Implementation of 1990 census population controls.
[h]CPS file for March 1992 (1991 data) was corrected after the release of the 1991 Income and Poverty reports. Weights for nine person records were omitted on the original file.
[i]Implementation of a new March CPS processing system.
[j]Implementation of Hispanic population weighting controls.
[k]Implemented three technical changes to the poverty definition.
[l]Implementation of 1980 census population controls. Questionnaire expanded to show 27 possible values from 51 possible sources of income.
[m]Implementation of a new March CPS processing system. Questionnaire expanded to ask eleven income questions.
[n]Implementation of 1970 census population controls.
[o]Implementation of a new March CPS processing system.
Note: Numbers in thousands. People as of March of the following year.

SOURCE: Adapted from "Table 2. Poverty Status of People by Family Relationship, Race, and Hispanic Origin: 1959 to 2013," in *Historical Poverty Tables—People*, U.S. Census Bureau, September 16, 2014, https://www.census.gov/hhes/www/poverty/data/historical/hstpov2.xls (accessed October 27, 2014)

FIGURE 1.1

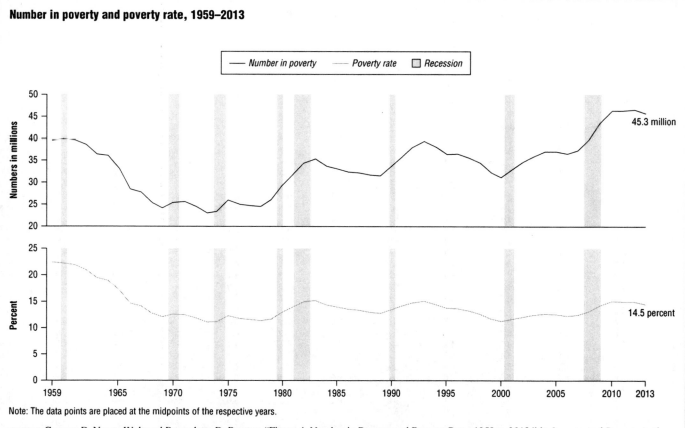

Number in poverty and poverty rate, 1959–2013

Note: The data points are placed at the midpoints of the respective years.

SOURCE: Carmen DeNavas-Walt and Bernadette D. Proctor, "Figure 4. Number in Poverty and Poverty Rate: 1959 to 2013," in *Income and Poverty in the United States: 2013*, U.S. Census Bureau, September 2014, https://www.census.gov/content/dam/Census/library/publications/2014/demo/p60-249.pdf (accessed October 27, 2014)

124% of the poverty level) and the nonpoor have an income-to-poverty ratio of 1.25 (125% of the poverty level) and above.

In 2013, 6.3% of the total U.S. population, or 19.9 million people, had income-to-poverty ratios under 0.5, or half of the poverty threshold. (See Table 1.6.) Fully

TABLE 1.5

Unemployment rate, 1948–September 2014

Year	Jan	Feb	Mar	Apr	May	Jun	Jul	Aug	Sep	Oct	Nov	Dec
1948	3.4	3.8	4.0	3.9	3.5	3.6	3.6	3.9	3.8	3.7	3.8	4.0
1949	4.3	4.7	5.0	5.3	6.1	6.2	6.7	6.8	6.6	7.9	6.4	6.6
1950	6.5	6.4	6.3	5.8	5.5	5.4	5.0	4.5	4.4	4.2	4.2	4.3
1951	3.7	3.4	3.4	3.1	3.0	3.2	3.1	3.1	3.3	3.5	3.5	3.1
1952	3.2	3.1	2.9	2.9	3.0	3.0	3.2	3.4	3.1	3.0	2.8	2.7
1953	2.9	2.6	2.6	2.7	2.5	2.5	2.6	2.7	2.9	3.1	3.5	4.5
1954	4.9	5.2	5.7	5.9	5.9	5.6	5.8	6.0	6.1	5.7	5.3	5.0
1955	4.9	4.7	4.6	4.7	4.3	4.2	4.0	4.2	4.1	4.3	4.2	4.2
1956	4.0	3.9	4.2	4.0	4.3	4.3	4.4	4.1	3.9	3.9	4.3	4.2
1957	4.2	3.9	3.7	3.9	4.1	4.3	4.2	4.1	4.4	4.5	5.1	5.2
1958	5.8	6.4	6.7	7.4	7.4	7.3	7.5	7.4	7.1	6.7	6.2	6.2
1959	6.0	5.9	5.6	5.2	5.1	5.0	5.1	5.2	5.5	5.7	5.8	5.3
1960	5.2	4.8	5.4	5.2	5.1	5.4	5.5	5.6	5.5	6.1	6.1	6.6
1961	6.6	6.9	6.9	7.0	7.1	6.9	7.0	6.6	6.7	6.5	6.1	6.0
1962	5.8	5.5	5.6	5.6	5.5	5.5	5.4	5.7	5.6	5.4	5.7	5.5
1963	5.7	5.9	5.7	5.7	5.9	5.6	5.6	5.4	5.5	5.5	5.7	5.5
1964	5.6	5.4	5.4	5.3	5.1	5.2	4.9	5.0	5.1	5.1	4.8	5.0
1965	4.9	5.1	4.7	4.8	4.6	4.6	4.4	4.4	4.3	4.2	4.1	4.0
1966	4.0	3.8	3.8	3.8	3.9	3.8	3.8	3.8	3.7	3.7	3.6	3.8
1967	3.9	3.8	3.8	3.8	3.8	3.9	3.8	3.8	3.8	4.0	3.9	3.8
1968	3.7	3.8	3.7	3.5	3.5	3.7	3.7	3.5	3.4	3.4	3.4	3.4
1969	3.4	3.4	3.4	3.4	3.4	3.5	3.5	3.5	3.7	3.7	3.5	3.5
1970	3.9	4.2	4.4	4.6	4.8	4.9	5.0	5.1	5.4	5.5	5.9	6.1
1971	5.9	5.9	6.0	5.9	5.9	5.9	6.0	6.1	6.0	5.8	6.0	6.0
1972	5.8	5.7	5.8	5.7	5.7	5.7	5.6	5.6	5.5	5.6	5.3	5.2
1973	4.9	5.0	4.9	5.0	4.9	4.9	4.8	4.8	4.8	4.6	4.8	4.9
1974	5.1	5.2	5.1	5.1	5.1	5.4	5.5	5.5	5.9	6.0	6.6	7.2
1975	8.1	8.1	8.6	8.8	9.0	8.8	8.6	8.4	8.4	8.4	8.3	8.2
1976	7.9	7.7	7.6	7.7	7.4	7.6	7.8	7.8	7.6	7.7	7.8	7.8
1977	7.5	7.6	7.4	7.2	7.0	7.2	6.9	7.0	6.8	6.8	6.8	6.4
1978	6.4	6.3	6.3	6.1	6.0	5.9	6.2	5.9	6.0	5.8	5.9	6.0
1979	5.9	5.9	5.8	5.8	5.6	5.7	5.7	6.0	5.9	6.0	5.9	6.0
1980	6.3	6.3	6.3	6.9	7.5	7.6	7.8	7.7	7.5	7.5	7.5	7.2
1981	7.5	7.4	7.4	7.2	7.5	7.5	7.2	7.4	7.6	7.9	8.3	8.5
1982	8.6	8.9	9.0	9.3	9.4	9.6	9.8	9.8	10.1	10.4	10.8	10.8
1983	10.4	10.4	10.3	10.2	10.1	10.1	9.4	9.5	9.2	8.8	8.5	8.3
1984	8.0	7.8	7.8	7.7	7.4	7.2	7.5	7.5	7.3	7.4	7.2	7.3
1985	7.3	7.2	7.2	7.3	7.2	7.4	7.4	7.1	7.1	7.1	7.0	7.0
1986	6.7	7.2	7.2	7.1	7.2	7.2	7.0	6.9	7.0	7.0	6.9	6.6
1987	6.6	6.6	6.6	6.3	6.3	6.2	6.1	6.0	5.9	6.0	5.8	5.7
1988	5.7	5.7	5.7	5.4	5.6	5.4	5.4	5.6	5.4	5.4	5.3	5.3
1989	5.4	5.2	5.0	5.2	5.2	5.3	5.2	5.2	5.3	5.3	5.4	5.4
1990	5.4	5.3	5.2	5.4	5.4	5.2	5.5	5.7	5.9	5.9	6.2	6.3
1991	6.4	6.6	6.8	6.7	6.9	6.9	6.8	6.9	6.9	7.0	7.0	7.3
1992	7.3	7.4	7.4	7.4	7.6	7.8	7.7	7.6	7.6	7.3	7.4	7.4
1993	7.3	7.1	7.0	7.1	7.1	7.0	6.9	6.8	6.7	6.8	6.6	6.5
1994	6.6	6.6	6.5	6.4	6.1	6.1	6.1	6.0	5.9	5.8	5.6	5.5
1995	5.6	5.4	5.4	5.8	5.6	5.6	5.7	5.7	5.6	5.5	5.6	5.6
1996	5.6	5.5	5.5	5.6	5.6	5.3	5.5	5.1	5.2	5.2	5.4	5.4
1997	5.3	5.2	5.2	5.1	4.9	5.0	4.9	4.8	4.9	4.7	4.6	4.7
1998	4.6	4.6	4.7	4.3	4.4	4.5	4.5	4.5	4.6	4.5	4.4	4.4
1999	4.3	4.4	4.2	4.3	4.2	4.3	4.3	4.2	4.2	4.1	4.1	4.0
2000	4.0	4.1	4.0	3.8	4.0	4.0	4.0	4.1	3.9	3.9	3.9	3.9
2001	4.2	4.2	4.3	4.4	4.3	4.5	4.6	4.9	5.0	5.3	5.5	5.7
2002	5.7	5.7	5.7	5.9	5.8	5.8	5.8	5.7	5.7	5.7	5.9	6.0
2003	5.8	5.9	5.9	6.0	6.1	6.3	6.2	6.1	6.1	6.0	5.8	5.7
2004	5.7	5.6	5.8	5.6	5.6	5.6	5.5	5.4	5.4	5.5	5.4	5.4
2005	5.3	5.4	5.2	5.2	5.1	5.0	5.0	4.9	5.0	5.0	5.0	4.9
2006	4.7	4.8	4.7	4.7	4.6	4.6	4.7	4.7	4.5	4.4	4.5	4.4
2007	4.6	4.5	4.4	4.5	4.4	4.6	4.7	4.6	4.7	4.7	4.7	5.0
2008	5.0	4.9	5.1	5.0	5.4	5.6	5.8	6.1	6.1	6.5	6.8	7.3
2009	7.8	8.3	8.7	9.0	9.4	9.5	9.5	9.6	9.8	10.0	9.9	9.9
2010	9.7	9.8	9.9	9.9	9.6	9.4	9.5	9.5	9.5	9.5	9.8	9.4
2011	9.1	9.0	9.0	9.1	9.0	9.1	9.0	9.0	9.0	8.8	8.6	8.5
2012	8.2	8.3	8.2	8.2	8.2	8.2	8.2	8.1	7.8	7.8	7.8	7.9
2013	7.9	7.7	7.5	7.5	7.5	7.5	7.3	7.2	7.2	7.2	7.0	6.7
2014	6.6	6.7	6.7	6.3	6.3	6.1	6.2	6.1	5.9			

SOURCE: "Unemployment Rate (Series ID LNS14000000)," in *Labor Force Statistics from the Current Population Survey*, U.S. Department of Labor, Bureau of Labor Statistics, http://data.bls.gov/timeseries/LNS14000000 (accessed October 27, 2014)

19.2% of the population, or 60.2 million people, were either poor or near-poor. Females were slightly more likely than males to be poor or near-poor, and poverty varied significantly by race and Hispanic origin. Whereas 13% of non-Hispanic whites and 14.7% of Asian Americans were poor or near-poor in 2013,

FIGURE 1.2

Poverty rates by age, 1959–2013

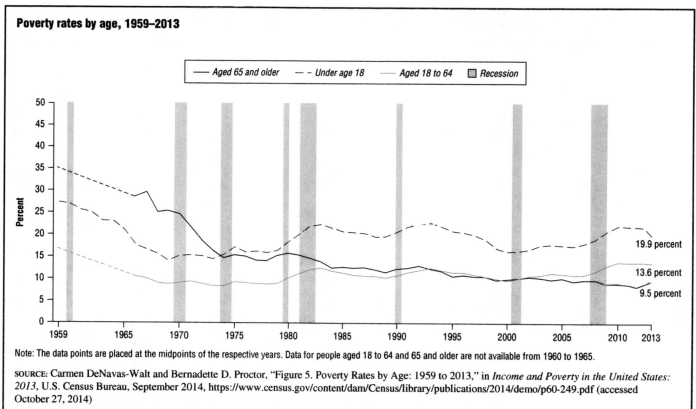

Note: The data points are placed at the midpoints of the respective years. Data for people aged 18 to 64 and 65 and older are not available from 1960 to 1965.

SOURCE: Carmen DeNavas-Walt and Bernadette D. Proctor, "Figure 5. Poverty Rates by Age: 1959 to 2013," in *Income and Poverty in the United States: 2013*, U.S. Census Bureau, September 2014, https://www.census.gov/content/dam/Census/library/publications/2014/demo/p60-249.pdf (accessed October 27, 2014)

31.6% of Hispanics and 34% of African Americans had incomes under 125% of poverty.

Children are also disproportionately likely to be poor. Although children under the age of 18 years accounted for only 23.5% of the total U.S. population in 2013, they accounted for 32.6% of those living at half of the poverty threshold or below and for 32.1% of those living at between 50% and 99% of poverty. (See Figure 1.3.) By contrast, adults aged 18 to 64 years, at 62.3% of the U.S. population, made up 61.2% of those living at half of the poverty threshold and 56.1% of those at 50% to 99% of poverty. Meanwhile, those aged 65 years and older were the least likely to be poor or near-poor. At 14.2% of the U.S. population, the elderly accounted for only 6.1% of those living below half of the poverty threshold and 11.8% of those at 50% to 99% of poverty.

HOW ACCURATE IS THE POVERTY LEVEL?

Almost every year since the Census Bureau first defined the poverty level, observers have been concerned about its accuracy. Since the early 1960s, when Orshansky defined the estimated poverty level based on an average family's food budget, living patterns have changed and food costs have become a smaller percentage of family spending. As Table 1.7 shows, in 2013 the average consumer unit (defined as a family, an economically independent single person, or two or more unrelated people who live together but share expenses) spent $51,100. By far the largest portion of this spending was on housing, which accounted for $17,148 (33.6%) of total spending, followed by transportation, which accounted for $9,004 (17.6%) of average consumer spending. Food accounted for $6,602 (12.9%) of the average consumer unit's spending, which was slightly more than spending on personal insurance and pensions, $5,528 (10.8%). The allocation of expenses for the lowest-earning 20% of American households, whose incomes are most directly relevant to the calculation of the poverty threshold, diverges somewhat from that of the average consumer unit. As Table 1.8 shows, this group's average (mean) annual expenditures totaled $22,393 in 2013, with 40% of that spending attributable to housing, 16.3% to food, 14.9% to transportation, and 8% to health care. Based on these changes in consumption patterns, many analysts ask: Should the amount spent on food be multiplied by a factor higher than three to arrive at a more accurate definition of poverty? Should the poverty level be based on housing, which is by far the most expensive need across all income brackets? Or should it be based on some other set of factors?

Other critics of the official poverty measure point to its insensitivity to geographical differences. Housing costs vary widely between, for example, rural Nebraska and New York City, as do costs for other basic necessities, including food, utilities, health care, and transportation. Even within one state, the differences between

TABLE 1.6

People with income below specified ratios of their poverty thresholds, by selected characteristics, 2013

[Data are based on the CPS ASEC (Current Population Survey, Annual Social and Economic Supplement) sample of 68,000 addresses.[a] Numbers in thousands. People as of March of the following year.]

Characteristic	Total	Income-to-poverty ratio							
		Under 0.50		Under 1.25		Under 1.50		Under 2.00	
		Number	Percent	Number	Percent	Number	Percent	Number	Percent
All people	312,965	19,870	6.3	60,215	19.2	76,077	24.3	106,024	33.9
Age									
Under age 18	73,625	6,484	8.8	19,215	26.1	23,656	32.1	31,364	42.6
Aged 18 to 64	194,833	12,165	6.2	34,298	17.6	43,073	22.1	59,911	30.7
Aged 65 and older	44,508	1,221	2.7	6,702	15.1	9,348	21.0	14,749	33.1
Sex									
Male	153,361	8,816	5.7	26,816	17.5	34,193	22.3	48,629	31.7
Female	159,605	11,054	6.9	33,399	20.9	41,885	26.2	57,395	36.0
Race[b] and Hispanic origin									
White	243,085	12,861	5.3	40,577	16.7	52,127	21.4	75,228	30.9
White, not Hispanic	195,167	8,383	4.3	25,420	13.0	33,332	17.1	49,843	25.5
Black	40,615	4,963	12.2	13,825	34.0	16,551	40.8	20,610	50.7
Asian	17,063	882	5.2	2,507	14.7	3,274	19.2	4,792	28.1
Hispanic (any race)	54,145	5,114	9.4	17,112	31.6	21,310	39.4	28,680	53.0
Family status									
In families	254,988	12,967	5.1	42,874	16.8	54,850	21.5	78,035	30.6
Householder	81,217	3,901	4.8	12,375	15.2	15,924	19.6	22,922	28.2
Related children under age 18	72,573	6,135	8.5	18,634	25.7	23,003	31.7	30,579	42.1
Related children under age 6	23,585	2,521	10.7	6,652	28.2	8,109	34.4	10,639	45.1
In unrelated subfamilies	1,413	377	26.7	722	51.1	830	58.7	1,045	73.9
Unrelated individuals	56,564	6,526	11.5	16,619	29.4	20,397	36.1	26,944	47.6

[a]The 2014 CPS ASEC included redesigned questions for income and health insurance coverage. All of the approximately 98,000 addresses were eligible to receive the redesigned set of health insurance coverage questions. The redesigned income questions were implemented to a subsample of these 98,000 addresses using a probability split panel design. Approximately 68,000 addresses were eligible to receive a set of income questions similar to those used in the 2013 CPS ASEC and the remaining 30,000 addresses were eligible to receive the redesigned income questions. The source of data for this table is the portion of the CPS ASEC sample which received the income questions consistent with the 2013 CPS ASEC, approximately 68,000 addresses.
[b]Federal surveys now give respondents the option of reporting more than one race. Therefore, two basic ways of defining a race group are possible. A group such as Asian may be defined as those who reported Asian and no other race (the race-alone or single-race concept) or as those who reported Asian regardless of whether they also reported another race (the race-alone-or-in-combination concept). This table shows data using the first approach (race alone). The use of the single-race population does not imply that it is the preferred method of presenting or analyzing data. The Census Bureau uses a variety of approaches. Information on people who reported more than one race, such as white *and* American Indian and Alaska Native or Asian *and* black or African American, is available from Census 2010 through American FactFinder. About 2.9 percent of people reported more than one race in Census 2010. Data for American Indians and Alaska Natives, Native Hawaiian and other Pacific Islanders, and those reporting two or more races are not shown separately.
Note: Details may not sum to totals because of rounding.

SOURCE: Adapted from Carmen DeNavas-Walt and Bernadette D. Proctor, "Table 5. People with Income below Specified Ratios of Their Poverty Thresholds by Selected Characteristics: 2013," in *Income and Poverty in the United States: 2013*, U.S. Census Bureau, September 2014, https://www.census.gov/content/dam/Census/library/publications/2014/demo/p60-249.pdf (accessed October 27, 2014)

rural, suburban, and urban costs of living can diverge widely. A family of four with an income approaching the official poverty measure of $23,850 would clearly be able to purchase more with that amount of money in rural Nebraska than in New York City, so why does the federal government define poverty identically for two such families?

Social changes, too, have altered the economic landscape in the 21st century, as critics of the official poverty measure point out. In families headed by two parents, both parents are far more likely to be working than they were a generation or two ago, and there is a much greater likelihood that a single parent, usually the mother, will be heading the family. Child care costs, which were of little concern during the 1950s, when stay-at home mothers were the norm, have become a major issue for working parents in the 21st century. Moreover, family life has become more complicated,

with complex financial consequences arising as parents living in one household may pay child support to another or receive support payments from another. Such incomes and expenses are not factored into the official poverty measure, which obscures the overall portrait of the nation's poor.

Moreover, if the goal is to measure U.S. poverty accurately, these are not the only expenses and forms of income that many analysts believe should be included in the poverty guidelines. The official poverty thresholds take into account only gross income, neglecting to account for that portion of income that must be spent on taxes and is therefore unavailable for spending on basic necessities. Although many low-income Americans pay no federal income taxes, they are frequently still subject to state and payroll taxes. Additionally, the poverty guidelines take no account of expenses that are accrued in the process of working or of out-of-pocket

FIGURE 1.3

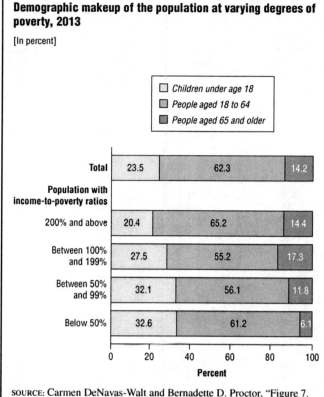

Demographic makeup of the population at varying degrees of poverty, 2013

[In percent]

- ☐ Children under age 18
- ▨ People aged 18 to 64
- ▤ People aged 65 and older

Total	23.5	62.3	14.2

Population with income-to-poverty ratios

200% and above	20.4	65.2	14.4
Between 100% and 199%	27.5	55.2	17.3
Between 50% and 99%	32.1	56.1	11.8
Below 50%	32.6	61.2	6.1

Percent (0 20 40 60 80 100)

SOURCE: Carmen DeNavas-Walt and Bernadette D. Proctor, "Figure 7. Demographic Makeup of the Population at Varying Degrees of Poverty: 2013," in *Income and Poverty in the United States: 2013*, U.S. Census Bureau, September 2014, https://www.census.gov/content/dam/Census/library/publications/2014/demo/p60-249.pdf (accessed October 27, 2014)

medical spending. Medical spending, too, is subject to another variable: age. The young spend far less money on health care than the elderly. Therefore, many critics argue that a poverty measure that does not take into account the burden of medical spending for the elderly does not accurately reflect economic realities.

Forms of income that are not factored into the official poverty thresholds include the various in-kind (or noncash) benefits that households receive from government sources, many of which can be used to meet basic expenses. Although some of these benefits, such as Medicaid, can be difficult to quantify, others, such as food assistance, have a more obvious cash value. Likewise, many poor and near-poor families benefit from the Earned Income Tax Credit, an Internal Revenue Service provision that allows working people to deduct certain dollar amounts from their tax bills if their incomes fall below annually updated thresholds. The deducted amounts function in the same way as government assistance, many analysts argue, and should therefore be included in poverty measurements.

THE SUPPLEMENTAL POVERTY MEASURE

Kathleen Short of the Census Bureau notes in *The Supplemental Poverty Measure: 2013* (October 2014, http://www.census.gov/content/dam/Census/library/publications/2014/demo/p60-251.pdf) that during the 1990s these widely publicized shortcomings in the official poverty measure led Congress to empower the National Academy

TABLE 1.7

Average annual consumer expenditures, 2011–13

				Percent change	
Item	2011	2012	2013	2011–2012	2012–2013
Average annual expenditures:					
Total	$49,705	$51,442	$51,100	3.5	−0.7
Food	6,458	6,599	6,602	2.2	0.0
At home	3,838	3,921	3,977	2.2	1.4
Away from home	2,620	2,678	2,625	2.2	−2.0
Housing	16,803	16,887	17,148	0.5	1.5
Apparel and services	1,740	1,736	1,604	−0.2	−7.6
Transportation	8,293	8,998	9,004	8.5	0.1
Healthcare	3,313	3,556	3,631	7.3	2.1
Entertainment	2,572	2,605	2,482	1.3	−4.7
Cash contributions	1,721	1,913	1,834	11.2	−4.1
Personal insurance and pensions	5,424	5,591	5,528	3.1	−1.1
All other expenditures	3,382	3,557	3,267	5.2	−8.2
Consumer unit characteristics:					
Number of consumer units (000's)	122,287	124,416	125,670		
Average age of reference person	49.7	50.0	50.1		
Average number in consumer unit					
People	2.5	2.5	2.5		
Earners	1.3	1.3	1.3		
Vehicles	1.9	1.9	1.9		
Percent homeowner	64.9	64.3	63.7		
Income before taxes	$63,685	$65,596	$63,784	3.0	−2.8

SOURCE: "Table A. Average Annual Expenditures and Characteristics of All Consumer Units and Percent Changes, 2011–2013," in "News Release: Consumer Expenditures—2013," U.S. Department of Labor, Bureau of Labor Statistics, September 9, 2014, http://www.bls.gov/news.release/pdf/cesan.pdf (accessed November 14, 2014)

TABLE 1.8

Average annual consumer expenditures, by income quintile, 2013

Item	All consumer units	Lowest 20 percent	Second 20 percent	Third 20 percent	Fourth 20 percent	Highest 20 percent
Number of consumer units (in thousands)	125,670	25,090	25,219	25,082	25,178	25,101
Lower limit	n.a.	n.a.	$17,883	$34,958	$57,968	$95,336
Consumer unit characteristics:						
Income before taxes						
Mean	$63,784	$9,658	$26,275	$45,826	$74,546	$162,720
Average annual expenditures						
Mean	$51,100	$22,393	$32,559	$42,495	$58,842	$99,237
Food						
Mean	6,602	3,655	4,781	5,728	7,655	11,184
Share	12.9	16.3	14.7	13.5	13.0	11.3
Housing						
Mean	17,148	8,963	11,994	14,808	19,084	30,901
Share	33.6	40.0	36.8	34.8	32.4	31.1
Apparel and services						
Mean	1,604	724	1,040	1,332	1,867	3,056
Share	3.1	3.2	3.2	3.1	3.2	3.1
Transportation						
Mean	9,004	3,327	5,856	8,071	10,908	16,860
Share	17.6	14.9	18.0	19.0	18.5	17.0
Healthcare						
Mean	3,631	1,790	2,850	3,375	4,386	5,755
Share	7.1	8.0	8.8	7.9	7.5	5.8
Entertainment						
Mean	2,482	1,002	1,416	1,997	2,866	5,133
Share	4.9	4.5	4.3	4.7	4.9	5.2
Personal care products and services						
Mean	608	275	412	503	706	1,147
Share	1.2	1.2	1.3	1.2	1.2	1.2
Reading						
Mean	102	37	68	84	117	207
Share	0.2	0.2	0.2	0.2	0.2	0.2
Education						
Mean	1,138	830	452	552	925	2,932
Share	2.2	3.7	1.4	1.3	1.6	3.0
Tobacco products and smoking supplies						
Mean	330	291	317	361	396	282
Share	0.6	1.3	1.0	0.9	0.7	0.3
Miscellaneous						
Mean	645	292	389	527	737	1,279
Share	1.3	1.3	1.2	1.2	1.3	1.3
Cash contributions						
Mean	1,834	577	1,054	1,304	2,095	4,143
Share	3.6	2.6	3.2	3.1	3.6	4.2
Personal insurance and pensions						
Mean	5,528	463	1,653	3,496	6,594	15,443
Share	10.8	2.1	5.1	8.2	11.2	15.6

n.a. = Notapplicable.

SOURCE: Adapted from "Table 1101. Quintiles of Income before Taxes: Annual Expenditure Means, Shares, Standard Errors, and Coefficient of Variation, Consumer Expenditure Survey, 2013," in *Consumer Expenditure Survey*, U.S. Department of Labor, Bureau of Labor Statistics, September 9, 2014, http://www.bls.gov/cex/2013/combined/quintile.pdf (accessed November 14, 2014)

of Sciences (NAS) to study the efficacy of the official measure and to recommend alternatives. The NAS assembled the Panel on Poverty and Family Assistance, and the panel's 1995 report, *Measuring Poverty: A New Approach*, recommended the creation of an alternate poverty measure to address many of the previously mentioned weaknesses in the official guidelines. During the late 1990s the Census Bureau began incorporating a number of experimental poverty measures in some of its reports and data sets. Taking into account various shortcomings of the official poverty measures, the data revealed different portraits of the poor population.

After continued research and discussion over the following decade, the U.S. Interagency Technical Working Group (ITWG) outlined the characteristics of a Supplemental Poverty Measure (SPM) that it proposed to begin using alongside the official measure. The new SPM specifies a poverty threshold that accounts not only for food expenses multiplied by three but also for the amount that is spent on a basic bundle of food, clothing, shelter, and utilities, as well as for additional household needs. The SPM further takes into account the needs of different family types and the needs of households in different geographic locations. In calculating income thresholds, the SPM includes not only cash income from all sources but also the value of various forms of government assistance and tax credits; and it takes into consideration necessary household expenses including income taxes, payroll taxes, child care, child support payments, and health care costs. (See Table 1.9.) There are no plans to use the SPM for the determination of funding for social welfare programs or as a replacement for the official measure in other contexts; rather, it is applied to Census Bureau data for the purpose of providing additional information about economic need to policy makers and analysts.

Short explains that the SPM poverty threshold differs from the official poverty threshold and that different SPM thresholds are provided depending on a household's housing status. (See Table 1.10.) These SPM thresholds, together with the additional variations in evaluating households, incomes, and expenditures, yield a different picture of the impoverished population than that rendered by use of the official measure. For example, according to the SPM 48.7 million people were poor in 2013, whereas according to the official poverty measure 45.8 million people were poor. The SPM also shows a different distribution of the impoverished population by age. (See Figure 1.4.) Considerably fewer children qualify as impoverished under the SPM, whereas more working-age adults and significantly more elderly adults do.

A number of policy experts have met the release of SPM data with skepticism. In "The Supplemental Poverty Measure: Is Child Poverty Really Less of a Problem Than We Thought?" (CEPR.net, August 3, 2012), Shawn Fremstad of the Center for Economic and Policy Research takes aim at the decreases in child poverty resulting from use of the SPM. Arguing that the SPM accurately shows an increase in poverty among the elderly because of its inclusion of out-of-pocket medical expenses in its calculations, Fremstad maintains that comparable adjustments are needed in the calculation of child poverty to account for "children's basic needs for care and healthy development."

Mark Levinson of the Service Employees International Union makes a more fundamental case for the SPM's inadequacy in "Mismeasuring Poverty" (Prospect.org, June 25, 2012). Faulting the official poverty measure for "setting the poverty bar so low that tens of millions of poor Americans are not accounted for," Levinson maintains that the SPM fails to fix this basic shortcoming. Noting that the original intent of President Johnson's War on Poverty was to aid "those whose basic needs exceed their means to satisfy them," he laments the fact that tens of millions of Americans fit this description and yet do not qualify for government assistance. In place of either the official poverty measure or the SPM, Levinson suggests that a more reasonable alternative would be a definition of poverty such as those used in European countries, where families earning less than 50% or 60% of the median income are considered to be poor.

THE U.S. POVERTY LINE IN A GLOBAL CONTEXT

Indeed, the poverty bar is set lower in the United States than in other comparably developed countries. Martin Ravallion of the World Bank reports in "A Relative Question" (*Finance and Development*, vol. 49, no. 4, December 2012) that most high-income countries peg their poverty lines to average incomes, so that the poverty line

TABLE 1.9

Official poverty measure vs. Supplemental Poverty Measure

	Official poverty measure	Supplemental Poverty Measure
Measurement units	Families and unrelated individuals	All related individuals who live at the same address, and any coresident unrelated children who are cared for by the family (such as foster children) and any cohabiters and their relatives
Poverty threshold	Three times the cost of a minimum food diet in 1963	The mean of the 30th to 36th percentile of expenditures on food, clothing, shelter, and utilities (FCSU) of consumer units with exactly two children multiplied by 1.2
Threshold adjustments	Vary by family size, composition, and age of householder	Geographic adjustments for differences in housing costs by tenure and a three-parameter equivalence scale for family size and composition
Updating thresholds	Consumer Price Index: all items	Five-year moving average of expenditures on FCSU
Resource measure	Gross before-tax cash income	Sum of cash income, plus noncash benefits that families can use to meet their FCSU needs, minus taxes (or plus tax credits), minus work expenses, minus out-of-pocket medical expenses and child support paid to another household

SOURCE: Kathleen Short, "Poverty Measure Concepts: Official and Supplemental," in *The Supplemental Poverty Measure: 2013*, U.S. Census Bureau, October 2014, http://www.census.gov/content/dam/Census/library/publications/2014/demo/p60-251.pdf (accessed October 27, 2014)

TABLE 1.10

Official and supplemental poverty thresholds for a two-adult, two-child household, 2012 and 2013

[In dollars]

Measure	2012	2013
Official poverty measure	23,283	23,624
Supplemental poverty measure		
Owners with a mortgage	25,784	25,639
Owners without a mortgage	21,400	21,397
Renters	25,105	25,144

SOURCE: Adapted from Kathleen Short, "Table 1. Two Adult, Two Child Poverty Thresholds: 2012 and 2013," in *The Supplemental Poverty Measure: 2013*, U.S. Census Bureau, October 2014, http://www.census.gov/content/dam/Census/library/publications/2014/demo/p60-251.pdf (accessed October 27, 2014)

FIGURE 1.4

Poverty rates using official and supplemental poverty measures, by age, 2013

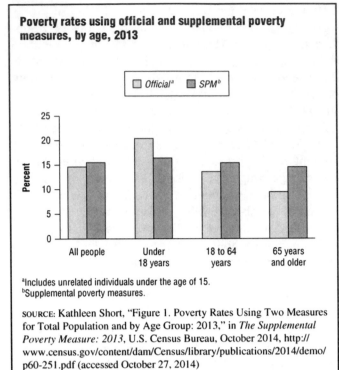

[a]Includes unrelated individuals under the age of 15.
[b]Supplemental poverty measures.

SOURCE: Kathleen Short, "Figure 1. Poverty Rates Using Two Measures for Total Population and by Age Group: 2013," in *The Supplemental Poverty Measure: 2013*, U.S. Census Bureau, October 2014, http://www.census.gov/content/dam/Census/library/publications/2014/demo/p60-251.pdf (accessed October 27, 2014)

rises as a country's economy grows. The rationale behind such systems is that one can feel poor in a rich country even when one's income is above the level required for basic subsistence and that poverty describes a condition of having too little money to participate in society.

To assess poverty, the World Bank uses a figure called purchasing power parity (PPP), which compares the ability of people to purchase basic necessities in different places and at different times. The poverty line is far lower in less-developed and developing countries than it is in the United States. As of 2012, the government of China maintained a poverty line that was equivalent to PPP of $1.80 per day, or double its previous poverty line of $0.90 per day. China's poverty measure was little different from the average poverty line of the world's 20 poorest countries (PPP of $1.25 per day), which is considered the absolute poverty line, or the amount needed for basic survival in the developing world. According to Ravallion, Luxembourg, the nation with the highest poverty line in the world in 2012, classified those living on less than the PPP equivalent of $43 per day as poor. Although U.S. citizens on average demonstrate consumption patterns similar to those in Luxembourg, meaning that participation in society would require roughly the same amount of income in both countries, the U.S. poverty line was equivalent to PPP of only $13 per day in 2012.

According to the World Bank, in *2014: World Development Indicators* (2014, http://data.worldbank.org/sites/default/files/wdi-2014-book.pdf), 20.6% of people in the developing world lived on less than $1.25 per day, down dramatically from 43.1% in 1990, largely as a result of rapid economic development in China and other countries. The World Bank expects continued economic growth in the developing world and predicts that the proportion of people living in extreme poverty will fall to 16% by 2015.

INCOME INEQUALITY

Whether considered globally or nationally, there is no mistaking the relative nature of poverty. Although the official U.S. poverty measure does not account for an individual's or family's poverty in terms of the country's average income, researchers in the fields of anthropology, psychology, and economics have established that people judge their own level of welfare not in absolute terms but relative to the prosperity of their society as a whole. For this and other reasons, many policy experts are concerned about a growing body of evidence suggesting that the gap between the rich and the poor in the United States widened considerably at the end of the 20th century and the beginning of the 21st century.

Utilizing Census Bureau data, Arloc Sherman and Chad Stone of the Center on Budget and Policy Priorities explain in *Income Gaps between Very Rich and Everyone Else More Than Tripled in Last Three Decades, New Data Show* (June 25, 2010, http://www.cbpp.org/files/6-25-10inc.pdf) that the gaps between the richest 1% of Americans and the middle and poorest fifths of Americans more than tripled between 1979 and 2007. During this period average after-tax incomes for the top 1% rose by 281%, whereas the middle fifth of households saw their incomes increase by only 25% and the lowest fifth of households saw their incomes increase by only 16%. In 2007, 17.1% of all after-tax income was earned by the wealthiest 1% of Americans.

Although the wealthiest Americans initially suffered significant financial setbacks during the Great Recession, income inequality continued to increase between 2010 and 2013. In the op-ed "Inequality, Unbelievably, Gets Worse" (NYTimes.com, November 16, 2014), Steven Rattner observes that according to the Federal Reserve System (the central banking and economic authority of the United States), incomes for the top 10% of earners rose 2% between 2010 and 2013, whereas incomes for the remaining 90% of earners declined. The declines varied by income strata. Those in the middle range of incomes (the 20th to the 60th percentiles) were hit the hardest: their incomes fell 6% to 7%. Those just below the top 10%, in the 80th to 90th percentiles, saw their incomes fall 3%; those in the 60th to 80th percentiles saw their incomes fall 2%; and those in the bottom 20% saw their incomes fall 4%.

Census data on income and earnings, which report pretax earnings, support this picture of increasing inequality. The accumulation of wealth by the highest quintile of earners, as Table 1.11 shows, proceeded most rapidly between 1977 and 2007, a period during which the richest 20% of Americans increased their share of all household income from 44% in 1977 to 49.7% in 2007. This upper quintile's accumulation of wealth did not dramatically accelerate relative to the other quintiles of earners during the Great Recession, but neither did it lose ground. However, after the recession its share of total income rose, reaching 51% by 2013. This increase of seven percentage points represents a 16% increase in the upper quintile's share of total income between 1977 and 2013. The accumulation of wealth by the top 5% of earners increased even more, proportionally speaking, than that of the top 20%. In 1977 the top 5% of earners accounted for 16.8% of total household income; by 2013 this group accounted for 22.2% of all income. The increase of 5.4 percentage points represents a 32% increase in the share of income held by this group.

These gains in the share of overall income by top earners naturally came at the expense of the remaining 80% of earners. The bottom four quintiles of income earners saw their shares of total income fall steadily. (See Table 1.11.) The lowest quintile's share of income was 4.2% in 1977 and 3.2% in 2013; the second-lowest quintile claimed 10.2% of all income in 1977 and 8.4% in 2013; the middle quintile of earners took home 16.9% of all income in 1977 and 14.4% in 2013; and the second-highest quintile's share was 24.7% in 1977 and 23% in 2013.

Why Is the Income Gap Growing?

Many reasons exist to explain the growing inequality, although observers disagree about which are more important. One reason is that the proportion of the elderly population, which is likely to earn less, is growing. According to the Census Bureau, 28.7 million of 123 million households, or 23.4%, were headed by a householder 65 years of age or older in 2013. (See Table 1.12; a household may consist of a single individual or a group of related or unrelated people living together, whereas a family consists of related individuals.) The median (the middle value—half are higher and half are lower) household income of households headed by a person aged 65 years or older was $35,611, compared with a median household income of $58,448 for households headed by someone under the age of 65 years.

In addition, more people than in previous years were living in nonfamily situations (either alone or with non-relatives). In 2013, 41.8 million of 123 million households, or 34%, were nonfamily households. (See Table 1.11.) These nonfamily households earned a median income of $31,178, compared with the $65,587 median income of family households.

The increase in the number of households headed by females and the increased labor force participation of women have also contributed to growing income inequality in the United States. In 2013, 15.2 million of 81.2 million family households, or 18.7%, were headed by women with no husband present, and 22.3 million of 41.8 million nonfamily households, or 53.3%, were headed by women. (See Table 1.11.) Female-headed households typically earn significantly less than other types of households. In 2013 the earnings of female-headed family households in which no husband was present were only 69.4% of the earnings of male-headed family households in which no wife was present ($35,154 and $50,625, respectively) and only 45.9% of the earnings of married-couple households ($35,154 and $76,509, respectively). Meanwhile, female nonfamily householders earned 71.7% of male nonfamily householders ($26,425 and $36,876, respectively). On average, female full-time workers earned only 78% of what male full-time workers earned in 2013. (See Figure 1.5.)

However, economists who study income and wealth inequality typically point to factors beyond these changes in the composition of households. Chrystia Freeland observes in "Income Inequality Sheds Its Taboo Status" (NYTimes.com, November 29, 2012) that most economists agree that the technology revolution and globalization, which have resulted in the loss of many of the highest-paying jobs available to those in the lower income quintiles, are important drivers of inequality. While incomes have stagnated for the lower quintiles, those at the extreme top of the income scale have seen unprecedented gains in their earnings. Freeland notes that as of 2012, "the wealth of the 400 richest Americans has increased more than fivefold over the past 20 years."

TABLE 1.11

Household income dispersion, selected years, 1967–2013

[Income in 2013 CPI-U-RS adjusted dollars]

Measures of income dispersion	2013[a]	2012	2011	2010[b]	2007	1997	1987[c]	1977	1967[d]
Measure									
Household income at selected percentiles									
10th percentile limit	12,401	12,414	12,429	12,672	13,664	13,335	12,234	12,262	9,940
20th percentile limit	20,900	20,898	20,986	21,368	22,797	22,286	21,185	20,078	18,294
40th percentile limit	40,187	40,342	39,896	40,599	43,928	42,256	40,212	37,817	35,674
50th (median)	51,939	51,759	51,842	52,646	56,436	53,551	51,121	47,523	43,558
60th percentile limit	65,501	65,520	64,664	65,706	69,656	66,568	62,771	57,642	50,632
80th percentile limit	105,910	105,609	105,211	106,870	112,348	103,469	94,868	84,037	72,201
90th percentile limit	150,000	148,122	148,742	148,269	152,793	141,329	125,157	107,182	91,715
95th percentile limit	196,000	193,934	192,645	192,829	198,856	183,133	158,747	133,058	115,863
Household income ratios of selected percentiles									
90th/10th	12.10	11.93	11.97	11.70	11.18	10.60	10.23	8.74	9.23
95th/20th	9.38	9.28	9.18	9.02	8.72	8.22	7.49	6.63	6.33
95th/50th	3.78	3.75	3.72	3.66	3.52	3.42	3.11	2.80	2.66
80th/50th	2.04	2.04	2.03	2.03	1.99	1.93	1.86	1.77	1.66
80th/20th	5.07	5.05	5.01	5.00	4.93	4.64	4.48	4.19	3.95
20th/50th	0.40	0.41	0.40	0.41	0.40	0.42	0.41	0.42	0.42
Mean household income of quintiles									
Lowest quintile	11,651	11,657	11,640	11,746	12,978	12,791	12,028	11,678	9,755
Second quintile	30,509	30,127	30,247	30,484	33,077	31,978	30,570	28,743	27,031
Third quintile	52,322	51,923	51,623	52,530	56,138	53,799	51,109	47,549	43,158
Fourth quintile	83,519	83,291	82,941	84,272	88,880	83,328	77,254	69,667	60,384
Highest quintile	185,206	184,548	184,380	180,977	188,712	177,654	146,916	124,233	108,669
Top 5 percent	322,343	322,674	322,571	306,844	322,654	311,763	231,467	190,054	171,414
Shares of household income of quintiles									
Lowest quintile	3.2	3.2	3.2	3.3	3.4	3.6	3.8	4.2	4.0
Second quintile	8.4	8.3	8.4	8.5	8.7	8.9	9.6	10.2	10.8
Third quintile	14.4	14.4	14.3	14.6	14.8	15.0	16.1	16.9	17.3
Fourth quintile	23.0	23.0	23.0	23.4	23.4	23.2	24.3	24.7	24.2
Highest quintile	51.0	51.0	51.1	50.3	49.7	49.4	46.2	44.0	43.6
Top 5 percent	22.2	22.3	22.3	21.3	21.2	21.7	18.2	16.8	17.2
Summary measures									
Gini index of income inequality	0.476	0.477	0.477	0.470	0.463	0.459	0.426	0.402	0.397
Mean logarithmic deviation of income	0.578	0.586	0.585	0.574	0.532	0.484	0.414	0.364	0.380
Theil	0.415	0.423	0.422	0.400	0.391	0.396	0.311	0.276	0.287
Atkinson:									
e = 0.25	0.100	0.101	0.101	0.097	0.095	0.094	0.077	0.069	0.071
e = 0.50	0.196	0.198	0.198	0.191	0.185	0.183	0.155	0.139	0.143
e = 0.75	0.298	0.300	0.300	0.293	0.281	0.272	0.238	0.213	0.220

CPI-U-RS = Consumer Price Index using Current Methods.
CPS ASEC = Current Population Survey, Annual Social and Economic Supplement.
[a]Data are based on the CPS ASEC sample of 68,000 addresses. The 2014 CPS ASEC included redesigned questions for income and health insurance coverage. All of the approximately 98,000 addresses were eligible to receive the redesigned set of health insurance coverage questions. The redesigned income questions were implemented to a subsample of these 98,000 addresses using a probability split panel design. Approximately 68,000 addresses were eligible to receive a set of income questions similar to those used in the 2013 CPS ASEC and the remaining 30,000 addresses were eligible to receive the redesigned income questions. The source of the 2013 data for this table is the portion of the CPS ASEC sample which received the income questions consistent with the 2013 CPS ASEC, approximately 68,000 addresses.
[b]Implementation of Census 2010-based population controls.
[c]Implementation of a new CPS ASEC processing system.
[d]Implementation of a new CPS ASEC processing system.

SOURCE: Adapted from Carmen DeNavas-Walt and Bernadette D. Proctor, "Table A-2. Selected Measures of Household Income Dispersion: 1967 to 2013," in *Income and Poverty in the United States: 2013*, U.S. Census Bureau, September 2014, https://www.census.gov/content/dam/Census/library/publications/2014/demo/p60-249.pdf (accessed October 27, 2014)

In *Wealth Inequality in the United States since 1913: Evidence from Capitalized Income Tax Data* (October 2014, http://gabriel-zucman.eu/files/SaezZucman2014.pdf), Emmanuel Saez and Gabriel Zucman focus on household wealth, as distinguished from household income, in an attempt to explain rising inequality. The researchers note that by 2012 the share of wealth owned by the wealthiest 0.1% of Americans was higher than it had been since 1929, the year that the Great Depression began. After almost 50 years of increasing equality (1929 to 1978), the top 0.1% saw its share of total wealth rise from 7% in 1979 to 22% in 2012, while the share of overall wealth held by the bottom 90% of Americans steadily declined between the mid-1980s and 2012. According to Saez and

TABLE 1.12

Income and earnings summary measures, by selected characteristics, 2012 and 2013

[Income in 2013 dollars. Households and people as of March of the following year.]

| Characteristic | 2012 | | 2013[a] | | Percentage change in real median income (2013 less 2012) |
	Number (thousands)	Median income (dollars) Estimate	Number (thousands)	Median income (dollars) Estimate	Estimate
Households					
All households	**122,459**	**51,759**	**122,952**	**51,939**	**0.3**
Type of household					
Family households	80,902	64,984	81,192	65,587	0.9
Married-couple	59,204	76,794	59,669	76,509	−0.4
Female householder, no husband present	15,469	34,496	15,193	35,154	1.9
Male householder, no wife present	6,229	49,341	6,330	50,625	2.6
Nonfamily households	41,558	31,329	41,760	31,178	−0.5
Female householder	21,810	26,394	22,266	26,425	0.1
Male householder	19,747	37,527	19,494	36,876	−1.7
Race[b] and Hispanic origin of householder					
White	97,705	54,487	97,774	55,257	1.4
White, not Hispanic	83,792	57,837	83,641	58,270	0.7
Black	15,872	33,805	16,108	34,598	2.3
Asian	5,560	69,633	5,759	67,065	−3.7
Hispanic (any race)	15,589	39,572	15,811	40,963	3.5
Age of householder					
Under 65 years	94,535	58,186	94,223	58,448	0.4
15 to 24 years	6,314	31,049	6,323	34,311	10.5
25 to 34 years	20,017	52,128	20,008	52,702	1.1
35 to 44 years	21,334	64,553	21,046	64,973	0.7
45 to 54 years	24,068	67,376	23,809	67,141	−0.3
55 to 64 years	22,802	59,478	23,036	57,538	−3.3
65 years and older	27,924	34,340	28,729	35,611	3.7
Nativity of householder					
Native born	104,909	52,556	105,328	52,779	0.4
Foreign born	17,550	46,136	17,624	46,939	1.7
Naturalized citizen	9,192	53,786	9,491	54,974	2.2
Not a citizen	8,358	38,269	8,133	40,578	6.0
Region					
Northeast	22,125	55,421	22,053	56,775	2.4
Midwest	27,093	51,213	27,214	52,082	1.7
South	45,938	48,731	46,499	48,128	−1.2
West	27,303	55,958	27,186	56,181	0.4
Residence					
Inside metropolitan statistical areas	102,784	53,758	103,573	54,042	0.5
Inside principal cities	41,152	46,570	41,359	46,778	0.4
Outside principal cities	61,631	59,634	62,213	59,497	−0.2
Outside metropolitan statistical areas[c]	19,676	41,796	19,379	42,881	2.6
Earnings of full-time, year-round workers					
Men with earnings	59,009	50,116	60,769	50,033	−0.2
Women with earnings	44,042	38,340	45,068	39,157	2.1

[a]Data are based on the CPS ASEC (Current Population Survey, Annual Social and Economic Supplement) sample of 68,000 addresses. The 2014 CPS ASEC included redesigned questions for income and health insurance coverage. All of the approximately 98,000 addresses were eligible to receive the redesigned set of health insurance coverage questions. The redesigned income questions were implemented to a subsample of these 98,000 addresses using a probability split panel design. Approximately 68,000 addresses were eligible to receive a set of income questions similar to those used in the 2013 CPS ASEC and the remaining 30,000 addresses were eligible to receive the redesigned income questions. The source of the 2013 data for this table is the portion of the CPS ASEC sample which received the income questions consistent with the 2013 CPS ASEC, approximately 68,000 addresses.
[b]Federal surveys give respondents the option of reporting more than one race. Therefore, two basic ways of defining a race group are possible. A group such as Asian may be defined as those who reported Asian and no other race (the race-alone or single-race concept) or as those who reported Asian regardless of whether they also reported another race (the race-alone-or-in-combination concept). This table shows data using the first approach (race alone). The use of the single-race population does not imply that it is the preferred method of presenting or analyzing data. The Census Bureau uses a variety of approaches. Information on people who reported more than one race, such as white *and* American Indian and Alaska Native or Asian *and* black or African American, is available from Census 2010 through American FactFinder. About 2.9 percent of people reported more than one race in Census 2010. Data for American Indians and Alaska Natives, Native Hawaiians and other Pacific Islanders, and those reporting two or more races are not shown separately.
[c]The "Outside metropolitan statistical areas" category includes both micropolitan statistical areas and territory outside of metropolitan and micropolitan statistical areas.

SOURCE: Adapted from Carmen DeNavas-Walt and Bernadette D. Proctor, "Table 1. Income and Earnings Summary Measures by Selected Characteristics: 2012 and 2013," in *Income and Poverty in the United States: 2013*, U.S. Census Bureau, September 2014, https://www.census.gov/content/dam/Census/library/publications/2014/demo/p60-249.pdf (accessed October 27, 2014)

Zucman, the increasing share of total wealth held by the richest 0.1% of Americans is a function both of ballooning incomes at the highest reaches of the economy and of the fact that the beneficiaries of such incomes are younger today than in past eras. Thus, they have more years to accumulate returns on their astronomical wealth

FIGURE 1.5

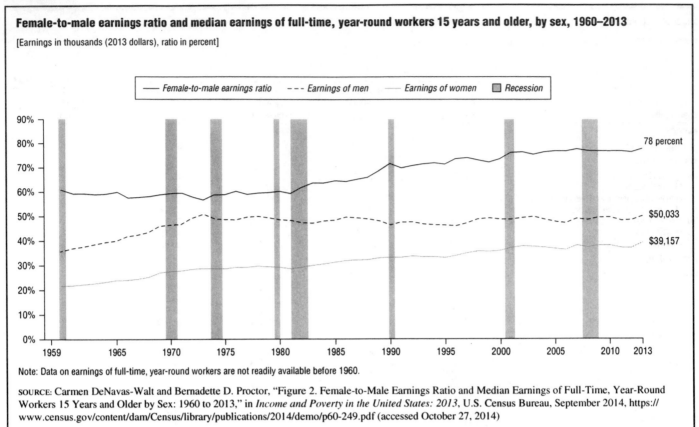

Female-to-male earnings ratio and median earnings of full-time, year-round workers 15 years and older, by sex, 1960–2013

[Earnings in thousands (2013 dollars), ratio in percent]

Note: Data on earnings of full-time, year-round workers are not readily available before 1960.

SOURCE: Carmen DeNavas-Walt and Bernadette D. Proctor, "Figure 2. Female-to-Male Earnings Ratio and Median Earnings of Full-Time, Year-Round Workers 15 Years and Older by Sex: 1960 to 2013," in *Income and Poverty in the United States: 2013*, U.S. Census Bureau, September 2014, https://www.census.gov/content/dam/Census/library/publications/2014/demo/p60-249.pdf (accessed October 27, 2014)

through savings and investment, thereby increasing the distance between their financial fortunes and those of the bottom 90%.

HOMELESSNESS

Homelessness is a complex social problem. Educators, sociologists, economists, and political scientists who have studied homelessness for decades agree that it is caused by a combination of poverty, misfortune, illness, and behavior. It is also evident that, for most people, homelessness is a temporary condition rather than a way of life and that the number of Americans who experience homelessness at some point in a given year has appreciably increased since the 1990s. Beyond these and other basic facts, however, the study of homelessness is complicated by methodological problems with counting the homeless and with disagreement over the definition of homelessness.

What Does It Mean to Be Homeless?

During a period of growing concern about homelessness in the mid-1980s, the first major piece of federal legislation aimed specifically at helping the homeless was adopted: the Stewart B. McKinney Homeless Assistance Act of 1987 (later renamed the McKinney-Vento Homeless Assistance Act). The act officially defines a homeless person as:

1. An individual who lacks a fixed, regular, and adequate nighttime residence; and

2. An individual who has a primary nighttime residence that is:

A. A supervised publicly or privately operated shelter designed to provide temporary living accommodations (including welfare hotels, congregate shelters, and transitional housing for the mentally ill);

B. An institution that provides a temporary residence for individuals intended to be institutionalized; or

C. A public or private place not designed for, or ordinarily used as, a regular sleeping accommodation for human beings.

The government definition of a homeless person focuses on whether a person is housed. Broader definitions of homelessness take into account whether a person has a home. For example, Martha Burt et al. report in *Helping America's Homeless: Emergency Shelter or Affordable Housing?* (2001) that as late as 1980 the Census Bureau identified people who lived alone and did not have a "usual home elsewhere"—in other words, a larger family—as homeless. In this sense the term *home* describes living within a family, rather than having a roof over one's head.

Burt et al. also state that homeless people themselves, when interviewed during the 1980s and 1990s, drew a distinction between having a house and having a home.

Even when homeless people had spent significant time in a traditional shelter, such as an apartment or rented room, if they felt those houses were transitional or insecure, they identified themselves as having been homeless while living there. According to Burt et al., these answers "reflect how long they have been without significant attachments to people."

Burt et al. and other homeless advocates disagree with the narrow government definition of a homeless person, which focuses on a person's sleeping arrangements. They assert that the definition should be broadened to include groups of people who, while they may have somewhere to live, do not really have a home in the conventional sense. Considerable debate has resulted over expanding the classification to include people in situations such as the following:

- People engaging in prostitution who spend each night in a different hotel room, paid for by clients

- Children in foster or relative care

- People living in stable but inadequate housing (e.g., having no plumbing or heating)

- People "doubled up" in conventional dwellings for the short term (the Census Bureau defines doubled-up households as those including one or more person over the age of 18 years who is not enrolled in school and is not the householder, spouse, or cohabiting partner of the householder)

- People in hotels paid for by vouchers to the needy

- Elderly people living with family members because they cannot afford to live elsewhere

Official definitions are important because total counts of the homeless influence the levels of funding that Congress authorizes for homeless programs. With the availability of federal funds since the passage of the McKinney-Vento Homeless Assistance Act, institutional constituencies have formed that advocate for additional funding, an effort in which more expansive definitions are helpful.

Causes of Homelessness

In 2014 the U.S. Conference of Mayors, a nonpartisan organization of cities with populations higher than 30,000, surveyed the mayors of major cities on the extent and causes of urban homelessness and published the results in *Hunger and Homelessness Survey: A Status Report on Hunger and Homelessness in America's Cities, a 25-City Survey* (December 2014, http://www.usmayors .org/pressreleases/uploads/2014/1211-report-hh.pdf). The mayors surveyed identified lack of affordable housing as the primary cause of homelessness among families, followed by unemployment, poverty, and low-wage jobs. Among unaccompanied homeless individuals, the leading

cause of homelessness in 2014 was lack of affordable housing, followed by unemployment, poverty, mental illness and the lack of needed services to address it, and substance abuse and the lack of needed services to address it.

Annie Lowery reports in "Homeless Rates in U.S. Held Level amid Recession, Study Says, but Big Gains Are Elusive" (NYTimes.com, December 10, 2012) that the U.S. Department of Housing and Urban Development (HUD) estimated that the overall number of the homeless did not rise over the course of the Great Recession and its aftermath, in spite of the large number of people who lost their home as a result of the housing crisis (the fall in real estate prices that, together with high unemployment, led many people to fall behind in their mortgage payments and often to lose their home). In fact, the number of chronically homeless fell 19% between 2007 and 2012 as a result, most likely, of targeted government efforts to reduce that portion of the homeless population. It is further believed that the problem of temporary homelessness was alleviated during this period thanks to emergency stimulus funding passed by Congress to address the consequences of the Great Recession. Part of this funding aimed to identify those who were vulnerable to homelessness as a result of foreclosure and the lack of affordable housing, and to find new housing for them; HUD estimates that more than 1 million people avoided homelessness as a result of this program. However, given the decrease in the number of chronically homeless, the relative steadiness of the overall homeless count suggests that the ranks of those who were forced into temporary homelessness by the economic downturn increased appreciably between 2007 and 2012, in spite of the success of the government's homeless prevention efforts.

In any event, there is no disputing that millions of Americans lost their home during the Great Recession. Rakesh Kochhar and D'Vera Cohn of the Pew Research Center observe in *Fighting Poverty in a Bad Economy, Americans Move in with Relatives* (October 3, 2011, http://www.pewsocialtrends.org/files/2011/10/Multigenerational-Households-Final1.pdf) that an unprecedented number of people left their own home and moved in with family members between 2007 and 2009. During that time the number of multigenerational households grew from 46.5 million to 51.4 million, for "the largest increase . . . in modern history." Although many advocates for the homeless would argue that such people should be counted among the homeless so that government aid might be more effective at meeting society's needs, these doubled-up families were not considered homeless.

Counting the Homeless

Crafting policies to combat homelessness depends heavily on the collection of reliable information regarding the number and attributes of the homeless population, but the very nature of homelessness makes accurate data collection difficult. Typically, researchers studying the U.S. population at large contact people in their home using in-person or telephone surveys to obtain information regarding income, education levels, household size, ethnicity, and other demographic data. Homeless people cannot be counted at home, of course, and researchers have struggled to address this methodological shortcoming.

The Census Bureau, in particular, has encountered difficulties in counting the homeless, and objections to its methodology during the 1990s led it to discontinue its efforts to comprehensively assess the homeless population in the 21st century. In its most recent decennial census (2010), the bureau released homeless population figures only as they relate to one category: people living in "emergency and transitional shelters." This count is openly incomplete, relative to the overall homeless population. Other people falling under the federal definition of homelessness, such as people who are counted at domestic violence shelters, family crisis centers, soup kitchens, mobile food vans, and targeted nonsheltered outdoor locations (i.e., street people, car dwellers, and so on), are included in the category of "other noninstitutional group quarters population." However, this category includes other groups, such as students living in college dormitories. As a result, the homeless portion of the category cannot be extracted. In 2010, 209,325

Americans were counted as occupants of emergency and transitional shelters. (See Table 1.13.)

In the 21st century HUD is widely seen as the sponsor of the most authoritative data on homelessness. The agency's attempts to collect data that accurately represent the U.S. homeless population at large center on its annual national point-in-time (PIT) studies of the homeless. These studies, which are undertaken in collaboration with local government officials and shelters across the United States, count the number of homeless people during a specific period and at specific places. The agency attempts to locate unsheltered as well as sheltered homeless people, and its yearly count is meant to provide a snapshot of the American homeless population on a given day.

HUD's assessment of the homeless population goes beyond PIT counts, as well. The department monitors the inventory of shelter beds to derive further information about the size of the homeless population and the nature of its needs. It also collaborates with state and municipal governments in the collection of longitudinal data about specific homeless populations. This longitudinal data, which is collected over time in an attempt to determine long-term patterns among the homeless, is stored in a database called the Homeless Management Information Systems (HMIS). PIT counts, shelter inventories, and HMIS data represent the three main data sets that are used by local governments, in partnership with HUD, to

TABLE 1.13

Decennial Census count of group quarters and emergency and transitional shelter populations, 2010

Sex and selected age group	Total population		Group quarters population		Emergency and transitional shelter population		
	Number	Percent	Number	Percent	Number	Percent	Percent of group quarters population
Both sexes	308,745,538	100.0	7,987,323	100.0	209,325	100.0	2.6
Male	151,781,326	49.2	4,858,210	60.8	129,969	62.1	2.7
Female	156,964,212	50.8	3,129,113	39.2	79,356	37.9	2.5
Both sexes, all ages	308,745,538	100.0	7,987,323	100.0	209,325	100.0	2.6
Under 18 years	74,181,467	24.0	260,586	3.3	42,290	20.2	16.2
18 to 64 years	194,296,087	62.9	6,269,031	78.5	161,578	77.2	2.6
65 years and over	40,267,984	13.0	1,457,706	18.3	5,457	2.6	0.4
Median age	37.2	(X)	28.8	(X)	39.2	(X)	(X)
Male, all ages	151,781,326	100.0	4,858,210	100.0	129,969	100.0	2.7
Under 18 years	37,945,136	25.0	165,477	3.4	21,325	16.4	12.9
18 to 64 years	96,473,230	63.6	4,239,142	87.3	104,834	80.7	2.5
65 years and over	17,362,960	11.4	453,591	9.3	3,810	2.9	0.8
Median age	35.8	(X)	29.5	(X)	43.9	(X)	(X)
Female, all ages	156,964,212	100.0	3,129,113	100.0	79,356	100.0	2.5
Under 18 years	36,236,331	23.1	95,109	3.0	20,965	26.4	22.0
18 to 64 years	97,822,857	62.3	2,029,889	64.9	56,744	71.5	2.8
65 years and over	22,905,024	14.6	1,004,115	32.1	1,647	2.1	0.2
Median age	38.5	(X)	25.4	(X)	29.7	(X)	(X)

(X) Not applicable.
Note: Percentages may not sum to 100.0 due to rounding.

SOURCE: Amy Symens Smith, Charles Holmberg, and Marcella Jones-Puthoff, "Table 1. Total, Group Quarters, and Emergency and Transitional Shelter Populations by Sex and Selected Age Groups: 2010," in *The Emergency and Transitional Shelter Population: 2010*, U.S. Census Bureau, September 2012, http://www.census.gov/prod/cen2010/reports/c2010sr-02.pdf (accessed November 18, 2014)

build a yearly portrait of the American homeless population. Each year HUD submits its findings in the *Annual Homeless Assessment Report* to Congress.

According to Meghan Henry et al., in *The 2014 Annual Homeless Assessment Report (AHAR) to Congress—Part 1: Point-in-Time Estimates of Homelessness* (October 2014, https://www.hudexchange.info/resources/documents/2014-AHAR-Part1.pdf), HUD conducted its PIT count on a single night in January 2014. On that night, HUD estimated that the U.S. homeless population was 578,424. (See Figure 1.6.) This number was down markedly from a recent peak of 651,142 in 2007. Since 2007 there had also been an increase in the number of sheltered homeless and a corresponding (but more dramatic) decrease in the number of unsheltered homeless. In 2007, 391,401 of the total homeless population of 651,142 (60.1%) were sheltered and 259,741 (39.9%) were unsheltered. By 2014, 401,051 (69.3%) of the total homeless population of 578,424 where sheltered and 177,373 (30.7%) were unsheltered. The changes in total homelessness, as well as the increase of sheltered homelessness relative to unsheltered homelessness, were likely influenced by an ongoing federal effort to retool the shelter system nationally to reduce chronic homelessness. Of the 578,424 homeless Americans counted on that January night in 2014, Henry et al. indicate that 36.2% were sheltered individuals and 33.2% were sheltered people in families. As in previous years, individuals were much more likely to be unsheltered than families. Of the total homeless count, 26.5% were unsheltered individuals and 4.2% were unsheltered people in families. (See Figure 1.7.)

THE ONGOING FIGHT AGAINST POVERTY AND HOMELESSNESS

In the many media commemorations of the 50th anniversary of the War on Poverty in 2014, pundits routinely recalled President Ronald Reagan's (1911–2004) witticism: "We fought a war on poverty, and poverty won." Reagan's intent in voicing this idea was to suggest that the liberal safety-net policies of the New Deal and the War on Poverty, which required large amounts of federal spending and correspondingly high rates of taxation on people at the upper end of the income spectrum, were ineffective and should be reduced or abolished. During the years of his presidency (from 1981 to 1989), Reagan spearheaded reductions in the size of many government programs, and his understanding of the War on Poverty informed the fight to reduce the scope of the U.S. welfare system during the 1990s.

In the 21st century many conservatives continue to argue that government-funded safety-net programs keep poverty entrenched, whereas business-friendly attempts to expand the economy through low taxes and minimal regulation are the most successful means of lifting people out of poverty. Meanwhile, many left-leaning experts suggest that President Johnson's War on Poverty was in many ways a success and that the inability to generate greater reductions in the poverty level since that time are a direct result of the cuts to the safety net imposed during the Reagan years and beyond.

There are, of course, many variations on these positions as well as many positions that adopt neither of these

FIGURE 1.6

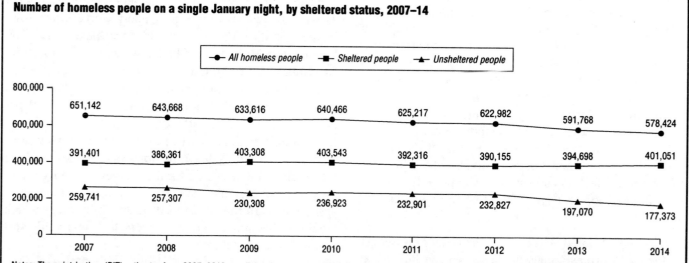

Number of homeless people on a single January night, by sheltered status, 2007–14

Notes: The point-in-time (PIT) estimates from 2007–2013 are slightly lower than those reported in past AHARs (Annual Homeless Assessment Report). The reduction reflects an adjustment to the estimates of unsheltered homeless people submitted by the Los Angeles City and County Continuum of Care. The adjustment removed: 20,746 people from 2007 and 2008; 9,451 people in 2009 and 2010; 10,800 people in 2011 and 2012; and 18,274 people from 2013. This change applies to all PIT estimates in this section.

SOURCE: Meghan Henry et al., "Exhibit 1.1. Estimates of Homeless People, by Sheltered Status, 2007–2014," in *The 2014 Annual Homeless Assessment Report (AHAR) to Congress—Part 1: Point-in-Time Estimates of Homelessness*, U.S. Department of Housing and Urban Development, Office of Community Planning and Development, October 2014, https://www.hudexchange.info/resources/documents/2014-AHAR-Part1.pdf (accessed October 31, 2014)

FIGURE 1.7

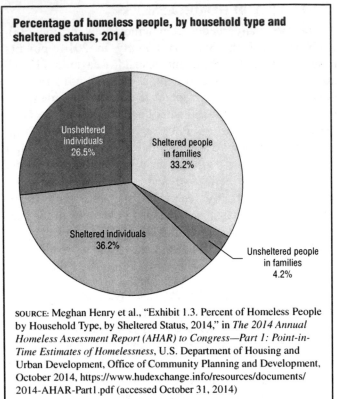

Percentage of homeless people, by household type and sheltered status, 2014

Unsheltered individuals 26.5%

Sheltered people in families 33.2%

Sheltered individuals 36.2%

Unsheltered people in families 4.2%

SOURCE: Meghan Henry et al., "Exhibit 1.3. Percent of Homeless People by Household Type, by Sheltered Status, 2014," in *The 2014 Annual Homeless Assessment Report (AHAR) to Congress—Part 1: Point-in-Time Estimates of Homelessness*, U.S. Department of Housing and Urban Development, Office of Community Planning and Development, October 2014, https://www.hudexchange.info/resources/documents/2014-AHAR-Part1.pdf (accessed October 31, 2014)

basic left–right poles. For example, in "Actually, We Won the War on Poverty" (Politico.com, January 24, 2014), Scott Winship updates the conservative interpretation of the War on Poverty. He argues that "the country has actually reduced poverty more than we often appreciate—and that decline in poverty has been less about the liberal programs of the New Deal and Great Society and more about economic growth and center-right welfare reforms than is widely recognized." He also suggests that the federal poverty line overstates the number of people in poverty because it fails "to account for food stamps, Medicaid, Medicare and public housing subsidies" as well as "for refundable tax credits that promote work." Winship maintains that the Census Bureau's techniques for adjusting for inflation overstate increases in the cost of living and thereby add to the overstatement of the size of the poor population. He cites the work of the economists Bruce Meyer and James Sullivan, who adjust for such statistical factors and find that the poverty rate fell from 32% in 1963 to 7% in 2000, before rising again to 8% in 2010.

By contrast, Jared Bernstein of the Center on Budget and Policy Priorities argues in "The War on Poverty at 50" (NYTimes.com, January 6, 2014) that the War on Poverty was a measured success but that structural changes in the economy stand in the way of eradicating poverty in the United States. In stark contrast to Winship, Bernstein argues that the official 2012 U.S. poverty rate of 15% undercounts the impoverished population and that

the actual poverty rate that year was 16%. He further notes that in the absence of food stamps, unemployment benefits, the Earned Income Tax Credit, and housing subsidies (among other government antipoverty programs), the 2012 poverty rate would have been 29%. Even so, these programs successfully lifted 40 million people, or 13% of the U.S. population, out of poverty in 2012. Their inability to do more to fight poverty, according to Bernstein, stems from the fact that "they've had to work much harder in an economy that has made it a lot tougher for those at the bottom to get ahead." The major structural forces keeping people in poverty were thus "inequality, globalization, deunionization, lower minimum wages, slack labor markets and decreasing returns to lower-end jobs."

Bernstein's conclusions are supported by data from the Economic Policy Institute (EPI), a nonpartisan think tank that is devoted to the interests of low- and middle-income workers. The EPI particularly singles out income inequality as a driver of poverty. For example, the EPI (September 26, 2014, http://stateofworkingamerica.org/chart/swa-poverty-figure-7q-impact-econonic-demographic) notes that income inequality increased the poverty rate by 7.1 percentage points between 1979 and 2013, outpacing other economic and demographic factors that cut the poverty rate. These antipoverty factors included income growth, which accounted for a decline in poverty of 3.4 percentage points, and the educational composition of households, which accounted for a decline of 2.9 percentage points.

Those who maintain that structural economic forces must be addressed if poverty and homelessness are to be combated tend to support a strengthening of the safety net as well as new measures to support workers and low-income families. For example, in "Anti-poverty Leaders Discuss the Need for a Shared Agenda" (Nation.com, November 25, 2013), Greg Kaufmann suggests a coordinated antipoverty campaign premised on three main demands: raising the minimum wage above $10.10 per hour, which would be sufficient for a full-time worker to lift a family of three out of poverty; the introduction of paid sick and family leave for low-wage workers, which would allow them to care for themselves or family members without risking their job; and the creation of a system for affordable and adequate child care, which would enable single parents to work full time while still caring for their children.

The stories of low-income workers themselves often illuminate the challenges of escaping poverty and homelessness in ways that cannot be captured by expert analysis. For example, Linda Tirado states in "Why Poor People Stay Poor" (Slate.com, December 5, 2014), "I once lost a whole truck over a few hundred bucks. It had been towed, and when I called the company they told me they'd need a few hundred dollars for the fee. I didn't have a few hundred dollars. . . . I was working two jobs at the time. Both were part time. Neither paid a hundred bucks a day, much less two." Without her truck, Tirado had to walk 6 miles (10 km) every day to her jobs, and once she had been paid, she went to reclaim the vehicle, only to be told that it would now cost her over a thousand dollars to do so because of the fees for storing the vehicle that had been imposed in the meantime. Eventually, both Tirado and her husband lost their jobs because of their lack of transportation, and because they could not pay their rent, they soon lost their apartment, as well. To avoid poverty and homelessness, explains Tirado, a low-income worker must either have good luck or substantial savings. "If I'm saving my spare five bucks a week, in the best-case scenario I will have saved $260 a year," Tirado writes. "If you deny yourself even small luxuries, that's the fortune you'll amass. Of course you will never manage to actually save it. . . . Something, I guarantee you, will happen in three months."

As Tirado's story illustrates, the poor are always at risk of becoming homeless. Thus, the fight against poverty is also a fight to prevent homelessness. However, once people have become homeless, they become the focus of a different set of aid efforts and government programs. Traditionally, private nonprofit groups that run shelters, soup kitchens, and other aid organizations have taken the lead in serving the needs of the homeless. These groups usually derive a large part of their funding from the federal government, often by applying for competitive grants awarded by HUD and other government agencies. Such efforts have been subject to many of the same criticisms as the larger safety-net programs that help the poor, and efforts to help the homeless have also sometimes run afoul of local residents who believe that feeding or helping the homeless encourages them to stay in the locality where they are being helped.

Whereas the predominant model for helping the homeless during the late 20th century involved a system of emergency shelters that housed the newly homeless and transitional shelters that put homeless individuals and families on a path toward self-sufficiency, a so-called housing-first approach increasingly characterizes the focus of government and nonprofit agencies in the 21st century. While funding remains in place for emergency shelters, the housing-first approach involves shifting government resources from transitional shelters to permanent housing. The chronically homeless are placed in permanent housing as quickly as possible and then matched with services to meet the health and behavioral needs that are often a primary cause of their having become homeless in the first place. Although this effort involves indefinitely subsidizing the housing costs of such individuals, it has been found to be more effective at helping the chronically homeless remain off the streets than any other previous aid effort. Furthermore, the housing-first approach has proven to be a fiscally responsible alternative to leaving chronically homeless people to fend for themselves on the streets. The federal funding that flows to state, local, and private groups implementing these efforts represents a reallocation of existing funds rather than an increase in overall funding, and the cost of permanent housing and services is significantly lower than the costs imposed by the chronically homeless on federal, state, and local governments, in the form of public funds spent on arrests, court fees, and emergency department bills.

Such programs, which combine fiscal priorities with effective aid to those in need, are more typical of the ongoing fight against poverty and homelessness than the simplistic left–right political debate might lead many ordinary citizens to believe. As the complexly interwoven social, economic, and political realities that drive poverty and homelessness change, the fight against poverty and homelessness will doubtless continue to change. However, contrary to Reagan's witticism, the fight is not over and it likely never will be.

CHAPTER 2

WHO ARE THE POOR?

CHARACTERISTICS OF THE POOR

Carmen DeNavas-Walt and Bernadette D. Proctor of the U.S. Census Bureau indicate in *Income and Poverty in the United States: 2013* (September 2014, https://www.census.gov/content/dam/Census/library/publications/2014/demo/p60-249.pdf) that in 2013, 45.3 million people, or 14.5% of the U.S. population, had income-to-poverty ratios under 1.00 and were therefore officially considered poor. As shown in Table 1.6 in Chapter 1, 60.2 million Americans, or 19.2% of the U.S. population, were poor or near-poor, meaning that they had income-to-poverty ratios of 1.25 or less.

Children under the age of 18 years are more likely than people of other ages to be poor. In 2013, 19.9% (14.7 million) of all American children were poor, compared with 13.6% (26.4 million) of adults aged 18 to 64 years and 9.5% (4.2 million) of adults aged 65 years and older. (See Table 2.1.) Children were also more likely than those in other age groups to experience income-to-poverty ratios of 1.25 or less. In 2013, 26.1% (19.2 million) of all children under the age of 18 years were either poor or near-poor, compared with 17.6% (34.3 million) of adults aged 18 to 64 years and 15.1% (6.7 million) of adults aged 65 years and older. (See Table 1.6 in Chapter 1.) Children were also disproportionately represented among the desperately poor (those whose incomes fall below half of the poverty line); 8.8% (6.5 million) of all children were in this category in 2013, compared with 6.2% (12.2 million) of adults aged 18 to 64 years and 2.7% (1.2 million) of adults over the age of 65 years.

Besides the previous statistics, which provide a yearly snapshot of poverty, the Census Bureau studies poverty longitudinally, surveying individuals at different points in time over multiple years. Publications based on these longitudinal studies provide additional insight into the experience of living in poverty. For example, according to Ashley N. Edwards of the Census Bureau, in *Dynamics of Economic Well-Being: Poverty, 2009–2011* (January 2014, http://www.census.gov/prod/2014pubs/p70-137.pdf), a much higher proportion of the U.S. population than that captured by the annual statistics experiences at least occasional poverty. In the three-year period from January 2009 to December 2011 nearly one-third (31.6%) of the total population lived below the poverty line for at least two months. Among those individuals who experienced poverty for at least two consecutive months, 44% lived below the poverty line for four months or less and 15.2% remained in poverty for more than two years. Some individuals exited and then reentered poverty during the survey period; overall, 35.4% of those individuals in poverty in 2009 were no longer in poverty in 2011. However, roughly half of those who had exited poverty by the end of the study period had incomes of less than 150% of poverty, a threshold at which they remained at risk of falling below the poverty line given a change in their personal circumstances, such as the loss of a job, a health problem, or a major property loss.

Race and Ethnicity

Historically, poverty rates have been consistently lower for whites than for minorities in the United States. According to DeNavas-Walt and Proctor, 28.5 million (18.1%) whites lived below the poverty level in 1959. The proportion of whites living below the poverty level fell markedly during the 1960s and early 1970s, reaching a low of 8.4% in 1973. The poverty rate for whites remained between 9% and 12% during the 1980s, 1990s, and early 2000s. In 2010 it reached its highest level (13%) since 1965. In 2013, 12.3% (29.9 million) of whites lived in poverty. (See Table 2.1.)

DeNavas-Walt and Proctor note that the poverty rate for African Americans started at a much higher level and has fallen more dramatically, but it has at all times been

TABLE 2.1

People in poverty, by selected characteristics, 2012 and 2013

[Numbers in thousands. People as of March of the following year.]

Characteristic	2012 Total	Below poverty Number	Below poverty Percent	2013[a] Total	Below poverty Number	Below poverty Percent	Change in poverty (2013 less 2012)[b] Number	Change in poverty (2013 less 2012)[b] Percent
People								
Total	310,648	46,496	15.0	312,965	45,318	14.5	−1,178	−0.5
Family status								
In families	252,863	33,198	13.1	254,988	31,530	12.4	−1,669	−0.8
Householder	80,944	9,520	11.8	81,217	9,130	11.2	−390	−0.5
Related children under age 18	72,545	15,437	21.3	72,573	14,142	19.5	−1,295	−1.8
Related children under age 6	23,604	5,769	24.4	23,585	5,231	22.2	−538	−2.3
In unrelated subfamilies	1,599	740	46.3	1,413	608	43.0	−132	−3.3
Reference person	641	278	43.3	595	246	41.3	−32	−2.0
Children under age 18	855	440	51.4	714	340	47.7	−99	−3.7
Unrelated individuals	56,185	12,558	22.4	56,564	13,181	23.3	623	1.0
Race[c] and Hispanic origin								
White	242,147	30,816	12.7	243,085	29,936	12.3	−880	−0.4
White, not Hispanic	195,112	18,940	9.7	195,167	18,796	9.6	−144	−0.1
Black	40,125	10,911	27.2	40,615	11,041	27.2	130	
Asian	16,417	1,921	11.7	17,063	1,785	10.5	−136	−1.2
Hispanic (any race)	53,105	13,616	25.6	54,145	12,744	23.5	−871	−2.1
Sex								
Male	152,058	20,656	13.6	153,361	20,119	13.1	−537	−0.5
Female	158,590	25,840	16.3	159,605	25,199	15.8	−641	−0.5
Age								
Under age 18	73,719	16,073	21.8	73,625	14,659	19.9	−1,415	−1.9
Aged 18 to 64	193,642	26,497	13.7	194,833	26,429	13.6	−68	−0.1
Aged 65 and older	43,287	3,926	9.1	44,508	4,231	9.5	305	0.4
Nativity								
Native born	270,570	38,803	14.3	271,968	37,921	13.9	−882	−0.4
Foreign born	40,078	7,693	19.2	40,997	7,397	18.0	−296	−1.2
Naturalized citizen	18,193	2,252	12.4	19,147	2,425	12.7	173	0.3
Not a citizen	21,885	5,441	24.9	21,850	4,972	22.8	−469	−2.1
Region								
Northeast	55,050	7,490	13.6	55,478	7,046	12.7	−444	−0.9
Midwest	66,337	8,851	13.3	66,785	8,590	12.9	−261	−0.5
South	115,957	19,106	16.5	116,961	18,870	16.1	−236	−0.3
West	73,303	11,049	15.1	73,742	10,812	14.7	−237	−0.4
Residence								
Inside metropolitan statistical areas	262,949	38,033	14.5	265,915	37,746	14.2	−287	−0.3
Inside principal cities	101,225	19,934	19.7	102,149	19,530	19.1	−404	−0.6
Outside principal cities	161,724	18,099	11.2	163,767	18,217	11.1	118	−0.1
Outside metropolitan statistical areas[d]	47,698	8,463	17.7	47,050	7,572	16.1	−891	−1.6
Work experience								
Total, aged 18 to 64	193,642	26,497	13.7	194,833	26,429	13.6	−68	−0.1
All workers	145,814	10,672	7.3	146,252	10,736	7.3	64	
Worked full-time, year-round	98,715	2,867	2.9	100,855	2,771	2.7	−96	−0.2
Less than full-time, year-round	47,099	7,805	16.6	45,397	7,965	17.5	160	1.0
Did not work at least 1 week	47,828	15,825	33.1	48,581	15,693	32.3	−132	−0.8
Disability status[e]								
Total, aged 18 to 64	193,642	26,497	13.7	194,833	26,429	13.6	−68	−0.1
With a disability	14,996	4,257	28.4	15,098	4,352	28.8	95	0.4
With no disability	177,727	22,189	12.5	178,761	22,023	12.3	−166	−0.2

much higher than that for whites. In 1959, 55.1% (9.9 million) of African Americans lived in poverty. By 1974 the rate had fallen to 30.3%. It fluctuated between 30% and 35% through the mid-1990s, before falling significantly during the late 1990s and reaching a new low of 22.5% in 2000. The rate rose slightly during the early 2000s and then, with the Great Recession (which officially lasted from December 2007 to June 2009), it returned to levels not seen since the mid-1990s. In 2013, 27.2% (11 million) of all African Americans lived below the poverty line. (See Table 2.1.)

According to DeNavas-Walt and Proctor, the Census Bureau began gathering poverty statistics by Hispanic origin in 1972 and found that in that year 22.8% (2.4 million) of Hispanics lived in poverty. The rate then

TABLE 2.1

People in poverty, by selected characteristics, 2012 and 2013 [CONTINUED]

[Numbers in thousands. People as of March of the following year.]

ªData are based on the CPS ASEC sample of 68,000 addresses. The 2014 CPS ASEC included redesigned questions for income and health insurance coverage. All of the approximately 98,000 addresses were eligible to receive the redesigned set of health insurance coverage questions. The redesigned income questions were implemented to a subsample of these 98,000 addresses using a probability split panel design. Approximately 68,000 addresses were eligible to receive a set of income questions similar to those used in the 2013 CPS ASEC and the remaining 30,000 addresses were eligible to receive the redesigned income questions. The source of the 2013 data for this table is the portion of the CPS ASEC sample which received the income questions consistent with the 2013 CPS ASEC, approximately 68,000 addresses.
ᵇDetails may not sum to totals because of rounding.
ᶜFederal surveys now give respondents the option of reporting more than one race. Therefore, two basic ways of defining a race group are possible. A group such as Asian may be defined as those who reported Asian and no other race (the race-alone or single-race concept) or as those who reported Asian regardless of whether they also reported another race (the race-alone-or-in-combination concept). This table shows data using the first approach (race alone). The use of the single-race population does not imply that it is the preferred method of presenting or analyzing data. The Census Bureau uses a variety of approaches. Information on people who reported more than one race, such as White *and* American Indian and Alaska Native or Asian *and* Black or African American, is available from Census 2010 through American FactFinder. About 2.9 percent of people reported more than one race in Census 2010. Data for American Indians and Alaska Natives, Native Hawaiians and Other Pacific Islanders, and those reporting two or more races are not shown separately.
ᵈThe "Outside metropolitan statistical areas" category includes both micropolitan statistical areas and territory outside of metropolitan and micropolitan statistical areas.
ᵉThe sum of those with and without a disability does not equal the total because disability status is not defined for individuals in the Armed Forces.
ᶠRepresents or rounds to zero.
CPS ASEC = Current Population Survey, Annual Social and Economic Supplement.

SOURCE: Adapted from Carmen DeNavas-Walt and Bernadette D. Proctor, "Table 3. People in Poverty by Selected Characteristics: 2012 and 2013," in *Income and Poverty in the United States: 2013*, U.S. Census Bureau, September 2014, https://www.census.gov/content/dam/Census/library/publications/2014/demo/p60-249.pdf (accessed October 27, 2014)

fluctuated from a low of 21.6% (1978) to a high of 30.7% (1994) over the following decades, before falling to sustained historic lows between 1999 and 2008, when it remained largely between 20% and 23%. As with other racial and ethnic groups, Hispanics experienced increasing poverty during in the Great Recession, with poverty rates rising to a high of 26.5% in 2010. In 2013, 23.5% (12.7 million) of all Hispanics lived in poverty. (See Table 2.1.)

DeNavas-Walt and Proctor indicate that the Census Bureau has been collecting data on poverty for Asian Americans since 2002. (Prior to 2002 the Census Bureau used the category "Asian and Pacific Islander," which yielded slightly different statistical outcomes.) Throughout this period the poverty rate for Asian Americans has more closely resembled that for whites than that for African Americans and Hispanics, fluctuating between 9.8% (2004) and 12.5% (2009). In 2013, 10.5% (1.8 million) of all Asian Americans lived in poverty. (See Table 2.1.)

African American and Hispanic children suffered even more disproportionately from poverty than African American and Hispanic adults and seniors. In 2012, 38.4% of non-Hispanic African Americans under the age of 18 years and 33.8% of Hispanics under the age of 18 years were poor, compared with only 12.3% of non-Hispanic white children in the same age group. (See Table 2.2.) Non-Hispanic African American and Hispanic children who were raised by a single mother were particularly likely to live in poverty in 2012. More than half of children in both groups (53.9% for non-Hispanic African Americans and 55.4% for Hispanics) lived in poverty. However, the difficulty of making ends meet as a single mother was a problem that extended across racial and ethnic boundaries. The poverty rate for non-Hispanic white children who were raised by single mothers was 37.3%—25 percentage points higher than the rate for non-Hispanic white children in general.

The rates of desperate poverty (having income-to-poverty ratios under 0.5, or half of the poverty threshold) were also much higher for non-Hispanic African American and Hispanic children than for non-Hispanic white children. Only 5.4% of non-Hispanic white children were desperately poor, compared with 13.7% of Hispanic children and 19.2% of non-Hispanic African American children. (See Table 2.2.) Again, single-parenting by females was a strong predictor of the likelihood of living in desperate poverty regardless of racial and ethnic identity. Nearly one out of five (19.2%) non-Hispanic white children who were raised by single mothers lived at half of the poverty line or less, compared with 27.1% of non-Hispanic African American children and 29.6% of Hispanic children in such households.

The median (the middle value—half are higher and half are lower) household income reflects the disparity in poverty levels between different groups. In 2013 Asian Americans had the highest median income among all racial and ethnic groups, at $72,472. (See Table 2.3.) The median income for non-Hispanic whites was significantly lower, at $57,684, and the median income for Hispanics was lower still, at $41,508. The median incomes for African Americans ($34,815) and for Native Americans and Alaskan Natives ($36,641) were roughly half that of Asian Americans.

Age

CHILD POVERTY. The United States has historically had one of the highest rates of child poverty in the developed world. In *Children of the Recession: The Impact of the Economic Crisis on Child Well-Being in*

TABLE 2.2

Percentage of children aged 0–17 living below selected poverty levels, by selected characteristics, selected years 1980–2012

Characteristic	1980	1985	1990	1995	2000	2005	2010	2011	2012
Below 100% poverty									
Total	18.3	20.7	20.6	20.8	16.2	17.6	22.0	21.9	21.8
Gender									
Male	18.1	20.3	20.5	20.4	16.0	17.4	22.2	21.6	21.3
Female	18.6	21.1	20.8	21.2	16.3	17.8	21.9	22.2	22.3
Age									
Ages 0–5	20.7	23.0	23.6	24.1	18.3	20.2	25.8	25.0	24.8
Ages 6–17	17.3	19.5	19.0	19.1	15.2	16.3	20.2	20.4	20.4
Race and Hispanic origin[a]									
White, non-Hispanic	11.8	12.8	12.3	11.2	9.1	10.0	12.3	12.5	12.3
Black, non-Hispanic	42.3	43.3	44.5	41.5	31.0	34.5	39.1	38.8	38.4
Hispanic	33.2	40.3	38.4	40.0	28.4	28.3	34.9	34.1	33.8
Region[b]									
Northeast	16.3	18.5	18.4	19.0	14.5	15.5	18.5	18.8	19.6
South	22.5	22.8	23.8	23.5	18.4	19.7	24.3	23.4	24.2
Midwest	16.3	20.7	18.8	16.9	13.1	15.9	20.5	20.8	19.9
West	16.1	19.3	19.8	22.1	16.9	17.5	22.2	22.5	21.2
Children in married-couple families, total	10.1	11.4	10.3	10.0	8.0	8.5	11.6	11.0	11.2
Ages 0–5	11.6	12.9	11.7	11.1	8.7	9.9	13.4	12.2	12.6
Ages 6–17	9.4	10.5	9.5	9.4	7.7	7.7	10.7	10.4	10.5
White, non-Hispanic	7.5	8.2	6.9	6.0	4.7	4.5	6.4	6.1	6.2
Black, non-Hispanic	19.7	17.2	17.8	12.0	8.5	12.4	16.0	15.6	14.9
Hispanic	23.0	27.2	26.6	28.4	20.8	20.1	25.1	23.3	23.6
Children in female-householder families, no husband present, total	51.4	54.1	54.2	50.7	40.5	43.1	47.1	48.0	47.6
Ages 0–5	65.4	65.7	65.9	61.9	50.7	52.9	58.7	57.7	56.3
Ages 6–17	46.2	49.1	48.4	45.2	36.3	38.9	41.9	43.5	43.7
White, non-Hispanic	38.6	39.1	41.4	34.9	29.3	33.8	36.0	36.5	37.3
Black, non-Hispanic	64.9	66.7	65.1	61.5	48.9	50.2	52.6	54.2	53.9
Hispanic	64.8	73.0	68.9	66.0	50.5	51.0	56.8	57.2	55.4
Below 50% poverty									
Total	6.9	8.6	8.8	8.5	6.7	7.7	9.9	9.8	9.7
Gender									
Male	6.9	8.6	8.8	8.4	6.6	7.3	10.0	9.7	9.3
Female	6.9	8.6	8.8	8.5	6.8	8.1	9.8	10.0	10.1
Age									
Ages 0–5	8.3	10.0	10.7	10.8	8.1	9.1	12.0	12.2	11.9
Ages 6–17	6.2	7.8	7.8	7.2	6.0	7.0	8.9	8.7	8.6
Race and Hispanic origin[a]									
White, non-Hispanic	4.3	5.0	5.0	3.9	3.7	4.1	5.1	5.6	5.4
Black, non-Hispanic	17.7	22.1	22.7	20.5	14.9	17.3	20.1	19.0	19.2
Hispanic	10.8	14.1	14.2	16.3	10.2	11.5	15.0	14.5	13.7
Region[b]									
Northeast	4.7	6.5	7.6	8.6	6.4	7.5	8.9	8.7	8.2
South	9.7	10.9	11.3	10.1	7.9	9.0	10.5	10.8	11.0
Midwest	6.3	9.5	8.9	6.6	5.5	6.5	9.8	10.0	9.2
West	5.1	5.6	6.1	7.8	6.2	7.0	9.8	8.9	9.0
Children in married-couple families, total	3.1	3.5	2.7	2.6	2.2	2.4	3.5	3.3	3.6
Ages 0–5	3.7	4.0	3.2	2.9	2.2	2.8	4.1	3.7	4.2
Ages 6–17	2.8	3.1	2.4	2.5	2.2	2.2	3.2	3.1	3.3
White, non-Hispanic	2.5	2.6	2.0	1.5	1.5	1.2	1.8	2.0	2.2
Black, non-Hispanic	4.2	5.2	3.9	2.5	2.9	4.5	5.7	5.1	5.8
Hispanic	6.2	7.4	6.7	8.6	4.5	5.2	7.5	6.4	6.0
Children in female-householder families, no husband present, total	22.3	27.0	28.7	24.4	19.7	22.5	25.3	25.5	24.6
Ages 0–5	31.4	35.8	37.7	34.3	28.4	29.4	33.3	34.1	32.0
Ages 6–17	18.8	23.2	24.2	19.7	16.1	19.6	21.7	21.6	21.3
White, non-Hispanic	15.3	17.5	21.1	14.5	13.4	16.4	18.6	19.7	19.2
Black, non-Hispanic	31.0	38.0	37.1	32.6	23.9	26.5	28.2	28.1	27.1
Hispanic	24.7	31.1	33.1	33.1	26.0	29.1	31.5	31.1	29.6

Rich Countries (September 2014, http://www.unicef-irc.org/publications/pdf/rc12-eng-web.pdf), the United Nations Children's Fund (UNICEF) provides an overview of government data from 41 of the world's richest countries to create a comparative portrait of child poverty in the developed world in 2008 and 2012. Although the U.S. economy outperformed other developed economies in the years after the Great Recession, UNICEF finds that U.S. children were far more likely to be impoverished than children in comparably wealthy countries. Setting

TABLE 2.2

Percentage of children aged 0–17 living below selected poverty levels, by selected characteristics, selected years 1980–2012 [CONTINUED]

Characteristic	1980	1985	1990	1995	2000	2005	2010	2011	2012
Below 150% poverty									
Total	**29.9**	**32.3**	**31.4**	**32.2**	**26.7**	**28.2**	**33.4**	**34.0**	**33.3**
Gender									
Male	29.6	32.2	31.3	31.7	26.6	28.0	33.6	33.6	32.8
Female	30.3	32.3	31.6	32.7	26.8	28.3	33.3	34.3	33.9
Age									
Ages 0–5	33.2	35.6	34.6	35.5	29.3	31.5	37.1	37.4	36.4
Ages 6–17	28.4	30.5	29.7	30.5	25.4	26.5	31.6	32.3	31.9
Race and Hispanic origin[a]									
White, non-Hispanic	21.7	22.6	21.4	20.1	16.4	17.2	20.5	21.5	20.7
Black, non-Hispanic	57.3	59.5	57.8	56.5	45.4	48.7	54.0	52.0	51.4
Hispanic	52.7	57.8	56.0	59.4	47.3	45.9	51.7	52.4	51.9
Region[b]									
Northeast	27.0	28.1	26.7	28.8	23.4	24.9	27.5	29.2	30.2
South	35.8	36.7	36.0	35.8	29.5	31.2	36.9	36.0	36.1
Midwest	26.0	31.0	28.7	26.8	21.8	25.0	31.1	31.5	30.6
West	27.9	30.4	31.4	35.0	29.3	28.8	34.2	36.1	33.5
Children in married-couple families, total	20.6	22.2	20.1	20.0	16.2	17.0	21.0	21.3	20.5
Ages 0–5	23.7	25.7	22.2	21.3	17.8	19.8	23.3	23.2	22.3
Ages 6–17	19.1	20.3	18.8	19.2	15.5	15.6	19.8	20.3	19.7
White, non-Hispanic	16.5	17.1	14.7	13.4	10.0	10.0	12.9	13.1	12.6
Black, non-Hispanic	34.6	37.1	31.6	25.3	20.0	22.9	27.0	26.3	24.3
Hispanic	43.4	47.3	46.6	49.8	39.4	38.5	42.3	42.6	41.6
Children in female-householder families, no husband present, total	66.7	68.1	67.6	65.7	57.6	58.9	63.2	63.6	63.5
Ages 0–5	79.1	77.4	77.1	75.3	67.2	68.8	72.9	72.5	71.5
Ages 6–17	62.0	64.1	62.9	61.0	53.7	54.7	58.9	59.5	59.9
White, non-Hispanic	53.6	54.4	56.1	50.1	45.1	47.8	50.1	52.3	52.6
Black, non-Hispanic	79.9	79.6	77.4	76.2	66.1	66.9	70.4	69.4	69.6
Hispanic	80.7	84.8	80.8	81.7	70.3	67.4	72.9	73.6	72.0
Below 200% poverty									
Total	**42.3**	**43.5**	**42.4**	**43.3**	**37.5**	**38.9**	**43.7**	**44.3**	**43.8**
Gender									
Male	42.3	43.2	42.5	43.1	37.5	38.6	43.7	44.1	43.3
Female	42.4	43.7	42.3	43.5	37.6	39.3	43.6	44.5	44.2
Age									
Ages 0–5	46.8	47.1	46.0	46.7	41.0	42.4	47.4	47.9	47.0
Ages 6–17	40.3	41.6	40.5	41.5	35.9	37.3	41.9	42.6	42.2
Race and Hispanic origin[a]									
White, non-Hispanic	33.8	33.6	32.3	30.5	25.5	26.2	29.1	30.4	30.0
Black, non-Hispanic	70.1	70.9	68.1	68.0	58.9	61.2	65.1	62.8	62.1
Hispanic	67.2	70.3	69.5	72.9	62.6	60.7	64.8	65.6	65.0
Region[b]									
Northeast	39.1	37.5	36.3	38.2	33.0	33.9	35.9	37.8	38.8
South	47.8	48.6	47.7	48.4	41.6	42.5	47.4	46.8	46.6
Midwest	39.1	42.5	39.6	36.9	31.2	35.3	41.2	42.0	41.3
West	40.5	41.7	42.7	46.1	40.5	40.5	45.5	46.8	44.9
Children in married-couple families, total	33.2	33.9	31.4	31.1	26.4	27.0	30.8	30.7	30.2
Ages 0–5	38.1	38.1	34.5	33.2	29.2	30.2	33.4	33.4	32.5
Ages 6–17	30.8	31.6	29.6	29.9	25.1	25.4	29.4	29.3	29.1
White, non-Hispanic	28.3	27.8	25.4	23.3	18.2	18.1	20.5	20.8	20.4
Black, non-Hispanic	50.9	52.5	44.7	38.3	35.3	35.3	40.4	36.0	36.3
Hispanic	60.5	62.8	62.1	66.0	55.5	54.1	56.0	56.3	56.0
Children in female-householder families, no husband present, total	78.2	77.4	77.6	76.4	69.7	71.2	73.9	75.5	74.7
Ages 0–5	87.9	84.5	85.4	84.3	78.6	80.2	82.4	82.4	81.8
Ages 6–17	74.5	74.4	73.7	72.5	66.0	67.4	70.1	72.3	71.6
White, non-Hispanic	67.8	66.6	68.0	62.6	57.1	60.2	62.0	65.3	66.3
Black, non-Hispanic	89.1	87.1	85.7	86.9	78.4	78.8	80.1	80.2	78.9
Hispanic	87.3	89.9	89.1	88.6	82.5	80.6	83.5	84.8	82.4

a poverty threshold for the purposes of the study of 60% of the median income in each country (which is consistent with the standards of many international studies that measure poverty), UNICEF finds that 30.1% of U.S. children were impoverished in 2008 and 32.2% were impoverished in 2012. (See Table 2.4.)

These rates were comparable to countries such as Turkey (33% in 2008 and 30.2% in 2012), Romania (32.9% and 30.6%), Israel (35.1% and 35.6%), and Mexico (29.3% and 34.3%). The country with the lowest rate of child poverty in 2012 was Norway, whose rate of 5.3% was more than six times lower than that of

TABLE 2.2

Percentage of children aged 0–17 living below selected poverty levels, by selected characteristics, selected years 1980–2012 [CONTINUED]

aFrom 1980 to 2002, following the 1977 Office of Management and Budget (OMB) standards for collecting and presenting data on race, the Current Population Survey (CPS) asked respondents to choose one race from the following: White, Black, American Indian or Alaskan Native, or Asian or Pacific Islander. An "Other" category was also offered. Beginning in 2003, the CPS allowed respondents to select one or more race categories. All race groups discussed in this table from 2002 onward refer to people who indicated only one racial identity within the categories presented. For this reason data from 2002 onward are not directly comparable with data from earlier years. People who reported only one race are referred to as the race-alone population. The use of the race-alone population in this table does not imply that it is the preferred method of presenting or analyzing data. Data on race and Hispanic origin are collected separately. Persons of Hispanic origin may be of any race.

bRegions: Northeast includes CT, MA, ME, NH, NJ, NY, PA, RI, and VT. South includes AL, AR, DC, DE, FL, GA, KY, LA, MD, MS, NC, OK, SC, TN, TX, VA, and WV. Midwest includes IA, IL, IN, KS, MI, MN, MO, ND, NE, OH, SD, and WI. West includes AK, AZ, CA, CO, HI, ID, MT, NM, NV, OR, UT, WA, and WY.

Note: Data for 2010 use the Census 2010-based population controls. The 2004 data have been revised to reflect a correction to the weights in the 2005 Annual Social and Economic Supplement (ASEC). Data for 1999, 2000, and 2001 use Census 2000 population controls. Data for 2000 onward are from the expanded Current Population Survey (CPS) sample. The poverty level is based on money income and does not include non-cash benefits, such as food stamps. Poverty thresholds reflect family size and composition and are adjusted each year using the annual average Consumer Price Index level. In 2012, the poverty threshold for a two-parent, two-child family was $23,283. The levels shown here are derived from the ratio of the family's income to the family's poverty threshold.

SOURCE: Adapted from "ECON1.A Child Poverty: Percentage of Children Ages 0–17 Living below Selected Poverty Levels by Selected Characteristics, 1980–2012," in *America's Children in Brief: Key National Indicators of Well-Being, 2014*, Federal Interagency Forum on Child and Family Statistics, 2014, http://www.childstats.gov/americaschildren/tables/econ1a.asp (accessed October 28, 2014)

TABLE 2.3

Median household income in the past 12 months, by race and Hispanic origin, 2013

| | United States | |
| | Total | Median income (dollars) |
Subject	Estimate	Estimate
Households	116,291,033	52,250
One race—		
White	77.6%	55,867
Black or African American	12.1%	34,815
American Indian and Alaska Native	0.7%	36,641
Asian	4.3%	72,472
Native Hawaiian and other Pacific Islander	0.1%	50,591
Some other race	3.3%	39,346
Two or more races	1.8%	46,709
Hispanic or Latino origin (of any race)	12.2%	41,508
White alone, not Hispanic or Latino	69.4%	57,684

Note: Data are based on a sample and are subject to sampling variability.

SOURCE: Adapted from "S1903. Median Income in the Past 12 Months (in 2013 Inflation-Adjusted Dollars)," in *2013 American Community Survey 1-Year Estimates*, U.S. Census Bureau, American FactFinder, 2014, http://factfinder2.census.gov/faces/tableservices/jsf/pages/productview.xhtml?pid=ACS_13_1YR_S1903&prodType=table (accessed October 28, 2014)

the United States. According to the Organisation for Economic Co-operation and Development (OECD; an organization consisting of 34 wealthy countries committed to promoting democracy and economic cooperation), in *OECD Better Life Index: Income* (2014, http://www.oecdbetterlifeindex.org/topics/income), the United States had the highest average net household disposable income (income after taxes and living expenses are paid) of any of the world's developed economies, at $39,531 per year. By comparison, Norway had an average net household disposable income of $32,093, and the average disposable incomes of the countries with which the United States' child poverty rate compares were far lower when adjusted for differences in the cost of living. Mexico's average disposable income was $12,850, Turkey's was $13,794,

and Israel's was $20,434 (Romania was not an OECD member as of 2014).

The United States' official poverty line is not pegged to median income as are most international developed-world statistics, so the Census Bureau's picture of child poverty is considerably less bleak than that indicated by UNICEF. However, even when applying the United States' comparatively low poverty threshold, some groups of children experience poverty at extremely high rates. As noted earlier, non-Hispanic African American and Hispanic children are disproportionately likely to live in poverty, as are children of all races who live in households headed by a single mother. What is more, much of the progress in combating poverty in single-mother families was reversed during the first and second decades of the 21st century. The poverty rate for children in female-householder families with no husband present fell steadily through the 1990s and the turn of the 21st century, from 54.2% in 1990 to 40.5% in 2000. (See Table 2.2.) The poverty rate for such children then rose to 43.1% in 2005, before rising still further during the Great Recession to 48% in 2011. Child poverty in single-mother families fell slightly in 2012, to 47.6%.

Younger children are more likely to be poor than older children, partly because parents themselves are more likely to be young (and not yet in their peak income-earning years) when children are young. A quarter (24.8%) of all children aged zero to five years lived in poverty in 2012. (See Table 2.2.) Furthermore, single mothers with young children often cannot obtain or keep jobs because of the constant care that children require before they are old enough to attend school. The child poverty rate for those aged zero to five years in single-mother households was 56.3% in 2012, and nearly one-third (32%) of such children were desperately poor, or living at 50% of poverty or less. More than seven out of 10 (71.5%) children aged zero to five years who were

TABLE 2.4

Child poverty rates in high-income countries, 2008 and 2012

Rank	Country	Change (2008–2012)
1	Chile	−8.67
2	Poland	−7.90
3	Australia	−6.27
4	Slovakia	−5.60
5	Switzerland	−4.80
6	Norway	−4.30
7	Republic of Korea	−3.40
8	Finland	−3.20
9	Turkey	−2.76
10	Japan	−2.70
11	Canada	−2.44
12	Romania	−2.30
13	Belgium	−0.80
14	Sweden	−0.80
15	Austria	−0.70
16	New Zealand	−0.40
17	Czech Republic	−0.40
18	Germany	−0.20
19	Israel	0.55
20	Bulgaria	0.60
21	Malta	0.60
22	Netherlands	1.00
23	Portugal	1.00
24	Denmark	1.10
25	United Kingdom	1.60
26	Slovenia	1.80
27	United States	2.06
28	Cyprus	2.70
29	Hungary	2.90
30	France	3.00
31	Mexico	5.00
32	Estonia	5.10
33	Italy	5.70
34	Luxembourg	6.50
35	Spain	8.10
36	Lithuania	8.30
37	Ireland	10.60
38	Croatia	11.80
39	Latvia	14.60
40	Greece	17.50
41	Iceland	20.40

Horizontal bar chart comparing child poverty rates (x-axis "Child poverty rate", 0 to 45) for 2008 and 2012 by country:

Country	2008	2012
Chile	31.4	22.8
Poland	22.4	14.5
Australia	19.2	13.0
Slovakia	16.7	11.1
Switzerland	19.5	14.7
Norway	9.6	5.3
Republic of Korea	16.8	13.4
Finland	12.0	8.8
Turkey	33.0	30.2
Japan	21.7	19.0
Canada	23.2	20.8
Romania	32.9	30.6
Belgium	17.2	16.4
Sweden	12.9	12.1
Austria	14.9	14.2
New Zealand	18.8	18.4
Czech Republic	13.2	12.8
Germany	15.2	15.0
Israel	35.1	35.6
Bulgaria	25.5	26.1
Malta	20.4	21.0
Netherlands	12.9	13.9
Portugal	22.8	23.8
Denmark	9.1	10.2
United Kingdom	24.0	25.6
Slovenia	11.6	13.4
United States	30.1	32.2
Cyprus	14.0	16.7
Hungary	19.7	22.6
France	15.6	18.6
Mexico	29.3	34.3
Estonia	17.1	22.2
Italy	24.7	30.4
Luxembourg	19.8	26.3
Spain	28.2	36.3
Lithuania	22.8	31.1
Ireland	18.0	28.6
Croatia	15.8	27.6
Latvia	23.6	38.2
Greece	23.0	40.5
Iceland	11.2	31.6

Legend: 2008, 2012

SOURCE: "League Table 1. Change in Child Poverty (Anchored in 2008)," in "Children of the Recession: The Impact of the Economic Crisis on Child Well-Being in Rich Countries," *Innocenti Report Card 12*, UNICEF Office of Research, September 2014, http://www.unicef-irc.org/publications/pdf/rc12-eng-web.pdf (accessed October 28, 2014)

raised by single mothers lived below 150% of poverty, a threshold at which households are at pronounced risk of falling into poverty—a statistic that indicates the difficulty in rising above poverty even when the household head is able to find work.

The poverty rate for children in married-couple households was comparatively stable prior to the Great Recession, and at all times it has been substantially lower than the total child poverty rate. In 2000 and 2005 the poverty rate for children in married-couple households was around 8%, but in 2010 it rose to 11.6%, a rate not seen since 1985. (See Table 2.2.) In 2012 the rate fell slightly to 11.2%.

Not only are children overrepresented among the poor but also they arguably suffer more from the deprivations of poverty than do adults. Strong evidence suggests that food insecurity and lack of good medical care caused by poverty can limit a child's physical and cognitive development. The higher incidence of poverty among children aged five years and younger is of particular concern to child advocates, given that the preschool years represent the most crucial period for brain development. In "Poverty during Early Childhood May Last a Lifetime" (Discovery.com, February 22, 2010), Jessica Marshall reports on several studies that show that early childhood poverty actually causes changes in the brain that lead to problems in adulthood, including lower adult income.

The Children's Defense Fund (CDF) argues in *Portrait of Inequality 2012—Black Children in America* (November 2012, http://www.childrensdefense.org/zzz-child-research-data-publications/data/portrait-of-inequality-2012.pdf) and in *Portrait of Inequality 2012—Hispanic Children in America* (November 2012, http://www.childrensdefense.org/library/data/a-portrait-of-inequality-2012.pdf), "Poverty destroys childhood and can destroy children." The CDF notes in both reports that children born into poverty are disproportionately likely to not receive prenatal care, be born underweight, lack family support systems, experience poor health, lack health insurance coverage, exhibit developmental delays, and fall behind in school at an early age. These children then attend schools that are disproportionately likely to be poorly funded and inadequate, leaving them ill-prepared for an increasingly competitive job market. All of these disadvantages add up to what the CDF calls the "Cradle to Prison Pipeline." According to E. Ann Carson of the Bureau of Justice Statistics, in *Prisoners in 2013* (September 2014, http://www.bjs.gov/content/pub/pdf/p13.pdf), there were nearly 1.6 million men and women in state and federal prisons as of December 31, 2013. Of that total, over 1.4 million were male prisoners, of which 526,000 (37%) were African American and 314,600 (22%) were Hispanic.

According to numerous sources, the problem of child poverty is increasingly affecting the U.S. public education system on a large scale. For example, Lyndsey Layton reports in "Study: Poor Children Are Now the Majority in American Public Schools in South, West" (WashingtonPost.com, October 16, 2013) that the Southern Education Foundation, a philanthropic organization devoted to educational issues, found that during the 2010–11 school year 48% of the 50 million students in U.S. public schools qualified for free or reduced-price meals through the federal school lunch and breakfast programs. Enrollment in these federal programs is considered broadly indicative of student poverty, and by this metric, student poverty has risen rapidly since the turn of the century. In 2001 poor children accounted for a majority of the public school population in only four states. By 2011 poor children accounted for a majority of the public school population in 17 states, including all states in the South (except Maryland and Virginia) and four of the largest western states (California, Oregon, Nevada, and New Mexico). The percentage of public school students who were poor was highest in Mississippi (71%), followed by New Mexico (68%) and Louisiana (66%).

In "Poverty and High School Dropouts" (APA.org, May 2013), Russell W. Rumberger of the University of California, Santa Barbara, indicates that the high rate of poverty in U.S. public schools translates into high dropout rates. A 2009 study found that students in the bottom 20% of households by income were five times more likely to drop out of high school than students in the top 20%, and in 2012 an estimated 1.1 million high school seniors failed to earn a diploma. In that year the U.S. high school graduation rate ranked 22nd in the world. High school dropouts are more likely than any other group, by education status, to be unemployed, have incomes below poverty, have numerous poor health outcomes, rely on public assistance programs, and engage in criminal activity.

POVERTY AMONG THE ELDERLY. In contrast with children, senior citizens are underrepresented among the poor. DeNavas-Walt and Proctor note that in 2013, 9.5% of adults aged 65 years and older were poor, up from 9.1% the year before. (See Table 2.1.) Between 1959 and 2013 the number of people aged 65 years and older living in poverty dropped significantly, from a high of about 35% to current levels. (See Figure 1.2 in Chapter 1.) Most observers credit Social Security for the sharp decline in poverty among the elderly. Although it was enacted in 1935, Social Security began paying substantially higher benefits in the era following World War II (1939–1945). Gary V. Engelhardt and Jonathan Gruber of the National Bureau of Economic Research maintain in *Social Security and the Evolution of Elderly Poverty* (May 2004, http://www.nber.org/papers/w10466.pdf) that increases in benefit levels between 1967 and 2000 account for the entirety of the reduction in poverty among the elderly.

Poverty rates among the elderly are the source of some dispute among analysts, however. Because the federal government's official poverty measure does not take into account out-of-pocket medical expenses, which are far higher on average for the elderly than for children and adults under the age of 65 years, many believe that the true poverty rate among the elderly is higher than Census Bureau estimates suggest. The Census Bureau has attempted to account for this issue in its formulation of the Supplemental Poverty Measure (SPM), which adjusts for expenses including out-of-pocket medical costs. According to Kathleen Short of the Census Bureau, in *The Supplemental Poverty Measure: 2013* (October 2014, http://www.census.gov/content/dam/Census/library/publications/2014/demo/p60-251.pdf), using the SPM to calculate poverty rates results in a poverty rate for the elderly of 14.6% in 2013, which is significantly higher than the rate of elderly poverty derived from the official measure (9.5%). Because there are no plans to use the SPM to administer government benefits, it is unclear how or even if the disparity between the two measures of elderly poverty will affect public policy.

Urban Areas

According to the official poverty thresholds, people living in cities are more likely to be poor than those living in rural areas, and people living in rural areas are more likely to be poor than those living in suburbs. In 2013, 19.1% of people living in cities (inside metropolitan statistical areas and inside principal cities) and 16.1% of people living in rural areas (outside metropolitan statistical areas) lived below the poverty line. (See Table 2.1.) Poverty in the suburbs (inside metropolitan statistical areas but outside principal cities) stood at a comparatively small 11.1% of the population.

Although urban and rural areas have similar official poverty rates, there is substantial doubt about whether the two populations truly experience the same levels of poverty. Because of sometimes dramatic differences in the cost of living between rural and urban areas, which are not accounted for in the official poverty measure, the equivalence between these two rates has perhaps been overstated. The Census Bureau's SPM, which attempts to account for geographical variation in the cost of living, provides different rates of poverty than the official measure. Short indicates the SPM yields a lower rate of rural poverty (13.2%), a higher rate of suburban poverty (13.4%), and a higher rate of urban poverty (20.1%) than the official measure.

Family Status

In 2013 people living in families (12.4%) were much less likely than people living in unrelated subfamilies (43%) or in households with unrelated individuals (23.3%) to suffer from poverty. (See Table 2.1.) However, there was a major variation in the poverty rate between different family structures. Whereas 9.1 million families in the United States (11.2% of the total number of families) were living in poverty in 2013, families headed by married couples had a dramatically lower poverty rate (5.8%) than other types of families. (See Table 2.5.) Almost one-third (30.6%) of families with a female householder and no husband present and 15.9% of households headed by a male with no wife present were living in poverty.

TABLE 2.5

Families in poverty, by type of family, 2012 and 2013

[Numbers in thousands. Families as of March of the following year.]

Characteristic	2012 Total	2012 Below poverty Number	2012 Below poverty Percent	2013[a] Total	2013[a] Below poverty Number	2013[a] Below poverty Percent	Change in poverty (2012 less 2013)[b] Number	Change in poverty (2012 less 2013)[b] Percent
Families								
Total	80,944	9,520	11.8	81,217	9,130	11.2	−390	−0.5
Type of family								
Married-couple	59,224	3,705	6.3	59,692	3,476	5.8	−228	−0.4
Female householder, no husband present	15,489	4,793	30.9	15,195	4,646	30.6	−147	−0.4
Male householder, no wife present	6,231	1,023	16.4	6,330	1,008	15.9	−15	−0.5

[a]Data are based on the CPS ASEC (Current Population Survey, Annual Social and Economic Supplement) sample of 68,000 addresses. The 2014 CPS ASEC included redesigned questions for income and health insurance coverage. All of the approximately 98,000 addresses were eligible to receive the redesigned set of health insurance coverage questions. The redesigned income questions were implemented to a subsample of these 98,000 addresses using a probability split panel design. Approximately 68,000 addresses were eligible to receive a set of income questions similar to those used in the 2013 CPS ASEC and the remaining 30,000 addresses were eligible to receive the redesigned income questions. The source of the 2013 data for this table is the portion of the CPS ASEC sample which received the income questions consistent with the 2013 CPS ASEC, approximately 68,000 addresses.
[b]Details may not sum to totals because of rounding.

SOURCE: Adapted from Carmen DeNavas-Walt and Bernadette D. Proctor, "Table 4. Families in Poverty by Type of Family: 2012 and 2013," in *Income and Poverty in the United States: 2013*, U.S. Census Bureau, September 2014, https://www.census.gov/content/dam/Census/library/publications/2014/demo/p60-249.pdf (accessed October 27, 2014)

SINGLE-PARENT FAMILIES. The proportion of single-parent families steadily increased between 1970 and the early 1990s, and the proportion of married-couple families correspondingly declined. Since then, the structure of U.S. households and families has remained relatively stable. According to the Census Bureau, there were 80.9 million families in the United States in 2013; of these, 59.2 million (73.2%) were headed by married couples. (See Table 2.6.)

TABLE 2.6

Households by type and selected characteristics, 2013

[Numbers in thousands]

	Total	Family households				Nonfamily households		
		Total	Married couple	Male householder	Female householder	Total	Male householder	Female householder
All households	**122,459**	**80,902**	**59,204**	**6,229**	**15,469**	**41,558**	**19,747**	**21,810**
Size of household								
One member	33,570	—	—	—	—	33,570	15,002	18,568
Two members	41,503	34,925	26,348	2,501	6,076	6,578	3,757	2,821
Three members	19,283	18,396	11,674	1,870	4,853	887	624	263
Four members	16,361	15,981	12,387	1057	2,537	380	263	118
Five members	7,425	7,342	5,657	491	1,194	83	60	23
Six members	2,735	2,695	1,996	188	511	41	32	8
Seven or more members	1,581	1,563	1,142	123	299	17	8	9
Number of nonrelatives in household								
No nonrelatives	109,614	76,044	58,334	4,496	13,214	33,570	15,002	18,568
One nonrelative	10,797	4,218	718	1,467	2,033	6,578	3,757	2,821
Two nonrelatives	1,300	413	100	177	135	887	624	263
Three or more nonrelatives	748	227	51	89	87	521	364	157
Race of householder								
White alone	97,705	64,714	50,155	4,591	9,968	32,991	15,693	17,298
Black alone	15,872	9,808	4,481	1040	4,287	6,063	2,766	3,297
Asian alone	5,560	4,118	3,269	327	522	1,442	728	713
All remaining single races and all race combinations	3,323	2,261	1,299	271	691	1062	560	502
Hispanic origin of householder								
Hispanic[a]	15,589	11,952	7,455	1,391	3,106	3,637	1,954	1,683
White alone, Non-Hispanic	83,792	54,004	43,299	3,388	7,317	29,787	13,955	15,833
Other non-Hispanic	23,079	14,946	8,450	1,451	5,045	8,133	3,839	4,295
White alone or combination householder								
White alone or in combination with one or more other races	99,273	65,720	50,749	4,716	10,255	33,553	15,981	17,572
Other	23,187	15,182	8,454	1,514	5,214	8,005	3,767	4,238
Black alone or combination householder								
Black alone or in combination with one or more other races	16,559	10,279	4,700	1,105	4,473	6,280	2,856	3,424
Other	105,900	70,623	54,503	5,124	10,996	35,277	16,891	18,386
Asian alone or combination householder								
Asian alone or in combination with one or more other races	5,872	4,320	3,409	346	565	1,552	794	758
Other	116,588	76,582	55,795	5,884	14,904	40,006	18,953	21,052
Marital status of householder								
Married, spouse present	59,204	59,204	59,204	—	—	—	—	—
Married, spouse absent[b]	2,085	865	—	230	636	1,219	681	538
Widowed	11,746	2,770	—	553	2,217	8,976	2,051	6,924
Divorced	19,094	6,834	—	1,912	4,922	12,260	6,027	6,233
Separated[c]	3,792	2,035	—	457	1,578	1,757	1021	736
Never married	26,539	9,194	—	3,078	6,116	17,345	9,967	7,378
Tenure								
Own/buying	79,474	58,148	47,567	3,412	7,169	21,326	9,468	11,858
Rent	41,337	21,958	11,203	2,713	8,042	19,379	9,824	9,555
No cash rent	1,649	797	434	105	258	852	455	397

Dash ("—") represents or rounds to zero.
[a]Hispanics may be of any race.
[b]In past reports: Married spouse absent—other (excluding separated).
[c]In past reports: Married spouse absent—separated.
Note: This table uses a person weight to describe characteristics of people living in households. As a result, estimates of the number of households do not match estimates of housing units from the Housing Vacancy Survey (HVS). The HVS is weighted to housing units, rather than the population, in order to more accurately estimate the number of occupied and vacant housing units.

SOURCE: "Table H1. Households by Type and Tenure of Householder for Selected Characteristics: 2013," in *America's Families and Living Arrangements: 2013*, U.S. Census Bureau, November 2013, http://www.census.gov/hhes/families/files/cps2013/tabH1-all.xls (accessed October 28, 2014)

Of the remaining families, 6.2 million (7.7%) were single-parent households headed by men and 15.5 million (19.1%) were single-parent households headed by women.

One factor in the rise of single-parent families is the rise in the divorce rate. Jason Fields of the Census Bureau indicates in *America's Families and Living Arrangements: 2003* (November 2004, http://www.census.gov/prod/2004pubs/p20-553.pdf) that in 1970 only 3.5% of men and 5.7% of women were separated or divorced. By 2013, 9% of men and 11.2% of women were divorced and had not remarried. (See Table 2.7.) The percentage of divorced women is consistently higher than the percentage of divorced men because divorced men are more likely to remarry, whereas divorced women are more likely to raise the children from the first marriage. As Table 2.8 shows, in 2011 there were an estimated 14.4 million custodial parents, or parents who were raising children in the absence of the second parent. Of these, 11.8 million were female and 2.6 million were male; in other words, 81.7% of custodial parents were mothers.

Another reason for the rise in single-parent families is the rise in people who never marry yet still have children. According to Fields, only 28.1% of males aged 15 years and older had never married in 1970; that figure stood at 34.4% in 2013. (See Table 2.7.) Likewise, the percentage of females aged 15 years and older who had never married rose from 22.1% in 1970 to 28.6% in 2013. The proportion of those who have never married has increased as young adults delay the age at which they marry. As Figure 2.1 shows, the median age at first marriage, after remaining relatively stable between 1890 and 1970, rose dramatically for both men and women between 1970 and 2013. The median age of women at first marriage was 20.8 years in 1970 and 26.6 years in 2013; and the median age of men at first marriage was 23.2 years in 1970 and 29 years in 2013. Besides these

trends, the proportion of all households that were unmarried-partner heterosexual households steadily rose between 1996 and 2013, from 2.9% to 6.6% of all households. As of 2013, there were 8.1 million households headed by opposite-sex unmarried couples; 3.1 million (39.1%) of these households had at least one biological child under the age of 18 years present. (See Table 2.9.)

Single-parent women were more likely than single-parent men to have never been married. In 2013, 49.2% of single mothers and 33.4% of single fathers had never been married. (See Table 2.10.)

African American children are far more likely to live with a single parent than are non-Hispanic white or Hispanic children. In 2013, 4.7 million (36.1%) of a total 13.1 million African American children (including only those children who had both African American and other racial characteristics) lived with married parents, and another 634,000 (4.8%) lived with unmarried parents who were both present. (See Table 2.11.) A larger share of African American children lived with a single-mother who had either never married (4.3 million, or 32.8%), was divorced (1.1 million, or 8.2%), was separated (653,000, or 5%), was widowed (119,000, or 0.9%), or whose married spouse was absent (209,000, or 1.6%). Together, these groups of children parented by single mothers accounted for 6.4 million, or nearly half (48.5%) of all African American children. An additional 606,000 (4.6%) African American children lived with their father only, and 774,000 (5.9%) lived in a household with neither parent present.

Although Hispanic children experienced rates of poverty similar to those of African American children, their living situations were dissimilar. A majority of Hispanic children (10.3 million, or 58.2%) lived with married parents, 4.9 million (27.9%) lived with their mother only, 570,000 (3.2%) lived with their father only, and 684,000

TABLE 2.7

Marital status of people aged 15 and over, 2013

[Numbers in thousands, except for percentages]

All races	Total Number	Married spouse present Number	Married spouse absent Number	Widowed Number	Divorced Number	Separated Number	Never married Number	Total Percent	Married spouse present Percent	Married spouse absent Percent	Widowed Percent	Divorced Percent	Separated Percent	Never married Percent
Both sexes														
Total 15+	249,893	122,590	3,465	14,349	25,388	5,600	78,499	100.0	49.1	1.4	5.7	10.2	2.2	31.4
Male														
Total 15+	121,067	61,295	1,639	3,124	10,954	2,435	41,620	100.0	50.6	1.4	2.6	9.0	2.0	34.4
Female														
Total 15+	128,826	61,295	1,827	11,225	14,434	3,165	36,879	100.0	47.6	1.4	8.7	11.2	2.5	28.6

SOURCE: Adapted from "Table A1. Marital Status of People 15 Years and over, by Age, Sex, Personal Earnings, Race, and Hispanic Origin, 2013," in *America's Families and Living Arrangements: 2013*, U.S. Census Bureau, November 2013, http://www.census.gov/hhes/families/files/cps2013/tabA1-all.xls (accessed October 28, 2014)

TABLE 2.8

Demographic characteristics of custodial parents by award status and payments received, 2011

[Numbers in thousands, as of spring 2012. Parents living with own children under 21 years of age whose other parent is not living in the home.]

				With child support agreements or awards							
				Due child support payments in 2011							
					Average due (in dollars)	Average received (in dollars)	Percent received	Received all payments		Did not receive payments	
Characteristic	Total	Total	Percent	Total				Total	Percent	Total	Percent
All custodial parents											
Total	14,440	7,057	48.9	6,262	6,052	3,771	62.3	2,716	43.4	1,621	25.9
Standard error	293	208	1.1	196	136	122	1.2	130	1.0	100	0.7
Sex											
Male	2,643	760	28.8	674	5,527	3,015	54.6	279	41.4	216	32.0
Female	11,797	6,297	53.4	5,588	6,115	3,862	63.2	2,438	43.6	1,405	25.1
Age											
Under 30 years	3,083	1,313	42.6	1,170	4,090	2,063	50.4	428	36.6	368	31.5
30 to 39 years	5,315	2,818	53.0	2,575	6,220	3,705	59.6	1,070	41.6	625	24.3
40 years and over	6,041	2,926	48.4	2,517	6,791	4,633	68.2	1,219	48.4	627	24.9
Race and ethnicity[a]											
White alone	9,829	5,257	53.5	4,664	6,158	3,895	63.3	2,046	43.9	1,167	25.0
White alone, not Hispanic	7,244	4,030	55.6	3,585	6,257	4,159	66.5	1,642	45.8	821	22.9
Black alone	3,677	1,390	37.8	1,265	5,442	3,309	60.8	532	42.1	340	26.9
Hispanic (any race)	3,021	1,378	45.6	1,202	6,086	3,147	51.7	450	37.4	386	32.1
Current marital status[b]											
Married	2,630	1,431	54.4	1,276	5,611	3,388	60.4	546	42.8	326	25.5
Divorced	4,772	2,669	55.9	2,404	6,811	4,435	65.1	1,164	48.4	559	23.3
Separated	1,813	804	44.3	666	6,017	3,947	65.6	327	49.1	153	23.0
Never married	5,060	2,076	41.0	1,857	5,438	3,131	57.6	652	35.1	564	30.4
Educational attainment											
Less than high school diploma	2,183	917	42.0	800	5,048	2,536	50.2	291	36.4	268	33.5
High school graduate	4,557	2,101	46.1	1,809	5,924	3,570	60.3	765	42.3	525	29.0
Less than 4 years of college	5,072	2,707	53.4	2,425	5,891	3,563	60.5	1,040	42.9	569	23.5
Bachelor's degree or more	2,628	1,332	50.7	1,228	7,212	5,281	73.2	621	50.6	259	21.1
Selected characteristics											
Family income below 2011 poverty level	4,180	1,992	47.7	1,707	5,448	3,273	60.1	676	39.6	466	27.3
Worked full-time, year-round	7,289	3,518	48.3	3,160	6,258	3,777	60.4	1,406	44.5	802	25.4
Public assistance program participation[c]	5,675	2,749	48.4	2,389	5,368	3,180	59.2	954	39.9	693	29.0
With one child	8,209	3,543	43.2	3,149	5,458	3,155	57.8	1,349	42.8	832	26.4
With two or more children	6,231	3,513	56.4	3,113	6,653	4,394	66.0	1,367	43.9	788	25.3
Child had contact with other parent in 2011	9,313	4,855	52.1	4,322	6,314	4,257	67.4	2,120	49.1	988	22.9
Child had no contact with other parent in 2011	5,127	2,202	42.9	1,940	5,467	2,689	49.2	596	30.7	632	32.6
Joint physical or legal custody	3,527	2,081	59.0	1,847	6,859	4,957	72.3	1,040	56.3	323	17.5

[a]Includes those reporting one race alone and not in combination with any other race.
[b]Excludes 165,000 with marital status of widowed.
[c]Received either Medicaid, food stamps, public housing or rent subsidy, TANF (Temporary Assistance for Needy Families), or general assistance.

SOURCE: Timothy Grall, "Table 2. Demographic Characteristics of Custodial Parents by Award Status and Payments Received: 2011," in *Custodial Mothers and Fathers and Their Child Support: 2011*, U.S. Census Bureau, October 2013, http://www.census.gov/prod/2013pubs/p60-246.pdf (accessed October 28, 2014)

(3.9%) lived with neither parent. (See Table 2.11.) Non-Hispanic white children were more likely to still live with married parents. In 2013, 28.9 million (74.4%) of a total 38.9 million non-Hispanic white children lived with married parents, 5.9 million (15.3%) lived with their mother only, 1.7 million (4.4%) lived with their father only, and 1.2 million (3%) lived with neither parent.

CHILD SUPPORT. Child support is often an important source of income for impoverished single parents. In *Custodial Mothers and Fathers and Their Child Support: 2011* (October 2013, http://www.census.gov/prod/2013pubs/p60-246.pdf), Timothy Grall of the Census Bureau notes that in 2011, 48.9% of all custodial parents had either legally binding or informal child-support agreements in place. (See Table 2.8.) Likewise, 47.7% of custodial parents below the poverty line had agreements in place. In 2011 a typical custodial parent below the poverty line was due an average $5,448; however, the average amount that was actually received was $3,273. Only 39.6% of impoverished custodial parents received all payments due to them and 27.3% received no payments at all.

FIGURE 2.1

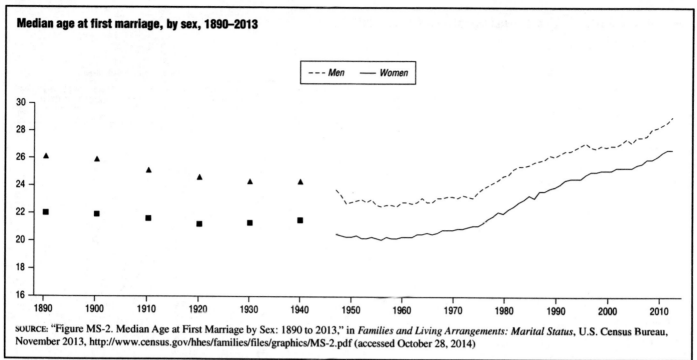

Median age at first marriage, by sex, 1890–2013

SOURCE: "Figure MS-2. Median Age at First Marriage by Sex: 1890 to 2013," in *Families and Living Arrangements: Marital Status*, U.S. Census Bureau, November 2013, http://www.census.gov/hhes/families/files/graphics/MS-2.pdf (accessed October 28, 2014)

The likelihood that custodial parents will receive a high proportion of the total amount of child support due to them varies strongly in proportion to age, current marital status, and educational attainment, as well as in proportion to the nature of the legal custody agreement and whether the child and the noncustodial parent are in contact with one another. In 2011 the average amount of child support due, as well as the average amount received, was lower for custodial parents below the poverty line than for all custodial parents. (See Table 2.8.) Similarly, the percentage of impoverished custodial parents who received all payments was below average, and the percentage of impoverished custodial parents who received no payments was above average. All these facts suggest another arena in which single parents living in poverty are disadvantaged relative to the population in general.

Studies indicate that a number of factors influence the rates of nonpayment of child support. Many researchers have focused specifically on fathers' willingness and ability to pay child support, given that the overwhelming majority of custodial parents are mothers. According to Lenna Nepomnyaschy and Irwin Garfinkel, in "Child Support Enforcement and Fathers' Contributions to Their Nonmarital Children" (*Social Service Review*, vol. 84, no. 3, September 2010), past studies have noted that a high level of trust between the parents correlates to higher levels of support payments. Additionally, fathers who have lived with the mother and child and fathers who maintain a regular visitation schedule with the child tend to satisfy their child-support obligations more fully

than those who have not cohabited and/or do not regularly see their child. Studies also show that child-support payments sometimes decline over time, especially when fathers have new biological children and when mothers move on to new romantic relationships and/or have new biological children.

Child support can be either informal or formal. Informal child-support agreements, wherein the father gives the mother money and in-kind awards without any legal encumbrances, are common during the first 15 months after a child is born. Studies show that informal support tends to decline over time and that formal child-support agreements, which are legally enforceable, become more important sources of income for custodial mothers beginning at 45 months after the child's birth. Enforcement of formal child-support agreements varies by state. Whether strong child-support enforcement, as is common in some states, leads to better outcomes for custodial mothers and their children has not been established, in part because strong enforcement is associated with declines in informal support.

Custodial parents are more likely to be poor than other Americans, and custodial mothers are significantly more likely to be poor than custodial fathers. According to Grall, the poverty rate of families headed by a custodial mother was 31.8% in 2011, compared with 16.2% for families headed by a custodial father. Among custodial-mother families in which the mother had less than a high school education, participated in one or more public assistance programs, or had three or more children, the poverty rate was around 57%. Between 1993 and 2001

TABLE 2.9

Opposite-sex unmarried couples, by selected characteristics, 2013

[Numbers in thousands]

	Total		Presence of biological children			
			No biological children		At least one biological child under 18, of either partner	
All opposite sex unmarried couples	N	%	N	%	N	%
Total	8,057	100.0	4,910	100.0	3,147	100.0
Age of male partner						
15–24 years	1,132	14.1	714	14.5	418	13.3
25–29 years	1,574	19.5	903	18.4	671	21.3
30–34 years	1,258	15.6	621	12.6	637	20.2
35–39 years	866	10.7	353	7.2	513	16.3
40–44 years	746	9.3	330	6.7	417	13.2
45–49 years	661	8.2	406	8.3	255	8.1
50–54 years	636	7.9	489	10.0	147	4.7
55–64 years	771	9.6	684	13.9	87	2.8
65+ years	414	5.1	410	8.4	3	0.1
Age of female partner						
15–24 years	1,703	21.1	1,030	21.0	674	21.4
25–29 years	1,698	21.1	957	19.5	741	23.5
30–34 years	1,056	13.1	436	8.9	620	19.7
35–39 years	797	9.9	332	6.8	465	14.8
40–44 years	688	8.5	332	6.8	355	11.3
45–49 years	614	7.6	443	9.0	171	5.4
50–54 years	535	6.6	444	9.0	91	2.9
55–64 years	669	8.3	638	13.0	31	1.0
65+ years	297	3.7	297	6.1	—	—
Age difference						
Male 10+ years older than female	856	10.6	521	10.6	335	10.6
Male 6–9 years older than female	967	12.0	543	11.1	424	13.5
Male 4–5 years older than female	923	11.5	534	10.9	389	12.4
Male 2–3 years older than female	1,325	16.4	809	16.5	515	16.4
Male and female within 1 year	2,326	28.9	1,431	29.1	895	28.4
Female 2–3 years older than male	655	8.1	409	8.3	246	7.8
Female 4–5 years older than male	338	4.2	198	4.0	140	4.4
Female 6–9 years older than male	342	4.2	236	4.8	106	3.4
Female 10+ years older than male	327	4.1	230	4.7	97	3.1
Race of male partner						
White alone—non-Hispanic	5,093	63.2	3,487	71.0	1,605	51.0
Black alone—non-Hispanic	1,046	13.0	563	11.5	483	15.4
Hispanic[a]	1,495	18.6	624	12.7	871	27.7
All remaining single races and all race combinations, non-Hispanic	423	5.3	236	4.8	187	6.0
Race of female partner						
White alone—non-Hispanic	5,203	64.6	3,491	71.1	1,712	54.4
Black alone—non-Hispanic	855	10.6	468	9.5	387	12.3
Hispanic[a]	1,447	18.0	614	12.5	833	26.5
All remaining single races and all race combinations, non-Hispanic	552	6.9	337	6.9	215	6.8
Race difference[b]						
Both white alone—non-Hispanic	4,600	57.1	3,140	63.9	1,460	46.4
Both black alone—non-Hispanic	756	9.4	422	8.6	334	10.6
Both other alone or any combination—non-Hispanic	257	3.2	145	2.9	112	3.6
Both Hispanic	1,086	13.5	404	8.2	682	21.7
Neither Hispanic	588	7.3	369	7.5	218	6.9
One Hispanic, other non-Hispanic	771	9.6	431	8.8	340	10.8
Race of male partner						
White alone	6,442	80.0	4,063	82.8	2,379	75.6
Black alone	1,105	13.7	579	11.8	526	16.7
Asian alone	190	2.4	116	2.4	73	2.3
All remaining single races and all race combinations	320	4.0	151	3.1	168	5.3
Race of female partner						
White alone	6,470	80.3	4,055	82.6	2,414	76.7
Black alone	940	11.7	489	10.0	452	14.4
Asian alone	271	3.4	173	3.5	99	3.1
All remaining single races and all race combinations	376	4.7	193	3.9	183	5.8

TABLE 2.9

Opposite-sex unmarried couples, by selected characteristics, 2013 [CONTINUED]

[Numbers in thousands]

All opposite sex unmarried couples	Total		Presence of biological children			
			No biological children		At least one biological child under 18, of either partner	
	N	%	N	%	N	%
Race difference						
Both white alone	6,132	76.1	3,862	78.7	2,270	72.1
Both black alone	854	10.6	447	9.1	407	12.9
Both Asian alone	137	1.7	75	1.5	62	2.0
Both other alone or any comb.	187	2.3	80	1.6	107	3.4
Partners identify as different races	747	9.3	446	9.1	302	9.6
Origin of male partner						
Hispanic	1,495	18.6	624	12.7	871	27.7
Non-Hispanic	6,562	81.4	4,286	87.3	2,276	72.3
Origin of female partner						
Hispanic	1,447	18.0	614	12.5	833	26.5
Non-Hispanic	6,610	82.0	4,296	87.5	2,314	73.5
Origin difference						
Neither Hispanic	6,201	77.0	4,075	83.0	2,125	67.5
Both Hispanic	1,086	13.5	404	8.2	682	21.7
Male Hispanic, female not	410	5.1	221	4.5	189	6.0
Female Hispanic, male not	361	4.5	210	4.3	151	4.8
Labor force status of male partner						
Not in labor force	1,356	16.8	996	20.3	360	11.4
In labor force	6,701	83.2	3,914	79.7	2,787	88.6
Labor force status of female partner						
Not in labor force	2,233	27.7	1,241	25.3	992	31.5
In labor force	5,824	72.3	3,669	74.7	2,155	68.5
Labor force difference						
Both in labor force	5,165	64.1	3,224	65.7	1,941	61.7
Only male in labor force	1,536	19.1	690	14.1	846	26.9
Only female in labor force	659	8.2	445	9.1	214	6.8
Neither in labor force	697	8.6	551	11.2	146	4.6
Employment of male partner						
Not employed	2,097	26.0	1,372	28.0	724	23.0
Employed	5,960	74.0	3,537	72.0	2,423	77.0
Employment of female partner						
Not employed	2,765	34.3	1,542	31.4	1,223	38.9
Employed	5,292	65.7	3,368	68.6	1,924	61.1
Employment difference						
Both in labor force—both employed	4,287	53.2	2,748	56.0	1,538	48.9
Both in labor force—only male employed	336	4.2	192	3.9	144	4.6
Both in labor force—only female employed	425	5.3	229	4.7	196	6.2
Both in labor force—both unemployed	117	1.5	54	1.1	63	2.0
Male in labor force—male employed	1,337	16.6	597	12.2	740	23.5
Male in labor force—male unemployed	199	2.5	93	1.9	106	3.4
Female in labor force—female employed	580	7.2	391	8.0	190	6.0
Female in labor force—female unemployed	79	1.0	54	1.1	25	0.8
Not in labor force—not employed	697	8.6	551	11.2	146	4.6
Male education						
Not high school graduate	1,143	14.2	507	10.3	636	20.2
High school graduate	2,985	37.0	1,683	34.3	1,302	41.4
Some college	2,331	28.9	1,429	29.1	902	28.7
Bachelor's degree or higher	1,598	19.8	1,290	26.3	307	9.8
Female education						
Not high school graduate	1,067	13.2	497	10.1	570	18.1
High school graduate	2,469	30.6	1,395	28.4	1,074	34.1
Some college	2,672	33.2	1,553	31.6	1,119	35.6
Bachelor's degree or higher	1,849	22.9	1,465	29.8	384	12.2
Education difference						
Neither has bachelor's degree	5,620	69.8	3,023	61.6	2,597	82.5
One has bachelor's degree, other has less	1,427	17.7	1,018	20.7	409	13.0
Both have bachelor's degree or more	1,010	12.5	869	17.7	141	4.5

TABLE 2.9

Opposite-sex unmarried couples, by selected characteristics, 2013 [CONTINUED]

[Numbers in thousands]

All opposite sex unmarried couples	Total		No biological children		At least one biological child under 18, of either partner	
	N	%	N	%	N	%
Personal earnings of male partner						
Under $5,000 or loss	301	3.7	189	3.8	112	3.6
Without income	1,425	17.7	1,010	20.6	416	13.2
$5,000 to $9,999	391	4.9	206	4.2	185	5.9
$10,000 to $14,999	423	5.2	220	4.5	203	6.4
$15,000 to $19,999	635	7.9	334	6.8	301	9.6
$20,000 to $24,999	645	8.0	341	6.9	304	9.7
$25,000 to $29,999	635	7.9	360	7.3	275	8.7
$30,000 to $39,999	1,086	13.5	571	11.6	515	16.4
$40,000 to $49,999	735	9.1	477	9.7	258	8.2
$50,000 to $74,999	1,045	13.0	695	14.2	350	11.1
$75,000 to $99,999	390	4.8	249	5.1	141	4.5
$100,000 and over	345	4.3	259	5.3	86	2.7
Personal earnings of female partner						
Under $5,000 or loss	470	5.8	242	4.9	227	7.2
Without income	2,174	27.0	1,235	25.1	939	29.9
$5,000 to $9,999	529	6.6	292	6.0	236	7.5
$10,000 to $14,999	708	8.8	386	7.9	321	10.2
$15,000 to $19,999	551	6.8	317	6.5	234	7.4
$20,000 to $24,999	661	8.2	395	8.0	266	8.5
$25,000 to $29,999	538	6.7	336	6.9	202	6.4
$30,000 to $39,999	905	11.2	608	12.4	297	9.4
$40,000 to $49,999	545	6.8	378	7.7	167	5.3
$50,000 to $74,999	649	8.1	462	9.4	187	5.9
$75,000 to $99,999	175	2.2	136	2.8	39	1.3
$100,000 and over	152	1.9	121	2.5	31	1.0
Personal earnings difference						
Male earns $50,000+ more	749	9.3	473	9.6	276	8.8
Male earns $30,000–$49,999 more	918	11.4	501	10.2	418	13.3
Male earns $10,000–$29,999 more	1,902	23.6	1,019	20.7	884	28.1
Male earns $5,000–$9,999 more	566	7.0	315	6.4	251	8.0
Male earns within $4,999 of female	1,945	24.1	1,301	26.5	644	20.5
Female earns $5,000–$9,999 more	402	5.0	251	5.1	151	4.8
Female earns $10,000–$29,999 more	969	12.0	615	12.5	354	11.3
Female earns $30,000–$49,999 more	390	4.8	273	5.6	117	3.7
Female earns $50,000+ more	215	2.7	163	3.3	52	1.7

Dash ("—") represents or rounds to zero.
[a]Hispanics may be of any race.
[b]"White" refers to Non-Hispanic white alone, "black" to Non-Hispanic black alone, and "other" to Non-Hispanic other alone or in combination.
Note: Excludes ever-married children under 18 years.

SOURCE: "Table UC3. Opposite Sex Unmarried Couples by Presence of Biological Children under 18, and Age, Earnings, Education, and Race and Hispanic Origin of Both Partners: 2013," in *America's Families and Living Arrangements: 2013*, November 2013, http://www.census.gov/hhes/families/files/cps2013/tabUC3-all.xls (accessed October 28, 2014)

the percentage of custodial parents and their children living below the poverty level declined from 33.3% to 23.4%, and then remained statistically unchanged between 2001 and 2007. (See Figure 2.2.) The poverty rate for both custodial mothers and custodial fathers rose markedly between 2007 and 2011 as a result of the Great Recession. The poverty rate of all custodial families, at 28.9% in 2011, was nearly double that of the total population, at 15% in 2011.

Work Experience

In strictly economic terms, the probability of a family living in poverty hinges on three primary factors: the size of the family, the number of workers, and the characteristics of the wage earners. As the number of wage earners in a family increases, the probability of poverty declines. The likelihood of a second wage earner is greatest in families that are headed by married couples; this is one of the key reasons that married-couple families consistently outperform single-parent families on measures of economic well-being. Additionally, in the late 20th and early 21st centuries many jobs in sectors such as manufacturing, which previously paid unskilled workers a middle-class wage, have been phased out as corporations move their operations overseas. As a result, many workers without a college education are forced into low-paying service jobs (e.g., jobs in food service, cleaning, and retail sales), some of which do not pay enough or offer workers enough hours to allow

TABLE 2.10

Single-parent family groups with own children under 18, by marital status and demographic characteristics, 2013

[Numbers in thousands]

	All one-parent unmarried family groups		Maintained by father										Maintained by mother									
			Total		Never married		Divorced		Separated*		Widowed		Total		Never married		Divorced		Separated*		Widowed	
	N	%	N	%	N	%	N	%	N	%	N	%	N	%	N	%	N	%	N	%	N	%
All family groups	12,007	100.0	2,000	100.0	667	33.4	869	43.5	380	19.0	83	4.2	10,007	100.0	4,928	49.2	2,993	29.9	1,774	17.7	313	3.1
Region																						
Northeast	1,987	16.5	338	100.0	142	42.0	106	31.4	81	24.1	9	2.6	1,649	100.0	861	52.2	431	26.1	308	18.7	49	3.0
Midwest	2,495	20.8	447	100.0	143	31.9	225	50.4	55	12.3	24	5.4	2,049	100.0	1,034	50.5	678	33.1	282	13.7	56	2.7
South	4,955	41.3	722	100.0	231	32.1	294	40.7	164	22.8	32	4.5	4,234	100.0	2,167	51.2	1,207	28.5	722	17.0	138	3.3
West	2,570	21.4	494	100.0	152	30.7	245	49.5	80	16.2	18	3.7	2,076	100.0	866	41.7	677	32.6	463	22.3	70	3.4
Size of family group																						
Two members	5,160	43.0	1,056	100.0	439	41.5	431	40.8	152	14.4	34	3.2	4,104	100.0	2,340	57.0	1,134	27.6	521	12.7	109	2.7
Three members	3,998	33.3	624	100.0	144	23.1	320	51.3	126	20.1	34	5.4	3,374	100.0	1,428	42.3	1,159	34.3	660	19.6	127	3.8
Four members	1,779	14.8	216	100.0	55	25.4	89	41.0	64	29.7	9	4.0	1,563	100.0	689	44.1	478	30.6	358	22.9	38	2.4
Five members	673	5.6	63	100.0	23	35.6	18	27.9	19	30.7	4	5.8	609	100.0	290	47.6	148	24.3	150	24.6	21	3.5
Six or more members	397	3.3	41	100.0	7	16.5	12	28.6	19	46.1	4	8.8	357	100.0	181	50.8	74	20.7	85	23.7	17	4.7
Age of reference person																						
Under 20 years	219	1.8	9	100.0	9	100.0	—	—	—	—	—	—	209	100.0	197	94.2	1	0.4	11	5.4	—	—
20–24 years	1,309	10.9	107	100.0	88	82.1	13	11.7	7	6.2	—	—	1,202	100.0	1,038	86.3	51	4.3	109	9.0	4	0.4
25–29 years	1,798	15.0	225	100.0	147	65.4	49	21.8	27	12.1	1	0.6	1,573	100.0	1,133	72.0	188	12.0	243	15.4	9	0.6
30–34 years	2,045	17.0	284	100.0	128	45.2	99	34.9	53	18.7	3	1.2	1,761	100.0	969	55.0	429	24.4	330	18.7	33	1.9
35–39 years	2,156	18.0	371	100.0	123	33.1	148	39.9	90	24.4	10	2.7	1,785	100.0	742	41.5	656	36.8	347	19.4	40	2.2
40–44 years	1,955	16.3	391	100.0	93	23.8	198	50.6	86	22.1	14	3.5	1,564	100.0	438	28.0	694	44.3	380	24.3	53	3.4
45–54 years	2,060	17.2	452	100.0	66	14.5	270	59.8	88	19.6	28	6.1	1,608	100.0	343	21.3	854	53.1	296	18.4	114	7.1
55+ years	465	3.9	161	100.0	13	8.2	93	57.4	28	17.5	27	16.8	304	100.0	68	22.2	119	39.2	59	19.3	59	19.3
Family income																						
Family income under $10,000	1,823	15.2	122	100.0	58	47.4	29	23.5	26	20.9	10	8.1	1,701	100.0	1,007	59.2	302	17.7	353	20.7	40	2.3
$10,000 to $14,999	1,130	9.4	114	100.0	56	49.4	28	24.6	22	19.2	8	6.9	1,017	100.0	592	58.2	201	19.8	196	19.3	28	2.8
$15,000 to $19,999	1,129	9.4	159	100.0	64	40.7	51	32.1	43	27.2	—	—	971	100.0	544	56.0	233	24.0	170	17.5	23	2.4
$20,000 to $24,999	985	8.2	129	100.0	54	41.8	41	31.8	27	20.7	7	5.8	856	100.0	449	52.5	220	25.7	166	19.4	21	2.5
$25,000 to $29,999	905	7.5	147	100.0	56	38.1	67	45.5	21	14.3	3	2.2	758	100.0	359	47.4	219	28.9	155	20.4	25	3.3
$30,000 to $39,999	1,603	13.4	324	100.0	99	30.6	145	44.6	66	20.3	15	4.5	1,280	100.0	609	47.6	453	35.4	164	12.8	53	4.2
$40,000 to $49,999	1,140	9.5	221	100.0	74	33.5	98	44.3	38	17.4	11	4.8	919	100.0	364	39.7	370	40.3	159	17.3	26	2.8
$50,000 to $74,999	1,679	14.0	356	100.0	104	29.1	188	52.7	58	16.3	7	1.9	1,323	100.0	494	37.4	557	42.1	224	17.0	47	3.6
$75,000 to $99,999	753	6.3	190	100.0	50	26.1	101	52.9	33	17.5	7	3.5	563	100.0	237	42.0	194	34.5	107	19.0	25	4.4
$100,000 and over	861	7.2	239	100.0	53	22.0	123	51.6	47	19.5	16	6.9	621	100.0	272	43.8	244	39.2	81	13.0	25	4.0
Poverty status																						
Below poverty level	4,200	35.0	382	100.0	170	44.5	105	27.4	86	22.5	21	5.6	3,818	100.0	2,239	58.7	720	18.9	767	20.1	91	2.4
At or above poverty level	7,807	65.0	1,618	100.0	497	30.7	765	47.3	294	18.2	62	3.8	6,190	100.0	2,688	43.4	2,273	36.7	1,007	16.3	221	3.6
Number of own children under 18																						
One own child under 18	6,582	54.8	1,279	100.0	506	39.5	529	41.3	202	15.8	43	3.4	5,302	100.0	2,801	52.8	1,548	29.2	769	14.5	185	3.5
Two own children under 18	3,619	30.1	536	100.0	118	22.0	271	50.5	115	21.4	33	6.1	3,083	100.0	1,367	44.3	1,004	32.6	617	20.0	95	3.1
Three own children under 18	1,290	10.7	139	100.0	35	25.0	55	39.3	44	31.5	6	4.1	1,151	100.0	518	45.0	335	29.2	275	23.9	23	2.0
Four or more own children under 18	516	4.3	45	100.0	9	18.8	15	33.6	20	44.7	1	2.9	471	100.0	241	51.3	105	22.4	113	24.1	11	2.3

TABLE 2.10

Single-parent family groups with own children under 18, by marital status and demographic characteristics, 2013 [CONTINUED]

[Numbers in thousands]

	All one-parent unmarried family groups		Maintained by father										Maintained by mother										
			Total		Never married		Divorced		Separated*		Widowed		Total		Never married		Divorced		Separated*		Widowed	
	N	%	N	%	N	%	N	%	N	%	N	%	N	%	N	%	N	%	N	%	N	%
Own children 6–17 years																						
Without own children 6–17	2,892	24.1	414	100.0	263	63.5	89	21.6	61	14.9	—	0.1	2,478	100.0	1,909	77.0	247	10.0	296	12.0	26	1.0
One own child 6–17	5,460	45.5	1,034	100.0	306	29.6	500	48.3	182	17.6	46	4.5	4,426	100.0	1,853	41.9	1,594	36.0	787	17.8	191	4.3
Two own children 6–17	2,635	21.9	441	100.0	78	17.7	237	53.6	98	22.1	29	6.6	2,194	100.0	812	37.0	835	38.1	474	21.6	73	3.3
Three own children 6–17	794	6.6	85	100.0	17	19.6	35	40.7	28	32.8	6	6.8	709	100.0	266	37.5	253	35.8	171	24.1	18	2.6
Four or more own children 6–17	227	1.9	26	100.0	4	15.3	9	34.9	12	44.7	1	5.1	201	100.0	87	43.3	64	31.9	46	22.8	4	2.0
Own children 12–17 years																						
Without own children 12–17	6,409	53.4	1,019	100.0	464	45.5	341	33.5	189	18.5	26	2.6	5,390	100.0	3,415	63.4	1,068	19.8	816	15.1	91	1.7
One own child 12–17	4,200	35.0	767	100.0	174	22.7	401	52.4	151	19.6	41	5.3	3,433	100.0	1,140	33.2	1,428	41.6	700	20.4	165	4.8
Two own children 12–17	1,201	10.0	189	100.0	25	13.1	118	62.3	31	16.6	15	8.0	1,012	100.0	319	31.5	425	42.0	218	21.5	50	5.0
Three or more own children 12–17	197	1.6	25	100.0	5	18.9	9	36.0	10	39.8	1	5.3	172	100.0	55	31.7	71	41.3	40	23.2	7	3.9
Own children 6–11 years																						
Without own children 6–11	6,779	56.5	1,168	100.0	424	36.3	508	43.5	193	16.5	43	3.7	5,611	100.0	2,858	50.9	1,650	29.4	894	15.9	208	3.7
One own child 6–11	3,837	32.0	630	100.0	203	32.2	278	44.1	122	19.4	28	4.4	3,207	100.0	1,536	47.9	953	29.7	630	19.6	89	2.8
Two own children 6–11	1,183	9.8	184	100.0	37	20.0	78	42.3	57	30.9	12	6.8	998	100.0	447	44.8	332	33.2	208	20.8	11	1.1
Three or more own children 6–11	208	1.7	18	100.0	4	19.6	5	30.5	9	49.9	—	—	191	100.0	86	45.2	58	30.6	42	22.3	4	1.9
Own children under 6 years																						
Without own children under 6	7,298	60.8	1,403	100.0	349	24.8	705	50.2	271	19.3	79	5.6	5,894	100.0	2,155	36.6	2,389	40.5	1,097	18.6	253	4.3
One own child under 6	3,687	30.7	510	100.0	285	55.8	142	27.8	80	15.6	4	0.8	3,177	100.0	2,139	67.3	492	15.5	501	15.8	45	1.4
Two own children under 6	887	7.4	81	100.0	33	40.3	23	28.2	26	31.6	—	—	806	100.0	544	67.5	104	12.8	150	18.6	9	1.1
Three or more own children under 6	135	1.1	5	100.0	1	19.1	—	—	4	77.0	—	—	130	100.0	90	69.2	8	6.5	26	20.1	5	4.2
Own children under 3 years																						
Without own children under 3	9,722	81.0	1,768	100.0	515	29.2	826	46.7	346	19.6	81	4.6	7,954	100.0	3,440	43.2	2,768	34.8	1,461	18.4	284	3.6
One own child under 3	2,071	17.2	218	100.0	146	67.1	39	17.8	31	14.0	2	1.1	1,853	100.0	1,337	72.2	212	11.4	278	15.0	26	1.4
Two or more own children under 3	214	1.8	14	100.0	6	40.2	4	30.1	4	29.8	—	—	200	100.0	150	75.2	12	6.2	35	17.7	2	0.9
Age of own children																						
With own children under 18 years	12,007	100.0	2,000	100.0	667	33.4	869	43.5	380	19.0	83	4.2	10,007	100.0	4,928	49.2	2,993	29.9	1,774	17.7	313	3.1
Without own children under 12 years	3,550	29.6	731	100.0	156	21.3	409	56.0	123	16.9	42	5.8	2,819	100.0	794	28.1	1,320	46.8	533	18.9	172	6.1
With own children under 12 years	8,457	70.4	1,269	100.0	511	40.3	460	36.3	257	20.3	41	3.2	7,188	100.0	4,134	57.5	1,673	23.3	1,241	17.3	140	2.0
Without own children under 6 years	7,298	60.8	1,403	100.0	349	24.8	705	50.2	271	19.3	79	5.6	5,894	100.0	2,155	36.6	2,389	40.5	1,097	18.6	253	4.3
With own children under 6 years	4,710	39.2	597	100.0	319	53.4	165	27.6	109	18.3	4	0.7	4,113	100.0	2,773	67.4	604	14.7	677	16.5	59	1.4
Without own children under 5 years	8,014	66.7	1,531	100.0	395	25.8	753	49.2	303	19.8	81	5.3	6,483	100.0	2,496	38.5	2,524	38.9	1,197	18.5	266	4.1
With own children under 5 years	3,993	33.3	469	100.0	273	58.1	116	24.8	78	16.6	2	0.5	3,524	100.0	2,432	69.0	469	13.3	577	16.4	46	1.3
Without own children under 3 years	9,722	81.0	1,768	100.0	515	29.2	826	46.7	346	19.6	81	4.6	7,954	100.0	3,440	43.2	2,768	34.8	1,461	18.4	284	3.6
With own children under 3 years	2,285	19.0	232	100.0	152	65.4	43	18.5	35	15.0	2	1.1	2,053	100.0	1,488	72.4	225	10.9	313	15.2	28	1.4
Without own children under 1 year	11,354	94.6	1,939	100.0	623	32.1	860	44.4	373	19.2	83	4.3	9,415	100.0	4,481	47.6	2,950	31.3	1,675	17.8	309	3.3
With own children under 1 year	653	5.4	61	100.0	45	72.8	9	14.6	8	12.6	—	—	592	100.0	446	75.4	43	7.2	99	16.8	4	0.6
Without own children 3–5 years	8,974	74.7	1,593	100.0	479	30.1	738	46.3	294	18.4	82	5.1	7,381	100.0	3,259	44.2	2,549	34.5	1,304	17.7	269	3.6
With own children 3–5 years	3,033	25.3	407	100.0	188	46.2	131	32.2	87	21.3	2	0.4	2,626	100.0	1,669	63.5	444	16.9	470	17.9	43	1.7
Without own children 6–11 years	6,779	56.5	1,168	100.0	424	36.3	508	43.5	193	16.5	43	3.7	5,611	100.0	2,858	50.9	1,650	29.4	894	15.9	208	3.7
With own children 6–11 years	5,228	43.5	832	100.0	243	29.2	361	43.4	188	22.6	40	4.8	4,396	100.0	2,069	47.1	1,343	30.5	880	20.0	104	2.4
Without own children 12–17 years	6,409	53.4	1,019	100.0	464	45.5	341	33.5	189	18.5	26	2.6	5,390	100.0	3,415	63.4	1,068	19.8	816	15.1	91	1.7
With own children 12–17 years	5,598	46.6	981	100.0	204	20.8	528	53.9	192	19.6	57	5.8	4,617	100.0	1,513	32.8	1,925	41.7	958	20.7	222	4.8
Without own children 6–17 years	2,892	24.1	414	100.0	263	63.5	89	21.6	61	14.9	—	0.1	2,478	100.0	1,909	77.0	247	10.0	296	12.0	26	1.0
With own children 6–17 years	9,116	75.9	1,586	100.0	405	25.5	780	49.2	319	20.1	83	5.2	7,529	100.0	3,019	40.1	2,746	36.5	1,478	19.6	287	3.8

TABLE 2.10

Single-parent family groups with own children under 18, by marital status and demographic characteristics, 2013 [CONTINUED]

[Numbers in thousands]

	All one-parent unmarried family groups		Maintained by father										Maintained by mother										
			Total		Never married		Divorced		Separated*		Widowed		Total		Never married		Divorced		Separated*		Widowed	
	N	%	N	%	N	%	N	%	N	%	N	%	N	%	N	%	N	%	N	%	N	%
Own children in specified age groups																						
Children in two or more age groups	4,619	38.5	545	100.0	135	24.8	249	45.7	134	24.7	26	4.8	4,074	100.0	1,773	43.5	1,220	29.9	941	23.1	141	3.5
Families with children 12–17 only	2,739	22.8	631	100.0	142	22.6	347	55.0	106	16.7	36	5.7	2,108	100.0	619	29.4	1,011	47.9	362	17.2	116	5.5
Families with children 6–11 only	2,185	18.2	443	100.0	143	32.3	192	43.4	87	19.6	21	4.7	1,742	100.0	887	50.9	564	32.4	250	14.4	41	2.4
Families with children 3–5 only	1,245	10.4	222	100.0	129	57.9	56	25.4	37	16.5	—	0.2	1,022	100.0	764	74.8	130	12.7	118	11.6	10	1.0
Families with children under 3 only	1,219	10.2	159	100.0	118	74.2	24	15.2	17	10.6	—	—	1,061	100.0	885	83.4	68	6.4	103	9.7	4	0.4
Under 6 only	2,892	24.1	414	100.0	263	63.5	89	21.6	61	14.9	—	0.1	2,478	100.0	1,909	77.0	247	10.0	296	12.0	26	1.0
Some under 6, some 6–17	1,818	15.1	183	100.0	56	30.6	76	41.3	48	26.2	3	1.9	1,635	100.0	864	52.8	357	21.8	381	23.3	34	2.1
6–17 only	7,298	60.8	1,403	100.0	349	24.8	705	50.2	271	19.3	79	5.6	5,894	100.0	2,155	36.6	2,389	40.5	1,097	18.6	253	4.3

Internet Release Date: November 2013.

*Includes "Married spouse absent".

Notes: Dash ("—") represents or rounds to zero. "Own children" exclude ever-married children under 18 years.

SOURCE: "Table FG6. One-Parent Unmarried Family Groups with Own Children under 18, by Marital Status of the Reference Person: 2013," in *America's Families and Living Arrangements: 2013*, November 2013, http://www.census.gov/hhes/families/files/cps2013/tabFG6-all_one.xls (accessed October 28, 2014)

TABLE 2.11

Living arrangements of children and marital status of parents, by selected characteristics, 2013

[Numbers in thousands]

	Total	Living with both parents		Living with mother only					Living with father only					Living with neither parent
		Married to each other	Not married to each other	Married spouse absent	Widowed	Divorced	Separated	Never married	Married spouse absent	Widowed	Divorced	Separated	Never married	No parent present
All children	**73,910**	**47,611**	**3,034**	**898**	**516**	**5,250**	**2,479**	**8,389**	**135**	**131**	**1,314**	**501**	**917**	**2,733**
Male	37,788	24,287	1,607	493	252	2,709	1,178	4,208	69	76	722	257	472	1,457
Female	36,122	23,325	1,427	405	264	2,540	1,301	4,181	65	55	593	245	446	1,276
Both sexes														
Total	**73,910**	**47,611**	**3,034**	**898**	**516**	**5,250**	**2,479**	**8,389**	**135**	**131**	**1,314**	**501**	**917**	**2,733**
Age of child														
Under 1 year	3,873	2,444	508	42	4	58	84	554	—	—	13	8	59	99
1–2 years	7,994	5,144	662	75	27	205	186	1,243	11	3	38	23	127	248
3–5 years	12,171	7,782	662	142	51	506	382	1,804	10	1	134	88	180	428
6–8 years	12,290	7,979	477	161	51	794	452	1,459	30	30	191	90	161	414
9–11 years	12,224	8,039	289	122	76	1,065	428	1,271	34	23	239	92	139	407
12–14 years	12,491	8,060	261	170	122	1,261	476	1,035	28	27	301	108	140	504
15–17 years	12,866	8,164	176	187	184	1,360	471	1,023	21	47	398	92	112	632
Race														
White alone	54,227	38,135	2,168	555	355	3,873	1,650	3,596	84	85	1,065	358	563	1,739
Black alone	11,086	3,813	490	190	107	930	563	3,809	29	21	114	84	257	678
Asian alone	3,591	2,983	64	89	23	121	53	99	9	13	31	26	11	69
All remaining single races and all race combinations	5,006	2,680	313	64	32	325	212	885	12	12	104	33	86	246
Race														
Hispanic*	17,709	10,300	1,221	385	121	1,096	939	2,394	31	22	144	120	253	684
White alone, non-Hispanic	38,880	28,935	1,157	234	249	2,934	827	1,695	57	74	939	259	363	1,158
All remaining single races and all race combinations, non-Hispanic	17,321	8,376	657	280	147	1,220	713	4,300	46	36	231	123	301	891
Race														
White alone or in combination with one or more other races	57,616	40,087	2,378	572	372	4,101	1,774	4,127	91	94	1,146	380	622	1,872
Other	16,294	7,524	657	326	144	1,149	705	4,263	43	37	168	121	295	861
Race														
Black alone or in combination with one or more other races	13,132	4,746	634	209	119	1,079	653	4,313	30	24	153	103	296	774
Other	60,778	42,866	2,401	689	397	4,171	1,826	4,076	105	108	1,161	399	621	1,958
Race														
Asian alone or in combination with one or more other races	4,551	3,708	92	91	24	174	102	153	16	13	44	31	20	83
Other	69,359	43,904	2,942	807	493	5,076	2,377	8,236	118	118	1,270	470	897	2,650
Presence of siblings														
None	15,238	7,217	764	158	125	1,134	374	2,475	32	35	424	130	441	1,931
One sibling	28,971	19,832	1,125	352	213	2,188	867	2,792	49	58	587	177	279	451
Two siblings	18,027	12,665	643	228	92	1,237	734	1,739	41	23	215	101	115	194
Three siblings	7,143	4,877	269	95	55	438	327	774	9	16	52	51	70	111
Four siblings	2,659	1,682	139	40	20	171	130	392	3	—	25	22	8	27
Five or more siblings	1,873	1,340	95	26	12	82	46	217	—	—	12	20	5	18

TABLE 2.11

Living arrangements of children and marital status of parents, by selected characteristics, 2013 [CONTINUED]

[Numbers in thousands]

		Living with both parents		Living with mother only					Living with father only					Living with neither parent
	Total	Married to each other	Not married to each other	Married spouse absent	Widowed	Divorced	Separated	Never married	Married spouse absent	Widowed	Divorced	Separated	Never married	No parent present
Presence of parent's unmarried partner														
Child's parent does not have opposite sex partner	68,624	47,611	261	877	466	4,439	2,333	7,577	124	105	1,037	449	613	2,733
Child's parent has opposite sex partner	5,286	—	2,773	22	50	811	146	812	11	26	278	52	305	—
Partner is also other parent	2,773	—	2,773	—	—	—	—	—	—	—	—	—	—	—
Partner is not other parent	2,513	—	—	22	50	811	146	812	11	26	278	52	305	—
Highest education of either parent														
No parents present	2,733	—	—	—	—	—	—	—	—	—	—	—	—	2,733
Less than 9th grade	2,329	1,386	146	73	28	105	138	357	9	9	17	24	36	—
9th to 12th grade, no diploma	4,917	1,907	274	149	70	308	376	1,475	11	7	89	112	140	—
High school graduate	15,535	8,095	1,145	234	136	1,219	746	2,932	43	58	384	163	381	—
Some college or AA (Associate of Arts) degree	20,761	12,317	1,073	269	167	2,214	892	2,884	45	42	491	126	243	—
Bachelor's degree	15,719	13,104	293	107	74	1,004	242	532	21	10	210	43	78	—
Prof. or graduate degree	11,916	10,804	104	65	41	400	86	209	5	6	123	34	40	—
Parent's labor force status														
Father in labor force, mother not present	2,678	—	—	—	—	—	—	—	123	105	1,219	424	807	—
Father not in labor force, mother not present	321	—	—	—	—	—	—	—	11	26	96	78	111	—
Mother in labor force, father not present	13,167	—	—	642	286	4,385	1,854	6,000	—	—	—	—	—	—
Mother not in labor force, father not present	4,365	—	—	256	230	865	625	2,390	—	—	—	—	—	—
Mother and father in labor force	30,402	28,803	1,599	—	—	—	—	—	—	—	—	—	—	—
Father in labor force, mother not in labor force	16,131	15,114	1,017	—	—	—	—	—	—	—	—	—	—	—
Mother in labor force, father not in labor force	2,527	2,293	234	—	—	—	—	—	—	—	—	—	—	—
Father not in labor force, mother not in labor force	1,586	1,401	184	—	—	—	—	—	—	—	—	—	—	—
No parents present	2,733	—	—	—	—	—	—	—	—	—	—	—	—	2,733
Family income														
Under $2,500	2,988	494	492	119	31	198	214	711	6	3	10	14	41	655
$2,500 to $4,999	884	150	94	40	15	113	72	311	2	2	9	10	10	55
$5,000 to $7,499	1,145	195	113	47	6	137	108	453	—	5	4	9	17	52
$7,500 to $9,999	1,229	258	120	30	19	158	139	404	4	4	14	8	19	50
$10,000 to $12,499	1,932	477	194	50	26	180	200	608	7	5	30	10	43	104
$12,500 to $14,999	1,523	380	134	55	30	185	103	508	2	2	8	12	27	76
$15,000 to $19,999	3,637	1,122	242	74	40	441	267	1,026	16	—	91	82	96	139
$20,000 to $24,999	3,630	1,476	269	73	35	388	254	799	16	11	55	30	65	157
$25,000 to $29,999	3,429	1,515	223	77	44	361	211	621	8	9	101	26	62	170
$30,000 to $39,999	6,813	3,540	341	53	89	821	241	979	25	20	210	87	153	255
$40,000 to $49,999	5,673	3,429	181	77	38	635	185	583	4	16	149	56	110	211
$50,000 to $74,999	12,274	8,911	316	77	65	946	305	736	15	11	305	77	142	367
$75,000 to $99,999	9,277	7,768	193	69	36	310	97	304	8	15	149	44	65	219
$100,00 and over	19,475	17,895	122	57	41	376	83	346	22	30	180	38	67	220
Health insurance coverage														
Covered by health insurance	67,360	44,091	2,682	764	444	4,815	2,174	7,576	107	112	1,171	449	812	2,164
Not covered by health insurance	6,550	3,520	353	134	72	435	305	814	27	20	143	53	106	568

TABLE 2.11

Living arrangements of children and marital status of parents, by selected characteristics, 2013 [CONTINUED]

[Numbers in thousands]

	Total	Living with both parents		Living with mother only					Living with father only					Living with neither parent
		Married to each other	Not married to each other	Married spouse absent	Widowed	Divorced	Separated	Never married	Married spouse absent	Widowed	Divorced	Separated	Never married	No parent present
Poverty status														
Below 100% of poverty	16,428	5,249	1,447	471	183	1,492	1,238	4,436	31	28	183	152	242	1,277
100% to 199% of poverty	16,131	8,896	829	195	147	1,580	703	2,293	55	25	360	130	275	645
200% of poverty and above	41,350	33,466	759	233	186	2,178	538	1,661	48	79	771	220	400	811
Household food stamp reciept														
No	58,264	42,453	1,945	501	367	3,661	1,337	3,721	97	98	1,133	354	683	1,912
Yes	15,646	5,159	1,089	397	149	1,588	1,142	4,668	37	33	181	148	234	820
Household public asst receipt														
No	70,978	46,989	2,826	814	485	5,003	2,235	7,302	121	119	1,276	478	872	2,458
Yes	2,931	623	208	84	31	247	244	1,087	13	12	38	24	46	274
100 percent of poverty														
Below 100% of poverty	16,428	5,249	1,447	471	183	1,492	1,238	4,436	31	28	183	152	242	1,277
100% of poverty and above	57,481	42,362	1,587	427	333	3,758	1,241	3,953	103	103	1,131	350	675	1,456
125 percent of poverty														
Below 125% of poverty	20,656	7,373	1,705	513	221	1,909	1,467	5,201	57	32	239	177	316	1,444
125% of poverty and above	53,254	40,238	1,330	385	295	3,341	1,012	3,188	77	99	1,075	325	601	1,288
Household tenure														
Own/buying	44,956	34,498	990	357	302	2,452	807	2,304	82	102	805	242	376	1,639
Rent	28,213	12,771	2,005	537	210	2,711	1,631	5,948	51	29	494	247	538	1,041
No cash rent	741	342	40	4	4	87	42	137	2	1	15	13	3	52

Dash "—" represents or rounds to zero.

*Hispanics may be of any race.

SOURCE: Adapted from "Table C3. Living Arrangements of Children under 18 Years and Marital Status of Parents, by Age, Sex, Race, and Hispanic Origin and Selected Characteristics of the Child for All Children: 2013," in *America's Families and Living Arrangements: 2013*, November 2013, http://www.census.gov/hhes/families/files/cps2013/tabC3-all.xls (accessed October 28, 2014)

FIGURE 2.2

Poverty status of custodial parents, 1993–2011

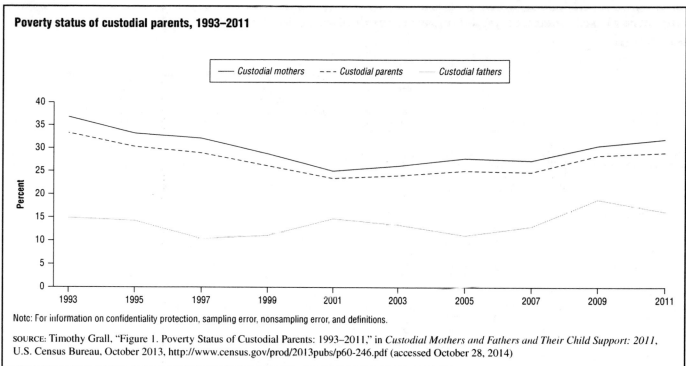

Note: For information on confidentiality protection, sampling error, nonsampling error, and definitions.

SOURCE: Timothy Grall, "Figure 1. Poverty Status of Custodial Parents: 1993–2011," in *Custodial Mothers and Fathers and Their Child Support: 2011*, U.S. Census Bureau, October 2013, http://www.census.gov/prod/2013pubs/p60-246.pdf (accessed October 28, 2014)

them to rise above the poverty line. Particularly in cases when a single parent must balance a low-paying job with the time-intensive demands of raising children, the likelihood of working and still failing to escape poverty increases markedly.

In 2012 most Americans aged 16 years and older worked at some point during the year (161.7 million of 245 million, or 66%). (See Table 2.12.) Approximately 92% (148.7 million) of those who had any labor force activity at all worked more than half of the weeks in the year (27 weeks or more), and among those who worked 27 weeks or more, 93% (138.1 million) lived at or above the poverty level. Some people who work less than this amount do so by choice; others do so because they cannot find full-time work or because they experience periods of unemployment.

In any event, employment does not always protect individuals and their families from poverty; 8.1% (13.2 million) of all those who worked lived in poverty in 2012, along with 22.5% (18.7 million) of the 16-and-older population that did not work. (See Table 2.12.) The poverty rate was higher for those who worked only 26 weeks or less (19.6%) than for those who worked 27 weeks or more (7.1%). The "working-poor rate" (as the U.S. Department of Labor calls the poverty rate of those who work 27 weeks or more per year) grew significantly during the Great Recession, jumping nearly two percentage points between 2007 and 2009 and then leveling off at around 7%. (See Table 2.13.)

Many poor children live in families in which one or more adults work. According to the U.S. Bureau of Labor Statistics (BLS), in *A Profile of the Working Poor, 2012* (March 2014, http://www.bls.gov/cps/cpswp2012.pdf), 5.5 million families with at least one member in the labor force lived below the poverty line in 2012. (See Table 2.14.) Among those families with a member in the labor force for at least 27 weeks, single-parent families headed by women were particularly likely to live in poverty. Over a quarter (26.8%) of working families headed by a single woman lived below the poverty line, compared with 16.8% of working families headed by a single man and 9.6% of working families headed by a married couple.

In 2012, 5.5 million working women and 5.1 million working men had incomes below the poverty level. (See Table 2.15.) Because there were fewer women in the labor force, working women had a higher poverty rate (7.9%) than working men (6.4%). Approximately 7.3 million (69%) of the working poor were white, 3.2 million (29.9%) were Hispanic, 2.4 million (22.6%) were African American, and 403,000 (3.8%) were Asian American. Although whites constituted the bulk of the working poor, African Americans and Hispanics experienced poverty while employed at much higher rates than whites. In 2012, 13.6% of African Americans in the labor force were below the poverty line, as were 13.8% of Hispanics, compared with 6.2% of whites and 4.9% of Asian Americans.

Workers between the ages of 16 and 24 years were much more likely to be in poverty than older workers in

TABLE 2.12

Poverty status and work experience of people in families and unrelated individuals, 2012

[Numbers in thousands]

Poverty status and work experience	Total people	In married-couple families				In families maintained by women			In families maintained by men			Unrelated individuals
		Husbands	Wives	Related children under 18 years	Other relatives	House holder	Related children under 18 years	Other relatives	House holder	Related children under 18 years	Other relatives	
Total												
All people[a]	244,993	58,546	59,178	5,746	20,666	15,455	2,252	13,199	6,206	643	6,216	56,884
With labor force activity	161,707	44,790	37,053	1,478	12,936	10,921	445	7,887	4,782	99	4,004	37,312
1 to 26 weeks	12,972	1,486	2,650	919	2,712	754	282	1,006	236	58	366	2,502
27 weeks or more	148,735	43,304	34,403	559	10,224	10,168	163	6,881	4,546	40	3,638	34,810
With no labor force activity	83,287	13,757	22,125	4,269	7,730	4,533	1,807	5,312	1,424	545	2,212	19,572
At or above poverty level												
All people[a]	213,108	54,870	55,474	5,269	19,359	10,666	1,528	10,705	5,188	525	5,488	44,035
With labor force activity	148,557	42,750	35,974	1,421	12,450	8,243	352	7,006	4,193	89	3,736	32,343
1 to 26 weeks	10,433	1,331	2,410	880	2,615	300	218	780	165	52	298	1,383
27 weeks or more	138,124	41,419	33,564	541	9,835	7,943	134	6,226	4,028	37	3,437	30,959
With no labor force activity	64,551	12,121	19,500	3,848	6,909	2,423	1,177	3,699	994	436	1,753	11,693
Below poverty level												
All people[a]	31,885	3,676	3,704	477	1,307	4,788	724	2,494	1,018	119	728	12,849
With labor force activity	13,150	2,040	1,079	57	486	2,678	94	881	589	10	268	4,970
1 to 26 weeks	2,538	155	240	38	97	453	65	226	71	7	67	1,119
27 weeks or more	10,612	1,885	839	18	389	2,225	29	655	518	—	201	3,851
With no labor force activity	18,735	1,636	2,626	421	821	2,110	631	1,613	430	109	460	7,879
Rate[b]												
All people[a]	13.0	6.3	6.3	8.3	6.3	31.0	32.1	18.9	16.4	18.5	11.7	22.6
With labor force activity	8.1	4.6	2.9	3.8	3.8	24.5	21.0	11.2	12.3	9.9	6.7	13.3
1 to 26 weeks	19.6	10.4	9.1	4.2	3.6	60.1	22.9	22.4	30.1	c	18.4	44.7
27 weeks or more	7.1	4.4	2.4	3.3	3.8	21.9	17.7	9.5	11.4	c	5.5	11.1
With no labor force activity	22.5	11.9	11.9	9.9	10.6	46.6	34.9	30.4	30.2	20.0	20.8	40.3

[a]Data on families include primary families that own or rent the housing unit as well as related and unrelated subfamilies that reside with them.
[b]Number below the poverty level as a percent of the total.
[c]Data not shown where base is less than 80,000.
Note: Dash represents or rounds to zero.

SOURCE: "Table 6. People in Families and Unrelated Individuals: Poverty Status and Work Experience, 2012," in *A Profile of the Working Poor, 2012*, U.S. Department of Labor, U.S. Bureau of Labor Statistics, March 2014, http://www.bls.gov/cps/cpswp2012.pdf (accessed October 28, 2014)

TABLE 2.13

Poverty status of people and primary families in the labor force for 27 or more weeks, 2007–12

[Numbers in thousands]

Characteristic	2007	2008	2009	2010	2011	2012
Total in the labor force[a]	**146,567**	**147,838**	**147,902**	**146,859**	**147,475**	**148,735**
In poverty	7,521	8,883	10,391	10,512	10,382	10,612
Working-poor rate	5.1	6.0	7.0	7.2	7.0	7.1
Unrelated individuals	**33,226**	**32,785**	**33,798**	**34,099**	**33,731**	**34,810**
In poverty	2,558	3,275	3,947	3,947	3,621	3,851
Working-poor rate	7.7	10.0	11.7	11.6	10.7	11.1
Primary families[b]	**65,158**	**65,907**	**65,467**	**64,931**	**66,225**	**66,541**
In poverty	4,169	4,538	5,193	5,269	5,469	5,478
Working-poor rate	6.4	6.9	7.9	8.1	8.3	8.2

[a]Includes individuals in families, not shown separately.
[b]Primary families with at least one member in the labor force for more than half the year.
Note: Updated population controls are introduced annually with the release of January data.

SOURCE: "Table A. Poverty Status of People and Primary Families in the Labor Force for 27 Weeks or More, 2007–2012," in *A Profile of the Working Poor, 2012*, U.S. Department of Labor, U.S. Bureau of Labor Statistics, March 2014, http://www.bls.gov/cps/cpswp2012.pdf (accessed October 28, 2014)

2012. Approximately 12.9% of workers aged 16 to 19 years and 13.8% of workers aged 20 to 24 years did not make enough income to rise above the poverty line, compared with 9.8% of workers aged 25 to 34 years and 7.4% of workers aged 35 to 44 years. (See Table 2.15.) Much of the reason for this is that many younger workers

TABLE 2.14

Poverty status and selected characteristics of families with one member in the labor force for 27 weeks or more, 2012

[Numbers in thousands]

Characteristic	Total families	At or above poverty level	Below poverty level	Rate*
Total primary families	**66,541**	**61,063**	**5,478**	**8.2**
With related children under 18 years	35,003	30,450	4,554	13.0
Without children	31,538	30,613	924	2.9
With one member in the labor force	28,836	24,369	4,467	15.5
With two or more members in the labor force	37,705	36,694	1,011	2.7
With two members	31,683	30,786	896	2.8
With three or more members	6,022	5,907	115	1.9
Married-couple families	**49,118**	**46,806**	**2,312**	**4.7**
With related children under 18 years	24,353	22,520	1,833	7.5
Without children	24,765	24,285	479	1.9
With one member in the labor force	17,067	15,423	1,644	9.6
Husband	12,139	10,883	1,256	10.3
Wife	4,185	3,901	283	6.8
Relative	744	639	105	14.1
With two or more members in the labor force	32,050	31,383	668	2.1
With two members	27,221	26,631	590	2.2
With three or more members	4,829	4,752	77	1.6
Families maintained by women	**12,075**	**9,542**	**2,532**	**21.0**
With related children under 18 years	7,817	5,582	2,235	28.6
Without children	4,257	3,960	297	7.0
With one member in the labor force	8,461	6,194	2,267	26.8
Householder	6,985	4,985	2,000	28.6
Relative	1,476	1,209	267	18.1
With two or more members in the labor force	3,614	3,348	265	7.3
Families maintained by men	**5,349**	**4,715**	**634**	**11.9**
With related children under 18 years	2,833	2,347	486	17.2
Without children	2,516	2,368	148	5.9
With one member in the labor force	3,308	2,752	556	16.8
Householder	2,715	2,261	453	16.7
Relative	593	491	102	17.3
With two or more members in the labor force	2,041	1,963	78	3.8

*Number below the poverty level as a percent of the total in the labor force for 27 weeks or more.
Note: Data relate to primary families with at least one member in the labor force for 27 weeks or more.

SOURCE: "Table 5. Primary Families: Poverty Status, Presence of Related Children, and Work Experience of Family Members in the Labor Force for 27 Weeks or More, 2012," in *A Profile of the Working Poor, 2012*, U.S. Department of Labor, U.S. Bureau of Labor Statistics, March 2014, http://www.bls.gov/cps/cpswp2012.pdf (accessed October 28, 2014)

are still in school and/or work at part-time or entry-level jobs that often do not pay well. In general, as age increases, the likelihood of being both in the labor force and poor decreases.

Educational levels typically correlate directly with the risk of poverty among workers. Among workers in the labor force for at least 27 weeks in 2012, 21.2% of those with less than a high school diploma fell below the poverty level, compared with 9.4% of high school graduates with no college experience. (See Table 2.16.) Lower poverty rates were reported for workers with some college or an associate's degree (6.7%), and workers with a bachelor's degree and higher were comparatively unlikely to live in poverty (2.1%). African American and Hispanic workers at all education levels had higher poverty rates than white workers, and women had a higher poverty rate than men at all educational levels and among all racial and ethnic groups (the one exception was Asian American women workers with a bachelor's

degree and higher). The highest poverty rate was for African American women workers without a high school diploma (38.2%). Hispanic women workers without a high school diploma experienced poverty at a rate of 27.8%.

Finally, labor market conditions play a major role in whether a working family lives in poverty. Three primary labor market problems contributed to poverty among workers in 2012: low earnings, unemployment, and involuntary part-time employment. Most full-time workers (81.2%) did not experience any of these three problems in 2012, and very few workers who experienced none of these problems (0.8%) were poor. (See Table 2.17.) By contrast, 23.5% of workers who had low earnings (and neither of the other two problems) lived in poverty. Unemployment alone accounted for the poverty of 7.7% of workers and involuntary part-time work for 2.4%. However, it was the combination of two or more factors that had the most devastating effect on families. Among

TABLE 2.15

Poverty status of people in the labor force for 27 weeks or more, by age, sex, race, and Hispanic origin, 2012

[Numbers in thousands]

Age and gender	Total	White	Black or African American	Asian	Hispanic or Latino ethnicity	Below poverty level Total	White	Black or African American	Asian	Hispanic or Latino ethnicity	Rate[a] Total	White	Black or African American	Asian	Hispanic or Latino ethnicity
Total, 16 years and older	**148,735**	**118,575**	**17,632**	**8,203**	**23,048**	**10,612**	**7,322**	**2,394**	**403**	**3,169**	**7.1**	**6.2**	**13.6**	**4.9**	**13.8**
16 to 19 years	3,293	2,608	414	111	601	425	307	92	11	97	12.9	11.8	22.3	10.1	16.2
20 to 24 years	13,302	10,133	1,990	573	2,850	1,840	1,223	485	47	472	13.8	12.1	24.4	8.2	16.6
25 to 34 years	32,477	25,000	4,201	2,044	6,352	3,185	2,169	746	89	985	9.8	8.7	17.8	4.3	15.5
35 to 44 years	31,942	24,760	4,043	2,157	5,842	2,350	1,646	517	95	883	7.4	6.6	12.8	4.4	15.1
45 to 54 years	34,117	27,620	3,938	1,782	4,547	1,680	1,160	345	97	484	4.9	4.2	8.8	5.4	10.6
55 to 64 years	25,289	21,251	2,387	1,210	2,272	981	708	185	54	193	3.9	3.3	7.8	4.5	8.5
65 years and older	8,316	7,203	659	326	584	150	109	23	10	56	1.8	1.5	3.5	3.0	9.5
Men, 16 years and older	**79,303**	**64,497**	**8,181**	**4,354**	**13,373**	**5,112**	**3,770**	**930**	**194**	**1,756**	**6.4**	**5.8**	**11.4**	**4.4**	**13.1**
16 to 19 years	1,619	1,300	180	63	319	197	143	43	6	50	12.2	11.0	24.1	[b]	15.5
20 to 24 years	7,025	5,516	921	278	1,621	857	601	199	16	248	12.2	10.9	21.6	5.7	15.3
25 to 34 years	17,583	13,827	1,982	1,115	3,846	1,443	1,067	270	38	528	8.2	7.7	13.6	3.4	13.7
35 to 44 years	17,354	13,803	1,842	1,174	3,438	1,206	924	191	39	531	7.0	6.7	10.4	3.3	15.4
45 to 54 years	17,962	14,795	1,819	944	2,567	847	609	136	65	270	4.7	4.1	7.5	6.9	10.5
55 to 64 years	13,070	11,134	1,108	609	1,261	489	374	80	24	104	3.7	3.4	7.2	3.9	8.3
65 years and older	4,691	4,123	331	171	321	72	52	11	6	24	1.5	1.3	3.4	3.6	7.5
Women, 16 years and older	**69,433**	**54,078**	**9,451**	**3,850**	**9,675**	**5,499**	**3,552**	**1,464**	**209**	**1,414**	**7.9**	**6.6**	**15.5**	**5.4**	**14.6**
16 to 19 years	1,674	1,308	234	48	283	228	164	49	5	48	13.6	12.5	20.9	[b]	16.9
20 to 24 years	6,277	4,617	1,069	295	1,229	983	622	287	31	224	15.7	13.5	26.8	10.5	18.2
25 to 34 years	14,894	11,174	2,220	929	2,506	1,742	1,103	476	51	457	11.7	9.9	21.4	5.4	18.2
35 to 44 years	14,588	10,957	2,201	982	2,403	1,144	722	326	56	352	7.8	6.6	14.8	5.7	14.6
45 to 54 years	16,155	12,825	2,119	838	1,980	833	550	210	32	213	5.2	4.3	9.9	3.8	10.8
55 to 64 years	12,220	10,117	1,279	602	1,011	492	333	105	31	89	4.0	3.3	8.2	5.1	8.8
65 years and older	3,625	3,080	329	155	263	78	58	12	3	32	2.2	1.9	3.5	2.2	12.0

[a]Number below the poverty level as a percent of the total in the labor force for 27 weeks or more.

[b]Data not shown where base is less than 80,000.

Note: Estimates for the race groups shown (white, black or African American, and Asian) do not sum to totals because data are not presented for all races. People whose ethnicity is identified as Hispanic or Latino may be of any race. Dash represents or rounds to zero.

SOURCE: "Table 2. People in the Labor Force for 27 Weeks or More: Poverty Status by Age, Gender, Race, and Hispanic or Latino Ethnicity, 2012," in A Profile of the Working Poor, 2012, U.S. Department of Labor, U.S. Bureau of Labor Statistics, March 2014, http://www.bls.gov/cps/cpswp2012.pdf (accessed October 28, 2014)

TABLE 2.16

Poverty status of people in the labor force for 27 weeks or more, by educational attainment, race, Hispanic origin, and sex, 2012

[Numbers in thousands]

Educational attainment, race, and Hispanic or Latino ethnicity	Total	Men	Women	Below poverty level			Rate[a]		
				Total	Men	Women	Total	Men	Women
Total, 16 years and older	**148,735**	**79,303**	**69,433**	**10,612**	**5,112**	**5,499**	**7.1**	**6.4**	**7.9**
Less than a high school diploma	13,132	8,260	4,871	2,781	1,572	1,209	21.2	19.0	24.8
Less than 1 year of high school	4,247	2,884	1,364	926	584	342	21.8	20.3	25.1
1–3 years of high school	7,160	4,311	2,848	1,520	795	724	21.2	18.5	25.4
4 years of high school, no diploma	1,725	1,066	659	335	192	143	19.4	18.0	21.6
High school graduates, no college[b]	40,616	23,263	17,352	3,805	1,898	1,907	9.4	8.2	11.0
Some college or associate's degree	44,251	21,841	22,410	2,970	1,167	1,803	6.7	5.3	8.0
Some college, no degree	28,388	14,540	13,848	2,199	896	1,303	7.7	6.2	9.4
Associate's degree	15,863	7,301	8,563	771	271	500	4.9	3.7	5.8
Bachelor's degree and higher[c]	50,737	25,938	24,798	1,055	475	581	2.1	1.8	2.3
White, 16 years and older	**118,575**	**64,497**	**54,078**	**7,322**	**3,770**	**3,552**	**6.2**	**5.8**	**6.6**
Less than a high school diploma	10,472	6,805	3,667	2,054	1,233	821	19.6	18.1	22.4
Less than 1 year of high school	3,568	2,504	1,064	769	502	267	21.5	20.0	25.1
1–3 years of high school	5,611	3,480	2,131	1,054	595	459	18.8	17.1	21.5
4 years of high school, no diploma	1,293	821	473	231	136	95	17.9	16.6	20.0
High school graduates, no college[b]	32,245	18,879	13,366	2,511	1,340	1,171	7.8	7.1	8.8
Some college or associate's degree	34,969	17,624	17,344	1,985	847	1,138	5.7	4.8	6.6
Some college, no degree	22,041	11,642	10,399	1,436	627	809	6.5	5.4	7.8
Associate's degree	12,928	5,982	6,946	549	220	329	4.2	3.7	4.7
Bachelor's degree and higher[c]	40,889	21,189	19,700	772	349	422	1.9	1.6	2.1
Black or African American, 16 years and older	**17,632**	**8,181**	**9,451**	**2,394**	**930**	**1,464**	**13.6**	**11.4**	**15.5**
Less than a high school diploma	1,585	845	740	513	230	283	32.3	27.2	38.2
Less than 1 year of high school	294	164	130	88	41	47	30.0	24.7	36.6
1–3 years of high school	999	521	478	343	142	201	34.3	27.3	41.9
4 years of high school, no diploma	293	160	133	82	47	35	28.0	29.5	26.2
High school graduates, no college[b]	5,662	2,909	2,752	979	411	568	17.3	14.1	20.6
Some college or associate's degree	6,148	2,670	3,477	739	228	511	12.0	8.5	14.7
Some college, no degree	4,333	1,910	2,422	584	200	383	13.5	10.5	15.8
Associate's degree	1,815	760	1,055	156	28	128	8.6	3.6	12.1
Bachelor's degree and higher[c]	4,238	1,757	2,481	163	61	102	3.8	3.5	4.1
Asian, 16 years and older	**8,203**	**4,354**	**3,850**	**403**	**194**	**209**	**4.9**	**4.4**	**5.4**
Less than a high school diploma	543	268	276	86	42	44	15.9	15.8	15.9
Less than 1 year of high school	210	88	121	32	21	12	15.5	23.3	9.7
1–3 years of high school	248	127	121	42	18	24	16.9	14.1	20.0
4 years of high school, no diploma	86	52	34	12	4	8	13.8	d	d
High school graduates, no college[b]	1,414	728	686	128	60	68	9.1	8.2	10.0
Some college or associate's degree	1,631	831	800	92	34	57	5.6	4.1	7.2
Some college, no degree	999	515	484	64	24	40	6.4	4.6	8.3
Associate's degree	632	316	316	28	11	17	4.4	3.4	5.4
Bachelor's degree and higher[c]	4,615	2,527	2,088	97	57	40	2.1	2.3	1.9
Hispanic or Latino ethnicity, 16 years and older	**23,048**	**13,373**	**9,675**	**3,169**	**1,756**	**1,414**	**13.8**	**13.1**	**14.6**
Less than a high school diploma	6,452	4,376	2,077	1,529	951	578	23.7	21.7	27.8
Less than 1 year of high school	3,157	2,212	945	769	499	270	24.3	22.5	28.5
1–3 years of high school	2,631	1,724	906	602	362	240	22.9	21.0	26.5
4 years of high school, no diploma	664	439	225	158	90	68	23.7	20.4	30.2
High school graduates, no college[b]	7,258	4,397	2,861	1,008	564	444	13.9	12.8	15.5
Some college or associate's degree	5,712	2,811	2,901	468	179	289	8.2	6.4	10.0
Some college, no degree	3,938	2,025	1,913	340	130	211	8.6	6.4	11.0
Associate's degree	1,775	787	988	128	50	78	7.2	6.3	7.9
Bachelor's degree and higher[c]	3,626	1,790	1,836	164	61	103	4.5	3.4	5.6

[a]Number below the poverty level as a percent of the total in the labor force for 27 weeks or more.
[b]Includes people with a high school diploma or equivalent.
[c]Includes people with bachelor's, master's, professional, and doctoral degrees.
[d]Data not shown where base is less than 80,000.
Note: Estimates for the race groups shown (white, black or African American, and Asian) do not sum to totals because data are not presented for all races. People whose ethnicity is identified as Hispanic or Latino may be of any race.

SOURCE: "Table 3. People in the Labor Force for 27 or More Weeks: Poverty Status by Educational Attainment, Race, Hispanic or Latino Ethnicity, and Gender, 2012," in *A Profile of the Working Poor, 2012*, U.S. Department of Labor, U.S. Bureau of Labor Statistics, March 2014, http://www.bls.gov/cps/cpswp2012.pdf (accessed October 28, 2014)

workers who experienced unemployment and low earnings, 44.5% were in poverty, as were 46.9% of those who experienced unemployment, low earnings, and involuntary part-time employment.

Education

Income and poverty levels correlate strongly with an individual's level of education. The BLS publishes quarterly statistics about the earnings of workers by various

TABLE 2.17

Poverty status and labor market problems of full-time wage and salary workers, 2012

[Numbers in thousands]

Labor market problems	Total	At or above poverty level	Below poverty level	Rate[a]
Total, full-time wage and salary workers	111,951	107,560	4,391	3.9
No unemployment, involuntary part-time employment, or low earnings[b]	90,879	90,159	720	0.8
Unemployment only	6,454	5,960	494	7.7
Involuntary part-time employment only	2,731	2,665	67	2.4
Low earnings only	7,448	5,699	1,749	23.5
Unemployment and involuntary part-time employment	1,341	1,200	141	10.5
Unemployment and low earnings	1,676	931	746	44.5
Involuntary part-time employment and low earnings	857	647	210	24.5
Unemployment, involuntary part-time employment, and low earnings	564	299	265	46.9
Unemployment (alone or with other problems)	10,035	8,390	1,646	16.4
Involuntary part-time employment (alone or with other problems)	5,493	4,811	682	12.4
Low earnings (alone or with other problems)	10,545	7,576	2,970	28.2

[a]Number below the poverty level as a percent of the total in the labor force for 27 weeks or more.
[b]The low-earnings threshold in 2012 was $337.92 per week.

SOURCE: "Table 8. People in the Labor Force for 27 Weeks or More: Poverty Status and Labor Market Problems of Full-Time Wage and Salary Workers, 2012," in *A Profile of the Working Poor, 2012*, U.S. Department of Labor, U.S. Bureau of Labor Statistics, March 2014, http://www.bls.gov/cps/cpswp2012.pdf (accessed October 28, 2014)

characteristics including education. For example, in the press release "Usual Weekly Earnings of Wage and Salary Workers, Fourth Quarter 2014" (January 21, 2015, http://www.bls.gov/news.release/pdf/wkyeng.pdf), the BLS notes that the median weekly earnings for the United States' 107.4 million full-time wage and salary workers were $799 during the fourth quarter of 2014. Full-time workers aged 25 years and older without a high school diploma had median weekly earnings ($491) well below the overall median earnings level, and those without a college diploma had median weekly earnings ($664) significantly below the overall level as well. By contrast, full-time workers over the age of 25 years with college degrees had median weekly earnings of $1,224.

Education alone does not necessarily correlate with avoidance of poverty, however. Yang Jiang, Mercedes Ekono, and Curtis Skinner of the National Center for Children in Poverty at Columbia University indicate in the fact sheet *Basic Facts about Low-Income Children: Children under 18 Years, 2012* (February 2014, http://nccp.org/publications/pdf/text_1089.pdf) that a majority of children who lived in poor families in 2012 had parents without any college education. Approximately 40% of poor families, however, were headed by parents with at least some college education. Thus, although lack of parental education was closely linked to the likelihood that a family will live in poverty, education was by no means a guarantee of prosperity in the early 21st century.

Chronic and Episodic Poverty

For most poor Americans poverty is not a static condition. Some people near the poverty level improve their economic status within two years or less, whereas others at near-poverty levels become poor through economic

catastrophes, such as an illness or job loss. Most data collected by the Census Bureau reflect a single point in time; in other words, they show how many people are in poverty or participating in a means-tested government program in a certain month or at a certain point in time each year. These snapshot surveys, while valuable, do not reflect the dynamic nature of poverty for individual people and families.

The Census Bureau collects longitudinal information (measurements over time for specific individuals or families) about poverty and government program participation rates in its Survey of Income and Program Participation (SIPP). The SIPP consists of interviews with a representative sample of U.S. households every four months, and it includes information about demographic characteristics, labor force status, participation in government programs, and a wide range of income data. Collecting such information over time from the same sample of people allows the Census Bureau to track the movement of individuals and families into and out of poverty (entry and exit rates), the duration of poverty spells (the number of months in poverty for those who were not poor during the first interview month, but who became poor at some point during the study), and the length of time individuals and families use government programs. Accordingly, SIPP data supplement the more commonly cited monthly and annual statistics by providing a detailed view of the experience of poverty.

Edwards uses data from the 2008 SIPP panel to examine poverty in the period from January 2009 to December 2011. Figure 2.3 shows Edwards's comparative analysis of data from the 2004 SIPP panel (covering January 2005 to December 2007) and the 2008 SIPP

FIGURE 2.3

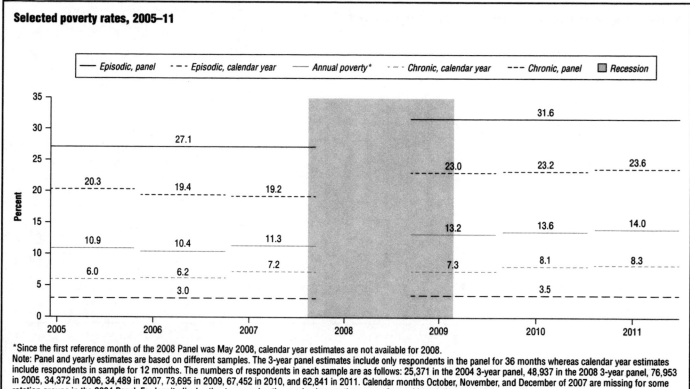

Selected poverty rates, 2005–11

*Since the first reference month of the 2008 Panel was May 2008, calendar year estimates are not available for 2008.

Note: Panel and yearly estimates are based on different samples. The 3-year panel estimates include only respondents in the panel for 36 months whereas calendar year estimates include respondents in sample for 12 months. The numbers of respondents in each sample are as follows: 25,371 in the 2004 3-year panel, 48,937 in the 2008 3-year panel, 76,953 in 2005, 34,372 in 2006, 34,489 in 2007, 73,695 in 2009, 67,452 in 2010, and 62,841 in 2011. Calendar months October, November, and December of 2007 are missing for some rotation groups in the 2004 Panel. For longitudinal estimates covering these calendar months, a carry forward imputation method was applied.

SOURCE: Ashley N. Edwards, "Figure 1. Selected Poverty Rates: 2005 to 2011," in *Dynamics of Economic Well-Being: Poverty, 2009–2011*, U.S. Census Bureau, January 2014, http://www.census.gov/prod/2014pubs/p70-137.pdf (accessed October 28, 2014)

panel (covering January 2009 to December 2011). The first period was one of economic expansion, and the second period was one in which the Great Recession peaked and came to an official end, while its aftereffects continued to be felt by ordinary people. Accordingly, the 2008 SIPP data reflect increased poverty levels no matter the form of measurement. The rate of episodic poverty (the percentage of survey respondents who lived below the poverty line for at least two months) over the entire three-year period of 2009–11 was 31.6%; and the episodic poverty rates for each individual calendar year were 23% (2009), 23.2% (2010), and 23.6% (2011). Likewise, the annual poverty rate (the percentage in poverty for a calendar year, determined by averaging monthly income) rose during this period, from 13.2% in 2009 to 14% in 2011. The chronic poverty rate for each calendar year (the percentage who were in poverty each month of the year) also rose, from 7.3% in 2009 to 8.3% in 2011. The rate of chronic poverty over the course of the entire panel period (the percentage who remained in poverty each month of the three-year period) was 3.5%. Although this level was comparatively small, as with all of the poverty measurements, it was noticeably higher than in the 2004 SIPP panel.

Figure 2.4 plots the degrees of both chronic and episodic poverty by selected demographic characteristics.

Among different racial and ethnic groups, African Americans had the highest rate of chronic poverty, whereas Hispanics had the highest rate of episodic poverty. Adults aged 18 to 64 years and 65 years and older both experienced below-average rates of chronic poverty. Working-aged adults experienced average levels of episodic poverty, while elderly adults experienced rates of episodic poverty far below the average. Meanwhile, children experienced above-average rates of both chronic and episodic poverty. Among all demographic subgroups, female-householder families had the highest rates of both types of poverty, once again suggesting that single motherhood is a major predictor of the likelihood that someone will live in poverty.

Figure 2.5 shows poverty entry rates (the percentage of survey respondents not in poverty in 2009 who had entered poverty by the end of the survey period in 2011) by demographic characteristics. Among racial and ethnic groups, Hispanics had the highest poverty entry rate, at 10.7%, or nearly double that of the rate for all people in the survey; and African Americans had the next highest entry rate, at 8.9%. The poverty entry rate for children (7.1%) was higher than the rates for either working-age adults (5.3%) or the elderly (3.1%). Female-householder families entered poverty at a rate (10%) more than double that of married-couple families

FIGURE 2.4

Chronic and episodic poverty, by selected characteristics, 2009–11

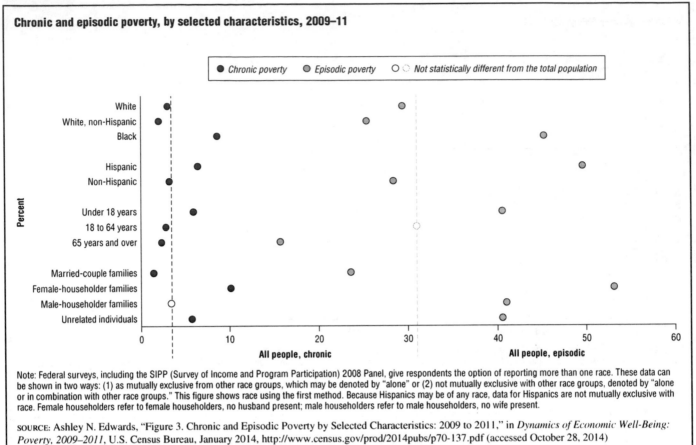

Note: Federal surveys, including the SIPP (Survey of Income and Program Participation) 2008 Panel, give respondents the option of reporting more than one race. These data can be shown in two ways: (1) as mutually exclusive from other race groups, which may be denoted by "alone" or (2) not mutually exclusive with other race groups, denoted by "alone or in combination with other race groups." This figure shows race using the first method. Because Hispanics may be of any race, data for Hispanics are not mutually exclusive with race. Female householders refer to female householders, no husband present; male householders refer to male householders, no wife present.

SOURCE: Ashley N. Edwards, "Figure 3. Chronic and Episodic Poverty by Selected Characteristics: 2009 to 2011," in *Dynamics of Economic Well-Being: Poverty, 2009–2011*, U.S. Census Bureau, January 2014, http://www.census.gov/prod/2014pubs/p70-137.pdf (accessed October 28, 2014)

(4%), but male-householder families also entered poverty at an elevated rate (8.6%).

The poverty exit rate (the percentage of people who were in poverty in 2009 and no longer in poverty in 2011) was 35.4% for all survey respondents. (See Figure 2.6.) African Americans were far less likely (22.7%) to have exited poverty over the three years of the survey than either whites (39.1%) or Hispanics (35.8%); both children (29.6%) and the elderly (31.5%) were less likely than working-age adults (39.7%) to have exited poverty over the three years of the survey; and female-householder families (25.2%) were far less likely than married-couple families (44.3%) to have exited poverty and significantly less likely than male-householder families (37.6%) to have exited poverty.

FIGURE 2.5

FIGURE 2.6

People not in poverty in 2009 but in poverty in 2011, by selected characteristics

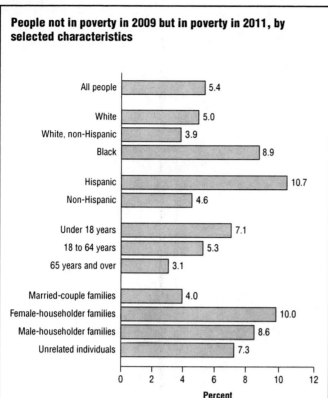

Note: Federal surveys, including the SIPP (Survey of Income and Program Participation) 2008 Panel, give respondents the option of reporting more than one race. These data can be shown in two ways: (1) as mutually exclusive from other race groups, which may be denoted by "alone" or (2) not mutually exclusive with other race groups, denoted by "alone or in combination with other race groups." This figure shows race using the first method. Because Hispanics may be of any race, data for Hispanics are not mutually exclusive with race. Female householders refer to female householders, no husband present; male householders refer to male householders, no wife present.

SOURCE: Ashley N. Edwards, "Figure 5. Poverty Entry Rates: People Not in Poverty in 2009 but in Poverty in 2011 by Selected Characteristics," in *Dynamics of Economic Well-Being: Poverty, 2009–2011*, U.S. Census Bureau, January 2014, http://www.census .gov/prod/2014pubs/p70-137.pdf (accessed October 28, 2014)

People in poverty in 2009 but not in poverty in 2011, by selected characteristics

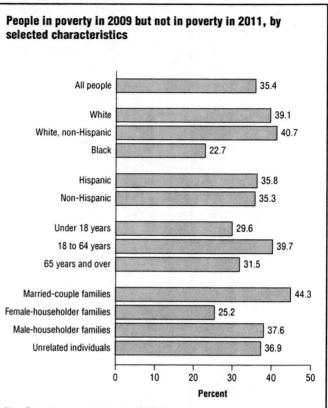

Note: Federal surveys, including the SIPP (Survey of Income and Program Participation) 2008 Panel, give respondents the option of reporting more than one race. These data can be shown in two ways: (1) as mutually exclusive from other race groups, which may be denoted by "alone" or (2) not mutually exclusive with other race groups, denoted by "alone or in combination with other race groups." This figure shows race using the first method. Because Hispanics may be of any race, data for Hispanics are not mutually exclusive with race. Female householders refer to female householders, no husband present; male householders refer to male householders, no wife present.

SOURCE: Ashley N. Edwards, "Figure 6. Poverty Exit Rates: People in Poverty in 2009 but Not in Poverty in 2011 by Selected Characteristics," in *Dynamics of Economic Well-Being: Poverty, 2009–2011*, U.S. Census Bureau, January 2014, http://www.census.gov /prod/2014pubs/p70-137.pdf (accessed October 28, 2014)

CHAPTER 3
PUBLIC PROGRAMS TO FIGHT POVERTY

The federal government and individual states use many methods and administer a variety of assistance programs to combat poverty, by helping those whose incomes are below the poverty line as well as those who are at risk of poverty. These programs are often collectively referred to as welfare. Some, such as Temporary Assistance for Needy Families (TANF), which offers cash assistance to the poor, are designed to help people improve their situation and escape poverty. A number of programs, including the Supplemental Nutrition Assistance Program (SNAP; previously called the Food Stamp Program), are designed to help those in poverty meet their basic needs. Meanwhile, the Supplemental Security Income (SSI) program provides assistance to people who have disabilities or conditions that make it difficult for them to earn a living. Besides welfare programs, the government has established policies such as the minimum wage and unemployment compensation that are intended to help people avoid poverty in the first place.

The first comprehensive welfare programs were established during the 1930s, and the overall welfare system was supplemented substantially during the 1960s. The most important change to the welfare system enacted since that time is the Personal Responsibility and Work Opportunity Reconciliation Act (PRWORA). First enacted in 1996 and renewed since, the PRWORA replaced a welfare system that was based primarily on the Aid to Families with Dependent Children (AFDC) program with one centered on TANF. Critics of the AFDC asserted that the system produced welfare dependency rather than temporary assistance to help recipients move into a job and off welfare. TANF was specifically designed to limit the amount of time individuals could receive benefits and to require them to work. The intention of the law was to reduce the number of people receiving welfare by bringing them into the workforce and out of poverty. The PRWORA also changed some

other welfare programs to place greater emphasis on these priorities. In *Policy Basics: An Introduction to TANF* (December 4, 2012, http://www.cbpp.org/files/7-22-10tanf2.pdf), Liz Schott of the Center on Budget and Policy Priorities (CBPP) notes that additional work requirements for TANF recipients put in place by the Deficit Reduction Act of 2005 further reduced the TANF caseload.

Far fewer families receive TANF cash assistance than received AFDC cash assistance. As Figure 3.1 shows, in 1996, 68 out of 100 families with children in poverty received cash assistance under the AFDC, but by 2012 that number stood at 25 out of 100. This decline in the distribution of cash assistance was not a result of decreasing poverty but of TANF's intentionally limited ability to serve the poor population.

In 2013 only 17.4% of all people below the poverty line lived with someone who received any form of means-tested cash assistance (TANF is the main source of means-tested cash assistance). (See Table 3.1.) As noted in Chapter 2, the poverty rate for children in female-householder families was 47.6% in 2012, the poverty rate for children aged zero to five years in such households was 56.3%, and the rate of desperate poverty (the percentage of such children in households earning less than 50% of poverty) was 32%. Nevertheless, in 2013 among people who lived below the poverty line in households headed by single women and including children, only 21.9% lived in households where any member received means-tested cash assistance. (See Table 3.1.) Among people who lived below the poverty line in households headed by single women and including children younger than six years, only 23.6% lived in households where any member received means-tested cash assistance. Thus, even desperately poor children were not guaranteed to live in a household that received cash assistance.

FIGURE 3.1

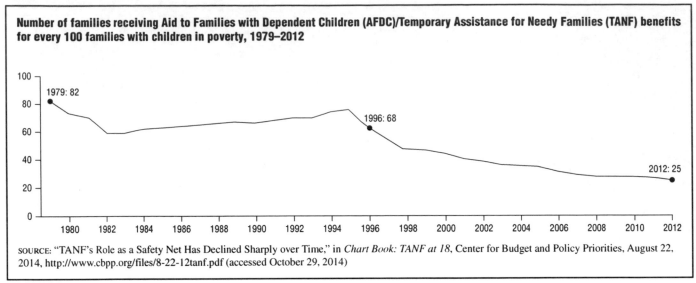

Number of families receiving Aid to Families with Dependent Children (AFDC)/Temporary Assistance for Needy Families (TANF) benefits for every 100 families with children in poverty, 1979–2012

SOURCE: "TANF's Role as a Safety Net Has Declined Sharply over Time," in *Chart Book: TANF at 18*, Center for Budget and Policy Priorities, August 22, 2014, http://www.cbpp.org/files/8-22-12tanf.pdf (accessed October 29, 2014)

Other government assistance programs were more responsive to overall levels of poverty. As Table 3.1 shows, nearly three-quarters (73.8%) of all people below the poverty level lived in a household where at least one person received some form of means-tested aid, including free or reduced-price school lunches, cash assistance, food stamps, Medicaid (free health care coverage available to the poor), or public or subsidized housing. Approximately half (49.5%) of people in poverty and 64.9% of children in poverty lived in households where someone received SNAP benefits, and 61.3% of people in poverty and 81.5% of children in poverty lived in households where someone was covered by Medicaid.

THE PERSONAL RESPONSIBILITY AND WORK OPPORTUNITY RECONCILIATION ACT

The following pages discuss the specific provisions of the PRWORA.

Title I: Block Grants

Under the PRWORA, each state receives a single block grant (a lump sum of money). States have considerable control over how they implement the programs that are covered by the block grant, but the act requires that:

- Families on welfare for five cumulative years no longer receive further cash assistance. States can set shorter time limits and can exempt up to 20% of their caseload from the time limits.

- To count toward meeting the work requirement, a state must require individuals to participate in employment (public or private), on-the-job training, community service, work experience, vocational training (up to 12 months), or child care for other workers for at least 20 hours per week. State and local communities are responsible for the development of

work, whether by creating community service jobs or by providing income subsidies or hiring incentives for potential employers.

- Unmarried parents under the age of 18 years must live with an adult or have adult supervision and must participate in educational or job training to receive benefits. In addition, the law encourages second-chance homes (group homes or apartment clusters with adult supervision) to provide teen parents with the skills and support they need. The law also provides $50 million per year in new funding for state abstinence education activities that are geared toward discouraging teen pregnancy through abstinence rather than through birth control.

None of the block grant funds can be used for adults who have been on welfare for over five years or who do not work after receiving benefits for two years. However, states are given some flexibility in how they spend their TANF funds.

Title II: Supplemental Security Income

The PRWORA redefined the term *disability* for children who receive SSI. A child is considered disabled if he or she has a medically determinable physical or mental impairment that results in marked and severe functional limitations that have lasted or can be expected to last at least 12 months or that can be expected to cause death. The PRWORA removed "maladaptive behavior" as a medical criterion from the listing of impairments used for evaluating mental disabilities in children.

Title III: Child Support

To be eligible for federal funds, each state must operate a Child Support Enforcement program that meets federal guidelines. The state must establish centralized

TABLE 3.1

Program participation status of households for people below poverty level, 2013

[All races—below poverty levels. Numbers in thousands. People who lived with someone (a non-relative or a relative) who received aid. Not every person tallied here received the aid themselves.]

All races below poverty levels	Total	In household that received means-tested assistance		In household that received means-tested assistance excluding school lunch		In household that received means-tested cash assistance		In household that received food stamps		In household in which one or more persons were covered by Medicaid		Lived in public or authorized housing	
		Number	Percent	Number	Percent	Number	Percent	Number	Percent	Number	Percent	Number	Percent
Both sexes													
Total (1)	45,318	33,450	73.8	31,958	70.5	7,881	17.4	22,418	49.5	27,758	61.3	6,702	14.8
Under 18 years	14,659	13,531	92.3	12,752	87.0	2,698	18.4	9,518	64.9	11,951	81.5	2,618	17.9
18 to 24 years	5,819	3,721	63.9	3,596	61.8	799	13.7	2,329	40.0	3,005	51.7	829	14.2
25 to 34 years	6,694	4,787	71.5	4,642	69.3	1,039	15.5	3,244	48.5	4,097	61.2	857	12.8
35 to 44 years	4,871	3,752	77.0	3,515	72.2	828	17.0	2,373	48.7	3,012	61.8	642	13.2
45 to 54 years	4,533	3,093	68.2	2,963	65.4	920	20.3	2,010	44.3	2,400	52.9	581	12.8
55 to 59 years	2,476	1,567	63.3	1,533	61.9	567	22.9	1,049	42.4	1,167	47.1	368	14.9
60 to 64 years	2,036	1,159	56.9	1,148	56.4	429	21.0	757	37.2	927	45.5	277	13.6
65 years and over	4,231	1,841	43.5	1,809	42.8	601	14.2	1,138	26.9	1,198	28.3	529	12.5
65 to 74 years	2,135	1,028	48.1	1,004	47.0	365	17.1	694	32.5	742	34.7	263	12.3
75 years and over	2,095	813	38.8	806	38.4	236	11.3	443	21.2	457	21.8	266	12.7
Male													
Total (1)	20,119	14,632	72.7	13,987	69.5	3,301	16.4	9,596	47.7	12,045	59.9	2,615	13.0
Under 18 years	7,416	6,848	92.3	6,481	87.4	1,272	17.1	4,807	64.8	6,041	81.4	1,327	17.9
18 to 24 years	2,622	1,584	60.4	1,524	58.1	342	13.0	955	36.6	1,235	47.1	298	11.4
25 to 34 years	2,712	1,692	62.4	1,652	60.9	362	13.4	1,044	38.5	1,393	51.4	258	9.5
35 to 44 years	2,044	1,507	73.7	1,428	69.8	340	16.6	877	42.9	1,179	57.6	183	9.0
45 to 54 years	2,009	1,292	64.3	1,235	61.5	402	20.0	802	39.9	976	48.6	186	9.3
55 to 59 years	1,145	715	62.4	693	60.5	272	23.8	472	41.2	513	44.8	152	13.3
60 to 64 years	820	470	57.3	467	56.9	164	19.9	305	37.2	366	44.7	85	10.3
65 years and over	1,349	524	38.9	507	37.6	147	10.9	328	24.3	342	25.4	125	9.3
65 to 74 years	824	340	41.3	325	39.4	95	11.5	220	26.7	233	28.3	70	8.5
75 years and over	524	184	35.1	182	34.7	52	10.0	108	20.6	109	20.8	55	10.5
Female													
Total (1)	25,199	18,818	74.7	17,971	71.3	4,580	18.2	12,822	50.9	15,713	62.4	4,087	16.2
Under 18 years	7,242	6,683	92.3	6,270	86.6	1,427	19.7	4,711	65.0	5,911	81.6	1,292	17.8
18 to 24 years	3,196	2,137	66.9	2,072	64.8	457	14.3	1,370	42.9	1,770	55.4	530	16.6
25 to 34 years	3,982	3,095	77.7	2,989	75.1	677	17.0	2,200	55.3	2,704	67.9	599	15.0
35 to 44 years	2,827	2,244	79.4	2,088	73.9	488	17.3	1,496	52.9	1,834	64.9	459	16.2
45 to 54 years	2,524	1,801	71.4	1,728	68.5	518	20.5	1,208	47.8	1,424	56.4	395	15.7
55 to 59 years	1,330	852	64.0	840	63.1	295	22.2	576	43.3	653	49.1	216	16.2
60 to 64 years	1,216	689	56.7	681	56.0	265	21.8	452	37.1	561	46.1	192	15.8
65 years and over	2,882	1,317	45.7	1,303	45.2	454	15.7	809	28.1	856	29.7	403	14.0
65 to 74 years	1,311	688	52.5	679	51.8	270	20.6	474	36.2	509	38.8	193	14.7
75 years and over	1,571	629	40.0	624	39.7	184	11.7	335	21.3	348	22.1	211	13.4

TABLE 3.1

Program participation status of households for people below poverty level, 2013 [CONTINUED]

[All races—below poverty levels. Numbers in thousands. People who lived with someone (a non-relative or a relative) who received aid. Not every person tallied here received the aid themselves.]

All races below poverty levels	Total	In household that received means-tested assistance		In household that received means-tested assistance excluding school lunch		In household that received means-tested cash assistance		In household that received food stamps		In household in which one or more persons were covered by Medicaid		Lived in public or authorized housing	
		Number	Percent	Number	Percent	Number	Percent	Number	Percent	Number	Percent	Number	Percent
Household relationship													
Total (1)	45,318	33,450	73.8	31,958	70.5	7,881	17.4	22,418	49.5	27,758	61.3	6,702	14.8
65 years and over	4,231	1,841	43.5	1,809	42.8	601	14.2	1,138	26.9	1,198	28.3	529	12.5
In families (2)	31,530	26,366	83.6	24,958	79.2	5,645	17.9	18,094	57.4	22,617	71.7	4,987	15.8
Householder	9,130	7,186	78.7	6,842	74.9	1,634	17.9	4,948	54.2	6,081	66.6	1,500	16.4
Under 65 years	8,161	6,744	82.6	6,420	78.7	1,501	18.4	4,687	57.4	5,754	70.5	1,433	17.6
65 years and over	970	442	45.6	421	43.5	133	13.7	261	27.0	326	33.7	67	6.9
Related children under 18 years (9)	14,142	13,073	92.4	12,323	87.1	2,610	18.5	9,272	65.6	11,536	81.6	2,588	18.3
Under 6 years	5,231	4,859	92.9	4,752	90.8	1,084	20.7	3,591	68.7	4,498	86.0	1,038	19.8
6 to 17 years	8,911	8,215	92.2	7,571	85.0	1,527	17.1	5,681	63.8	7,038	79.0	1,550	17.4
Own children 18 years and over (15)	2,893	2,372	82.0	2,262	78.2	599	20.7	1,589	54.9	1,917	66.3	428	14.8
In married-couple families (11)	12,832	9,621	75.0	8,926	69.6	1,587	12.4	5,934	46.2	8,062	62.8	1,131	8.8
Husbands (11)	3,476	2,250	64.7	2,106	60.6	422	12.1	1,397	40.2	1,838	52.9	290	8.3
Under 65 years	2,815	2,036	72.3	1,905	67.7	367	13.0	1,277	45.3	1,699	60.3	249	8.8
65 years and over	661	214	32.4	201	30.4	55	8.4	120	18.2	140	21.1	41	6.2
Wives (11)	3,476	2,250	64.7	2,106	60.6	422	12.1	1,397	40.2	1,838	52.9	290	8.3
Under 65 years	2,977	2,101	70.6	1,960	65.8	374	12.6	1,317	44.2	1,737	58.3	256	8.6
65 years and over	500	149	29.8	147	29.4	48	9.6	80	16.1	101	20.3	34	6.8
Related children under 18 years (9)	4,699	4,201	89.4	3,847	81.9	567	12.1	2,685	57.1	3,602	76.7	490	10.4
Under 6 years	1,662	1,515	91.2	1,448	87.1	237	14.3	1,044	62.8	1,368	82.3	228	13.7
6 to 17 years	3,037	2,686	88.4	2,399	79.0	330	10.9	1,641	54.0	2,234	73.6	262	8.6
Own children 18 years and over (15)	929	714	76.9	664	71.4	133	14.4	345	37.1	587	63.1	47	5.0
In families with male householder, no spouse present	3,091	2,437	78.8	2,308	74.6	534	17.3	1,455	47.1	2,025	65.5	358	11.6
Householder	1,008	763	75.7	728	72.2	179	17.8	453	44.9	619	61.5	119	11.8
Under 65 years	953	723	75.8	688	72.2	175	18.4	426	44.7	588	61.7	117	12.3
65 years and over	54	40	74.4	39	72.6	4	7.5	27	49.0	31	57.1	2	3.3
Related children under 18 years (9)	1,138	1,031	90.5	971	85.3	225	19.7	636	55.9	929	81.6	162	14.2
Under 6 years	430	386	89.9	384	89.3	107	24.8	258	60.1	372	86.5	78	18.1
6 to 17 years	709	644	90.9	587	82.9	118	16.7	377	53.3	557	78.7	84	11.9
Own children 18 years and over (15)	227	172	75.8	163	71.9	36	15.7	103	45.4	129	56.7	18	8.0
In families with female householder, no spouse present	15,606	14,308	91.7	13,725	87.9	3,524	22.6	10,705	68.6	12,530	80.3	3,498	22.4
Householder	4,646	4,173	89.8	4,008	86.3	1,033	22.2	3,098	66.7	3,623	78.0	1,091	23.5
Under 65 years	4,340	3,963	91.3	3,808	87.7	958	22.1	2,965	68.3	3,455	79.6	1,064	24.5
65 years and over	306	210	68.5	200	65.4	74	24.3	133	43.6	168	54.8	28	9.1
Related children under 18 years (9)	8,305	7,841	94.4	7,505	90.4	1,819	21.9	5,952	71.7	7,005	84.4	1,936	23.3
Under 6 years	3,139	2,957	94.2	2,920	93.0	740	23.6	2,289	72.9	2,758	87.9	732	23.3
6 to 17 years	5,165	4,884	94.6	4,585	88.8	1,079	20.9	3,663	70.9	4,247	82.2	1,204	23.3
Own children 18 years and over (15)	1,737	1,487	85.6	1,436	82.7	430	24.8	1,141	65.7	1,202	69.2	363	20.9

TABLE 3.1

Program participation status of households for people below poverty level, 2013 [CONTINUED]

[All races—below poverty levels. Numbers in thousands. People who lived with someone (a non-relative or a relative) who received aid. Not every person tallied here received the aid themselves.]

All races below poverty levels	Total	In household that received means-tested assistance		In household that received means-tested assistance excluding school lunch		In household that received means-tested cash assistance		In household that received food stamps		In household in which one or more persons were covered by Medicaid		Lived in public or authorized housing	
		Number	Percent	Number	Percent	Number	Percent	Number	Percent	Number	Percent	Number	Percent
In unrelated subfamilies (3)	608	559	92.1	530	87.2	103	17.0	342	56.4	520	85.6	27	4.5
Under 18 years	340	316	92.9	298	87.5	61	17.8	197	57.8	293	86.0	16	4.8
Under 6 years	122	116	95.3	112	91.6	22	17.8	63	51.8	109	89.4	1	0.6
6 to 17 years	218	200	91.6	186	85.2	39	17.8	133	61.1	184	84.1	15	7.1
18 years and over	267	243	91.0	232	86.9	43	15.9	146	54.6	227	85.1	11	4.1
Unrelated individuals (4)	13,181	6,525	49.5	6,470	49.1	2,132	16.2	3,981	30.2	4,621	35.1	1,688	12.8
Male	5,810	2,878	49.5	2,854	49.1	979	16.8	1,779	30.6	2,007	34.5	619	10.7
Under 65 years	5,274	2,659	50.4	2,635	50.0	895	17.0	1,628	30.9	1,869	35.4	540	10.2
Living alone	2,202	1,113	50.5	1,106	50.2	474	21.5	754	34.2	755	34.3	340	15.4
65 years and over	536	219	40.8	219	40.8	83	15.6	151	28.1	139	25.8	79	14.7
Living alone	417	158	37.8	158	37.8	71	17.0	113	27.1	93	22.2	76	18.3
Female	7,371	3,647	49.5	3,616	49.1	1,153	15.6	2,202	29.9	2,614	35.5	1,069	14.5
Under 65 years	5,501	2,851	51.8	2,821	51.3	872	15.9	1,701	30.9	2,146	39.0	737	13.4
Living alone	2,441	1,373	56.2	1,373	56.2	531	21.7	965	39.5	948	38.8	587	24.0
65 years and over	1,870	795	42.5	795	42.5	281	15.0	501	26.8	468	25.0	332	17.7
Living alone	1,656	681	41.1	681	41.1	244	14.8	449	27.1	384	23.2	311	18.8

Notes: The 2014 Current Population Survey (CPS) Annual Social and Economic Supplement (ASEC) included redesigned questions for income and health insurance coverage. All of the approximately 98,000 addresses were eligible to receive the redesigned set of health insurance coverage questions. The redesigned income questions were implemented to a subsample of these 98,000 addresses using a probability split panel design. Approximately 58,000 addresses were eligible to receive a set of income questions similar to those used in the 2013 CPS ASEC and the remaining 30,000 addresses were eligible to receive the redesigned income questions. The source of data for this table is the portion of the CPS ASEC sample which received the income questions consistent with the 2013 CPS ASEC, approximately 68,000 addresses.

SOURCE: "POV26. Program Participation Status of Household—Poverty Status of People: 2013—All Races—Below Poverty Levels," in Current Population Survey (CPS) 2014 Annual Social and Economic Supplement, U.S. Census Bureau, September 2014, http://www.census.gov/hhes/www/cpstables/032014/pov/pov26_002_1.xls (accessed October 28, 2014)

registries of child support orders and centers for the collection and disbursement of child support payments, and parents must sign their child support rights over to the state to be eligible for TANF benefits. The state must also establish enforcement methods, such as revoking the driver's and professional licenses of delinquent parents. The Administration for Children and Families' Office of Child Support Enforcement notes in "OCSE Fact Sheet" (2015, http://www.acf.hhs.gov/programs/css/resource/ocse-fact-sheet) that in fiscal year (FY) 2013 the program served 16.9 million children at a cost of $3.9 billion.

To receive full benefits, a mother must cooperate with state efforts to establish paternity. She may be denied assistance if she refuses to disclose the father.

Title IV: Restricting Welfare and Public Benefits for Noncitizens

The PRWORA originally severely limited or banned benefits to most legal immigrants who entered the country on or after August 22, 1996, when the bill became law. Ineligibility continued for a five-year period or until the legal immigrants attained citizenship. In addition, states had the option of withholding eligibility for Medicaid, TANF, and other social services from legal immigrants already residing in the United States.

Immigrants who were not authorized to be in the country no longer had any entitlement to benefit programs, such as TANF or Medicaid. They could receive emergency medical care, short-term disaster relief, immunizations, and treatment for communicable diseases (in the interest of public health). They could also use community services such as soup kitchens and shelters, some housing programs, and school lunches/breakfasts if their children were eligible for free public education. States have established programs to verify the legal residence of immigrants before paying benefits and may elect to deny Special Supplemental Food Program for Women, Infants, and Children benefits and other child nutrition programs to unauthorized immigrants.

Title V: Child Protection

The PRWORA gave states the authority to use current federal funds to pay for foster care for children in child care institutions. It extended the enhanced federal match for statewide automated child welfare information systems. It also increased the funding and visibility of abstinence-only sex education to combat teen pregnancy.

Title VI: Child Care

The law required that states maintain spending for child care for low-income families at the level of FY 1994 or FY 1995, whichever was greater, to be eligible for federally matched funds. Mandatory funding was set at $13.9 billion through June 30, 2004, with states receiving an estimated $1.2 billion per year before matching

began. The remainder of the funds was available for state matching at the Medicaid rate.

Liz Schott, LaDonna Pavetti, and Ife Finch of the CBPP explain in *How States Have Spent Federal and State Funds under the TANF Block Grant* (August 7, 2012, http://www.cbpp.org/files/8-7-12tanf.pdf) that the child care portion of TANF was one of the program's bright spots in the early years after welfare reform. Federal and state spending on child care rose from $1.1 billion in 1997 to $5.9 billion in 2000. Spending remained stagnant over the following 11 years, however, fluctuating between $5 billion and $6 billion. When taking inflation into account, the 2011 spending total of $5.5 billion represented a 29% decline from the 2000 figure of $5.9 billion.

Title VII: Child Nutrition Programs

The PRWORA continued existing child nutrition programs, such as the National School Lunch Program and the School Breakfast Program. However, maximum reimbursement was reduced for the Summer Food Service Program and for some institutional food programs. States were allowed to decide whether to include or exclude legal immigrants from these programs.

Title VIII: Supplemental Nutrition Assistance Program

The PRWORA reduced maximum benefits for the Food Stamp Program, which became known as SNAP in 2008. The act set SNAP benefits at the level of the Thrifty Food Plan, an index set by the U.S. Department of Agriculture (USDA) that reflects the amount of money needed to purchase food to meet minimal nutrition requirements. Benefits were indexed to the rate of inflation so that they increase as inflation rises.

The law also restructured the way certain expenses and earnings were counted in establishing eligibility for food stamps. Under the PRWORA, when recipients' benefits are calculated, their countable monthly income is reduced by several deductions, including a standard deduction, a deduction for excessively high shelter expenses, a dependent care deduction, and medical expenses for the elderly and disabled. These deductions raised food stamp allotments.

In response to the Great Recession (which officially lasted from December 2007 to June 2009), President Barack Obama (1961–) signed the American Recovery and Reinvestment Act (ARRA) in February 2009. According to the USDA, in the memo "Economic Stimulus— Adjustments to the Maximum Supplemental Nutrition Assistance Program (SNAP) Monthly Allotments" (February 18, 2009, http://www.fns.usda.gov/sites/default/files/021809.pdf), the act increased SNAP benefits by 13.6% over the June value of the Thrifty Food Plan. The maximum monthly benefits for a family of four in the continental United States increased to $668, and the maximum monthly allotment for a family of three increased to $526.

The ARRA increases in SNAP monthly benefits expired in October 2013. In *SNAP Benefits Will Be Cut for Nearly All Participants in November 2013* (August 2, 2013, http://www.cbpp.org/files/2-8-13fa.pdf), Stacy Dean and Dottie Rosenbaum of the CBPP note that without the additional funding provided by the ARRA, the average amount of SNAP benefits fell below $1.40 per person per meal.

By law, all SNAP recipients who are 18 to 50 years old and without children (known as able-bodied adults without dependents [ABAWD]) must work at least part time or be limited to three months of assistance during a 36-month period. Recipients who were in a workfare program (a welfare program that usually requires recipients to perform public service duties) for 30 days but lost their placement may qualify for an additional three months of food assistance. (This provision was revised to allow states to exempt 15% of ABAWD recipients from this restriction.)

Reauthorization of the PRWORA

The PRWORA was reauthorized through 2010 when President George W. Bush (1946–) signed the Deficit Reduction Act in February 2006. The CBPP explains in *Implementing the TANF Changes in the Deficit Reduction Act: "Win-Win" Solutions for Families and States* (February 2007, http://www.cbpp.org/files/2-9-07tanf.pdf) that this bill did not increase funding for TANF programs; however, it did make the eligibility requirements stricter. The basic TANF block grant did not increase with inflation but remained capped at $16 billion. Thus, actual TANF funding has measurably decreased since that time. The reauthorization bill required 50% of TANF recipients to work in 2006, increasing by 5% each year to 70% in 2010. Funding for child care was set at $2 billion for each year between 2006 and 2010. Child support enforcement funding was reduced. Drug testing became required for every TANF applicant and recipient. Finally, the bill allowed TANF funds to be used to promote the value of marriage through public advertising and high school and adult classes and mentoring programs.

Although the law was scheduled for full-scale reauthorization in 2010, which would have entailed opportunities to enhance or alter its components, Congress instead passed short-term funding extensions in the years that followed. As of February 2015, TANF policies were operating under an extension that was attached to the so-called Cromnibus spending bill, which funded basic government operations through September 2015.

ELIGIBILITY FOR TANF AND BENEFIT PAYMENTS

Under TANF, states decide how much to aid a needy family. No federal guidelines exist for determining eligibility, and no requirement mandates that states aid all needy families. TANF does not require states to have a need standard or a gross income limit, as the AFDC did, but many states base their TANF programs in part on their earlier practices.

The maximum benefit is the amount paid to a family with no countable income. (Federal law specifies what income counts toward figuring benefits and what income, such as child support, is to be disregarded by the state.) The maximum benefit is to be paid only to those families that comply with TANF's work requirements or other program requirements established by the state, such as parental and personal responsibility rules.

Most states vary benefits according to family size, such as by eliminating or restricting benefit increases due to the birth of a new child to a recipient already receiving benefits. In 16 states benefits depend on family size at the time of enrollment. Idaho pays a flat monthly grant that is the same regardless of family size. Wisconsin pays benefits based on work activity of the recipient and not on family size. Five states provide an increase in benefits to TANF families following the birth of an additional child. The CBPP points out in *Chart Book: TANF at 18* (August 22, 2014, http://www.cbpp.org/files/8-22-12tanf.pdf) that in 2013 the median benefit level for a family of three was $428 per month (or $5,136 per year, an amount equal to 26.3% of poverty in that year), and in 14 states a family of three received less than $300 per month. In 2014 TANF benefit levels for a family of three were below 50% of poverty in all 50 states, and in 16 states they were between 10% and 20% of poverty. (See Figure 3.2.)

As Table 3.2 shows, most states have not changed their maximum benefit levels appreciably since 1996, despite the major changes brought about by the PRWORA, and despite the fact that inflation means that these steady amounts represent yearly reductions in benefits. The average (mean) maximum TANF benefit for a family of three was $394 in 1996 and $431 in 2013. According to the U.S. Bureau of Labor Statistics (BLS), in "CPI Inflation Calculator" (http://data.bls.gov/cgi-bin/cpicalc.pl?cost1=394.00&year1=1996&year2=2013), had benefit levels kept pace with inflation, the average maximum TANF award would have been $585 in 2013. The value of the average maximum TANF benefit in 2013 was thus only 73.7% of the average maximum TANF benefit in 1996.

Many families receiving TANF benefits are also eligible for SNAP. A single benefit determination is made for both cash and food assistance. Whereas TANF eligibility and benefit amounts are determined by the states, SNAP eligibility and benefit amounts are determined by federal law and are consistent in all states. Because SNAP benefits are determined in relation to income and are not contingent on a recipient's employment status, the program is generally regarded as much more responsive to the changing financial status of households during periods such as the Great Recession.

FIGURE 3.2

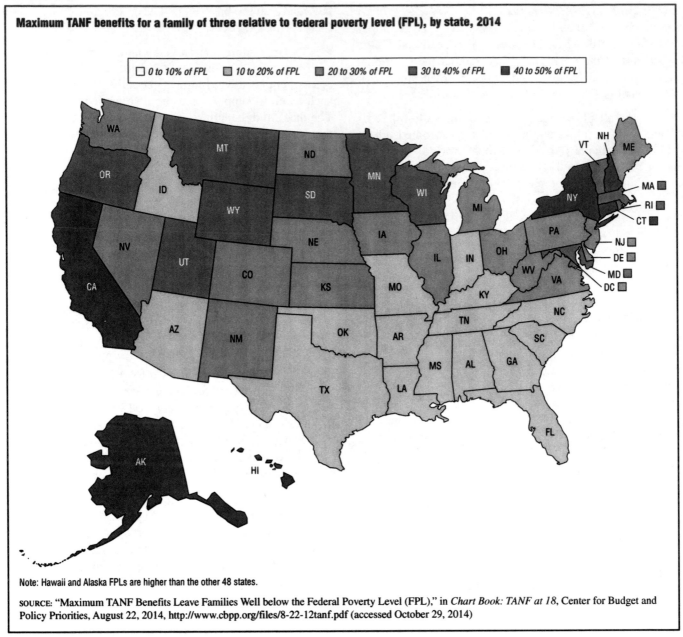

Maximum TANF benefits for a family of three relative to federal poverty level (FPL), by state, 2014

□ 0 to 10% of FPL   ▢ 10 to 20% of FPL   ▢ 20 to 30% of FPL   ▮ 30 to 40% of FPL   ▮ 40 to 50% of FPL

Note: Hawaii and Alaska FPLs are higher than the other 48 states.

SOURCE: "Maximum TANF Benefits Leave Families Well below the Federal Poverty Level (FPL)," in *Chart Book: TANF at 18*, Center for Budget and Policy Priorities, August 22, 2014, http://www.cbpp.org/files/8-22-12tanf.pdf (accessed October 29, 2014)

SNAP benefit levels vary less from state to state than do TANF benefit levels. In FY 2013 the average monthly SNAP benefit nationally was $274.98 per household, and the average monthly benefits ranged from a low of $230.79 (Oregon) to a high of $428.88 (Hawaii). (See Table 3.3.) The U.S. territory of Guam ($652.23) had an even higher average monthly benefit than Hawaii, due not only to high levels of poverty there but also to differences in the administration of the social welfare system relative to the 50 states.

THE WELFARE-TO-WORK CONCEPT

TANF recipients are expected to participate in work activities while receiving benefits. After 24 months of assistance, states must require recipients to work at least part time to continue to receive cash benefits. States are permitted to exempt certain groups of people from the work-activity requirements, including parents of very young children (up to one year) and disabled adults. TANF defines the work activities that count when determining a state's work participation rate.

As part of their plans, states must require parents to work after two years of receiving benefits. In 2000 states were required to have 40% of all parents and at least one adult in 90% of all two-parent families engaged in a work activity for a minimum of 20 hours per week for single parents and 35 hours per week for at least one adult in two-parent families. This work requirement became stricter with the 2006 reauthorization of the PRWORA, which required 50% of all single-parent TANF recipients to work.

TABLE 3.2

Maximum TANF benefits for a family of three with no income, by state, selected years 1996–2013

State	1996	2002	2007	2013
Alabama	$164	$164	**$215**	$215
Alaska	$923	$923	$923	$923
Arizona	$347	$347	$347	**$277**
Arkansas	$204	$204	$204	$204
California	$596			
Nonexempt	$594	**$679**	**$750**	**$638**
Exempt	$663	**$758**	**$838**	**$714**
Colorado	$356	$356	$356	**$462**
Connecticut	$543	$543	$543	**$576**
Delaware	$338	$338	$338	$338
DC	$415	**$379**	**$407**	**$428**
Florida	$303	$303	$303	$303
Georgia	$280	$280	$280	$280
Hawaii	$712	**$570ᵉ**	$570ᵃ	**$610ᵇ**
Idaho	$317	**$309**	$309	$309
Illinois	$377	**$396**	$396	**$432**
Indiana	$288	$288	$288	$288
Iowa	$426	$426	$426	$426
Kansas	$429	$429	$429	$429
Kentucky	$262	$262	$262	$262
Louisiana	$190	**$240**	$240	$240
Maine	$418	**$485**	$485	$485
Maryland	$373	**$472**	**$549**	**$576**
Massachusetts				
Exempt	$579	**$633**	$633	$633
Nonexempt	$565	**$618**	$618	$618
Michigan	$459	**$459ᶜ**	**$489ᶜ**	**$492**
Minnesota	$532	$532	$532	$532
Mississippi	$120	**$170**	$170	$170
Missouri	$292	$292	$292	$292
Montana	$425	**$507**	**$472**	**$510**
Nebraska	$364	$364	$364	$364
Nevada	$348	$348	**$383**	$383
New Hampshire	$550	**$625**	$625	**$675**
New Jersey	$424	$424	$424	$424
New Mexico	$389	**$389**	$389	**$380**
New York	$577	$577	**$691**	**$789**
North Carolina	$272	$272	$272	$272
North Dakota	$431	**$477ᵈ**	$477ᵈ	$477ᵈ
Ohio	$341	**$373**	**$410**	**$458**
Oklahoma	$307	**$292**	$292	$292
Oregon	$460	**$503**	**$514**	**$506**
Pennsylvania	$403	$403	$403	$403
Rhode Island	$554	$554	$554	$554
South Carolina	$200	**$204**	**$240**	**$223**
South Dakota	$430	$483	**$508**	**$582**
Tennessee	$185	**$185ᵉ**	$185ᵉ	$185ᵉ
Texas	$188	**$208**	**$236**	**$271**
Utah	$426	**$474**	$474	**$498**
Vermont	$597	**$638**	**$640**	$640
Virginia	$291	**$320**	$320	$320
Washington	$546	$546	$546	**$478**
West Virginia	$253	**$453**	**$340**	$340
Wisconsin	$518			
W-2 transition	—	**$628**	$628	**$608**
Community service jobs	—	**$673**	$673	**$653**
Trial jobs/unsubsidized Employment	—	—ᶠ	—ᶠ	—ᵍ
Wyoming	$360	**$340**	$340	**$616**
Meanʰ	$394	**$413**	**$419**	**$431**
Medianʰ	$377	**$396**	**$403**	**$427**

TANF recipients required to work must spend a minimum number of hours per week engaged in one of the following activities:

- An unsubsidized job (no government help)
- A subsidized private job
- A subsidized public job

TABLE 3.2

Maximum TANF benefits for a family of three with no income, by state, selected years 1996–2013 [CONTINUED]

TANF = Temporary Assistance for Needy Families.
ᵃApplies to units who have received assistance for two or more months in a lifetime. For units applying for their first or second months of benefits, the maximum monthly benefit for a family of three is $712.
ᵇApplies to units who have received assistance for two or more months in a lifetime. For units applying for their first or second months of benefits, the maximum monthly benefit for a family of three is $763.
ᶜApplies to units that have at least one employable adult. For units where all adults either receive Social Security income (SSI) or are exempt from work requirements for reasons other than caring for a child under three months old, the maximum monthly benefit for a family of three is $477.
ᵈThis amount includes a $50 increase to the payment standard given to units who pay for shelter.
ᵉFor units where the caretaker is over 65, disabled, caring full-time for a disabled family member, or excluded from the assistance unit, the maximum monthly benefit for a family of three is $232.
ᶠThe benefits in these components are based on the wages earned by individual recipients.
ᵍ"Trial jobs" was discontinued as a component in June 2013.
ʰThe calculations only include one value per state (the policy affecting the largest percent of the caseload).
Notes: Maximum benefits are calculated assuming that the unit contains one adult and two children who are not subject to a family cap, has no special needs, pays for shelter, and lives in the most populated area of the state.
Bolded text indicates a change from the previous year shown.

SOURCE: Erika Huber, David Kassabian, and Elissa Cohen, "Table L5. Maximum Monthly Benefit for a Family of Three with No Income, 1996–2013 (July)," in *Welfare Rules Databook: State TANF Policies as of July 2013*, Urban Institute, September 2014, http://anfdata.urban.org/databooks/Welfare%20Rules%20Databook%202013.pdf (accessed October 29, 2014)

- Work experience
- On-the-job training
- Job search and job readiness (a usual maximum of six weeks total)
- Community service
- Vocational educational training (a 12-month maximum)
- Job skills training
- Education related to employment
- High school or a general equivalency diploma completion
- Providing child care for a community service participant

Additional provisions apply to young parents who are under the age of 20 years and are either household heads or married and who lack a high school diploma. They are considered "engaged in work" if they either maintain satisfactory attendance in high school (no hours specified) or participate in education directly related to work (20 hours per week).

The PRWORA imposed strict limits on the number of TANF recipients who may get work credit through participation in education and training. No more than 30% of TANF families who are counted as engaged in work may consist of people who are participating in vocational educational training. Vocational educational

TABLE 3.3

Supplemental Nutrition Assistance Program (SNAP) average monthly benefit per household, by state/territory, fiscal years 2009–13

[Data as of October 3, 2014]

State/territory	Fiscal year 2009	Fiscal year 2010	Fiscal year 2011	Fiscal year 2012	Fiscal year 2013
Alabama	288.33	296.32	307.35	281.33	279.88
Alaska	430.24	436.40	419.10	409.13	412.68
Arizona	299.21	301.14	295.25	293.29	288.14
Arkansas	275.19	289.44	285.67	277.68	271.71
California	325.19	340.90	334.92	332.08	330.49
Colorado	302.70	325.09	317.73	305.27	296.46
Connecticut	249.36	263.07	262.18	264.11	252.91
Delaware	267.36	282.40	276.50	271.42	271.11
District of Columbia	234.88	247.22	251.12	243.85	239.12
Florida	246.94	268.56	258.62	255.24	253.19
Georgia	302.81	313.54	305.11	295.57	292.69
Guam	685.23	694.93	678.77	661.43	652.23
Hawaii	394.20	430.04	431.82	427.08	428.88
Idaho	307.48	318.49	313.02	299.54	295.10
Illinois	285.85	299.40	290.33	285.17	276.75
Indiana	296.39	309.35	303.08	299.86	293.04
Iowa	258.11	280.10	272.70	259.30	246.24
Kansas	252.06	272.91	271.62	266.15	264.83
Kentucky	264.36	279.87	275.25	268.71	264.35
Louisiana	307.50	303.21	297.31	305.50	289.72
Maine	245.01	259.83	252.36	239.38	234.63
Maryland	262.53	275.27	262.74	255.26	250.45
Massachusetts	229.53	238.54	240.76	237.93	233.08
Michigan	252.86	270.43	271.43	268.60	266.70
Minnesota	237.96	248.19	236.99	235.94	234.40
Mississippi	268.98	284.52	281.14	275.44	271.33
Missouri	263.06	277.56	276.16	275.89	272.20
Montana	274.02	287.64	281.96	272.67	269.73
Nebraska	259.78	280.66	280.55	279.71	277.82
Nevada	256.39	267.87	264.88	258.81	255.40
New Hampshire	251.24	255.39	250.43	246.17	241.65
New Jersey	257.53	282.65	272.77	271.07	273.60
New Mexico	286.76	299.42	294.07	290.26	286.91
New York	267.54	283.92	278.56	274.94	273.87
North Carolina	267.69	282.46	269.70	257.95	264.10
North Dakota	276.40	290.76	286.57	277.11	271.32
Ohio	288.95	303.22	293.68	286.76	273.88
Oklahoma	278.22	298.40	290.04	282.26	277.98
Oregon	228.81	237.85	236.13	233.54	230.79
Pennsylvania	250.80	262.61	270.45	265.86	263.30
Rhode Island	275.54	271.85	265.08	252.97	251.01
South Carolina	275.99	291.21	285.56	278.39	276.32
South Dakota	300.09	318.48	310.00	305.71	303.53
Tennessee	272.23	285.58	279.18	271.50	267.75
Texas	309.84	322.62	310.50	300.39	295.36
Utah	297.64	309.45	299.09	297.67	311.72
Vermont	233.56	244.13	243.04	238.53	238.92
Virginia	260.05	277.19	273.48	265.90	263.32
Virgin Islands	447.73	439.79	426.30	416.58	397.18
Washington	232.26	243.41	245.70	241.96	236.66
West Virginia	246.53	261.99	257.90	254.22	251.72
Wisconsin	241.25	263.00	251.50	243.92	239.57
Wyoming	276.22	297.54	288.77	288.64	292.91
Total	**275.51**	**289.60**	**283.99**	**278.48**	**274.98**

Note: The following outlying areas receive Nutrition Assistance Grants which provide benefits analogous to the Supplemental Nutrition Assistance Program: Puerto Rico, American Samoa, and the Northern Marianas. Annual averages are total benefits divided by total annual household participation. All data are subject to revision.

SOURCE: "Supplemental Nutrition Assistance Program: Average Monthly Benefit per Household," in *Supplemental Nutrition Assistance Program (SNAP)*, U.S. Department of Agriculture, Food and Nutrition Service, October 2014, http://www.fns.usda.gov/sites/default/files/pd/19SNAPavg$HH.pdf (accessed October 29, 2014)

training is the only creditable work activity not explicitly confined to high school dropouts.

In 2012 the states of Utah and Nevada appealed to the federal government, requesting that certain TANF work requirements be waived because the rigidity of the rules was making it increasingly difficult for them to fulfill the spirit of the law, which was to help people find permanent jobs. For example, the rules relating to job training, educational programs, and work in government-subsidized jobs made it difficult for states to help TANF recipients simultaneously meet the PRWORA work requirements and prepare themselves for the forms of long-term employment that would lift them out of poverty for good. In July 2012 the U.S. Department of Health and Human Services granted the states waivers provided they devised better solutions for helping TANF benefit recipients find permanent jobs. This established a path for other states to address deficiencies in the work requirements and propose alternative plans.

Finding and Creating Jobs for TANF Recipients

Job availability is one of the most difficult challenges that states face when moving recipients from welfare to work. Welfare recipients, who often lack job skills and work experience, are at a pronounced disadvantage in the labor pool. In *TANF Recipients with Barriers to Employment* (August 2011, http://www.urban.org/UploadedPDF/412567-TANF-Recipients-with-Barriers-to-Employmentz.pdf), Dan Bloom, Pamela J. Loprest, and Sheila R. Zedlewski of the Urban Institute note that numerous surveys estimate that approximately 40% of TANF recipients lack a high school diploma and that many lack current work experience. The labor-market disadvantages of welfare recipients increase during recessionary periods, when unemployment is high and even well-qualified workers find themselves out of work. Even when the national unemployment rate is low, unemployment in some areas of the country might be much higher, or available jobs might not match the skills of those welfare recipients who are looking for work. TANF work requirements, which are designed to keep people from becoming dependent on welfare, can thus burden states unduly. States can lose funding even though benefits administrators and welfare recipients alike are doing everything possible to obtain jobs.

If suitable jobs cannot be found, states must create work-activity placements and may use TANF block grant funds to do so. Welfare agencies have had to change their focus and train staff to function more as job developers and counselors than as caseworkers. They make an initial assessment of recipients' skills as required by TANF. They may then develop personal responsibility plans for recipients, identifying what is needed (e.g., training, job-placement services, and support services) to move them into the workforce.

Addressing Other Barriers to Work

Low-income adults and public assistance recipients face multiple barriers to working that put them at a disadvantage relative to other participants in the labor market. Beyond the lack of education and job experience described earlier, a number of other barriers to work are common among welfare recipients. These include mental and physical health issues, child care, and transportation. In many cases, federal funding can be used to address these problems, but states are granted a wide degree of latitude. Some states employ specialized strategies to help beneficiaries overcome barriers, whereas others do little to address such problems.

HEALTH OF RECIPIENTS AND THEIR CHILDREN. Bloom, Loprest, and Zedlewski note that numerous estimates place the proportion of TANF recipients with work-limiting health conditions at between 25% and 30%. Additionally, one study has estimated the proportion of the TANF recipient population with poor mental/emotional health at 13.8%, and another has estimated it at 24.4%. Still other TANF families (between 3.2% and 7.6%, depending on the study) have children on SSI (i.e., children with severe disabilities or other conditions that entitle them to federal benefits); these children often require round-the-clock parental care long after infancy.

No obvious or widely validated solutions to increasing the work participation of such welfare recipients exist. However, Bloom, Loprest, and Zedlewski indicate that some states use federal TANF funds to promote intensive case management approaches that connect recipients with mental health professionals, substance abuse treatment, and domestic violence counseling, among other services. According to Bloom, Loprest, and Zedlewski, these states "struggle with integrating services while maintaining a work focus and operating with limited resources."

State welfare caseworkers also sometimes facilitate referrals to the SSI program for those TANF recipients whose health problems rise to the level of a qualifying disability. The process for applying to receive SSI benefits is intricate, requiring a large amount of documentation and legal hearings. Welfare agencies can connect TANF recipients to nonprofit and other agencies that can help them with this time-consuming process, and recipients are generally exempt from the TANF work requirements while their SSI applications are being processed.

CHILD CARE. Access to affordable child care is one critical element in encouraging low-income parents to seek and keep jobs. In *Child Care in America: 2014 State Fact Sheets* (2014, http://usa.childcareaware.org/sites/default/files/19000000_state_fact_sheets_2014_v04.pdf), Child Care Aware of America, a leading nonprofit devoted to extending access to affordable child care, noted that in 2014 the average yearly cost for full-time infant care in a child care center ranged from $5,496 in Mississippi to $16,549 in Massachusetts. The full-time costs for a four-year-old ranged from $4,515 in Tennessee to $12,320 in Massachusetts. Full-time infant care in an accredited home-based business ranged from $4,560 in Mississippi to $12,272 in Virginia, and full-time four-year-old care in a home-based business ranged from $4,039 in South Carolina to $9,962 in Massachusetts. These costs put full-time child care out of reach not only for families living in poverty but also for families well above poverty. For example, a Massachusetts single mother of one infant with an income of twice the 2014 poverty level ($31,460) would have to spend over half ($16,549, or 53%) of her income to enroll her child in full-time center-based care or one-third ($10,535, or 33%) of her income in full-time home-based care.

The 1996 welfare reform law created a block grant to states for child care. The amount of the block grant was equivalent to what states received under the AFDC. However, states that maintain the amount that they spent for child care under the AFDC are eligible for additional matching funds. The block grant and the supplemental matching funds are referred to as the Child Care Development Fund. In addition, states were given the option of transferring some of their TANF funds to the Child Care Development Fund or spending them directly on child care services.

Because states can use TANF funds for child care, they have more flexibility to design child care programs, not only for welfare recipients but also for working-poor families who may need child care support to continue working and stay off welfare. States determine who is eligible for child care support, how much those parents will pay (often using a sliding fee scale), and the amount the state will reimburse providers of subsidized care. Children under the age of 13 years are eligible for child care subsidies; depending on the state, families with incomes up to 85% of the state's median income for a family of that size are eligible, although few states guarantee payments to all eligible families.

The Administration for Children and Families' Office of Child Care reports in "Characteristics of Families Served by Child Care and Development Fund (CCDF) Based on Preliminary FY 2013 Data" (November 17, 2014, http://www.acf.hhs.gov/programs/occ/resource/char acteristics-of-families-served-by-child-care-and-develop ment-fund-ccdf) that in FY 2013 states provided child care subsidies to nearly 1.5 million low-income children in 874,200 families. Of the families served by the program, 52% were below the poverty level, 26% had incomes between 100% and 150% of poverty, and 13% had incomes above 150% of poverty. Of the children served, 34% were aged six years and older, 11% were aged five years, 28% were aged three to four years, and 27% were aged three years and younger. Furthermore, 70% were cared for in a child care center, 19% in home-based care, 6% in a group home, and 4% in the child's own home. Approximately 73% of families were responsible for a copayment in addition to the subsidized amount, and these copayments averaged 7% of the family income. Almost all (93%) families stated they needed care because of parental employment, education, or training; the remainder sought out care because of the need for protective services.

TRANSPORTATION. Transportation is another critical factor facing welfare recipients moving into a job. Recipients without a car must depend on public transportation. However, when available jobs are in suburban areas outside the range of public transportation, when job locations are accessible to public transportation but day care centers and schools are not, or when jobs require work at times when public transportation schedules are limited, welfare recipients may find a lack of transportation options to be a significant barrier to employment. Even for those recipients with cars, the expense of gas and repairs can deplete earnings. For low-income rural families, many of these problems are even more forbidding, due to a lack of any public transportation options.

Most states enforce asset limits on welfare recipients (restrictions regarding how much personal wealth, in the form of savings and possessions, an individual or household may have while still qualifying for benefits). To promote employment, TANF's vehicle asset limits are broader than they were under the AFDC. Each state has the flexibility to determine its own vehicle asset level, but all states have chosen to increase the limit for the value of the primary automobile in the family beyond that set under the AFDC. Some states offer transportation-specific assistance to individuals transitioning off TANF and into the job market. As with many aspects of TANF, the wide latitude granted to states means that no one-size-fits-all approach exists.

GOVERNMENT PROGRAMS TO COMBAT HUNGER
Supplemental Nutrition Assistance Program

SNAP, which is administered by the USDA, is the largest food assistance program in the United States. SNAP is designed to help low-income families purchase a nutritionally adequate, low-cost diet. Generally, SNAP may only be used to buy food to be prepared at home. It cannot be used for alcohol, tobacco, or hot foods that are intended to be consumed immediately, such as restaurant or delicatessen food. Because TANF benefits have declined and fewer families receive cash assistance, SNAP has increasingly become (with Medicaid) the centerpiece of the U.S. welfare system.

SNAP calculates 30% of each recipient family's earnings and then issues enough food credits to make up the difference between that amount and the amount that is needed to buy an adequate diet. These monthly allotments are usually provided electronically through an electronic benefit transfer, a debit card that is similar to a bank card. The cash value of these benefits is based on the size of the household and how much the family earns. Households without an elderly or disabled member generally must have a monthly total (gross) cash income at or below 130% of the poverty level and may not have

TABLE 3.4

SNAP eligibility income thresholds, by household size, 2014–15

[October 1, 2014 through September 30, 2015]

Household size	Gross monthly income (130 percent of poverty)	Net monthly income (100 percent of poverty)
1	$1,265	$973
2	1,705	1,311
3	2,144	1,650
4	2,584	1,988
5	3,024	2,326
6	3,464	2,665
7	3,904	3,003
8	4,344	3,341
Each additional member	+440	+339

SOURCE: "Income," in *Supplemental Nutrition Assistance Program (SNAP): Eligibility*, U.S. Department of Agriculture, Food and Nutrition Service, October 2014, http://www.fns.usda.gov/snap/eligibility#Income (accessed October 29, 2014)

liquid assets (cash, savings, or other assets that can be easily sold) of more than $2,000. (If the household has a member aged 60 years or older, the asset limit is $3,000.) The net monthly income limit (gross income minus any approved deductions for child care, some housing costs, and other expenses) must be 100% or less of the poverty level, or $1,988 per month for a family of four between October 2014 and September 2015. (See Table 3.4.)

With some exceptions, SNAP is automatically available to SSI and TANF recipients. SNAP benefits are higher in states with lower TANF benefits because those benefits are considered a part of a family's countable income. To receive SNAP, certain household members must register for work, accept suitable job offers, or fulfill work or training requirements (such as looking or training for a job).

Although the federal government sets guidelines and provides funding, SNAP is administered by the states. State agencies certify eligibility as well as calculate and issue benefit allotments. Most often, the welfare agency and staff that administer the TANF and Medicaid programs also run SNAP. The program operates in all 50 states, the District of Columbia, Guam, and the Virgin Islands. (Puerto Rico is covered under a separate nutrition assistance program.)

Except for some small differences in Alaska, Hawaii, and the territories, the program is run the same way throughout the United States. The states pay 50% of the administrative costs, and the federal government pays 100% of SNAP benefits and the other 50% of the administrative costs.

Unlike TANF, SNAP is responsive to fluctuations in unemployment and the poverty level, with participation increasing in times of economic distress and decreasing as unemployment and poverty rates fall. In FY 2000, at a time of economic expansion and low unemployment, the federal government paid $15 billion in SNAP benefits. (See Table 3.5.) In FY 2013, as the U.S. economy continued to suffer the aftereffects of the Great Recession and many unemployed people had given up looking for work, the federal government spent $76.1 billion on SNAP benefits, or an estimated average monthly benefit of $133.07 per recipient. The ARRA supplemented SNAP's structural responsiveness to the recession by providing an additional $500 million to support participation in the program and by increasing benefit levels to 113.6% of the value of the Thrifty Food Plan. This supplemental funding expired in October 2013.

National School Lunch and School Breakfast Programs

The National School Lunch Program (NSLP) and the School Breakfast Program provide federal cash and commodity support to participating public and private schools and to nonprofit residential institutions that serve meals to children. Children from households with incomes at or below 130% of the poverty line receive free meals. Children from households with incomes between 130% and 185% of the poverty level receive meals at a reduced price (no more than $0.40). Table 3.6 shows the income eligibility guidelines, based on the poverty guidelines, effective from July 1, 2014, to June 30, 2015. The levels were higher in Alaska and Hawaii than in the 48 contiguous states, the District of Columbia, Guam, and other U.S. territories. Children in TANF families are automatically eligible to receive free breakfasts and lunches. Almost 90% of federal funding for the NSLP is used to subsidize free and reduced-price lunches for low-income children.

The NSLP, which was created in 1946 under the National School Lunch Act, supplies subsidized lunches to children in almost all schools and in 6,000 residential and day care institutions. During the 1996–97 school year the USDA changed certain policies so that school meals would meet the recommendations of the Dietary Guidelines for America, the federal standards for what constitutes a healthy diet. The program has grown steadily since its introduction. In FY 2013 the program served free lunches to 18.9 million children and reduced-price lunches to another 2.6 million. (See Table 3.7.)

The School Breakfast Program, which was created under the Child Nutrition Act of 1966, serves far fewer students than does the NSLP. The School Breakfast Program also differs from the NSLP in that most schools offering the program are in low-income areas, and the children who participate in the program are mainly from low- and moderate-income families. In FY 2013 the program served free breakfasts to 10.2 million children and reduced-price breakfasts to another 1 million. (See Table 3.8.)

TABLE 3.5

SNAP participation and costs, fiscal years 1969–2013

[Data as of October 3, 2014]

Fiscal year	Average participation Thousands	Average benefit per person[a] Dollars	Total benefits Millions of dollars	All other costs[b] Millions of dollars	Total costs Millions of dollars
1969	2,878	6.63	228.80	21.70	250.50
1970	4,340	10.55	549.70	27.20	576.90
1971	9,368	13.55	1,522.70	53.20	1,575.90
1972	11,109	13.48	1,797.30	69.40	1,866.70
1973	12,166	14.60	2,131.40	76.00	2,207.40
1974	12,862	17.61	2,718.30	119.20	2,837.50
1975	17,064	21.40	4,385.50	233.20	4,618.70
1976	18,549	23.93	5,326.50	359.00	5,685.50
1977	17,077	24.71	5,067.00	394.00	5,461.00
1978	16,001	26.77	5,139.20	380.50	5,519.70
1979	17,653	30.59	6,480.20	459.60	6,939.80
1980	21,082	34.47	8,720.90	485.60	9,206.50
1981	22,430	39.49	10,629.90	595.40	11,225.20
1982[c]	21,717	39.17	10,208.30	628.40	10,836.70
1983	21,625	42.98	11,152.30	694.80	11,847.10
1984	20,854	42.74	10,696.10	882.60	11,578.80
1985	19,899	44.99	10,743.60	959.60	11,703.20
1986	19,429	45.49	10,605.20	1,033.20	11,638.40
1987	19,113	45.78	10,500.30	1,103.90	11,604.20
1988	18,645	49.83	11,149.10	1,167.70	12,316.80
1989	18,806	51.71	11,669.78	1,231.81	12,901.59
1990	20,049	58.78	14,142.79	1,304.47	15,447.26
1991	22,625	63.78	17,315.77	1,431.50	18,747.27
1992	25,407	68.57	20,905.68	1,556.66	22,462.34
1993	26,987	67.95	22,006.03	1,646.94	23,652.97
1994	27,474	69.00	22,748.58	1,744.87	24,493.45
1995	26,619	71.27	22,764.07	1,856.30	24,620.37
1996	25,543	73.21	22,440.11	1,890.88	24,330.99
1997	22,858	71.27	19,548.86	1,958.68	21,507.55
1998	19,791	71.12	16,890.49	2,097.84	18,988.32
1999	18,183	72.27	15,769.40	2,051.52	17,820.92
2000	17,194	72.62	14,983.32	2,070.70	17,054.02
2001	17,318	74.81	15,547.39	2,242.00	17,789.39
2002	19,096	79.67	18,256.20	2,380.82	20,637.02
2003	21,250	83.94	21,404.28	2,412.01	23,816.28
2004	23,811	86.16	24,618.89	2,480.14	27,099.03
2005	25,628	92.89	28,567.88	2,504.24	31,072.11
2006	26,549	94.75	30,187.35	2,715.72	32,903.06
2007	26,316	96.18	30,373.27	2,800.25	33,173.52
2008	28,223	102.19	34,608.40	3,031.26	37,639.66
2009	33,490	125.31	50,359.92	3,260.09	53,620.01
2010	40,302	133.79	64,702.16	3,581.78	68,283.94
2011	44,709	133.85	71,810.92	3,876.30	75,687.23
2012	46,609	133.41	74,619.34	3,836.08	78,455.42
2013	47,636	133.07	76,066.28	3,863.19	79,929.47

[a]Represents average monthly benefits per person.
[b]Includes the federal share of state administrative expenses, nutrition education, and employment and training programs. Also includes federal costs (e.g., benefit and retailer redemption and monitoring, payment accuracy, EBT (Electronic Benefits Transfer) systems, program evaluation and modernization, program access, health and nutrition pilot projects.)
[c]Puerto Rico initiated food stamp operations during fiscal year 1975 and participated through June of fiscal year 1982. A separate nutrition assistance grant began in July 1982.
Note: All data are subject to revision.

SOURCE: "Supplemental Nutrition Assistance Program Participation and Costs," in *Supplemental Nutrition Assistance Program (SNAP)*, U.S. Department of Agriculture, Food and Nutrition Service, October 2014, http://www.fns.usda.gov/sites/default/files/pd/SNAPsummary.pdf (accessed October 30, 2014)

In December 2010 President Obama signed the Healthy, Hunger-Free Kids Act into law. This act upgraded nutritional standards for school meal programs and required schools to make information on the nutritional quality of meals available to parents. The act provided several ways to certify additional children for the free and reduced meal programs, such as using Medicaid data to directly certify children rather than relying on paper applications or using census data in high-poverty communities to certify school-wide income eligibility. In addition, the act expanded the school meal program to after-school meals through the existing Child and Adult Care Food Program providers across the nation.

Special Supplemental Food Program for Women, Infants, and Children

The Special Supplemental Food Program for Women, Infants, and Children (WIC) provides food assistance as well as nutrition counseling and health services to low-income pregnant women, to women who have just given birth and their babies, and to low-income children up to five years old. Participants in the

TABLE 3.6

Income eligibility guidelines for free and reduced-price school meals, 2014–15

Household size	Federal poverty guidelines Annual	Reduced price meals—185%					Free meals—130%				
		Annual	Monthly	Twice per month	Every two weeks	Weekly	Annual	Monthly	Twice per month	Every two weeks	Weekly
				48 Contiguous states, District of Columbia, Guam, and Territories							
1	11,670	21,590	1,800	900	831	416	15,171	1,265	633	584	292
2	15,730	29,101	2,426	1,213	1,120	560	20,449	1,705	853	787	394
3	19,790	36,612	3,051	1,526	1,409	705	25,727	2,144	1,072	990	495
4	23,850	44,123	3,677	1,839	1,698	849	31,005	2,584	1,292	1,193	597
5	27,910	51,634	4,303	2,152	1,986	993	36,283	3,024	1,512	1,396	698
6	31,970	59,145	4,929	2,465	2,275	1,138	41,561	3,464	1,732	1,599	800
7	36,030	66,656	5,555	2,778	2,564	1,282	46,839	3,904	1,952	1,802	901
8	40,090	74,167	6,181	3,091	2,853	1,427	52,117	4,344	2,172	2,005	1,003
For each add'l family member, add	4,060	7,511	626	313	289	145	5,278	440	220	203	102
				Alaska							
1	14,580	26,973	2,248	1,124	1,038	519	18,954	1,580	790	729	365
2	19,660	36,371	3,031	1,516	1,399	700	25,558	2,130	1,065	983	492
3	24,740	45,769	3,815	1,908	1,761	881	32,162	2,681	1,341	1,237	619
4	29,820	55,167	4,598	2,299	2,122	1,061	38,766	3,231	1,616	1,491	746
5	34,900	64,565	5,381	2,691	2,484	1,242	45,370	3,781	1,891	1,745	873
6	39,980	73,963	6,164	3,082	2,845	1,423	51,974	4,332	2,166	1,999	1,000
7	45,060	83,361	6,947	3,474	3,207	1,604	58,578	4,882	2,441	2,253	1,127
8	50,140	92,759	7,730	3,865	3,568	1,784	65,182	5,432	2,716	2,507	1,254
For each add'l family member, add	5,080	9,398	784	392	362	181	6,604	551	276	254	127
				Hawaii							
1	13,420	24,827	2,069	1,035	955	478	17,446	1,454	727	671	336
2	18,090	33,467	2,789	1,395	1,288	644	23,517	1,960	980	905	453
3	22,760	42,106	3,509	1,755	1,620	810	29,588	2,466	1,233	1,138	569
4	27,430	50,746	4,229	2,115	1,952	976	35,659	2,972	1,486	1,372	686
5	32,100	59,385	4,949	2,475	2,285	1,143	41,730	3,478	1,739	1,605	803
6	36,770	68,025	5,669	2,835	2,617	1,309	47,801	3,984	1,992	1,839	920
7	41,440	76,664	6,389	3,195	2,949	1,475	53,872	4,490	2,245	2,072	1,036
8	46,110	85,304	7,109	3,555	3,281	1,641	59,943	4,996	2,498	2,306	1,153
For each add'l family member, add	4,670	8,640	720	360	333	167	6,071	506	253	234	117

SOURCE: "Income Eligibility Guidelines," in "Child Nutrition Programs—Income Eligibility Guidelines," *Federal Register*, vol. 79, no. 43, March 5, 2014, http://www.fns.usda.gov/sites/default/files/2014-04788.pdf (accessed October 30, 2014)

program must have incomes at or below 185% of the poverty level (all but five states use this cutoff level) and must be nutritionally at risk.

As explained by the Child Nutrition Act of 1966, nutritional risk includes abnormal nutritional conditions, medical conditions related to nutrition, health-impairing dietary deficiencies, or conditions that might predispose a person to these conditions. Pregnant women may receive benefits throughout their pregnancies and for up to six months after childbirth or up to one year for nursing mothers.

Those receiving WIC benefits get supplemental food each month in the form of actual food items or, more commonly, vouchers (coupons) for the purchase of specific items at the store. Permitted foods contain high amounts of protein, iron, calcium, vitamin A, and vitamin C. Items that may be purchased include milk, cheese, eggs, infant formula, cereals, and fruit or vegetable juices. Mothers participating in WIC are encouraged to breast-feed their infants if possible, but state WIC agencies will provide formula for mothers who choose to use it.

The USDA estimates that the national average monthly cost of a WIC food package in FY 2013 was $43.26 per participant. (See Table 3.9.) The federal government spent an estimated $6.5 billion to operate WIC in FY 2013, which was down significantly from previous years, and program participation had fallen from a high of 9.2 million women, infants, and children in FY 2010 to 8.7 million. WIC works in conjunction with the Farmers' Market Nutrition Program, which was established in 1992 to provide WIC recipients with increased access, in the form of vouchers, to fresh fruits and vegetables.

OTHER PUBLIC PROGRAMS TO FIGHT POVERTY

Unemployment Insurance

The federal government and the states combine to offer a system of unemployment insurance, often called unemployment compensation, that provides a temporary source of income to those who have lost their jobs. Besides giving workers support as they seek new jobs, unemployment compensation is intended to exert a stabilizing

TABLE 3.7

National school lunch program participation and lunches served, fiscal years 1969–2013

[Data as of October 3, 2014]

Fiscal year	Average participation Free (Millions)	Reduced price (Millions)	Full price (Millions)	Total (Millions)	Total lunches served (Millions)	Percent free/reduced price of total (%)
1969	2.9	*	16.5	19.4	3,368.2	15.1
1970	4.6	*	17.8	22.4	3,565.1	20.7
1971	5.8	0.5	17.8	24.1	3,848.3	26.1
1972	7.3	0.5	16.6	24.4	3,972.1	32.4
1973	8.1	0.5	16.1	24.7	4,008.8	35.0
1974	8.6	0.5	15.5	24.6	3,981.6	37.1
1975	9.4	0.6	14.9	24.9	4,063.0	40.3
1976	10.2	0.8	14.6	25.6	4,147.9	43.1
1977	10.5	1.3	14.5	26.2	4,250.0	44.8
1978	10.3	1.5	14.9	26.7	4,294.1	44.4
1979	10.0	1.7	15.3	27.0	4,357.4	43.6
1980	10.0	1.9	14.7	26.6	4,387.0	45.1
1981	10.6	1.9	13.3	25.8	4,210.6	48.6
1982	9.8	1.6	11.5	22.9	3,755.0	50.2
1983	10.3	1.5	11.2	23.0	3,803.3	51.7
1984	10.3	1.5	11.5	23.4	3,826.2	51.0
1985	9.9	1.6	12.1	23.6	3,890.1	49.1
1986	10.0	1.6	12.2	23.7	3,942.5	49.1
1987	10.0	1.6	12.4	23.9	3,939.9	48.6
1988	9.8	1.6	12.8	24.2	4,032.9	47.4
1989	9.7	1.6	12.9	24.2	4,004.9	47.2
1990	9.8	1.7	12.6	24.1	4,009.0	48.3
1991	10.3	1.8	12.2	24.2	4,050.7	50.4
1992	11.2	1.7	11.7	24.6	4,101.4	53.1
1993	11.7	1.7	11.4	24.9	4,137.7	54.8
1994	12.2	1.8	11.3	25.3	4,201.6	55.9
1995	12.4	1.9	11.4	25.7	4,253.3	56.4
1996	12.6	2.0	11.3	25.9	4,313.2	56.9
1997	12.9	2.1	11.3	26.3	4,409.0	57.6
1998	13.0	2.2	11.4	26.6	4,425.0	57.8
1999	13.0	2.4	11.6	27.0	4,513.6	57.6
2000	13.0	2.5	11.9	27.3	4,575.0	57.1
2001	12.9	2.6	12.0	27.5	4,585.2	56.8
2002	13.3	2.6	12.0	28.0	4,716.6	57.6
2003	13.7	2.7	11.9	28.4	4,762.9	58.5
2004	14.1	2.8	12.0	29.0	4,842.4	59.1
2005	14.6	2.9	12.2	29.6	4,976.4	59.4
2006	14.8	2.9	12.4	30.1	5,027.9	59.3
2007	15.0	3.1	12.6	30.6	5,071.3	59.3
2008	15.4	3.1	12.5	31.0	5,208.5	60.1
2009	16.3	3.2	11.9	31.3	5,186.1	62.6
2010	17.6	3.0	11.1	31.8	5,278.3	65.3
2011	18.4	2.7	10.8	31.8	5,274.5	66.6
2012	18.7	2.7	10.2	31.7	5,214.8	68.2
2013	18.9	2.6	9.2	30.7	5,097.7	70.5

*Included with free meals.

Note: Fiscal year 2013 data are preliminary; all data are subject to revision. Participation data are 9 month averages (summer months are excluded).

SOURCE: "National School Lunch Program: Participation and Lunches Served," in *Child Nutrition Tables*, U.S. Department of Agriculture, Food and Nutrition Service, October 2014, http://www.fns.usda.gov/sites/default/files/pd/slsummar.pdf (accessed October 30, 2014)

TABLE 3.8

National school breakfast program participation and meals served, fiscal years 1969–2013

[Data as of October 3, 2014]

Fiscal years	Total participation[a] Free (Millions)	Reduced price (Millions)	Paid (Millions)	Total (Millions)	Meals served (Millions)	Free/reduced price of total meals (Percent)
1969	—	—	—	0.22	39.70	71.0
1970	—	—	—	0.45	71.80	71.5
1971	0.60	b	0.20	0.80	125.50	76.3
1972	0.81	b	0.23	1.04	169.30	78.5
1973	0.99	b	0.20	1.19	194.10	83.4
1974	1.14	b	0.24	1.37	226.70	82.8
1975	1.45	0.04	0.33	1.82	294.70	82.1
1976	1.76	0.06	0.37	2.20	353.60	84.2
1977	2.02	0.11	0.36	2.49	434.30	85.7
1978	2.23	0.16	0.42	2.80	478.80	85.3
1979	2.56	0.21	0.54	3.32	565.60	84.1
1980	2.79	0.25	0.56	3.60	619.90	85.2
1981	3.05	0.25	0.51	3.81	644.20	86.9
1982	2.80	0.16	0.36	3.32	567.40	89.3
1983	2.87	0.15	0.34	3.36	580.70	90.3
1984	2.91	0.15	0.37	3.43	589.20	89.7
1985	2.88	0.16	0.40	3.44	594.90	88.6
1986	2.93	0.16	0.41	3.50	610.60	88.7
1987	3.01	0.17	0.43	3.61	621.50	88.4
1988	3.03	0.18	0.47	3.68	642.50	87.5
1989	3.11	0.19	0.51	3.81	658.45	86.8
1990	3.30	0.22	0.55	4.07	707.49	86.7
1991	3.61	0.25	0.58	4.44	771.86	87.3
1992	4.05	0.26	0.61	4.92	852.43	88.0
1993	4.41	0.28	0.66	5.36	923.56	87.9
1994	4.76	0.32	0.75	5.83	1,001.52	87.4
1995	5.10	0.37	0.85	6.32	1,078.92	86.8
1996	5.27	0.41	0.90	6.58	1,125.74	86.5
1997	5.52	0.45	0.95	6.92	1,191.21	86.5
1998	5.64	0.50	1.01	7.14	1,220.90	86.1
1999	5.72	0.56	1.09	7.37	1,267.62	85.4
2000	5.73	0.61	1.21	7.55	1,303.35	84.2
2001	5.80	0.67	1.32	7.79	1,334.51	83.2
2002	6.03	0.70	1.41	8.15	1,404.76	82.9
2003	6.22	0.74	1.47	8.43	1,447.90	82.8
2004	6.52	0.80	1.58	8.90	1,524.91	82.4
2005	6.80	0.86	1.70	9.36	1,603.88	82.1
2006	6.99	0.92	1.86	9.76	1,663.07	81.2
2007	7.15	0.98	1.99	10.12	1,713.96	80.6
2008	7.48	1.04	2.08	10.61	1,812.41	80.6
2009	7.99	1.07	2.01	11.08	1,866.66	82.1
2010	8.68	1.05	1.94	11.67	1,968.02	83.5
2011	9.20	0.98	2.00	12.17	2,048.16	83.7
2012	9.77	1.04	2.05	12.87	2,145.19	84.2
2013	10.16	1.02	2.02	13.20	2,223.01	84.8

[a]Nine month average: October–May plus September.
[b]Included with free participation.

Notes: Fiscal year 2013 data are preliminary; all data are subject to revision.

SOURCE: "School Breakfast Program Participation and Meals Served," in *Child Nutrition Tables*, U.S. Department of Agriculture, Food and Nutrition Service, October 2014, http://www.fns.usda.gov/sites/default/files/pd/sbsummar.pdf (accessed October 30, 2014)

influence on the economy. When workers lose their jobs, unemployment benefits allow them to continue satisfying their consumer needs, which keeps demand for goods and services from dropping precipitately in times of economic crisis or stagnation.

The unemployment insurance system was designed in 1935 during the administration of President Franklin D. Roosevelt (1882–1945) with the intent of giving states wide latitude in operating their own programs. For the basic system, states set their own eligibility criteria and benefit levels with minimal intervention so long as they operate within broad federal guidelines. The federal government pays for administrative costs, but the states manage their own funds for actual payments to those who have lost their jobs. Both state and federal spending on unemployment compensation is generated via taxes on employers, but economists note that this money

TABLE 3.9

Special Supplemental Program for Women, Infants, and Children (WIC) program participation and costs, fiscal years 1974–2013

[Data as of October 3, 2014]

Fiscal year	Total participation[a] (Thousands)	Program costs			Average monthly food cost per person (Dollars)
		Food (Millions of dollars)	NSA (Millions of dollars)	Total[b] (Millions of dollars)	
1974	88	8.2	2.2	10.4	15.68
1975	344	76.7	12.6	89.3	18.58
1976	520	122.3	20.3	142.6	19.60
1977	848	211.7	44.2	255.9	20.80
1978	1,181	311.5	68.1	379.6	21.99
1979	1,483	428.6	96.8	525.4	24.09
1980	1,914	584.1	140.5	727.7	25.43
1981	2,119	708.0	160.6	871.6	27.84
1982	2,189	757.6	190.5	948.8	28.83
1983	2,537	901.8	221.3	1,126.0	29.62
1984	3,045	1,117.3	268.8	1,388.1	30.58
1985	3,138	1,193.2	294.4	1,489.3	31.69
1986	3,312	1,264.4	316.4	1,582.9	31.82
1987	3,429	1,344.7	333.1	1,679.6	32.68
1988	3,593	1,434.8	360.6	1,797.5	33.28
1989	4,119	1,489.4	416.5	1,910.9	30.13
1990	4,517	1,636.8	478.7	2,122.4	30.20
1991	4,893	1,751.9	544.0	2,301.0	29.84
1992	5,403	1,960.5	632.7	2,600.6	30.24
1993	5,921	2,115.1	705.6	2,828.6	29.77
1994	6,477	2,325.2	834.4	3,169.3	29.92
1995	6,894	2,511.6	904.6	3,436.2	30.36
1996	7,186	2,689.9	985.1	3,695.4	31.19
1997	7,407	2,815.5	1,008.2	3,843.8	31.68
1998	7,367	2,808.1	1,061.4	3,890.4	31.76
1999	7,311	2,851.6	1,063.9	3,938.1	32.50
2000	7,192	2,853.1	1,102.6	3,982.1	33.06
2001	7,306	3,007.9	1,110.6	4,149.4	34.31
2002	7,491	3,129.7	1,182.3	4,339.8	34.82
2003	7,631	3,230.3	1,260.0	4,524.4	35.28
2004	7,904	3,562.0	1,272.4	4,887.3	37.55
2005	8,023	3,602.8	1,335.5	4,992.6	37.42
2006	8,088	3,598.2	1,402.6	5,072.7	37.07
2007	8,285	3,881.1	1,479.0	5,409.6	39.04
2008	8,705	4,534.0	1,607.6	6,188.8	43.40
2009	9,122	4,640.9	1,788.0	6,471.6	42.40
2010	9,175	4,562.8	1,907.9	6,687.3	41.44
2011	8,961	5,020.2	1,961.3	7,178.2	46.69
2012	8,908	4,809.9	1,877.6	6,799.7	45.00
2013	8,663	4,497.3	1,882.1	6,455.4	43.26

NSA = Nutrition Services and Administrative costs. Nutrition Services includes nutrition education, preventative and coordination services (such as health care), and promotion of breastfeeding and immunization.

[a]Participation data are annual averages (6 months in fiscal year 1974; 12 months all subsequent years).

[b]In addition to food and NSA costs, total expenditures includes funds for program evaluation, Farmers' Market Nutrition Program (fiscal year 1989 onward), special projects and infrastructure.

Note: Fiscal year 2013 data are preliminary; all data are subject to revision.

SOURCE: "WIC Program Participation and Costs," in *WIC Program*, U.S. Department of Agriculture, Food and Nutrition Service, October 2014, http://www.fns .usda.gov/sites/default/files//pd/wisummary.pdf (accessed October 30, 2014)

ultimately comes from the workers themselves because employers reduce the wages they pay in proportion to the taxes they are required to contribute to unemployment insurance funds. Most states offer up to 26 weeks of unemployment insurance benefits, although the duration of benefits is often shorter because of irregularities in an individual's employment history. Qualifying workers typically receive approximately half of the amount of money they made on the job.

The general criteria for unemployment compensation eligibility are consistent across the states. A qualifying worker must have met certain thresholds for the amount of time on the job and the income generated during that time, and he or she must have lost the job through no fault of his or her own. Additionally, the person must be ready and willing to work, and he or she must be actively seeking a new job. Unemployment insurance is not intended to cover numerous classes of workers, including self-employed workers, temporary workers, and those who voluntarily leave their jobs.

Different states, however, interpret these general criteria very differently. In some states it is more difficult for employees to prove that they were fired through no fault of their own than in other, more pro-worker states.

The period of employment used to calculate eligibility and benefits varies by state, compensation levels vary by state, and the degree to which part-time workers are covered varies by state. According to Chad Stone and William Chen of the CBPP, in *Introduction to Unemployment Insurance* (July 30, 2014, http://www.cbpp.org/files/12-19-02ui.pdf), since the 1950s basic unemployment compensation has provided support for fewer than half of unemployed workers. The researchers note that a "growing percentage of unemployed workers who meet the basic criteria... yet fail to satisfy their *state's* eligibility criteria—often established decades ago (in a very different labor market)—has made it harder for [the unemployment insurance system] to fulfill its mission."

Besides the basic unemployment insurance system, there is a permanent Extended Benefits program that covers workers for an additional period in states whose job markets are poor. The length of the extension of benefits varies based on the state's unemployment rate and the laws governing its unemployment insurance program. Historically, Extended Benefits is funded by both the federal government and the states, and the program operates even when the overall national economy is strong. However, with the Great Recession and the passage of the ARRA in 2009, the federal government began fully funding the Extended Benefits program. This measure was kept in place through 2013.

Additionally, the federal government has created numerous other temporary programs meant to supplement the basic state programs during periods of high unemployment nationwide. In 2008 Congress created the Emergency Unemployment Compensation program to respond to the massive job losses during the Great Recession. Because of lingering unemployment even after the recession officially ended in June 2009, the Emergency Unemployment Compensation program was repeatedly reauthorized, and it remained in operation through 2013. In states with particularly high unemployment during the recession and its aftermath, some workers were able to collect benefits for as long as 99 weeks. As the unemployment rate climbed from below 5% in 2007 to a peak of 10% in 2009, the average duration of a worker's unemployment compensation rose from 15 weeks to almost 20 weeks, according to statistics available at the website of the U.S. Department of Labor's Employment and Training Administration (http://www.ows.doleta.gov/unemploy/chartbook.asp).

Federal Minimum Wage

The federal minimum wage dates back to the passage of the Fair Labor Standards Act of 1938, which established basic national standards for minimum wages, overtime pay, and the employment of child workers. (The minimum wage is a cash wage only and does not include any fringe benefits. Consequently, the total compensation for minimum-wage workers is even lower than the total compensation for higher-paid workers, who generally receive some kind of benefits besides wages. Most minimum-wage workers do not receive any benefits.) The provisions of the act have been extended to cover many other areas of employment since 1938.

The first minimum wage instituted in 1938 was $0.25 per hour. (See Table 3.10.) It gradually increased over the years, reaching $4.25 in 1991. In July 1996 Congress passed legislation that raised the minimum wage to $5.15 in 1997 by means of two $0.45 increases. In July 2007 the minimum wage was raised to $5.85, in July 2008 it was raised to $6.55, and in July 2009 it was raised to $7.25. As of 2014, a person working 40 hours per week for 50 weeks per year at minimum wage ($7.25 per hour) would gross $290 per week, or $14,500 per year, an income below the poverty level for a family of two ($15,730 in 2014) and substantially below the poverty level for a family of three ($19,790). (See Table 1.1 in Chapter 1.)

WHO WORKS FOR MINIMUM WAGE? Although workers must receive at least the minimum wage for most jobs, there are some exceptions in which a person may be paid less than the minimum wage. Full-time students working on a part-time basis in the service and retail industries or at the students' academic institution, certain disabled people, and workers who are "customarily and regularly" tipped may receive less than the minimum wage. According to the BLS, in *Characteristics of Minimum Wage Workers, 2013* (March 2014, http://www.bls.gov/cps/minwage2013.pdf), 1.5 million workers earned exactly the federal minimum wage in 2013 and 1.8 million earned below the minimum. The percentage of workers earning at or below the minimum wage was substantially higher than in the prerecession years. In 2006 only 2.2% of all salary and wage workers made at or below minimum wage; this percentage rose to 6% in 2010, the highest level since the late 1990s, before falling to 4.3% in 2013.

The BLS notes that in 2013, 63.6% of all U.S. workers who made the minimum wage or less were in the service occupations and that a majority of those service workers were in food preparation and serving jobs. The industry with the highest percentage of hourly workers making at or below minimum wage was leisure and hospitality, at 19%. Many of these workers receive tips in addition to their base pay of minimum wage or less.

Earnings at or below the minimum wage were more common among part-time hourly workers (10.4% of whom were paid at or below the minimum wage) than full-time workers (2.1%). (See Table 3.11.) Young workers hold minimum-wage jobs at rates that are disproportionate with their numbers as a share of the overall labor force. Just over half (50.4%) of the total number of workers making the

TABLE 3.10

Federal minimum wage rates under the Fair Labor Standards Act, 1938–2014

Effective date	1938 Act[a]	1961 amendments[b]	1966 & subsequent amendments[c]	
			Nonfarm	Farm
Oct. 24, 1938	$0.25			
Oct. 24, 1939	$0.30			
Oct. 24, 1945	$0.40			
Jan. 25, 1950	$0.75			
Mar. 1, 1956	$1.00			
Sept. 3, 1961	$1.15	$1.00		
Sept. 3, 1963	$1.25			
Sept. 3, 1964		$1.15		
Sept. 3, 1965		$1.25		
Feb. 1, 1967	$1.40	$1.40	$1.00	$1.00
Feb. 1, 1968	$1.60	$1.60	$1.15	$1.15
Feb. 1, 1969			$1.30	$1.30
Feb. 1, 1970			$1.45	
Feb. 1, 1971			$1.60	
May 1, 1974	$2.00	$2.00	$1.90	$1.60
Jan. 1, 1975	$2.10	$2.10	$2.00	$1.80
Jan. 1, 1976	$2.30	$2.30	$2.20	$2.00
Jan. 1, 1977			$2.30	$2.20
Jan. 1, 1978	$2.65 for all covered, nonexempt workers			
Jan. 1, 1979	$2.90 for all covered, nonexempt workers			
Jan. 1, 1980	$3.10 for all covered, nonexempt workers			
Jan. 1, 1981	$3.35 for all covered, nonexempt workers			
Apr. 1, 1990[d]	$3.80 for all covered, nonexempt workers			
Apr. 1, 1991	$4.25 for all covered, nonexempt workers			
Oct. 1, 1996[e]	$4.75 for all covered, nonexempt workers			
Sept. 1, 1997	$5.15 for all covered, nonexempt workers			
Jul. 24, 2007	$5.85 for all covered, nonexempt workers			
Jul. 24, 2008	$6.55 for all covered, nonexempt workers			
Jul. 24, 2009	$7.25 for all covered, nonexempt workers			

[a]The 1938 act was applicable generally to employees engaged in interstate commerce or in the production of goods for interstate commerce.

[b]The 1961 amendments extended coverage primarily to employees in large retail and service enterprises as well as to local transit, construction, and gasoline service station employees.

[c]The 1966 amendments extended coverage to state and local government employees of hospitals, nursing homes, and schools, and to laundries, dry cleaners, and large hotels, motels, restaurants, and farms. Subsequent amendments extended coverage to the remaining federal, state and local government employees who were not protected in 1966, to certain workers in retail and service trades previously exempted, and to certain domestic workers in private household employment.

[d]Grandfather clause: Employees who do not meet the tests for individual coverage, and whose employers were covered by the Fair Labor Standards Act on March 31, 1990, and fail to meet the increased annual dollar volume (ADV) test for enterprise coverage, must continue to receive at least $3.35 an hour.

[e]A subminimum wage—$4.25 an hour—is established for employees under 20 years of age during their first 90 consecutive calendar days of employment with an employer.

SOURCE: "Federal Minimum Wage Rates under the Fair Labor Standards Act," U.S. Department of Labor, Wage, and Hour Division, http://www.dol.gov/whd/minwage/chart.pdf (accessed October 30, 2014)

minimum wage or less in 2013 were under the age of 25 years, even though this age group represented only 20% (15.1 million) of the 75.9 million U.S. workers who were paid by the hour. The pool of workers making the minimum wage or less was disproportionately female: 2.1 million such workers were women and 1.2 million were men. White workers accounted for 2.6 million (77.4%) of the 3.3 million total workers making at or below the minimum wage, which was consistent with the percentage of white hourly workers among all hourly workers (59.5 million of 75.9 million, or 78.4%). Hispanic workers accounted for 643,000 (19.5%) of all those who earned at or below minimum wage, African American workers for 500,000 (15.2%), and Asian American workers for 114,000 (3.5%).

THE INSUFFICIENCY OF MINIMUM WAGE TO MEET EXPENSES. Minimum wage is insufficient to meet the living expenses in almost all locations of the United States, and even full-time minimum-wage workers are eligible for public assistance programs. For example, in *Fast Food, Poverty Wages: The Public Cost of Low-Wage Jobs in the Fast-Food Industry* (October 15, 2013, http://laborcenter.berkeley.edu/pdf/2013/fast_food_poverty_wages.pdf), Sylvia Allegretto et al. find that 52% of people in the families of fast-food workers (one of the industries with the largest number of minimum-wage workers) are enrolled in at least one government assistance program. The researchers also find that 20% of these families live below poverty and 43% have incomes below 200% of poverty. Some of the workers in these families did not work full time; however, even among those who did work 40 or more hours per week, more than half were enrolled in government assistance programs.

As a result of such facts, a nationwide movement of fast-food workers emerged during the second decade of the 21st century. Steven Greenhouse reports in "Strong Voice in 'Fight for 15' Fast-Food Wage Campaign" (NYTimes.com, December 4, 2014) that in 2012, 200 fast-food workers in New York City walked off the job to protest their low pay, and such walkouts spread across the country. In the following years the organizers of these protests combined forces, creating the Fight for 15 movement (http://strikefastfood.org), which united fast-food workers in 150 cities, 33 countries, and six continents. One of the movement's key leaders and spokespersons was Terrance Wise, a Kansas City, Missouri, father of three who worked 16 hours a day at two fast-food jobs. In spite of spending all of his waking hours at work, Wise did not make enough money to pay for housing, and when his fiancée was injured and could no longer work, the family was evicted from their apartment and spent three months homeless.

Supplemental Security Income

SSI is a means-tested income assistance program authorized in 1972 by Title XVI of the Social Security Act. The SSI program replaced the combined federal-state programs of Old Age Assistance, Aid to the Blind, and Aid to the Permanently and Totally Disabled in the 50 states and the District of Columbia. These programs, however, still exist in the U.S. territories of Guam, Puerto Rico, and the Virgin Islands. Since the first payments in 1974, SSI has provided monthly cash payments to needy aged, blind, and disabled individuals who meet the eligibility requirements. States may supplement the basic federal SSI payment.

A number of requirements must be met to receive financial benefits from SSI. Applicants must be U.S. residents, although citizenship is not always necessary; some noncitizens who are lawfully residing in the United

TABLE 3.11

Workers paid hourly rates at or below minimum wage, by selected characteristics, 2013

Characteristic	Number of workers (in thousands)				Percent distribution				Percentage of workers paid hourly rates		
	Total paid hourly rates	At or below minimum wage			Total paid hourly rates	At or below minimum wage			At or below minimum wage		
		Total	At minimum wage	Below minimum wage		Total	At minimum wage	Below minimum wage	Total	At minimum wage	Below minimum wage
Age and gender											
Total, 16 years and older	75,948	3,300	1,532	1,768	100.0	100.0	100.0	100.0	4.3	2.0	2.3
16 to 24 years	15,110	1,663	855	808	19.9	50.4	55.8	45.7	11.0	5.7	5.3
16 to 19 years	4,089	797	476	321	5.4	24.2	31.1	18.2	19.5	11.6	7.9
25 years and older	60,838	1,638	677	961	80.1	49.6	44.2	54.4	2.7	1.1	1.6
Men, 16 years and older	37,544	1,243	622	621	49.4	37.7	40.6	35.1	3.3	1.7	1.7
16 to 24 years	7,558	655	382	273	10.0	19.8	24.9	15.4	8.7	5.1	3.6
16 to 19 years	1,975	332	205	127	2.6	10.1	13.4	7.2	16.8	10.4	6.4
25 years and older	29,985	587	240	347	39.5	17.8	15.7	19.6	2.0	0.8	1.2
Women, 16 years and older	38,404	2,058	910	1,148	50.6	62.4	59.4	64.9	5.4	2.4	3.0
16 to 24 years	7,552	1,007	473	534	9.9	30.5	30.9	30.2	13.3	6.3	7.1
16 to 19 years	2,115	466	272	194	2.8	14.1	17.8	11.0	22.0	12.9	9.2
25 years and older	30,852	1,051	437	614	40.6	31.8	28.5	34.7	3.4	1.4	2.0
Race and Hispanic or Latino ethnicity											
White[a]	59,515	2,554	1,160	1,394	78.4	77.4	75.7	78.8	4.3	1.9	2.3
Men	29,947	950	470	480	39.4	28.8	30.7	27.1	3.2	1.6	1.6
Women	29,569	1,605	691	914	38.9	48.6	45.1	51.7	5.4	2.3	3.1
Black or African American[a]	10,233	500	276	224	13.5	15.2	18.0	12.7	4.9	2.7	2.2
Men	4,590	208	121	87	6.0	6.3	7.9	4.9	4.5	2.6	1.9
Women	5,643	292	155	137	7.4	8.8	10.1	7.7	5.2	2.7	2.4
Asian[a]	3,495	114	43	71	4.6	3.5	2.8	4.0	3.3	1.2	2.0
Men	1,606	44	18	26	2.1	1.3	1.2	1.5	2.7	1.1	1.6
Women	1,888	70	25	45	2.5	2.1	1.6	2.5	3.7	1.3	2.4
Hispanic or Latino	14,706	643	318	325	19.4	19.5	20.8	18.4	4.4	2.2	2.2
Men	8,365	280	123	157	11.0	8.5	8.0	8.9	3.3	1.5	1.9
Women	6,341	363	195	168	8.3	11.0	12.7	9.5	5.7	3.1	2.6
Full-and part-time status											
Full-time workers[b]	55,387	1,173	447	726	72.9	35.5	29.2	41.1	2.1	0.8	1.3
Men	30,309	475	184	291	39.9	14.4	12.0	16.5	1.6	0.6	1.0
Women	25,078	698	263	435	33.0	21.2	17.2	24.6	2.8	1.0	1.7
Part-time workers[b]	20,453	2,125	1,085	1,040	26.9	64.4	70.8	58.8	10.4	5.3	5.1
Men	7,188	766	438	328	9.5	23.2	28.6	18.6	10.7	6.1	4.6
Women	13,265	1,359	648	711	17.5	41.2	42.3	40.2	10.2	4.9	5.4

[a]Estimates for the race groups—white, black or African American, and Asian—do not sum to totals because data are not presented for all races. Persons whose ethnicity is identified as Hispanic or Latino may be of any race.

[b]The distinction between full- and part-time workers is based on hours usually worked. These data will not sum to totals because full- or part-time status on the principal job is not identifiable for a small number of multiple jobholders. Full time is 35 hours or more per week; part time is less than 35 hours.

Note: Data exclude all self-employed persons whether or not their businesses are incorporated.

SOURCE: "Table 1. Wage and Salary Workers Paid Hourly Rates with Earnings at or below the Prevailing Federal Minimum Wage, by Selected Characteristics, 2013 Annual Averages," in *Characteristics of Minimum Wage Workers, 2013*, U.S. Department of Labor, Bureau of Labor Statistics, March 2014, http://www .bls.gov/cps/minwage2013.pdf (accessed October 30, 2014).

States are eligible. The applicant must meet the program criteria for age, blindness, or disability. The aged, or elderly, are people aged 65 years and older. To be considered legally blind, a person must have vision of 20/200 or less in the better eye with the use of corrective lenses, have tunnel vision of 20 degrees or less (can only see a small area straight ahead), or have met state qualifications for the earlier Aid to the Blind program. A person is disabled if he or she cannot earn money at a job because of a physical or mental illness or injury that may cause his or her death, or if the condition lasts for 12 months or longer. Those who met earlier state Aid to the Permanently and Totally Disabled requirements may also qualify for assistance.

Unmarried children under the age of 18 years (or age 22 if a full-time student) may qualify for SSI if they have a medically determinable physical or mental impairment that substantially reduces their ability to function independently or to engage in age-appropriate activities. This impairment must be expected to last for a continuous period of more than 12 months or to result in death.

Because SSI is a means-tested benefit, a person's income and property must be counted before he or she can receive benefits. The income thresholds for SSI eligibility vary by state. Income included in the determination of benefits includes any money earned, any Social Security or private pension benefits, and the value of the applicant's shelter and food, if the applicant gets those things from someone else. The applicant must not own assets (excluding the house one lives in and, in most cases, one's car) worth more than $2,000. A couple applying for SSI must not have assets exceeding $3,000. When applying for SSI, applicants must also apply for other forms of government assistance, including SNAP and Medicaid.

Although the income and property eligibility thresholds vary by state, the baseline monthly SSI payment is the same nationwide. According to the Social Security Administration, in "You May Be Able to Get Supplemental Security Income (SSI)" (2015, http://www.social security.gov/pubs/EN-05-11069.pdf), the basic payment for one person in 2015 was $733 per month, and the basic payment per couple was $1,100 per month. The actual amount an applicant may receive often varies from this basic level. Most states pay a supplement to the federal SSI benefit, increasing the overall disability benefit that eligible applicants receive. Other applicants receive less than the nationwide basic payment because they or their family members have other sources of income or because of other factors related to location and household characteristics.

Tax Relief for the Poor

Both conservatives and liberals hailed the Tax Reform Act of 1986 as a major step toward relieving the tax burden of low-income families, one group of Americans whose wages and benefits have been eroding since 1979. The law enlarged and inflation-proofed the Earned Income Tax Credit (EITC), which provides a refundable tax credit that both offsets taxes and often operates as a wage supplement. Only those who work can qualify, and household earnings must fall below a certain threshold, which varies depending on whether the taxpayer is a single head of household or married and filing jointly, as well as on the number of children in the household. Children must be under age 19 or under age 24 and enrolled full time in college.

The Internal Revenue Service provides information about income thresholds and the corresponding size of tax credit amounts in "Income Limits and Range of EITC" (November 24, 2014, http://www.eitc.irs.gov/ EITC-Central/abouteitc/ranges). A childless individual making less than $14,590 was eligible for an EITC of $2 to $496 in tax year 2014. An individual with one child

and an income of less than $38,511, or a couple with one child and an income of less than $43,941, was eligible for a credit of $9 to $3,305. An individual with two children and an income of less than $43,756, or a couple with two children and an income of less than $49,186, was eligible for a credit of $10 to $5,460. An individual with three or more children and an income of less than $46,997, or a couple with three or more children and an income of less than $52,427, was eligible for a credit of $11 to $6,143.

Although income must be below these thresholds, families with incomes below the poverty line do not necessarily receive the most generous EITC amounts because they may receive other forms of public assistance. The largest EITC benefits go to working families that are not eligible for most forms of means-tested benefits, and the EITC is considered an effective tool at helping former welfare recipients transition away from government assistance. The gradual phase-out and availability of the EITC at above-poverty income levels helps stabilize a parent's employment by providing additional money to cover expenses that are associated with working, such as child care and transportation. Research finds that the EITC has been an effective work incentive and has significantly increased work participation among single mothers.

Those who do not owe income tax, or who owe an amount smaller than the credit, receive a check directly from the Internal Revenue Service for the credit due them. Most recipients claim the credit when they file an income tax form. In "Statistics for Tax Returns with EITC" (January 29, 2015, http://www.eitc.irs.gov/EITC-Central/eitcstats), the Internal Revenue Service indicates that for tax year 2013 nearly 28 million U.S. taxpayers filed EITC claims for a total credit amount of over $66 billion. The average credit amount per tax return varied by state from $1,894 (Vermont) to $2,817 (Mississippi). (See Table 3.12.)

Although the Tax Reform Act of 1986 has helped ease the burden of federal taxes, most of the poor still pay a substantial share of their income in state and local taxes. To address the needs of such low-income families, 26 states and the District of Columbia have enacted a state EITC to supplement the federal credit, as the CBPP reports in "Policy Basics: State Earned Income Tax Credits" (January 28, 2015, http://www.cbpp.org/files/ policybasics-seitc.pdf).

TABLE 3.12

Earned Income Tax Credit (EITC) claims and dollar values, by state, 2013

State[a]	Number of EITC claims[a]	Total EITC amount[a]	Average EITC amount[a]
Alabama	516 K	$1.4 B	$2,732
Alaska	49 K	$99.5 M	$2,049
Arizona	566 K	$1.4 B	$2,530
Arkansas	302 K	$771 M	$2,552
California	3.1 M	$7.3 B	$2,373
Colorado	358 K	$777 M	$2,174
Connecticut	221 K	$472 M	$2,140
Delaware	73 K	$170 M	$2,309
District of Columbia	54 K	$125 M	$2,316
Florida	2 M	$5.2 B	$2,450
Georgia	1.1 M	$2.9 B	$2,692
Hawaii	110 K	$239 M	$2,175
Idaho	135 K	$307 M	$2,283
Illinois	1 M	$2.5 B	$2,437
Indiana	558 K	$1.3 B	$2,346
Iowa	212 K	$462 M	$2,182
Kansas	214 K	$494 M	$2,307
Kentucky	409 K	$961 M	$2,351
Louisiana	519 K	$1.4 B	$2,741
Maine	102 K	$207 M	$2,035
Maryland	417 K	$958 M	$2,297
Massachusetts	406 K	$833 M	$2,050
Michigan	823 K	$1.96 B	$2,387
Minnesota	344 K	$732 M	$2,124
Mississippi	390 K	$1.1 B	$2,817
Missouri	519 K	$1.2 B	$2,377
Montana	80 K	$168 M	$2,096
Nebraska	136 K	$310 M	$2,271
Nevada	244 K	$579 M	$2,372
New Hampshire	79 K	$153 M	$1,926
New Jersey	596 K	$1.4 B	$2,281
New Mexico	214 K	$515 M	$2,405
New York	1.8 M	$4.1 B	$2,309
North Carolina	931 K	$2.3 B	$2,462
North Dakota	43 K	$87.3 M	$2,051
Ohio	963 K	$2.3 B	$2,364
Oklahoma	337 K	$825 M	$2,449
Oregon	279 K	$586 M	$2,101
Pennsylvania	936 K	$2.0 B	$2,185
Rhode Island	84 K	$190 M	$2,264
South Carolina	494 K	$1.2 B	$2,504
South Dakota	66 K	$141 M	$2,143
Tennessee	657 K	$1.6 B	$2,492
Texas	2.6 M	$7.0 B	$2,661
Utah	195 K	$452 M	$2,320
Vermont	45 K	$86 M	$1,894
Virginia	614 K	$1.4 B	$2,287
Washington	448 K	$960 M	$2,145
West Virginia	158 K	$349 M	$2,211
Wisconsin	391 K	$848 M	$2,167
Wyoming	39 K	$79.5 M	$2,038
International	24 K	$55 M	$2,326

[a]Calendar year report, July 2014.

SOURCE: "Statistics for Tax Returns with EITC," in *EITC Central*, Internal Revenue Service, October 2014, http://www.eitc.irs.gov/EITC-Central/eitcstats (accessed October 30, 2014)

CHAPTER 4
WHO RECEIVES GOVERNMENT BENEFITS?

A variety of government programs exist to assist low-income and impoverished families as well as those unable to work either permanently, due to disability, or temporarily, due to job loss. Means-tested assistance programs (programs that are only available to individuals or households whose incomes are below certain thresholds), such as Temporary Assistance for Needy Families (TANF) and the Supplemental Nutrition Assistance Program (SNAP; previously called the Food Stamp Program), provide the most assistance to the largest proportion of impoverished families, and they are particularly important sources of support for children. Meanwhile, Supplemental Security Income (SSI) provides assistance to disabled Americans of all ages. Other forms of government assistance, such as unemployment compensation and tax credits, are aimed specifically at working Americans. Collectively, these programs represent an important safety net for a wide variety of the country's citizens.

Assistance programs are among the most controversial of the federal government's operations, in large part due to conservative opposition to the notion of redistribution—the transfer of money from one group of people to another. In the case of means-tested public assistance programs, middle-class and wealthy households pay money via taxes that are used to fund the government programs that aid the poor. In spite of the fact that U.S. antipoverty programs are modest by international standards, and in spite of the cutbacks in assistance that have come in the wake of welfare reform, a growing population of poor people has translated into steady growth in federal spending on most programs. The Heritage Foundation, a conservative advocacy group, notes in "Spending on the Largest Anti-poverty Programs" (August 20, 2013, http://www.heritage.org/multimedia/infographic/2013/08/federalspendingbynumbers2013/page-9-chart-1) that between 2003 and 2013 SNAP spending rose 160%, spending on the Children's Health Insurance Program

(discussed at greater length in Chapter 8) rose 84%, and spending on the U.S. Department of Agriculture's (USDA) Child Nutrition Programs rose 54%. In all, the federal government spent $566.7 billion on its 10 major antipoverty programs in 2013. The largest of these by spending was Medicaid, which cost $266.6 billion; the second-largest program by spending, SNAP, was much smaller at $82.6 billion.

However, spending on the 10 major antipoverty programs was far lower than spending on the other programs that represented the federal government's largest outlays. In *Federal Spending by the Numbers, 2014: Government Spending Trends in Graphics, Tables, and Key Points (Including 51 Examples of Government Waste)* (December 8, 2014, http://thf_media.s3.amazonaws.com/2014/pdf/SR162.pdf), Romina Boccia of the Heritage Foundation indicates that Social Security represented the largest single outlay among all government programs in 2013, at $813.6 billion, followed by national defense, at $633.4 billion. Spending on these programs had risen since 2003 at rates comparable to those by which antipoverty spending had risen.

Although assumptions about aid recipients' unwillingness to work are common, a sizable proportion of even the poorest welfare beneficiaries typically derive some amount of their income through work. In fact, Arloc Sherman, Robert Greenstein, and Kathy Ruffing of the Center on Budget and Policy Priorities (CBPP) report in *Contrary to "Entitlement Society" Rhetoric, over Nine-Tenths of Entitlement Benefits Go to Elderly, Disabled, or Working Households* (February 10, 2012, http://www.cbpp.org/files/2-10-12pov.pdf) that 91% of the recipients of government aid in 2010 were either elderly, disabled, or employed. According to the researchers, "People who are neither elderly nor disabled—and do not live in a working household—received only 9 percent of the benefits" from entitlement programs in 2010.

Conservative opposition to spending on antipoverty programs also focuses on notions of these programs' inability to solve the problems they address. In contrast, supporters of safety-net programs point to statistics showing that the programs are indeed effective and that their limitations typically reflect the low levels of spending on aid relative to the size of the poor population and the depth of poverty. For example, Danilo Trisi of the CBPP demonstrates the effectiveness of two key antipoverty programs in "SNAP and Unemployment Insurance Kept Millions out of Poverty Last Year, Census Supplemental Poverty Measure Shows" (Offthechartsblog.org, November 6, 2013). Using the U.S. Census Bureau's Supplemental Poverty Measure, which includes public benefits in its calculations of household income, SNAP kept 4.9 million people (including 2.2 million children) above the poverty line in 2012, and unemployment insurance kept 2.5 million people (including 600,000 children) out of poverty in 2012.

Other programs that function as antipoverty programs even though they are available to people living above the poverty level are also effective at lifting people above poverty. Social Security is widely credited with drastic reductions in poverty among the elderly between 1967 and 2000, as noted in Chapter 2. Additionally, the Earned Income Tax Credit (EITC), which benefited more than 27 million people in 2013 (see Table 3.12 in Chapter 3), is widely believed to have multiple and long-term impacts on poverty. According to Chuck Marr, Chye-Ching Huang, and Arloc Sherman of the CBPP, in *Earned Income Tax Credit Promotes Work, Encourages Children's Success at School, Research Finds* (April 15, 2014, http://www.cbpp.org/files/6-26-12tax.pdf), studies show that the EITC has done as much to increase the labor-force participation of single mothers since the 1990s as the welfare-to-work requirements of the Personal Responsibility and Work Opportunity Reconciliation Act (PRWORA). Women benefiting from the EITC saw higher wage growth than similar low-income women who did not, and this wage growth translates into higher Social Security payments in old age, because Social Security benefit amounts are calculated according to a worker's career earnings.

This chapter focuses on the populations that benefit from the most prominent antipoverty programs in the U.S. social welfare system: TANF, SNAP, unemployment compensation, and SSI. Beneficiaries of other prominent antipoverty programs that focus on health are discussed in Chapter 8.

TEMPORARY ASSISTANCE FOR NEEDY FAMILIES
Who Receives TANF Benefits?

In *Temporary Assistance for Needy Families Program (TANF): Tenth Report to Congress* (December 12, 2013,

http://www.acf.hhs.gov/sites/default/files/ofa/10th_tanf _report_congress.pdf), the U.S. Department of Health and Human Services' Office of Family Assistance (OFA) describes the TANF caseload as of the end of fiscal year (FY) 2011. Over the course of the full fiscal year, 4.6 million individuals received assistance—1.2 million (25.3%) of whom were adults and 3.4 million (74.7%) of whom were children. (See Table 4.1.) A monthly average of 1.9 million families participated in TANF. With an average monthly caseload of 602,027, California accounted for 31.3% of the total TANF caseload, followed by New York, with a monthly caseload of 157,623, and Ohio, with a monthly caseload of 99,471. Whites accounted for 34.7% of the TANF caseload in FY 2011; African Americans, 34.5%; and Hispanics, 24.2%. Furthermore, 84.7% of adult TANF recipients were female and 15.3% were male.

There are three basic types of TANF cases: single-parent cases, two-parent cases, and child-only cases (cases in which no adult in the household is a recipient of TANF benefits). Pamela J. Loprest of the Urban Institute explains in *How Has the TANF Caseload Changed over Time?* (March 2012, http://www.urban.org/Uploaded PDF/412565-How-Has-the-TANF-Caseload-Changed-Over-Time.pdf) that the proportion of each case type in the overall caseload has changed substantially in the years since the 1996 passage of the PRWORA, which replaced Aid to Families with Dependent Children (AFDC) with TANF. In 1997 single-parent families accounted for 72% of the caseload, child-only cases for 20%, and two-parent families for 7%. By 2009 single-parent households represented 47% of the national caseload, child-only cases represented 48%, and two-parent families represented 5%.

These changes in the caseload composition do not correspond to increases in the child-only caseload, however, but to massive declines in the overall caseload. As Figure 4.1 shows, the AFDC caseload peaked in FY 1994 at a monthly average of 5.1 million families and then fell precipitously in the years after welfare reform, to 2.4 million TANF families in 2000. According to the OFA, a significant portion of this decline in the caseload was attributable to a sharp increase in the number of single mothers leaving the TANF rolls. The caseload continued to decline in the years that followed, although it rose slightly between 2008 and 2010 as a result of the Great Recession (which officially lasted from December 2007 to June 2009). After reaching a recession-era peak of 2 million families in December 2010, the TANF caseload began falling again. Between October 2013 and December 2014 the average monthly caseload stood at 1.5 million families and demonstrated a downward trend from late 2013 through the early months of 2014. (See Table 4.2.) With few exceptions, the trend toward declining caseloads was evident across most of the states.

TABLE 4.1

Number of adults and number of children receiving TANF and SSP benefits, by state, fiscal year 2011

	Total recipients	Adults	Children	Percentage adults	Percentage children
U.S. totals	**4,599,846**	**1,164,628**	**3,435,218**	**25.3%**	**74.7%**
Alabama	56,495	14,894	41,601	26.4%	73.6%
Alaska	10,045	3,207	6,837	31.9%	68.1%
Arizona	41,395	11,574	29,821	28.0%	72.0%
Arkansas	18,437	5,306	13,132	28.8%	71.2%
California	1,474,923	329,623	1,145,300	22.3%	77.7%
Colorado	30,668	8,027	22,642	26.2%	73.8%
Connecticut	32,427	9,586	22,841	29.6%	70.4%
Delaware	15,696	5,996	9,700	38.2%	61.8%
Dist. of Col.	24,374	5,906	18,468	24.2%	75.8%
Florida	98,854	18,409	80,445	18.6%	81.4%
Georgia	37,201	3,783	33,418	10.2%	89.8%
Guam	3,117	808	2,309	25.9%	74.1%
Hawaii	29,719	9,804	19,915	33.0%	67.0%
Idaho	2,850	216	2,633	7.6%	92.4%
Illinois	83,012	13,884	69,129	16.7%	83.3%
Indiana	66,304	15,825	50,479	23.9%	76.1%
Iowa	53,732	17,144	36,588	31.9%	68.1%
Kansas	38,451	12,541	25,910	32.6%	67.4%
Kentucky	63,073	13,556	49,517	21.5%	78.5%
Louisiana	23,983	3,754	20,229	15.7%	84.3%
Maine	40,049	13,919	26,129	34.8%	65.2%
Maryland	61,601	17,119	44,482	27.8%	72.2%
Massachusetts	99,289	33,188	66,101	33.4%	66.6%
Michigan	172,972	49,016	123,955	28.3%	71.7%
Minnesota	54,231	13,588	40,643	25.1%	74.9%
Mississippi	24,865	6,741	18,123	27.1%	72.9%
Missouri	94,401	30,140	64,262	31.9%	68.1%
Montana	8,706	2,555	6,152	29.3%	70.7%
Nebraska	19,795	4,234	15,561	21.4%	78.6%
Nevada	27,675	7,121	20,554	25.7%	74.3%
New Hampshire	12,903	3,681	9,222	28.5%	71.5%
New Jersey	83,753	25,332	58,421	30.2%	69.8%
New Mexico	52,395	14,895	37,499	28.4%	71.6%
New York	395,242	109,661	285,581	27.7%	72.3%
North Carolina	43,923	6,833	37,090	15.6%	84.4%
North Dakota	4,642	1,136	3,506	24.5%	75.5%
Ohio	225,452	61,756	163,696	27.4%	72.6%
Oklahoma	20,217	3,760	16,457	18.6%	81.4%
Oregon	88,903	28,957	59,947	32.6%	67.4%
Pennsylvania	145,977	38,425	107,551	26.3%	73.7%
Puerto Rico	41,305	13,860	27,445	33.6%	66.4%
Rhode Island	15,473	4,817	10,657	31.1%	68.9%
South Carolina	41,994	10,451	31,544	24.9%	75.1%
South Dakota	6,814	1,076	5,737	15.8%	84.2%
Tennessee	158,576	44,463	114,113	28.0%	72.0%
Texas	112,777	15,878	96,899	14.1%	85.9%
Utah	15,962	4,725	11,237	29.6%	70.4%
Vermont	7,666	2,365	5,301	30.9%	69.1%
Virgin Islands	1,326	369	956	27.8%	72.2%
Virginia	79,431	22,922	56,509	28.9%	71.1%
Washington	149,412	45,459	103,952	30.4%	69.6%
West Virginia	23,642	6,778	16,864	28.7%	71.3%
Wisconsin	63,108	15,467	47,641	24.5%	75.5%
Wyoming	617	99	519	16.0%	84.0%

AFDC = Aid to Families with Dependent Children.
TANF = Temporary Assistance for Needy Families.

SOURCE: "Figure 2-E. TANF and SSP Average Monthly Number of Adults and Children, FY 2011," in *Temporary Assistance to Needy Families (TANF): Tenth Report to Congress*, U.S. Department of Health and Human Services, Administration for Children and Families, Office of Family Assistance, December 12, 2013, http://www.acf.hhs.gov/sites/default/files/ofa/10th_tanf_report_congress.pdf (accessed October 30, 2014)

Amid this overall trend toward declining caseloads between 1994 and 2014, the percentage of child-only cases among the total caseload grew steadily. Numerous adults became ineligible for TANF during this time due to rising incomes, work requirements, benefit time limits, and other factors related both to changes in the economy and to welfare reform. Many of the households that received child-only benefits likely included an adult TANF recipient whose eligibility expired, who no longer qualified for benefits, or who had chosen not to enroll due to the eligibility restrictions. Child-only cases are subject to fewer eligibility restrictions and time limits than adult cases, so much of the changing composition of the TANF caseload reflects the fact that the need for

FIGURE 4.1

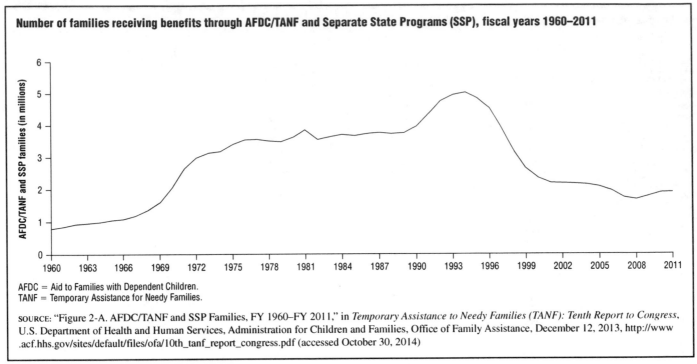

Number of families receiving benefits through AFDC/TANF and Separate State Programs (SSP), fiscal years 1960–2011

AFDC = Aid to Families with Dependent Children.
TANF = Temporary Assistance for Needy Families.

SOURCE: "Figure 2-A. AFDC/TANF and SSP Families, FY 1960–FY 2011," in *Temporary Assistance to Needy Families (TANF): Tenth Report to Congress,* U.S. Department of Health and Human Services, Administration for Children and Families, Office of Family Assistance, December 12, 2013, http://www .acf.hhs.gov/sites/default/files/ofa/10th_tanf_report_congress.pdf (accessed October 30, 2014)

assistance has remained relatively constant even though many adults have been removed from the welfare rolls.

Between FYs 2000 and 2011 the distribution of adult TANF recipients by age shifted noticeably toward younger adults. Adults aged 20 to 29 years accounted for 42.5% of all beneficiaries in FY 2000 and for 51.8% in FY 2011, whereas the proportion of teenaged recipients remained flat and the proportions of adults aged 30 to 39 years and adults over the age of 39 years declined. (See Table 4.3.) Over this same period, the proportion of the caseload accounted for by white recipients increased slightly (from 32.8% to 34.7%), the proportion accounted for by African American recipients declined slightly (from 37.9% to 34.5%), and the proportion accounted for by Hispanic recipients was flat (at 23.7% in FY 2000 and 24.2% in FY 2011). (See Table 4.4.)

Children who receive TANF benefits, either as part of the family of an adult TANF recipient or under a child-only designation, are overwhelmingly young. In FY 2011, 74.9% of TANF children were aged 11 years and younger, whereas 8.5% were aged 16 years and older. (See Table 4.5.) Children two years old and younger represented 15.7% of the child caseload, and children between two and five years old represented 28.9% of the caseload. The proportion of the child caseload has shifted slightly toward the younger end of the age spectrum. In FY 2000 children aged five years and younger accounted for 38.7% of the total child caseload, and in FY 2011 they accounted for 44.6%. The proportion of the caseload consisting of children aged six to 11 years fell

accordingly, while the proportions consisting of older children remained relatively constant.

In FY 2011 white children accounted for 27.1% of the child TANF caseload, African American children for 31.4%, and Hispanic children for 34.7%. (See Table 4.6.) Although the white proportion of the overall child caseload changed little between FYs 2000 and 2011, the proportion of Hispanic recipients increased significantly and the proportion of African American recipients decreased significantly.

According to the OFA, approximately 18% of TANF families had income from other sources in FY 2011. Those who had such income made a monthly average of $725 beyond their TANF benefits. About 9% of TANF families had income from child support, with an average monthly payment of $221, and 10% had cash assets, with an average balance of $220. Over one out of five (22.3%) TANF adults were employed in FY 2011; this was a dramatic increase over the AFDC employment rate of 6.6% in FY 1992 but a decrease from the peak TANF employment rate of 27.6% in FY 1999. (See Table 4.7.)

Duration of TANF Benefits

According to Loprest, the majority of adult TANF recipients collect benefits for short periods. Setting aside child-only cases, which generally are not subject to time limits, 41% of TANF recipients in FY 2009 had been collecting benefits for less than one year and 23% of beneficiaries had been collecting benefits for less than two years; 12% of the overall caseload consisted of adults who had been receiving benefits for more than four years.

TABLE 4.2

Families receiving TANF benefits, by state, October 2013–December 2014

[Fiscal and calendar year 2014 average monthly number families, as of 7/1/2014]

State	Oct-13	Nov-13	Dec-13	Jan-14	Feb-14	Mar-14	Average fiscal year 2014	Average calendar year 2014
U.S. totals	1,594,965	1,580,247	1,548,566	1,538,866	1,527,453	1,518,121	1,551,370	1,528,147
Alabama	18,832	18,561	18,394	18,016	17,656	17,232	18,115	17,635
Alaska	3,401	3,384	3,439	3,593	3,667	3,681	3,528	3,647
Arizona	15,071	14,619	14,036	13,571	13,020	12,557	13,812	13,049
Arkansas	6,720	6,450	6,395	6,304	6,132	5,963	6,327	6,133
California	553,945	553,437	533,081	536,226	536,783	537,178	541,775	536,729
Colorado	17,562	17,383	17,270	17,042	17,011	16,960	17,205	17,004
Connecticut	14,604	14,627	14,335	14,455	14,426	14,421	14,478	14,434
Delaware	4,947	4,866	4,792	4,657	4,649	4,627	4,756	4,644
District of Columbia	6,401	6,061	4,388	7,176	6,738	6,151	6,153	6,688
Florida	51,791	52,138	53,087	52,663	50,319	49,391	51,565	50,791
Georgia	17,087	16,705	16,481	16,123	15,549	15,280	16,204	15,651
Guam	1,355	1,332	1,342	1,288	1,278	1,254	1,308	1,273
Hawaii	8,880	8,802	8,865	8,756	8,604	8,441	8,725	8,600
Idaho	1,830	1,842	1,843	1,845	1,865	1,867	1,849	1,859
Illinois	20,522	20,069	20,354	20,095	19,673	20,206	20,153	19,991
Indiana	11,342	11,025	10,719	10,444	10,425	10,248	10,701	10,372
Iowa	14,431	14,150	13,777	13,372	13,287	13,251	13,711	13,303
Kansas	7,810	7,581	7,553	7,398	7,178	7,027	7,425	7,201
Kentucky	30,168	29,720	29,488	29,255	28,962	28,785	29,396	29,001
Louisiana	6,502	6,280	6,151	6,201	5,732	5,604	6,078	5,846
Maine	6,175	6,074	5,942	5,818	5,914	5,890	5,969	5,874
Maryland	21,498	21,147	21,306	20,297	20,484	20,360	20,849	20,380
Massachusetts	45,712	44,414	43,420	42,954	42,890	42,858	43,708	42,901
Michigan	31,460	30,787	30,316	29,139	28,698	28,048	29,741	28,628
Minnesota	20,514	20,630	20,421	20,366	20,271	20,144	20,391	20,260
Mississippi	9,604	9,487	9,260	8,933	8,864	8,637	9,131	8,811
Missouri	29,888	29,027	28,889	28,376	28,097	27,720	28,666	28,064
Montana	3,413	3,423	3,487	3,494	3,421	3,339	3,430	3,418
Nebraska	5,405	5,248	5,188	5,238	5,069	5,048	5,199	5,118
Nevada	11,543	11,734	11,913	11,937	11,889	11,960	11,829	11,929
New Hampshire	3,328	3,248	3,221	3,230	3,185	3,158	3,228	3,191
New Jersey	29,695	29,316	28,894	27,699	28,470	28,327	28,734	28,165
New Mexico	13,606	13,197	13,206	12,698	12,830	12,693	13,038	12,740
New York	117,806	117,139	116,483	114,581	114,562	114,595	115,861	114,579
North Carolina	20,013	19,514	18,575	17,997	17,429	16,688	18,369	17,371
North Dakota	1,411	1,393	1,366	1,328	1,327	1,280	1,351	1,312
Ohio	65,907	65,149	64,371	63,770	63,090	62,519	64,134	63,126
Oklahoma	7,443	7,408	7,270	7,249	7,147	6,987	7,251	7,128
Oregon	24,058	24,160	24,134	24,443	24,032	24,078	24,151	24,184
Pennsylvania	71,586	70,690	69,667	68,639	68,010	68,008	69,433	68,219
Puerto Rico	12,195	12,178	12,088	11,711	11,475	11,381	11,838	11,522
Rhode Island	5,951	5,937	5,815	5,775	5,675	5,523	5,779	5,658
South Carolina	12,373	12,210	11,770	11,428	11,230	11,089	11,683	11,249
South Dakota	3,215	3,228	3,204	3,185	3,170	3,117	3,187	3,157
Tennessee	51,376	50,691	50,222	48,391	48,034	47,089	49,301	47,838
Texas	40,337	39,361	38,460	37,686	36,500	35,950	38,049	36,712
Utah	4,337	4,201	4,111	4,155	4,128	4,119	4,175	4,134
Vermont	3,115	3,020	3,083	3,029	3,070	2,889	3,034	2,996
Virgin Islands	446	444	432	432	428	420	434	427
Virginia	28,134	27,721	27,140	26,842	26,176	25,831	26,974	26,283
Washington	43,165	42,473	42,747	43,381	43,044	42,521	42,889	42,982
West Virginia	9,053	8,957	8,862	8,744	8,677	8,535	8,805	8,652
Wisconsin	27,618	27,243	27,133	27,073	26,825	26,833	27,121	26,910
Wyoming	384	366	380	368	388	363	375	373

Notes: Fiscal year average is based on data October 2013 through March 2014. Calendar year average is based on data January 2014 through March 2014. TANF = Temporary Assistance for Needy Families.

SOURCE: "TANF: Total Number of Families," in *TANF Caseload Data 2014*, U.S. Department of Health and Human Services, Office of the Administration for Children and Families, Office of Family Assistance, July 31, 2014, http://www.acf.hhs.gov/sites/default/files/ofa/2014_family_tan.pdf (accessed October 30, 2014)

The PRWORA limited the duration that a family can collect TANF benefits to a lifetime maximum of 60 months, and states have the freedom to set shorter maximum time limits. In *Many States Cutting TANF Benefits Harshly Despite High Unemployment and Unprecedented Need* (October 3, 2011, http://www.cbpp.org/files/5-19-11 tanf.pdf), Liz Schott and LaDonna Pavetti of the CBPP explain that fiscal pressures at the state level during the Great Recession led to numerous cuts in TANF benefits, including reductions in the program time limits. For example, in 2010 Arizona cut its TANF time limit from the federally established 60 months to 36 months, before

TABLE 4.3

Trend in adult TANF recipients, by age, fiscal years 2000–11

	Under 20	20–29	30–39	Over 39
2000	7.1%	42.5%	32.1%	18.3%
2001	7.4%	42.4%	31.2%	19.0%
2002	7.5%	44.9%	29.9%	17.7%
2003	7.7%	46.8%	28.7%	16.8%
2004	7.4%	47.6%	28.2%	16.8%
2005	7.3%	47.1%	28.1%	17.4%
2006	7.2%	48.5%	26.8%	17.5%
2007	7.3%	48.7%	27.0%	17.0%
2008	7.3%	50.1%	26.4%	16.1%
2009	8.0%	50.0%	26.0%	16.0%
2010	7.9%	51.3%	25.4%	15.4%
2011	6.9%	51.8%	26.6%	14.7%

TANF = Temporary Assistance for Needy Families.

SOURCE: "Figure 10-E. Trend in TANF Adult Recipients by Age Group, FY 2000–FY 2011," in *Temporary Assistance to Needy Families (TANF): Tenth Report to Congress*, U.S. Department of Health and Human Services, Administration for Children and Families, Office of Family Assistance, December 12, 2013, http://www.acf.hhs.gov/sites/default/files/ofa/10th_tanf_report_congress.pdf (accessed October 30, 2014)

TABLE 4.4

Trend in adult TANF recipients, by race and Hispanic origin, fiscal years 2000–11

	White	Black or African American	Hispanic*
2000	32.8%	37.9%	23.7%
2001	32.2%	39.0%	23.6%
2002	34.2%	38.9%	21.6%
2003	35.1%	38.6%	20.5%
2004	36.7%	38.9%	19.1%
2005	36.3%	38.6%	19.8%
2006	37.9%	37.2%	19.9%
2007	35.9%	36.4%	22.6%
2008	35.2%	35.0%	23.3%
2009	35.4%	34.1%	24.2%
2010	36.8%	33.0%	23.7%
2011	34.7%	34.5%	24.2%

*Can be of any race.

SOURCE: Adapted from "Figure 10-D. Trend in TANF Adults by Race/Ethnicity, FY 2000–FY 2011," in *Temporary Assistance to Needy Families (TANF): Tenth Report to Congress*, U.S. Department of Health and Human Services, Administration for Children and Families, Office of Family Assistance, December 12, 2013, http://www.acf.hhs.gov/sites/default/files/ofa/10th_tanf_report_congress.pdf (accessed October 30, 2014)

TABLE 4.5

Trend in child TANF recipients, by age, fiscal years 2000–11

	Under 2	2–5	6–11	12–15	16–19
2000	13.1%	25.6%	36.2%	17.4%	7.6%
2001	13.4%	24.9%	35.8%	18.4%	7.5%
2002	14.6%	25.1%	34.4%	18.3%	7.6%
2003	14.6%	25.4%	33.4%	18.8%	7.7%
2004	14.7%	25.7%	32.2%	19.4%	8.0%
2005	14.5%	25.0%	31.8%	19.9%	8.8%
2006	14.5%	25.5%	31.1%	19.7%	9.2%
2007	15.4%	25.3%	30.5%	19.2%	9.5%
2008	16.0%	25.5%	30.4%	18.5%	9.5%
2009	16.1%	26.9%	29.9%	17.9%	9.2%
2010	16.0%	28.0%	30.1%	16.7%	9.2%
2011	15.7%	28.9%	30.3%	16.6%	8.5%

SOURCE: "Figure 10-F. Trend in TANF Recipient Children by Age Group, FY 2002 [*sic*]–FY 2011," in *Temporary Assistance to Needy Families (TANF): Tenth Report to Congress*, U.S. Department of Health and Human Services, Administration for Children and Families, Office of Family Assistance, December 12, 2013, http://www.acf.hhs.gov/sites/default/files/ofa/10th_tanf_report_congress.pdf (accessed October 30, 2014)

TABLE 4.6

Trend in child TANF recipients, by race and Hispanic origin, fiscal years 2000–11

	White	Black or African American	Hispanic*
2000	25.9%	37.9%	30.6%
2001	25.6%	40.8%	27.8%
2002	26.8%	39.8%	27.4%
2003	27.0%	39.1%	27.5%
2004	27.8%	38.6%	27.1%
2005	27.7%	37.5%	28.6%
2006	28.8%	36.4%	29.2%
2007	27.6%	36.2%	30.1%
2008	26.2%	34.1%	32.5%
2009	26.1%	33.1%	33.9%
2010	27.1%	31.4%	34.7%
2011	27.1%	31.4%	34.7%

*Can be of any race.
TANF = Temporary Assistance for Needy Families.

SOURCE: Adapted from "Figure 10-G. Trend in TANF Children by Race/Ethnicity, FY 2000—FY 2011," in *Temporary Assistance to Needy Families (TANF): Tenth Report to Congress*, U.S. Department of Health and Human Services, Administration for Children and Families, Office of Family Assistance, December 12, 2013, http://www.acf.hhs.gov/sites/default/files/ofa/10th_tanf_report_congress.pdf (accessed October 30, 2014)

further shortening the lifetime maximum period to 24 months in 2011. California, which is home to approximately one-third of the entire TANF caseload, also shortened its time limit from 60 to 48 months in 2011. Schott and Pavetti suggest that "the TANF block grant has been in place long enough for us to know that families who reach time limits are among the most vulnerable families. They are far more likely than other TANF recipients to face employment barriers such as physical and mental health problems and to have lower levels of education that significantly reduce their chances of finding jobs."

SUPPLEMENTAL NUTRITION ASSISTANCE PROGRAM

In the years since the passage of the PRWORA in 1996, SNAP has increasingly functioned as a central part of the U.S. welfare system. The AFDC/TANF, formerly the centerpiece of the national safety net, contracted following welfare reform and then proved relatively unresponsive to increasing levels of poverty during the Great Recession. Unlike TANF, SNAP is not tied to work requirements, which can be especially hard to meet during times of recession and high unemployment. SNAP is also available to a wider proportion of the impoverished

TABLE 4.7

TABLE 4.8

Trend in employment rate of adult TANF recipients, fiscal years 1992–2011

	Employment rate
1992	6.6%
1993	6.9%
1994	8.3%
1995	9.3%
1996	11.3%
1997	13.2%*
1998	22.8%
1999	27.6%
2000	26.4%
2001	26.7%
2002	25.3%
2003	22.9%
2004	22.0%
2005	23.2%
2006	21.6%
2007	24.9%
2008	25.9%
2009	23.5%
2010	22.3%
2011	22.3%

TANF = Temporary Assistance for Needy Families.
AFDC = Aid to Families with Dependent Children.
*Based on AFDC data from the first three quarters of fiscal year 1997.

SOURCE: "Figure 10-H. Trend in Employment Rate of TANF Adult Recipients, FY 1992–FY 2011," in *Temporary Assistance to Needy Families (TANF): Tenth Report to Congress*, U.S. Department of Health and Human Services, Administration for Children and Families, Office of Family Assistance, December 12, 2013, http://www.acf.hhs.gov/sites/default/files/ofa/10th_tanf_report_congress.pdf (accessed October 30, 2014)

SNAP maximum benefits, 2014–15

[October 1, 2014 through September 30, 2015]

People in household	Maximum monthly allotment
1	$194
2	$357
3	$511
4	$649
5	$771
6	$925
7	$1,022
8	$1,169
Each additional person	$146

Note: SNAP = Supplemental Nutrition Assistance Program.

SOURCE: "Benefits," in *Supplemental Nutrition Assistance Program (SNAP): Eligibility*, U.S. Department of Agriculture, Food and Nutrition Service, October 2014, http://www.fns.usda.gov/snap/eligibility (accessed October 30, 2014)

population than other social welfare programs, including nonelderly adults, nondisabled adults, and childless adults.

SNAP is overseen by the USDA's Food and Nutrition Service (FNS) and is the largest of 15 food and nutrition assistance programs in the United States. SNAP issues an electronic debit card that may be used at participating U.S. grocery stores, farmers' markets, homeless meal providers, treatment centers, group homes, and other authorized outlets. According to the FNS, in *SNAP Retailer Management: 2013 Annual Report* (June 2014, http://www.fns.usda.gov/sites/default/files/snap/2013-annual-report.pdf), approximately $76 billion in SNAP benefits were redeemed in FY 2013 at 252,962 retailers and other outlets that accepted the SNAP debit card. The value of an individual household's benefits varies according to family size and income: maximum amounts for October 2014 through September 2015 ranged from $194 per month for one person to $1,169 for a family of eight. (See Table 4.8.)

SNAP has grown significantly since the 1980s, broadly tracking changes in the larger economy, in particular the number of individuals whose gross incomes are at or below 130% of poverty (the level at which one may become eligible for SNAP, depending on other eligibility variables). (See Figure 4.2.) The number of SNAP beneficiaries declined slightly between 1985 and 1989, grew rapidly during the early 1990s before peaking

in 1994, and then declined again through 2000. Growth in the number of beneficiaries has been steady since that time, rising from 17.2 million individuals in FY 2000 to 46.6 million individuals in FY 2012. Sheila Zedlewski, Elaine Waxman, and Craig Gundersen of the Urban Institute observe in *SNAP's Role in the Great Recession and Beyond* (July 2012, http://www.urban.org/Uploaded PDF/412613-SNAPs-Role-in-the-Great-Recession-and-Beyond.pdf) that "SNAP does more than combat hunger. It is an antipoverty program, a work support, a promoter of health and nutrition, and an automatic stabilizer in recessions—filling in the gaps that other safety net programs leave behind."

SNAP is without a doubt the most important program to that portion of the population that experiences food insecurity. This group includes most people living below the poverty line as well as many whose incomes are marginally higher than the poverty line.

Measuring Levels of Food Insecurity

Since 1995 the FNS and the Census Bureau have conducted annual surveys of food security, low food security (or food insecurity), and very low food security (previously called hunger). Alisha Coleman-Jensen, Christian Gregory, and Anita Singh of the USDA's Economic Research Service indicate in *Household Food Security in the United States in 2013* (September 2014, http://www.ers.usda.gov/media/1565415/err173.pdf) that the agency uses 18 questions to assess a family's level of food security (questions 11 to 18 are asked only if the household includes children aged 17 years and younger):

1. "We worried whether our food would run out before we got money to buy more." Was that often, sometimes, or never true for you in the last 12 months?

FIGURE 4.2

SNAP participants, unemployed individuals, individuals in poverty, and individuals at or below 130% of poverty, 1985–2012

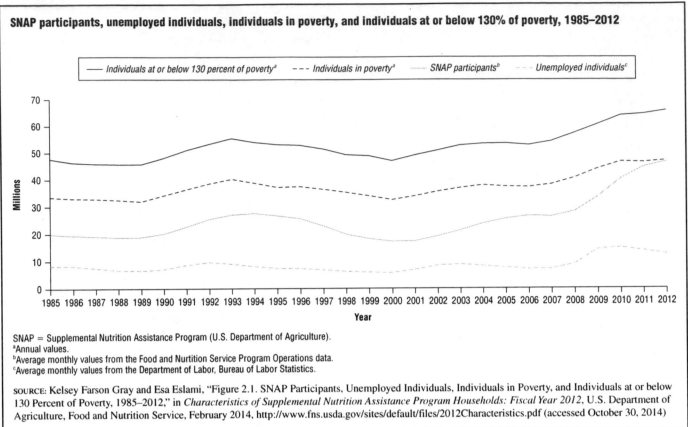

SNAP = Supplemental Nutrition Assistance Program (U.S. Department of Agriculture).
[a]Annual values.
[b]Average monthly values from the Food and Nurtition Service Program Operations data.
[c]Average monthly values from the Department of Labor, Bureau of Labor Statistics.

SOURCE: Kelsey Farson Gray and Esa Eslami, "Figure 2.1. SNAP Participants, Unemployed Individuals, Individuals in Poverty, and Individuals at or below 130 Percent of Poverty, 1985–2012," in *Characteristics of Supplemental Nutrition Assistance Program Households: Fiscal Year 2012*, U.S. Department of Agriculture, Food and Nutrition Service, February 2014, http://www.fns.usda.gov/sites/default/files/2012Characteristics.pdf (accessed October 30, 2014)

2. "The food that we bought just didn't last and we didn't have money to get more." Was that often, sometimes, or never true for you in the last 12 months?

3. "We couldn't afford to eat balanced meals." Was that often, sometimes, or never true for you in the last 12 months?

4. In the last 12 months, did you or other adults in the household ever cut the size of your meals or skip meals because there wasn't enough money for food? (Yes/No)

5. (If yes to question 4) How often did this happen— almost every month, some months but not every month, or in only one or two months?

6. In the last 12 months, did you ever eat less than you felt you should because there wasn't enough money for food? (Yes/No)

7. In the last 12 months, were you ever hungry, but didn't eat, because there wasn't enough money for food? (Yes/No)

8. In the last 12 months, did you lose weight because there wasn't enough money for food? (Yes/No)

9. In the last 12 months, did you or other adults in your household ever not eat for a whole day because there wasn't enough money for food? (Yes/No)

10. (If yes to question 9) How often did this happen— almost every month, some months but not every month, or in only one or two months?

11. "We relied on only a few kinds of low-cost food to feed our children because we were running out of money to buy food." Was that often, sometimes, or never true for you in the last 12 months?

12. "We couldn't feed our children a balanced meal, because we couldn't afford that." Was that often, sometimes, or never true for you in the last 12 months?

13. "The children were not eating enough because we just couldn't afford enough food." Was that often, sometimes, or never true for you in the last 12 months?

14. In the last 12 months, did you ever cut the size of any of the children's meals because there wasn't enough money for food? (Yes/No)

15. In the last 12 months, were the children ever hungry but you just couldn't afford more food? (Yes/No)

16. In the last 12 months, did any of the children ever skip a meal because there wasn't enough money for food? (Yes/No)

17. (If yes to question 16) How often did this happen— almost every month, some months but not every month, or in only one or two months?

18. In the last 12 months did any of the children ever not eat for a whole day because there wasn't enough money for food? (Yes/No)

Food-secure households are those that have access at all times to enough food for an active, healthy life. Low-food-security households are uncertain of having, or unable to acquire, enough food to meet basic needs at all times during the year. Households with very low food security often worry that their food will run out, report that their food does run out before they have money to buy more, cannot afford to eat balanced meals, often have adults who skip meals because there is not enough money for food, and report that they eat less than they should because of a lack of money.

In 2013, 14.3% of U.S. households reported some level of food insecurity during the year—8.7% of U.S. households reported low food security and 5.6% reported very low food security. (See Figure 4.3.) The prevalence of food insecurity in 2013 was high by historical standards, as it had been since the onset of the Great Recession in late 2007. Figure 4.4 shows that the levels of food insecurity steadily rose from 1999 to 2004, but dropped in 2005 before rising again. Then food insecurity rose precipitously between 2007 and 2008, as the effects of the Great Recession began to be felt, and remained high through 2013. The prevalence rate of very low food security followed a similar pattern, although the recession-era increase was less pronounced.

Poor and low-income households were more likely to experience food insecurity and very low food security during the year than were households with higher incomes. In 2013, 23.5% of households with an income below the poverty line reported low food security and 18.5% reported very low food security. (See Table 4.9.) Moreover, food insecurity did not decrease substantially until households reached income levels well above the

FIGURE 4.3

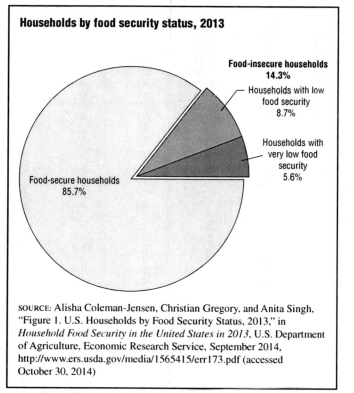

Households by food security status, 2013

Food-insecure households
14.3%

Households with low food security
8.7%

Households with very low food security
5.6%

Food-secure households
85.7%

SOURCE: Alisha Coleman-Jensen, Christian Gregory, and Anita Singh, "Figure 1. U.S. Households by Food Security Status, 2013," in *Household Food Security in the United States in 2013*, U.S. Department of Agriculture, Economic Research Service, September 2014, http://www.ers.usda.gov/media/1565415/err173.pdf (accessed October 30, 2014)

FIGURE 4.4

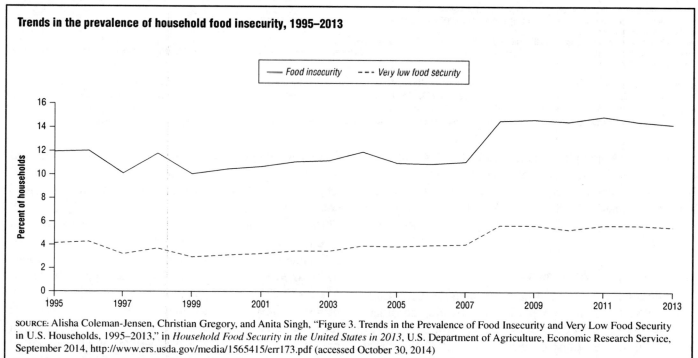

Trends in the prevalence of household food insecurity, 1995–2013

— Food insecurity - - - Very low food security

SOURCE: Alisha Coleman-Jensen, Christian Gregory, and Anita Singh, "Figure 3. Trends in the Prevalence of Food Insecurity and Very Low Food Security in U.S. Households, 1995–2013," in *Household Food Security in the United States in 2013*, U.S. Department of Agriculture, Economic Research Service, September 2014, http://www.ers.usda.gov/media/1565415/err173.pdf (accessed October 30, 2014)

TABLE 4.9

Households by food security status and selected characteristics, 2013

	Total[a]	Food secure		Food insecure All		With low food security		With very low food security	
	1,000	1,000	Percent	1,000	Percent	1,000	Percent	1,000	Percent
Category									
All households	122,579	105,070	85.7	17,509	14.3	10,664	8.7	6,845	5.6
Household composition:									
With children <18 yrs	38,486	30,979	80.5	7,507	19.5	5,240	13.6	2,267	5.9
With children <6 yrs	16,942	13,405	79.1	3,537	20.9	2,556	15.1	981	5.8
Married-couple families	24,896	21,700	87.2	3,196	12.8	2,283	9.2	913	3.7
Female head, no spouse	10,025	6,577	65.6	3,448	34.4	2,362	23.6	1,086	10.8
Male head, no spouse	3,025	2,327	76.9	698	23.1	501	16.6	197	6.5
Other household with child[b]	540	374	69.3	166	30.7	95	17.6	71	13.1
With no children <18 yrs	84,093	74,092	88.1	10,001	11.9	5,423	6.4	4,578	5.4
More than one adult	50,145	45,201	90.1	4,944	9.9	2,913	5.8	2,031	4.1
Women living alone	18,686	15,853	84.8	2,833	15.2	1,453	7.8	1,380	7.4
Men living alone	15,263	13,038	85.4	2,225	14.6	1,058	6.9	1,167	7.6
With elderly	33,244	30,354	91.3	2,890	8.7	1,866	5.6	1,024	3.1
Elderly living alone	12,341	11,232	91.0	1,109	9.0	657	5.3	452	3.7
Race/ethnicity of households:									
White, non-Hispanic	83,496	74,636	89.4	8,860	10.6	5,033	6.0	3,827	4.6
Black, non-Hispanic	15,311	11,322	73.9	3,989	26.1	2,442	15.9	1,547	10.1
Hispanic[c]	15,648	11,939	76.3	3,709	23.7	2,660	17.0	1,049	6.7
Other	8,124	7,175	88.3	949	11.7	528	6.5	421	5.2
Household income-to-poverty ratio:									
Under 1.00	14,819	8,583	57.9	6,236	42.1	3,489	23.5	2,747	18.5
Under 1.30	20,715	12,657	61.1	8,058	38.9	4,589	22.2	3,469	16.7
Under 1.85	29,809	19,429	65.2	10,380	34.8	6,089	20.4	4,291	14.4
1.85 and over	62,985	58,774	93.3	4,211	6.7	2,784	4.4	1,427	2.3
Income unknown	29,786	26,869	90.2	2,917	9.8	1,790	6.0	1,127	3.8
Area of residence:[d]									
Inside metropolitan area	102,936	88,384	85.9	14,552	14.1	8,857	8.6	5,695	5.5
In principal cities[e]	34,425	28,667	83.3	5,758	16.7	3,593	10.4	2,165	6.3
Not in principal cities	51,077	44,904	87.9	6,173	12.1	3,721	7.3	2,452	4.8
Outside metropolitan area	19,643	16,686	84.9	2,957	15.1	1,807	9.2	1,150	5.9
Census geographic region:									
Northeast	21,894	19,190	87.6	2,704	12.4	1,636	7.5	1,068	4.9
Midwest	27,097	23,420	86.4	3,677	13.6	2,198	8.1	1,479	5.5
South	46,256	38,974	84.3	7,282	15.7	4,421	9.6	2,861	6.2
West	27,331	23,486	85.9	3,845	14.1	2,408	8.8	1,437	5.3

[a]Totals exclude households for which food security status is unknown because they did not give a valid response to any of the questions in the food security scale. In 2013, these exclusions represented 433,000 households (0.4 percent of all households).
[b]Households with children in complex living arrangements, e.g., children of other relatives or unrelated roommate or boarder.
[c]Hispanics may be of any race.
[d]Metropolitan area residence is based on 2003 Office of Management and Budget delineation.
[e]Households within incorporated areas of the largest cities in each metropolitan area. Residence inside or outside of principal cities is not identified for about 17 percent of households in metropolitan statistical areas.

SOURCE: Alisha Coleman-Jensen, Christian Gregory, and Anita Singh, "Table 2. Households by Food Security Status and Selected Household Characteristics, 2013," in *Household Food Security in the United States in 2013*, U.S. Department of Agriculture, Economic Research Service, September 2014, http://www.ers .usda.gov/media/1565415/err173.pdf (accessed October 30, 2014)

poverty line. Among households under 130% of the poverty line, 22.2% experienced low food security and 16.7% experienced very low food security. Among households under 185% of poverty, 20.4% experienced low food security and 14.4% experienced very low food security.

Who Receives SNAP Benefits?

Although not all food-insecure households participate in SNAP, the two population sets overlap considerably. In *Characteristics of Supplemental Nutrition Assistance Program Households: Fiscal Year 2012* (February 2014, http://www.fns.usda.gov/sites/default/files/2012

Characteristics.pdf), Kelsey Farson Gray and Esa Eslami of the FNS provide detailed information about SNAP recipients. In FY 2012 approximately 22 million households received SNAP benefits. (See Table 4.10.) One-fifth (20.5%, or 4.5 million) of these households had zero gross income, another one-fifth (20.2%, or 4.5 million) received SSI benefits, nearly one-third (31.3%, or 6.9 million) had earned income of some kind, and approximately a quarter (23.3%, or 5.1 million) received Social Security benefits. Only 1.6 million (7.1%) SNAP households received cash assistance through TANF. Over eight out of 10 (82.5%) SNAP households contained either children, elderly individuals, or disabled nonelderly

TABLE 4.10

Characteristics of SNAP recipient households, fiscal year 2012

Households with:	All households Number (000)	Percent	Earned income Number (000)	Percent	Households with countable: Social Security Number (000)	Percent	SSI Number (000)	Percent	Zero gross income Number (000)	Percent	TANF Number (000)	Percent	General assistance Number (000)	Percent
Total[a]	**22,046**	**100.0**	**6,909**	**100.0**	**5,142**	**100.0**	**4,452**	**100.0**	**4,515**	**100.0**	**1,572**	**100.0**	**708**	**100.0**
Children	**9,984**	**45.3**	**5,063**	**73.3**	**903**	**17.6**	**1,170**	**26.3**	**1,221**	**27.0**	**1,536**	**97.7**	**123**	**17.3**
Single-adult household	5,651	25.6	2,303	33.3	530	10.3	668	15.0	859	19.0	968	61.6	81	11.4
Multiple-adult household	3,014	13.7	1,909	27.6	348	6.8	442	9.9	231	5.1	314	19.9	31	4.4
Married head household	1,857	8.4	1,298	18.8	183	3.6	206	4.6	130	2.9	154	9.8	13	1.9
Other multiple-adult Household	1,157	5.2	611	8.8	165	3.2	237	5.3	101	2.2	160	10.2	18	2.5
Children only	1,318	6.0	851	12.3	25	0.5	60	1.3	131	2.9	254	16.2	11	1.5
Elderly individuals	**3,799**	**17.2**	**242**	**3.5**	**2,625**	**51.0**	**1,488**	**33.4**	**250**	**5.5**	**40**	**2.5**	**144**	**20.4**
Living alone	3,074	13.9	129	1.9	2,142	41.7	1,213	27.2	228	5.0	1	0.0	115	16.3
Not living alone	725	3.3	114	1.6	482	9.4	275	6.2	22	0.5	39	2.5	29	4.1
Disabled nonelderly individuals	**4,409**	**20.0**	**448**	**6.5**	**2,273**	**44.2**	**3,048**	**68.5**	**0**	**0.0**	**286**	**18.2**	**135**	**19.1**
Living alone	2,567	11.6	95	1.4	1,472	28.6	1,637	36.8	0	0.0	1	0.1	73	10.3
Not Living alone	1,841	8.4	353	5.1	801	15.6	1,411	31.7	—	—	285	18.1	62	8.7
Other households[b]	**5,527**	**25.1**	**1,473**	**21.3**	**46**	**0.9**	—	—	**3,050**	**67.5**	**27**	**1.7**	**359**	**50.7**
Single-person household	5,024	22.8	1,177	17.0	32	0.6	—	—	2,950	65.3	23	1.5	343	48.4
Multi-person household	503	2.3	296	4.3	14	0.3	—	—	100	2.2	4	0.3	16	2.3
Single-person households	**11,081**	**50.3**	**1,667**	**24.1**	**3,660**	**71.2**	**2,850**	**64.0**	**3,233**	**71.6**	**93**	**5.9**	**536**	**75.6**

SSI = Social Security Income. TANF = Temporary Assistance for Needy Families.

[a]The sums of the household types do not match the numbers in the "Total" row because a household can have more than one of the characteristics.
[b]Households not containing children, elderly individuals, or disabled nonelderly individuals.
—No sample households are found in this category.

SOURCE: Kelsey Farson Gray and Esa Eslami, "Table 3.2. Household Composition and Selected Characteristics of Participating Households, Fiscal Year 2012," in *Characteristics of Supplemental Nutrition Assistance Program Households: Fiscal Year 2012*, U.S. Department of Agriculture, Food and Nutrition Service, February 2014, http://www.fns.usda.gov/sites/default/files/2012Characteristics.pdf (accessed October 30, 2014)

individuals. SNAP households with children were the largest subgroup, at nearly 10 million (45.3%) of the total, followed by the disabled nonelderly (4.4 million, or 20%) and the elderly (3.8 million, or 17.2%).

As Table 4.11 shows, the composition of SNAP participant households has changed along with the absolute number of households. In FY 1989, 7.1% of SNAP households had zero gross income and 18.3% had zero net income. Meanwhile, 41.9% of SNAP households received cash assistance through the AFDC/TANF. The dramatic increase in the percentage of SNAP households in FY 2012 with zero gross income (20.5%) and zero net income (38.4%) corresponds with a dramatic decline in the percentage of SNAP households receiving cash assistance through TANF (7.1%). Other notable changes in the composition of the SNAP caseload include an increase in the percentage of households with earned income, from 19.6% in FY 1989 to 31.3% in FY 2012; an increase in the proportion of disabled individuals,

from 9.1% to 20%; and a decline in the proportion of households with children, from 60.4% to 45.3%.

In FY 2012, 16.5 million (35.8%) of SNAP's 46 million individual recipients were non-Hispanic white, 11 million (23.8%) were African American, and 6.5 million (14.1%) were Hispanic. (See Table 4.12.) Just over 3% of SNAP individual recipients were Native American, and just under 3% were Asian American. Children under the age of 18 years accounted for 20.5 million (44.5%) of SNAP's 46 million individual recipients, and nonelderly adults accounted for 21.4 million (46.4%). These nonelderly adults were split almost equally between people aged 18 to 35 years (11 million) and people aged 36 to 59 years (10.3 million). Those aged 60 years and older accounted for 4.2 million (9%) of the SNAP individual recipient population. Except among children, where there were no statistically significant disparities by sex, females were substantially more likely to receive SNAP benefits than males. Nearly 7.2

TABLE 4.11

Characteristics of SNAP recipient households, fiscal years 1989–2012

| Time period | Total households (000) | Percentage of households with: | | | | | | | | | |
		Zero gross income	Zero net income[a]	Minimum benefit	Elderly individuals	Children	Disabled individuals[b]	AFDC/TANF	Earnings	SSI	Any noncitizen
Fiscal year 1989	7,217	7.1	18.3	7.5	19.3	60.4	9.1	41.9	19.6	20.6	9.8
Fiscal year 1990	7,811	7.4	19.3	5.0	18.1	60.3	8.9	42.0	19.0	19.6	10.3
Fiscal year 1991	8,863	8.3	20.5	4.1	16.5	60.4	9.0	40.5	19.8	18.6	11.8
Fiscal year 1992	10,059	9.6	21.9	3.6	15.4	62.2	9.5	39.5	20.2	18.4	10.4
Fiscal year 1993	10,791	9.7	23.7	4.0	15.5	62.1	10.7	39.4	20.6	19.4	11.6
Fiscal year 1994	11,091	10.2	23.8	4.5	15.8	61.1	12.5	38.1	21.4	21.4	10.7
Fiscal year 1995	10,883	9.7	25.0	4.3	16.0	59.7	18.9	38.3	21.4	22.6	10.7
Fiscal year 1996	10,552	10.2	24.9	4.5	16.2	59.5	20.2	36.6	22.5	24.1	10.5
Fiscal year 1997	9,452	9.2	22.7	6.6	17.6	58.3	22.3	34.6	24.2	26.5	8.4
Fiscal year 1998	8,246	8.8	20.8	8.3	18.2	58.3	24.4	31.4	26.3	28.1	4.3
Fiscal year 1999	7,670	8.5	20.6	9.7	20.1	55.7	26.4	27.3	26.8	30.2	6.0
Fiscal year 2000	7,335	8.4	20.1	10.9	21.0	53.9	27.5	25.8	27.2	31.7	6.4
Fiscal year 2001	7,450	9.4	22.2	11.2	20.4	53.6	27.7	23.1	27.0	31.8	5.4
Fiscal year 2002	8,201	10.5	24.3	10.7	18.7	54.1	27.0	20.9	28.0	29.5	5.2
Fiscal year 2003	8,971	12.7	27.7	7.0	17.1	55.1	22.1	17.2	27.5	26.3	5.4
Fiscal year 2004	10,069	13.1	29.7	5.9	17.3	54.3	22.7	16.2	28.5	26.8	6.2
Fiscal year 2005	10,852	13.7	30.0	5.2	17.1	53.7	23.0	14.5	29.1	26.4	6.2
Fiscal year 2006	11,313	14.1	31.0	6.2	17.9	52.0	23.1	13.0	29.5	26.8	6.1
Fiscal year 2007	11,561	14.7	31.4	6.6	17.8	51.0	23.8	12.1	29.6	27.7	5.7
Fiscal year 2008	12,464	16.2	33.6	6.7	18.5	50.6	22.6	10.6	28.9	26.2	5.6
Fiscal year 2009	14,981	17.6	36.0	4.1	16.6	49.9	21.2	9.7	29.4	23.6	5.9
Fiscal year 2010	18,369	19.7	38.3	3.8	15.5	48.7	19.8	8.0	29.9	20.9	5.9
Fiscal year 2011	20,803	20.0	39.4	4.2	16.5	47.1	20.2	7.6	30.5	20.2	5.8
Fiscal year 2012	22,046	20.5	38.4	4.8	17.2	45.3	20.0	7.1	31.3	20.2	5.7

[a]Beginning in 2004, net income is not calculated for Minnesota Family Investment Program (MFIP) households or SSI-CAP (Combined Application Project) households in states that use standardized SSI-CAP benefits.
[b]The substantial increase in 1995 and decrease in 2003 are in part of a result of the changes in the definition of a household with a disabled member. Prior to 1995, these households were defined as those with SSI and no members over age 59. In 1995, that definition changed to households with at least one member under age 65 who received SSI, or at least one member age 18 to 61 who received Social Security, veterans benefits, or other government benefits as a result of a disability. Due to changes in the SNAP QC data in 2003, the definition of a disabled household changed again, to households with either SSI income or a medical expense deduction and without an elderly person, and households with a nonelderly adult who works fewer than 30 hours a week and receives Social Security, veterans benefits, or workers' compensation.
Notes: Fiscal year analysis files were not developed for the years before 1989. The fiscal year 2003 through fiscal year 2012 estimates differ methodologically from estimates for earlier years and, in some cases, from estimates presented in reports prior to 2009. Under the current methodology, the weighting of the SNAP QC (Supplemental Nutrition Assistance Program Quality Control System) data reflects adjustments to U.S. Department of Agriculture, Food and Nutrition Service Program Operations counts of households to account for receipt of benefits in error or for disaster assistance. In addition, the weighted SNAP QC data match adjusted Program Operations counts of households, individuals, and benefit amounts. Beginning with the fiscal year 2009 report, corrected SNAP Program Operations data from Missouri was incorporated for every fiscal year from 2003 to 2008. AFDC = Aid to Families with Dependent Children. TANF = Temporary Assistance for Needy Families. SSI = Social Security Income.

SOURCE: Kelsey Farson Gray and Esa Eslami, "Table A. 26. Comparison of Participating Households with Key SNAP Household Characteristics for Fiscal Years 1989 to 2012," in *Characteristics of Supplemental Nutrition Assistance Program Households: Fiscal Year 2012*, U.S. Department of Agriculture, Food and Nutrition Service, February 2014, http://www.fns.usda.gov/sites/default/files/2012Characteristics.pdf (accessed October 30, 2014)

TABLE 4.12

Individual SNAP recipients, by selected demographic characteristic, fiscal year 2012

Participant Characteristic	Total participants		Female participants		Male participants		Prorated benefits[b]	
	Number (000)	Percent[a]	Number (000)	Percent[a]	Number (000)	Percent[a]	Dollars (000)	Percent
Total	**46,022**	**100.0**	**25,945**	**56.4**	**20,076**	**43.6**	**6,046,191**	**100.0**
Age								
Child	20,500	44.5	10,149	22.1	10,352	22.5	2,644,671	43.7
Preschool (4 or less)	6,770	14.7	3,322	7.2	3,448	7.5	916,428	15.2
School age (5–17)	13,730	29.8	6,826	14.8	6,904	15.0	1,728,243	28.6
Nonelderly adult	21,367	46.4	13,086	28.4	8,281	18.0	2,936,807	48.6
18–35	11,031	24.0	7,193	15.6	3,838	8.3	1,532,692	25.3
36–59	10,337	22.5	5,893	12.8	4,443	9.7	1,404,115	23.2
Elderly individual (60 or more)	4,154	9.0	2,710	5.9	1,444	3.1	464,713	7.7
Citizenship								
U. S. born citizen	42,697	92.8	23,939	52.0	18,758	40.8	5,597,782	92.6
Naturalized citizen	1,587	3.4	1,016	2.2	571	1.2	217,981	3.6
Refugee	338	0.7	167	0.4	171	0.4	41,644	0.7
Other noncitizen	1,400	3.0	823	1.8	577	1.3	188,784	3.1
Citizen children living with noncitizen adults[c]	3,828	8.3	1,865	4.1	1,963	4.3	533,268	8.8
Disabled nonelderly individuals	5,456	11.9	2,997	6.5	2,459	5.3	591,652	9.8
Disabled children	1,067	2.3	411	0.9	656	1.4	104,118	1.7
Disabled nonelderly adults	4,390	9.5	2,586	5.6	1,804	3.9	487,534	8.1
Nondisabled adults age 18–49 in childless households[d]	4,794	10.4	2,041	4.4	2,753	6.0	820,699	13.6
Race and Hispanic status[e]								
White, not Hispanic	16,475	35.8	9,278	20.2	7,197	15.6	2,086,097	34.5
African American, not Hispanic	10,955	23.8	6,327	13.7	4,627	10.1	1,466,391	24.3
Hispanic, any race	6,493	14.1	3,647	7.9	2,846	6.2	902,920	14.9
Asian, not Hispanic	1,258	2.7	691	1.5	567	1.2	174,417	2.9
Native American, not Hispanic	1,565	3.4	868	1.9	697	1.5	214,416	3.5
Multiple races reported, not Hispanic	129	0.3	65	0.1	63	0.1	19,311	0.3
Race unknown	9,147	19.9	5,068	11.0	4,079	8.9	1,182,638	19.6

SNAP = Supplemental Nutrition Assistance Program.

[a]Percent of all participants.

[b]Prorated benefits equal the benefits paid to households multiplied by the ratio of participants with selected characteristic to total household size.

[c]Noncitizens may be inside or outside the SNAP unit.

[d]These participants are subject to work requirements and a time limit. For this report, we incorporated a newly-developed methodology to better identify nondisabled individuals when defining these participants.

[e]Codes to allow reporting of multiple races were implemented beginning in April 2007. We have grouped the codes together to form general race and ethnicity categories. "White, not Hispanic" includes "White, not Hispanic or Latino"; "African American, not Hispanic" includes "Black or African American, not Hispanic or Latino" and "(Black or African American) and white"; "Hispanic, any race" includes "Hispanic" and "(Hispanic or Latino) with any race or race combination"; "Asian, not Hispanic" includes "Asian," "Native Hawaiian or other Pacific Islander," and "Asian and white"; "Native American, not Hispanic" includes "American Indian or Alaska Native," "(American Indian or Alaska Native) and white," and "(American Indian or Alaska Native) and (black or African American)"; "Multiple races reported, not Hispanic" includes individuals who reported more than one race and who do not fit into any previously mentioned value; and, "Race unknown" includes "Racial/ethnic data not available" and "Racial/ethnic data not recorded." Reporting of race and ethnicity is now voluntary and was missing for 20 percent of participants in fiscal year 2012. As a result, fiscal year 2012 race and ethnicity distributions are not comparable to distributions for years prior to fiscal year 2007.

SOURCE: Kelsey Farson Gray and Esa Eslami, "Table A.23. Gender and SNAP Benefits of Participants by Selected Demographic Characteristic," in *Characteristics of Supplemental Nutrition Assistance Program Households: Fiscal Year 2012*, U.S. Department of Agriculture, Food and Nutrition Service, February 2014, http://www.fns.usda.gov/sites/default/files/2012Characteristics.pdf (accessed October 30, 2014)

million women aged 18 to 35 years received SNAP benefits, compared with 3.8 million men; 5.9 million women aged 36 to 59 years received benefits, compared with 4.4 million men; and 2.7 million women aged 60 years and older received benefits, compared with 1.4 million men.

According to Zedlewski, Waxman, and Gunderson, between 2000 and 2009 SNAP was responsible for an average annual decrease in the poverty rate of 4.4% and an average annual decrease in the child poverty rate of 5.6%. More pronounced than its effects on moving individuals out of poverty, however, was SNAP's ability to ameliorate the depth and severity of poverty. Most families

do not exit poverty as a result of food assistance, but studies show that those families whose incomes are far below the poverty line see significant increases in well-being due to SNAP.

UNEMPLOYMENT COMPENSATION

The U.S. Department of Labor's Bureau of Labor Statistics (BLS), which collects data on the labor force (the total number of employed and unemployed people), defines an unemployed person as someone who is jobless, looking for a job, and available for work. Those who are jobless but not looking for work are not considered unemployed; they are classified as not being part of the labor force. The unemployment rate, as it is publicized each month in the media, is often mistakenly assumed to represent the number of jobless workers who have filed for unemployment compensation. Many workers who are jobless, actively looking for work, and available for work, however, have either come to the end of their unemployment benefits, are not eligible for benefits, or fail to apply for benefits. The BLS's official unemployment rate, then, is derived not from unemployment compensation records but from the monthly Current Population Surveys that are conducted in partnership with the Census Bureau. A separate agency of the Department of Labor, the Employment and Training Administration, maintains and publishes data on those who file claims for unemployment insurance.

Table 4.13 shows the differences, on a state-by-state basis, between total unemployment and insured unemployment. As the data indicate, the insured unemployed made up only a fraction of the total unemployed in most states during the second quarter of 2014. In California, for example, the state with the largest civilian labor force in the United States, the unemployment rate was 7.2%, but the insured unemployment rate (the unemployment rate among those qualifying for unemployment compensation) was only 3%. Larger gaps were in evidence in some states experiencing above-average unemployment, such as Georgia (7.4% total unemployed and 1.3% insured unemployed), Illinois (7.2% and 2.4%), Kentucky (7.4% and 1.6%), Michigan (7.5% and 2.1%), Mississippi (7.9% and 1.9%), Nevada (7.6% and 2.7%), and Rhode Island (7.7% and 2.5%). Although the unemployment insurance program provides a key form of support for covered workers, a large number among the total labor force do not qualify for benefits.

Who Receives Unemployment Insurance Benefits?

In 2010 the Employment and Training Administration released a wide range of reports resulting from a landmark five-year study of the unemployment compensation program. Conducted by the research firm IMPAQ International, the study assessed many aspects of the program, including the characteristics of those receiving unemployment insurance (UI) benefits, between the 1950s and 2007. In *UI Benefits Study: Recent Changes in the Characteristics of Unemployed Workers* (August 2009, http://wdr.doleta.gov), Marios Michaelides of IMPAQ International provides an overview of gender, racial, and ethnic disparities in unemployment and the collection of unemployment compensation over that period. Michaelides finds that, after controlling for industry and occupation differences:

1. women have higher unemployment rates than men but are equally likely to receive UI benefits;

2. the racial unemployment rate gap is smaller than in earlier years but remains substantial, yet nonwhites are only marginally more likely to receive UI benefits; and

3. there is a dramatic convergence in the unemployment rates between Hispanics and non-Hispanics, although Hispanics remain less likely to receive UI benefits.

Michaelides points out that although there was a sizable gap in the unemployment rate for men and women between 1953 and 1957, that gap closed by the mid-1980s, and in the period 1993 to 2007 the unemployment rate for women was slightly less than that for men. The gap in the unemployment rate for white and nonwhite workers remained wide over the course of those same 54 years, however. Between 1953 and 1967 the rate averaged 4.1% for white workers and 8.6% for nonwhite workers. By the first decade of the 21st century the gap had closed only marginally, with 4.6% of white workers and 8.2% of nonwhite workers experiencing unemployment between 2003 and 2007. Moreover, the gap had widened in the interim, peaking during the mid-1980s, when 6.5% of white workers were unemployed, compared with 14.1% of nonwhite workers. The gap between non-Hispanic workers and Hispanic workers closed more significantly: from a difference of 3.3 percentage points during the mid-1970s to a 1.4-point separation between 2003 and 2007.

The explanations for these phenomena are complex. Uneven distribution in different industries and occupations likely explains some portion of the changing dynamic between unemployment for men and unemployment for women. Some of the industries and occupations subject to the highest levels of unemployment over time, such as the construction industry, are heavily dominated by men. By contrast, women are far more likely to work in white-collar jobs than men. Thus, although women may face lingering disadvantages due to workplace bias, their overall unemployment rate has converged with that of men.

Michaelides notes that between 1992 and 2007 whites and nonwhites were approximately equally likely to work in both blue-collar and white-collar jobs, but nonwhites were far more likely to be unemployed in all occupation categories. Thus, the gap in the employment rate cannot be attributed to the differing concentrations of whites and nonwhites in various industries. Instead, social factors are likely to play a role in the disparity.

Nonwhite workers, in spite of their significantly higher rates of unemployment in almost all occupations between 1992 and 2007, were not substantially more likely than white workers to receive unemployment compensation. Michaelides states, "Since UI is only available to the experienced labor force, we might expect higher

TABLE 4.13

Unemployment compensation recipiency rates, by state, second quarter 2014

[In thousands]

State	IUR (%)	TUR (%)	Covered employment[a]	Civilian labor force	Total unemployment	Insured unemployment	
						Regular programs[b]	All programs[c]
Alabama	1.6	6.5	1,805	2,135	138.9	28.3	28.3
Alaska	3.6	6.4	305	367	23.6	11.1	11.1
Arizona	1.7	6.8	2,495	3,029	205.7	41.3	41.3
Arkansas	2.0	6.3	1,137	1,315	82.5	23.0	23.0
California	3.0	7.2	15,409	18,563	1,345.3	458.8	460.5
Colorado	1.7	5.5	2,318	2,791	152.9	37.8	37.8
Connecticut	2.8	6.7	1,642	1,878	125.1	45.4	45.4
Delaware	1.9	6.0	414	448	26.8	7.9	7.9
District of Columbia	0.9	7.1	524	370	26.4	4.6	6.5
Florida	1.3	6.0	7,539	9,606	578.9	92.7	92.7
Georgia	1.3	7.4	3,883	4,774	351.4	48.1	48.1
Hawaii	1.8	4.5	595	663	29.8	10.5	10.5
Idaho	1.6	4.6	628	780	35.7	10.1	10.1
Illinois	2.4	7.2	5,676	6,539	469.3	133.0	133.0
Indiana	1.3	5.8	2,858	3,237	188.6	35.2	35.2
Iowa	1.3	4.2	1,496	1,698	70.9	19.9	19.9
Kansas	1.5	4.7	1,333	1,500	70.8	19.7	19.7
Kentucky	1.6	7.4	1,773	2,059	151.4	27.5	27.5
Louisiana	1.1	5.1	1,883	2,115	108.0	20.3	20.3
Maine	2.0	5.6	577	708	39.8	11.6	11.6
Maryland	2.2	5.7	2,411	3,113	179.0	53.3	53.3
Massachusetts	2.4	5.5	3,288	3,496	191.3	78.5	78.5
Michigan	2.1	7.5	4,032	4,741	356.1	82.8	82.9
Minnesota	1.8	4.4	2,698	2,998	132.9	49.0	49.0
Mississippi	1.9	7.9	1,080	1,268	99.6	19.9	19.9
Missouri	1.4	6.2	2,621	3,047	189.3	37.3	37.3
Montana	1.9	4.4	428	521	23.0	8.1	8.1
Nebraska	0.9	3.4	928	1,030	35.5	7.9	7.9
Nevada	2.7	7.6	1,162	1,369	104.2	30.6	30.6
New Hampshire	1.2	4.3	620	744	32.2	7.3	7.3
New Jersey	3.1	6.5	3,831	4,497	291.6	118.0	123.1
New Mexico	2.1	6.4	767	924	59.1	16.0	18.3
New York	2.2	6.3	8,755	9,603	609.5	187.1	189.2
North Carolina	1.4	6.4	3,973	4,695	299.8	54.9	54.9
North Dakota	0.6	2.7	429	413	11.1	2.5	2.5
Ohio	1.4	5.5	5,101	5,732	316.2	69.2	69.6
Oklahoma	1.1	4.5	1,536	1,801	80.9	16.7	16.7
Oregon	2.4	6.7	1,680	1,928	129.1	39.3	39.3
Pennsylvania	2.9	5.5	5,554	6,400	353.0	158.6	158.8
Puerto Rico	3.2	13.3	923	1,145	152.7	29.0	29.0
Rhode Island	2.5	7.7	454	555	42.7	11.0	11.0
South Carolina	1.0	5.3	1,839	2,179	116.1	18.6	20.1
South Dakota	0.5	3.6	397	456	16.6	1.9	1.9
Tennessee	1.1	6.5	2,697	3,041	198.5	30.0	30.0
Texas	1.4	5.1	11,015	12,977	659.8	150.2	150.2
Utah	1.0	3.4	1,246	1,445	49.7	12.1	12.1
Vermont	1.9	3.6	299	350	12.7	5.5	5.5
Virgin Islands	2.1		37			0.8	0.8
Virginia	1.1	5.2	3,493	4,330	223.2	36.9	36.9
Washington	2.1	5.7	2,924	3,468	197.1	59.5	59.5
West Virginia	2.2	6.2	688	808	49.8	14.9	14.9
Wisconsin	2.2	5.8	2,728	3,081	178.1	59.8	59.8
Wyoming	1.1	4.0	273	312	12.4	3.1	3.1
United States	**1.9**	**6.1**	**134,200**	**155,894**	**9,472.0**	**2,557.0**	**2,572.7**

IUR = insured unemployment rate.
TUR = total unemployment rate.
[a]Wages and covered employment lag the rest of the data summary information by 6 months.
[b]Includes state Unemployment Insurance (UI), Unemployment Compensation for Federal Civilian Employees (UCFE), and Unemployment Compensation for Ex-Service Members (UCX).
[c]Includes Emergency Unemployment Compensation (EUC08) + Extended Benefits (EB).
Note: Blank cells appearing in any section of this report indicates that information is unavailable.

SOURCE: "Labor Force Information by State (Levels in Thousands) for CYQ 2014.2," in *Unemployment Insurance Data Summary*, U.S. Department of Labor, Employment and Training Administration, 2014, http://workforcesecurity.doleta.gov/unemploy/content/data_stats/datasum14/DataSum_2014_2.pdf (accessed October 31, 2014)

unemployment among experienced nonwhites to lead to greater levels of UI receipt. On the other hand, however, even in the same industries and occupations nonwhites suffer greater employment instability and lower earnings, making them less likely to meet states' minimum earnings or employment requirements. They may also be more likely to separate from jobs under circumstances that make them ineligible for benefits."

Hispanics were also overrepresented among the unemployed in the years surveyed by Michaelides and the Department of Labor. The trend of Hispanic unemployment relative to the group's presence in the overall labor force had begun to resemble that of the trend between women and men, however, in the later years considered in the study. During the 1980s and 1990s the proportion of Hispanics among the unemployed grew more rapidly than the proportion of Hispanics in the labor force, but by 2000 the proportion of Hispanics among the unemployed had stopped increasing, even though the proportion of Hispanics in the labor force continued to grow.

Hispanics' likelihood of receiving unemployment compensation has changed over time. During the early 1990s Hispanics were more likely to receive unemployment benefits than non-Hispanics, in keeping with the fact that they experienced unemployment at a higher rate than non-Hispanics. After 2000, however, non-Hispanic workers became marginally more likely to receive unemployment compensation than Hispanics, even though Hispanics were more likely to be unemployed. Michaelides hypothesizes that this gap, which is not explained by differing distributions across industries, may be attributable to unfamiliarity, on the part of some Hispanic workers, with U.S. laws regarding their eligibility for unemployment benefits.

In the years following the period studied by Michaelides and the Department of Labor, unemployment rose dramatically as a result of the Great Recession, and many of the same trends described by Michaelides persisted. Nonwhites and Hispanics continued to be overrepresented among the unemployed. As Table 4.14 shows, the 2013 unemployment rate for white male workers aged 16 years and older was 6.8% and for Asian American male workers of the same age it was 5.6%, compared with 14.2% for African American male workers and 8.8% for Hispanic male workers. Overall, women were slightly less likely to be unemployed than men in 2013, and white (6.2%) and Asian American (4.8%) women were less likely than African American (12.1%) and Hispanic (9.5%) women to be unemployed. Across all categories, single people were generally more likely to be unemployed than married people, with the never-married proportion of each demographic group experiencing dramatically higher rates of unemployment than any other subset.

SUPPLEMENTAL SECURITY INCOME

SSI is a means-tested income assistance program that was created in 1972 to provide monthly cash assistance to senior citizens, blind people, and disabled individuals. A number of requirements must be met before an applicant can receive financial benefits from SSI. First, a person must meet the program criteria for age, blindness, or disability. In addition, because SSI is a means-tested program, only those who meet the income eligibility requirements receive payments. Total SSI payments to all recipients grew steadily from $5.1 billion in 1974 to $52.1 billion in 2012. (See Table 4.15.) During that period, the number of SSI recipients grew from 3.2 million to 8.3 million. (See Table 4.16). According to the CBPP, in *Introduction to the Supplemental Security Income (SSI) Program* (February 27, 2014, http://www.cbpp.org/files/1-10-11socsec.pdf), this growth has come as a result of the program's shifting emphasis. SSI's main function during its early years was to supplement the incomes of elderly beneficiaries of the primary Social Security program, whose official name is Old Age, Survivors, and Disability Insurance (OASDI). Since that time, SSI has become a broader antipoverty program, serving as a primary resource for children and adults who are both poor and disabled.

Who Receives Supplemental Security Income Benefits?

Of the 8.3 million recipients in December 2012, approximately 7 million (85.2%) were disabled and 1.2 million (14%) were aged; less than 1% (67,725) were blind. (See Table 4.17.) Among these three eligibility categories, the disabled and the blind received the highest average monthly payments from SSI in December 2012, at $537.41 and $532.41, respectively. Aged beneficiaries (most of whom were also entitled to OASDI benefits) received an average monthly payment of $409.31. Approximately 4.9 million (58.9%) of the total number of SSI beneficiaries were between the ages of 18 and 64 years, 1.3 million (15.9%) were aged 17 years and younger, and 2.1 million (25.2%) were aged 65 years and older. Among the different age groups, children received the highest average monthly payment from SSI, due largely to an absence of other income sources.

Although SSI benefits are not enough to lift recipients out of poverty, the CBPP and others credit the program with a high level of effectiveness in lifting recipients out of extreme poverty, or 50% of the poverty line.

TABLE 4.14

Unemployed persons, by selected demographic characteristics, 2012 and 2013

[Numbers in thousands]

Marital status, race, Hispanic or Latino ethnicity, and age	Men				Women			
	Unemployed		Unemployment rates		Unemployed		Unemployment rates	
	2012	2013	2012	2013	2012	2013	2012	2013
Total, 16 years and over	**6,771**	**6,314**	**8.2**	**7.6**	**5,734**	**5,146**	**7.9**	**7.1**
Married, spouse present	2,274	1,993	4.9	4.3	1,915	1,653	5.3	4.6
Widowed, divorced, or separated	1,005	923	9.4	8.7	1,286	1,112	8.7	7.7
Never married	3,492	3,398	13.7	13.0	2,533	2,381	11.8	10.8
White, 16 years and over	4,931	4,520	7.4	6.8	3,985	3,513	7.0	6.2
Married, spouse present	1,764	1,534	4.6	4.0	1,539	1,288	5.1	4.3
Widowed, divorced, or separated	767	708	8.8	8.2	947	810	8.3	7.2
Never married	2,399	2,278	12.2	11.5	1,499	1,416	9.9	9.2
Black or African American, 16 years and over	1,292	1,236	15.0	14.2	1,252	1,192	12.8	12.1
Married, spouse present	303	265	8.4	7.4	200	202	6.8	7.1
Widowed, divorced, or separated	177	166	13.3	12.8	252	225	10.9	9.8
Never married	812	805	22.1	21.0	800	765	17.5	16.2
Asian, 16 years and over	249	253	5.8	5.6	234	195	6.1	4.8
Married, spouse present	122	116	4.4	4.1	111	95	4.8	3.9
Widowed, divorced, or separated	25	17	7.2	4.8	37	29	6.3	5.3
Never married	102	119	8.5	9.0	86	71	8.9	6.7
Hispanic or Latino ethnicity, 16 years and over	1,383	1,263	9.9	8.8	1,130	994	10.9	9.5
Married, spouse present	498	428	6.9	5.9	396	335	8.6	7.4
Widowed, divorced, or separated	166	137	9.3	7.7	243	193	11.0	8.7
Never married	720	699	14.2	13.3	491	466	13.8	12.7
Total, 25 years and over	**4,821**	**4,425**	**6.8**	**6.2**	**4,234**	**3,711**	**6.8**	**5.9**
Married, spouse present	2,207	1,931	4.9	4.3	1,815	1,558	5.1	4.4
Widowed, divorced, or separated	961	883	9.2	8.5	1,229	1,066	8.6	7.5
Never married	1,654	1,611	10.6	10.1	1,189	1,087	9.4	8.4
White, 25 years and over	3,555	3,238	6.1	5.6	3,003	2,559	6.1	5.3
Married, spouse present	1,710	1,486	4.5	3.9	1,459	1,221	4.9	4.2
Widowed, divorced, or separated	737	679	8.6	8.0	904	774	8.2	7.1
Never married	1,107	1,072	9.4	9.0	640	564	7.7	6.6
Black or African American, 25 years and over	883	809	12.3	11.1	878	833	10.6	10.0
Married, spouse present	292	256	8.3	7.3	188	185	6.6	6.7
Widowed, divorced, or separated	167	157	13.0	12.3	242	216	10.7	9.6
Never married	424	396	17.9	15.9	448	432	14.2	13.1
Asian, 25 years and over	198	190	5.0	4.6	187	156	5.4	4.3
Married, spouse present	121	115	4.4	4.1	108	92	4.7	3.9
Widowed, divorced, or separated	24	17	7.0	4.8	35	28	6.1	5.2
Never married	53	57	6.4	6.2	44	36	6.9	5.1
Hispanic or Latino ethnicity, 25 years and over	941	842	8.1	7.1	805	685	9.5	8.1
Married, spouse present	476	409	6.9	5.8	367	312	8.4	7.3
Widowed, divorced, or separated	153	131	8.9	7.6	222	184	10.5	8.5
Never married	312	302	10.6	9.7	216	189	10.8	9.2

Note: Estimates for the above race groups (white, black or African American, and Asian) do not sum to totals because data are not presented for all races. Persons whose ethnicity is identified as Hispanic or Latino may be of any race. Updated population controls are introduced annually with the release of January data.

SOURCE: "24. Unemployed Persons by Marital Status, Race, Hispanic or Latino Ethnicity, Age, and Sex," in *Labor Force Statistics from the Current Population Survey*, U.S. Department of Labor, Bureau of Labor Statistics, 2014, http://www.bls.gov/cps/cpsaat24.pdf (accessed October 31, 2014)

TABLE 4.15

Total Supplemental Security Income (SSI) payments, by eligibility category, selected years 1974–2012

[In thousands of dollars]

Year	Total	Federal Social Security Income	Federally administered state supplementation
All recipients			
1974	5,096,813	3,833,161	1,263,652
1975	5,716,072	4,313,538	1,402,534
1980	7,714,640	5,866,354	1,848,286
1985	10,749,938	8,777,341	1,972,597
1990	16,132,959	12,893,805	3,239,154
1995	27,037,280	23,919,430	3,117,850
1996	28,252,474	25,264,878	2,987,596
1997	28,370,568	25,457,387	2,913,181
1998	29,408,208	26,404,793	3,003,415
1999	30,106,132	26,805,156	3,300,976
2000	30,671,699	27,290,248	3,381,451
2001	32,165,856	28,705,503	3,460,353
2002	33,718,999	29,898,765	3,820,234
2003	34,693,278	30,688,029	4,005,249
2004	36,065,358	31,886,509	4,178,849
2005	37,235,843	33,058,056	4,177,787
2006	38,888,961	34,736,088	4,152,873
2007	41,204,645	36,884,066	4,320,579
2008	43,040,481	38,655,780	4,384,701
2009	46,592,308	42,628,709	3,963,606
2010	48,194,514	44,605,122	3,589,392
2011	49,520,299	45,999,647	3,520,652
2012	52,074,525	48,769,579	3,304,947

SOURCE: Adapted from "Table 7.A4. Total Federally Administered Payments, by Eligibility Category, Selected Years 1974–2012," in *Annual Statistical Supplement to the Social Security Bulletin, 2013*, U.S. Social Security Administration, Office of Retirement and Disability Policy, February 2014, http://www.ssa.gov/policy/docs/statcomps/supplement/2013/supplement13.pdf (accessed October 31, 2014)

TABLE 4.16

Number of recipients of SSI payments, by eligibility category, selected years 1974–2012

Month and year	Total*	Federal Social Security Income	Federally administered state supplementation	State supplementation only
All recipients				
January 1974	3,215,632	2,955,959	1,480,309	259,673
December				
1975	4,314,275	3,893,419	1,684,018	420,856
1980	4,142,017	3,682,411	1,684,765	459,606
1985	4,138,021	3,799,092	1,660,847	338,929
1990	4,817,127	4,412,131	2,058,273	404,996
1995	6,514,134	6,194,493	2,517,805	319,641
2000	6,601,686	6,319,907	2,480,637	281,779
2001	6,688,489	6,410,138	2,520,005	278,351
2002	6,787,857	6,505,227	2,461,652	282,630
2003	6,902,364	6,614,465	2,467,116	287,899
2004	6,987,845	6,694,577	2,497,589	293,268
2005	7,113,879	6,818,944	2,242,112	294,935
2006	7,235,583	6,938,690	2,268,579	296,893
2007	7,359,525	7,061,234	2,302,130	298,291
2008	7,520,501	7,219,012	2,343,599	301,489
2009	7,676,686	7,422,879	2,339,346	253,807
2010	7,912,266	7,655,667	2,385,933	256,599
2011	8,112,773	7,866,390	2,389,113	246,383
2012	8,262,877	8,039,984	2,215,840	222,893

*Total equals the sum of "Federal Social Security Income" and "State supplementation only."

SOURCE: Adapted from "Table 7.A3. Number of Recipients of Federally Administered Payments, by Eligibility Category, January 1974 and December 1975–2012, Selected Years," in *Annual Statistical Supplement to the Social Security Bulletin, 2013*, U.S. Social Security Administration, Office of Retirement and Disability Policy, February 2014, http://www.ssa.gov/policy/docs/statcomps/supplement/2013/supplement13.pdf (accessed October 31, 2014)

TABLE 4.17

Number of SSI recipients, total payments, and average monthly payment, by eligibility category, December 2012

Source of payment	Total	Category			Age		
		Aged	Blind	Disabled	Under 18	18–64	65 or older[a]
				Number of recipients			
Total	**8,262,877**	**1,156,188**	**67,725**	**7,038,964**	**1,311,861**	**4,869,484**	**2,081,532**
Federal payment only	6,047,037	619,717	43,515	5,383,805	1,077,394	3,752,903	1,216,740
Federal payment and state supplementation	1,992,947	465,726	20,856	1,506,365	233,290	1,004,546	755,111
State supplementation only	222,893	70,745	3,354	148,794	1,177	112,035	109,681
Total with—							
Federal payment	8,039,984	1,085,443	64,371	6,890,170	1,310,684	4,757,449	1,971,851
State supplementation	2,215,840	536,471	24,210	1,655,159	234,467	1,116,581	864,792
				Total payments[b] (thousands of dollars)			
Total	**4,598,945**	**474,662**	**36,865**	**4,087,418**	**858,185**	**2,870,381**	**870,380**
Federal payments	4,314,795	403,804	32,445	3,878,545	845,875	2,713,542	755,378
State supplementation	284,151	70,858	4,419	208,873	12,310	156,839	115,001
				Average monthly payment[c] (dollars)			
Total	**519.43**	**409.31**	**532.41**	**537.41**	**620.77**	**536.06**	**416.80**
Federal payments	500.29	371.17	494.06	520.73	612.68	518.39	382.15
State supplementation	121.79	130.66	175.72	118.12	48.61	129.58	131.56

[a]Includes approximately 14,000 blind and 911,300 disabled persons aged 65 or older.
[b]Includes retroactive payments.
[c]Excludes retroactive payments.
Note: Totals do not necessarily equal the sum of rounded components.

SOURCE: "Table 7.A1. Number of Recipients of Federally Administered Payments, Total Payments, and Average Monthly Payment, by Source of Payment, Eligibility Category, and Age, December 2012," in *Annual Statistical Supplement to the Social Security Bulletin, 2013*, U.S. Social Security Administration, Office of Retirement and Disability Policy, February 2014, http://www.ssa.gov/policy/docs/statcomps/supplement/2013/supplement13.pdf (accessed October 31, 2014)

CHAPTER 5
CHARACTERISTICS OF THE HOMELESS

ESTIMATING THE SIZE OF THE HOMELESS POPULATION

Lacking fixed residences and regular means of contact, the homeless population is uniquely resistant to comprehensive data collection and research. As discussed in Chapter 1, the U.S. Census Bureau's efforts to count the homeless population have been fraught with methodological problems, in large part because its decennial counts have historically failed to count unsheltered homeless people and thus underestimated the overall scope of homelessness. The Census Bureau no longer attempts to count the entire homeless population, explicitly limiting its decennial count to the occupants of emergency and transitional shelters.

The U.S. Department of Housing and Urban Development (HUD) attempts to arrive at a more complete picture of homelessness through its annual point-in-time (PIT) counts, which estimate the size of both the sheltered and unsheltered homeless populations across the country on a single night. These efforts combine actual counting of the homeless with statistical sampling, and they supply much of the data in the annual reports on homelessness that HUD has delivered to Congress since 2001. Called the *Annual Homeless Assessment Report* (*AHAR*), each annual report also includes data on shelter availability and occupancy levels. Part 1 of each *AHAR* presents PIT count and shelter availability data and is typically released before the end of the year in which the count takes place. Part 2 adds a range of longitudinal data collected in the Homeless Management Information Systems (HMIS), an electronic system that collects nationally representative information about homeless people who use shelters and subsidized housing programs over the course of a given year. The publication of part 2 typically lags well behind the publication of part 1. For example, as of February 2015 part 1 of the 2014 *AHAR* had been released, but part 2 of the 2013 *AHAR* had not.

Thus, HUD data in this chapter are focused on the 2014 PIT count as well as on the HMIS statistics from 2012, the most recent year for which the second *AHAR* installment was available.

Although HUD's PIT counts are widely considered to be the most authoritative sources of up-to-date information on the U.S. homeless population, these counts are best viewed not as comprehensive resources but as estimated snapshots of homelessness on one particular day each year. In fact, some advocacy groups maintain that even highly accurate PIT counts drastically underestimate the scope of homelessness. Defining the homeless as those who are without a home on any given night results in a much smaller number than would a definition that encompasses a larger time horizon, such as a year. Individuals are continuously joining the population of those who are homeless on any given night, and others are continuously leaving this population. If all people who are homeless during a given year were counted, the official homeless population would be much higher.

Meghan Henry et al. note in *The 2014 Annual Homeless Assessment Report (AHAR) to Congress—Part 1: Point-in-Time Estimates of Homelessness* (October 2014, https://www.HUDexchange.info/resources/documents/2014-AHAR-Part1.pdf) that between 2007 and 2014 the homeless population on any given night ranged from a high of 651,142 (2007) to a low of 578,424 (2014). In the fact sheet "How Many People Experience Homelessness?" (July 2009, http://www.nationalhomeless.org/factsheets/How_Many.html), the National Coalition for the Homeless (NCH) indicates that estimates conducted during the late 1990s, at which point PIT counts ranged from 440,000 to 842,000, suggested that the population of those who experienced homelessness during a given year was between 2.3 million and 3.5 million. Because HUD's 2007 to 2014 PIT counts fall within the range of the PIT counts cited by the NCH, it is reasonable to assume that comparable numbers of people continue to experience homelessness in the course of a year.

These figures are also consistent with HUD's HMIS data as presented in *The 2012 Annual Homeless Assessment Report (AHAR) to Congress—Volume II: Estimates of Homelessness in the United States* (September 2013, https://www.HUDexchange.info/resources/documents/2012-AHAR-Volume-2.pdf) by Claudia D. Solari, Alvaro Cortes, and Scott Brown. This installment of the *AHAR* suggests that in 2012 approximately 1.5 million people were homeless in shelters. The HMIS does not count unsheltered homeless people, but HUD's PIT count for 2012 set the percentage of the sheltered population at 62.6% (390,155) of the total homeless population (622,982) on one night in January of that year. (See Figure 1.6 in Chapter 1.) If this percentage was roughly accurate for 2012 as a whole, it can be estimated that approximately 2.4 million people experienced homelessness over the course of the year, according to the best available HUD data.

However, as discussed in Chapter 1, some homeless advocates dispute estimates of homelessness not simply on methodological grounds but on the grounds that the definition of homelessness is too narrow, leading HUD to forgo counting many people who experience homelessness by most commonsense definitions. The current official definition of homelessness, which specifies the homeless as those without a proper shelter of their own on any given night, leaves out many people who may consider themselves without a home and who do not have a home in the sense that the term is conventionally understood. Such people include prostitutes who spend their nights in different hotel rooms, children in foster care, people who have shelter that lacks essential services such as plumbing or heating, people living temporarily with relatives, and people living "doubled-up" (the Census Bureau defines doubled-up households as those including one or more person over the age of 18 years who is not enrolled in school and is not the householder, spouse, or cohabiting partner of the householder).

One source of reliable data employing a broadened definition of homelessness is the National Center for Homeless Education (NCHE), a nonprofit organization that acts as the U.S. Department of Education's technical assistance and information center on matters concerning the education of homeless youth. The NCHE collects data on homeless children in public schools rather than in the places where the homeless spend their nights, and the resulting publications count students who are living doubled-up as well as students who are living temporarily in hotels and motels. The NCHE statistics also estimate student homelessness over the course of an entire school year. Accordingly, the NCHE's yearly data releases identify a drastically larger population of homeless children than do HUD statistics, even though the NCHE does not account for infants and many preschool-aged children who are homeless (because the information is collected in schools). Because of the expanded definition of homelessness the NCHE uses, the group's data are considered superior to HUD data by many advocates for homeless children.

Several other organizations periodically collect and publish data on the homeless population. The National Alliance to End Homelessness (NAEH) collects information and analyzes HUD data in ways that enable a broader understanding of homelessness in the United States. In 2014 the NAEH released the fourth in its ongoing series of reports, *The State of Homelessness in America*, each of which makes use of and supplements HUD PIT count data, with the goal of promoting efforts to eradicate homelessness. Although the NAEH and HUD both attempt to estimate the size and characteristics of the homeless population and in many cases use the same data, the two organizations sometimes arrive at different figures and conclusions. The Association of Gospel Rescue Missions (AGRM), an association of more than 300 Christian-oriented missions that offer emergency shelter and services to the homeless, regularly undertakes its own surveys of those whom it serves. However, AGRM missions do not serve the homeless exclusively, and the portion of the homeless population that makes use of shelters with a religious orientation may differ from the homeless population at large. Thus, like the NAEH reports, the AGRM annual surveys supplement rather than rival HUD data.

AN OVERVIEW OF THE HOMELESS POPULATION

Common conceptions of the homeless usually involve images of people, including children, who live on the street permanently and sleep under bridges and in cardboard boxes. There are, of course, people in this category, but they are the minority among the homeless. HUD, the NAEH, and other experts call such people the chronically homeless. Most of the homeless are not chronically homeless but are temporarily without a residence. After some period of homelessness, during which they often occupy emergency or transitional shelters, they often find a more permanent home of their own or move in with relatives.

CHANGES IN THE SIZE OF THE HOMELESS POPULATION

Henry et al. note that an estimated 578,424 people were homeless nationwide on one night in January 2014. (See Figure 1.6 in Chapter 1.) The number of homeless people had declined considerably since 2007, when

651,142 were counted on one night in January of that year. The level of decline was minimal between 2007 and 2010, when the effects of the Great Recession (which officially lasted from December 2007 to June 2009) were being felt most severely, and then the rate of decline accelerated between 2010 and 2014.

Much of the decrease in homeless numbers since 2010 is likely a result of two factors: improving economic conditions and a concerted federal effort to reduce levels of chronic homelessness as well as homelessness among military veterans, who are disproportionately likely to be chronically homeless. In May 2009 Congress enacted the Homeless Emergency Assistance and Rapid Transition to Housing Act to combat homelessness, charging the U.S. Interagency Council on Homelessness (USICH), a consortium of 19 federal agencies and their state and local partners, to produce a national strategic plan for ending homelessness. In June 2010 the USICH released *Opening Doors: Federal Strategic Plan to Prevent and End Homelessness* (http://usich.gov/PDF/OpeningDoors_2010_FSPPreventEndHomeless.pdf), which set leadership and collaboration goals among agencies; called for increased investment in employment and health services for the homeless, as well as investment in affordable housing and permanent supportive housing (PSH; long-term housing with support services for disabled, previously homeless people); and attempted to reconfigure the ways that agencies respond to homelessness. This national strategic plan enhanced efforts already under way to combat chronic and veteran homelessness, and in 2012 the plan was amended to include a focus on educational outcomes for homeless children.

The new strategic direction in homeless policy involved a pronounced shift away from transitional housing (TH; temporary housing for formerly homeless people, usually including support services and available for up to two years) and toward PSH. As its name suggests, PSH represents a permanent intervention in the lives of homeless individuals and families, allowing even those with debilitating conditions to live on their own and stay off the streets on a long-term basis. As Figure 5.1 shows, in 2007 there were 188,636 PSH beds and 211,205 TH beds nationally. By 2014 there were 300,282 PSH beds (an increase of 111,646, or 59.2%) and 173,224 TH beds (a decrease of 37,981, or 18%). Meanwhile, the number of emergency shelter beds (beds available to homeless people on a nightly or short-term basis) also increased, from 211,451 in 2007 to 249,497 in 2014, a gain of 18%.

This shift to an emphasis on PSH represents a corresponding evolution in the thinking of homelessness experts. Robert Samuels describes this evolution in "This Group Thinks It's Found a Way to End Chronic Homelessness. It's Working" (WashingtonPost.com, June 11, 2014), which profiles Community Solutions, a nonprofit organization that has pioneered the shift to PSH in partnership with local governments (and drawing on federal funding from HUD and the U.S. Department of Veterans Affairs [VA], among other agencies). According to Samuels, groups such as Community Solutions locate

FIGURE 5.1

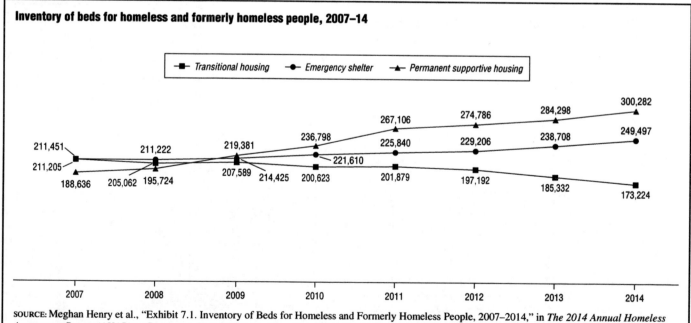

Inventory of beds for homeless and formerly homeless people, 2007–14

SOURCE: Meghan Henry et al., "Exhibit 7.1. Inventory of Beds for Homeless and Formerly Homeless People, 2007–2014," in *The 2014 Annual Homeless Assessment Report (AHAR) to Congress—Part 1: Point-in-Time Estimates of Homelessness*, U.S. Department of Housing and Urban Development, Office of Community Planning and Development, October 2014, https://www.hudexchange.info/resources/documents/2014-AHAR-Part1.pdf (accessed October 31, 2014)

the chronically homeless on the streets and place them in permanent housing immediately. Whereas TH focuses on readying the homeless to become permanently housed (often by connecting them with mental health providers, caseworkers, and employment or training opportunities), PSH focuses on housing people first and then finding case managers and counselors who can help them manage the problems that may have caused them to become homeless. Samuels explains, "The homeless person never has to leave the apartment, so long as they keep the place clean or follow whatever plan has been decided by the case manager. Government pays the rent. The group charts the success of keeping the formerly homeless off the streets at about 80 percent."

The PSH inventory targeted to chronically homeless people increased by 149.4% between 2007 and 2014, from 37,807 beds to 94,282 beds. (See Figure 5.2.) During this same period the chronically homeless population declined by 30%, from 120,488 to 84,291. (See Figure 5.3.)

These successes in combating chronic homelessness have not been duplicated among the majority of the homeless population, whose fate is more often tied to trends in the broader economy than to disabilities and mental health or substance abuse issues, as is often the case with the chronically homeless. Although improving economic conditions between 2010 and 2014 likely drove some portion of the overall reductions in homelessness, unemployment declined only gradually through 2014, and the poverty rate barely changed at all during these years. (See Table 1.5 [unemployment rates] and Figure 1.1 [poverty rates] in Chapter 1.) In *The State of Homelessness in America 2014* (May 2014, http://b.3cdn.net/naeh/d1b106237807ab260f_qam6ydz02.pdf), the NAEH states, "The overall economy is starting to recover, but this improvement does not appear to be penetrating lower-income populations. The pool of people at risk of homelessness, those in poverty, those living with friends and family, and those paying over half of their income for housing, has remained high despite improvements in unemployment and the overall economy."

The AGRM makes a similar point in "Stalemate in War on Homelessness" (November 12, 2014, http://www.agrm.org/NewsBot.asp?MODE=VIEW&ID=661), noting that in an October 2014 survey of more than 20,000 people being served at 135 North American rescue missions, 37% of respondents reported that they had never been homeless before. (See Table 5.1.) People who find themselves homeless for the first time are typically members of low-income households (often families) that experience phenomena such as job loss, illness, and increased housing costs. In times of low unemployment, adequate wages, and affordable housing costs, such people can more easily avoid homelessness. The percentage of those experiencing homelessness for the first time in 2014 remained unchanged since 2013 and was up slightly since 2011. This suggests that the economic trends driving homelessness for most of those who experience it had not been significantly ameliorated since the end of the Great Recession.

FIGURE 5.2

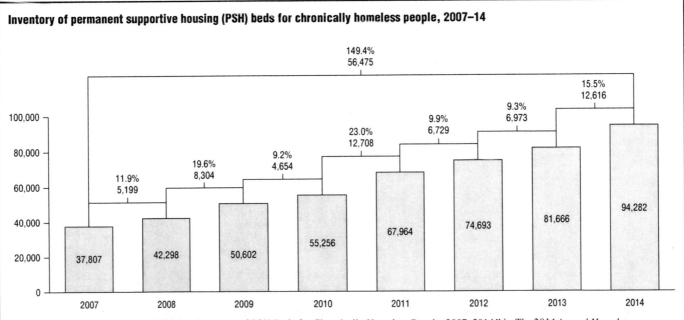

Inventory of permanent supportive housing (PSH) beds for chronically homeless people, 2007–14

SOURCE: Meghan Henry et al., "Exhibit 7.5. Inventory of PSH Beds for Chronically Homeless People, 2007–2014," in *The 2014 Annual Homeless Assessment Report (AHAR) to Congress—Part 1: Point-in-Time Estimates of Homelessness*, U.S. Department of Housing and Urban Development, Office of Community Planning and Development, October 2014, https://www.hudexchange.info/resources/documents/2014-AHAR-Part1.pdf (accessed October 31, 2014)

FIGURE 5.3

Estimates of chronically homeless people, by sheltered status, 2007–14

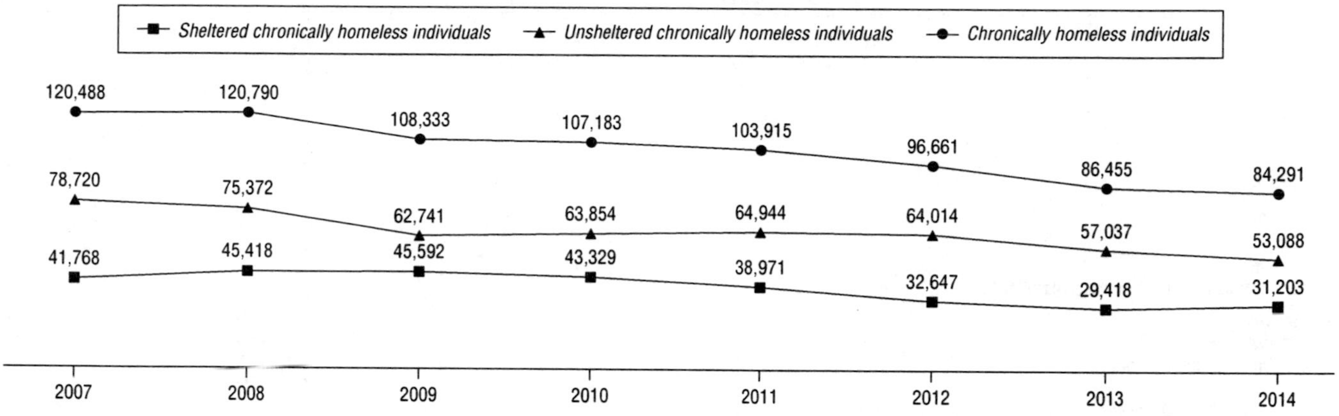

Note: The point-in-time (PIT) estimates from 2007–2013 are slightly lower than estimates reported in past Annual Homeless Assessment Reports (AHARs). The reduction reflects an adjustment to the estimates of unsheltered homeless individuals submitted by the Los Angeles City and County Continuum of Care. The adjustment removed: 3,345 chronically homeless individuals from 2007 and 2008; 2,584 chronically homeless individuals in 2009 and 2010; 3,233 chronically homeless individuals in 2011 and 2012; and 6,138 chronically homeless individuals form 2013.

SOURCE: Meghan Henry et al., "Exhibit 6.1. Estimates of Chronically Homeless Individuals, by Sheltered Status, 2007–2014," in *The 2014 Annual Homeless Assessment Report (AHAR) to Congress—Part 1: Point-in-Time Estimates of Homelessness*, U.S. Department of Housing and Urban Development, Office of Community Planning and Development, October 2014, https://www.hudexchange.info/resources/documents/2014-AHAR-Part1.pdf (accessed October 31, 2014)

Individuals and Families

A majority of the homeless people counted on one night in January 2014 were living alone as homeless individuals rather than as part of a family. Such individuals accounted for 362,163 (62.6%) of the total homeless population of 578,424. (See Figure 5.4.) Homeless individuals were more likely to be sheltered than unsheltered (209,148, or 57.7%, occupied shelters at the time of HUD's PIT count), but individuals constituted most of the total unsheltered homeless population. As Figure 1.6 in Chapter 1 shows, there were 177,373 unsheltered homeless people in 2014, and as Figure 5.4 shows, 153,015 (86.3%) of these unsheltered people were living as individuals. The number of unsheltered homeless individuals declined dramatically between 2007 and 2014, however, likely as a result of increasing access to emergency shelter beds and PSH beds for the chronically homeless, as discussed earlier. By contrast, the number of sheltered homeless individuals remained steady over this period, fluctuating between a low of 199,159 (2012) and a high of 215,995 (2009). The 2014 sheltered individual population of 209,148 represented progress in the sense that a higher proportion of homeless individuals were now sheltered rather than living in locations such as cars, abandoned buildings, and under bridges. However, the fact that the sheltered population was not falling points to the challenges that remain in eradicating homelessness.

As Figure 5.5 shows, an estimated 216,261 (37.4%) of the total homeless population on one night in January 2014 consisted of people living in families. Homeless families were much more likely to be sheltered than were homeless individuals: 191,903 (88.7%) were sheltered and only 24,358 (11.3%) were unsheltered. Homeless families are also only rarely among the chronically homeless. According to Henry et al., 15,143 homeless people in families, or 7% of all homeless people in families, were chronically homeless, and 9,362 (61.8%) of these people lived in shelters. Children accounted for 59.2% of all homeless people in families, 60.4% of sheltered homeless people in families, and 49.8% of unsheltered homeless people in families. (See Figure 5.6.)

Between 2007 and 2014 the number of homeless people living in families declined less dramatically than the number of homeless individuals. From a population of 235,545 in 2007, the number of people in homeless families fell to 216,261 by 2014, a decline of 8.2%. (See Figure 5.5.) Moreover, this decline was entirely attributable to a decline in the unsheltered portion of the homeless family population, which fell from 57,217 to 24,358, while the sheltered homeless family population rose from 178,328 to 191,903. As with the homeless individual population, the movement of families from unsheltered to sheltered status was something of a mixed achievement. Sheltered families typically enjoy better living conditions than unsheltered ones, but persistently high levels of overall family homelessness were cause for continuing concern.

Homeless Children and Youth

Homeless children have always received special attention from the public and welfare agencies. In the

TABLE 5.1

Demographic overview of the homeless population served by the Association of Gospel Rescue Missions, 2010–14

	2014	2013	2012	2011
Gender (of total mission population)				
Male	73%	72%	72%	74%
Female	27%	28%	28%	26%
Age groups (of total mission population)				
Under 18	6%	6%	7%	7%
18–25	9%	9%	9%	9%
26–35	18%	18%	18%	18%
36–45	22%	22%	23%	25%
46–65	42%	41%	39%	39%
65+	4%	4%	3%	3%
Race/ethnic groups (of total mission population)				
White/Caucasian	49%	49%	50%	50%
Black or African American	34%	32%	34%	34%
Hispanic, Latin, or Spanish origin	9%	11%	10%	9%
Asian	1%	1%	1%	1%
American Indian or Alaskan Native	3%	3%	2%	2%
Native Hawaiian or other Pacific Islander	1%	0%	0%	0%
Other or 2+ races	2%	4%	3%	3%
Single individuals (of total mission population)	86%	82%	81%	86%
Women/children/families (of family units identified)				
Couples	20%	19%	23%	20%
Women with children	54%	52%	51%	52%
Men with children	11%	12%	11%	12%
Intact families	15%	17%	16%	17%
Veteran status (of total mission population)				
Veterans (male)	11%	11%	13%	13%
Veterans (female)	2%	1%	2%	1%
Homeless status (of total mission population)				
Not currently homeless	16%	19%	17%	17%
Currently homeless	84%	81%	83%	83%
Of currently homeless:				
Less than 3 months	31%	30%	30%	31%
3 to 6 months	20%	21%	24%	21%
6 months to 1 year	20%	19%	20%	20%
More than 1 year	29%	30%	27%	27%
Never before homeless	37%	37%	34%	35%
Homeless once previously	24%	24%	26%	24%
Homeless twice previously	16%	16%	17%	17%
Homeless three-plus times previously	23%	23%	22%	24%
Other information (of total mission population)				
Struggles with mental illness	32%	31%	30%	30%
Victim of physical violence in last 12 months	20%	19%	24%	21%
Prefer spiritual emphasis in services	81%	79%	81%	80%
Comes daily to the mission	84%	81%	84%	82%

SOURCE: "AGRM's 2014 Snapshot Survey: Homeless Statistical Comparison," Association of Gospel and Rescue Missions, 2014, http://www.agrm.org/agrm/2014_Snapshot_Survey_Yearly_Comparison.asp (accessed December 4, 2014)

terminology of previous centuries, children are considered "worthy poor" (i.e., "worthy" of help from society) because they have no control over their financial circumstances. Homeless youth (those aged 18 to 24 years) are also often considered a population of particular concern. Both children and youth who find themselves homeless are considered at enhanced risk of sexual and physical abuse and other forms of violence. Additionally, the privations and stresses of homelessness can traumatize and scar young people in irreversible ways, leaving them more likely to be poor or homeless as adults.

HUD PIT COUNT ESTIMATES. An estimated 135,701 children under the age of 18 years were homeless on one night in January 2014, 94.4% of whom were living in families, 4.6% of whom were living as unaccompanied individuals, and 1% of whom were living in multichild families in which no member of the family was over the age of 18 years. (See Figure 5.7.) Meanwhile, young people aged 18 to 24 years were much more likely to live unaccompanied than in families. Of the estimated 58,601 homeless youth, 33.6% lived in families and 66.4% lived as unaccompanied individuals. Unaccompanied children and youth are among the most vulnerable of all homeless people, and their vulnerability is exacerbated by their disproportionate likelihood of living in unsheltered locations. As Figure 5.8 shows, only 40.7% of unaccompanied children and 54.4% of unaccompanied youth were counted in sheltered locations in January 2014. By contrast, 57.7% of homeless individuals and

FIGURE 5.4

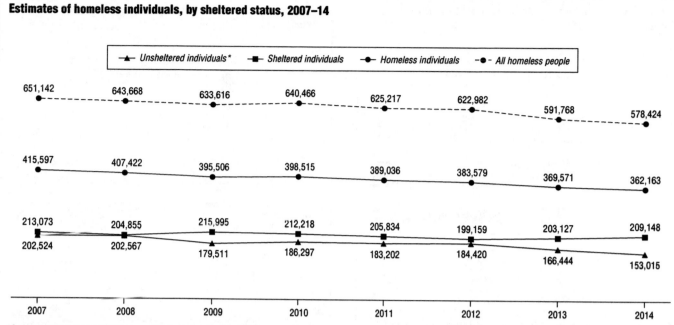

Estimates of homeless individuals, by sheltered status, 2007–14

*Counts for unsheltered individuals are labeled below the trend line.

Note: The point-in-time (PIT) estimates from 2007–2013 are slightly lower than estimates reported in past Annual Homeless Assessment Reports (AHARs). The reduction reflects an adjustment to the estimates of unsheltered homeless individuals submitted by the Los Angeles City and County Continuum of Care. The adjustment removed: 7,780 individuals from 2007 and 2008; 9,451 individuals in 2009 and 2010; 10,800 individuals in 2011 and 2012; and 18,274 individuals from 2013. This change applies to all PIT estimates in this section.

SOURCE: Meghan Henry et al., "Exhibit 2.1. Estimates of Homeless Individuals, by Sheltered Status, 2007–2014," in *The 2014 Annual Homeless Assessment Report (AHAR) to Congress—Part 1: Point-in-Time Estimates of Homelessness*, U.S. Department of Housing and Urban Development, Office of Community Planning and Development, October 2014, https://www.hudexchange.info/resources/documents/2014-AHAR-Part1.pdf (accessed October 31, 2014)

FIGURE 5.5

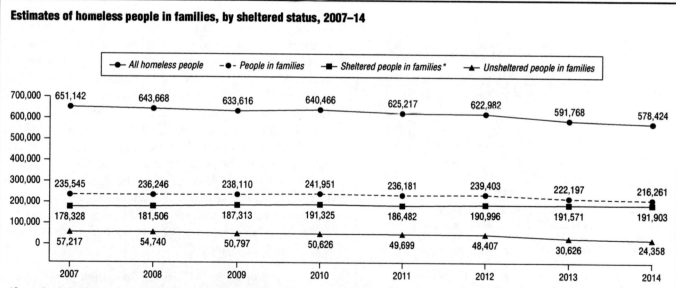

Estimates of homeless people in families, by sheltered status, 2007–14

*Counts for sheltered people in families are labeled below the trend line.

Note: The point-in-time (PIT) estimates from 2007–2013 are slightly lower than estimates reported in past Annual Homeless Assessment Reports (AHARs). The reduction reflects an adjustment to the estimates of unsheltered homeless individuals submitted by the Los Angeles City and County Continuum of Care. The adjustment removed 12,966 homeless people in families and 5,073 homeless family households in 2007 and 2008. This change applies to all PIT estimates in this section.

SOURCE: Meghan Henry et al., "Exhibit 3.1. Estimates of Homeless People in Families, by Sheltered Status, 2007–2014," in *The 2014 Annual Homeless Assessment Report (AHAR) to Congress—Part 1: Point-in-Time Estimates of Homelessness*, U.S. Department of Housing and Urban Development, Office of Community Planning and Development, October 2014, https://www.hudexchange.info/resources/documents/2014-AHAR-Part1.pdf (accessed October 31, 2014)

FIGURE 5.6

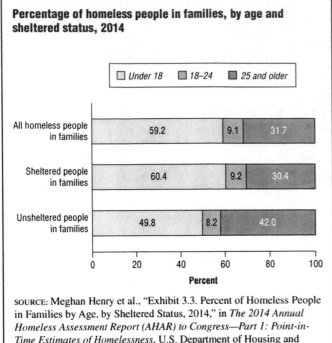

Percentage of homeless people in families, by age and sheltered status, 2014

SOURCE: Meghan Henry et al., "Exhibit 3.3. Percent of Homeless People in Families by Age, by Sheltered Status, 2014," in *The 2014 Annual Homeless Assessment Report (AHAR) to Congress—Part 1: Point-in-Time Estimates of Homelessness*, U.S. Department of Housing and Urban Development, Office of Community Planning and Development, October 2014, https://www.hudexchange.info/resources/documents/2014-AHAR-Part1.pdf (accessed October 31, 2014)

FIGURE 5.7

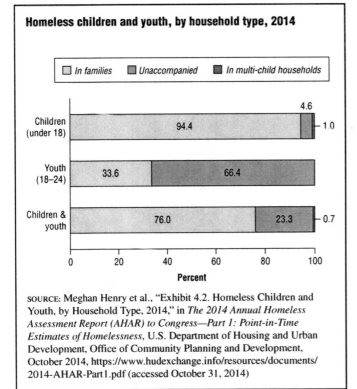

Homeless children and youth, by household type, 2014

SOURCE: Meghan Henry et al., "Exhibit 4.2. Homeless Children and Youth, by Household Type, 2014," in *The 2014 Annual Homeless Assessment Report (AHAR) to Congress—Part 1: Point-in-Time Estimates of Homelessness*, U.S. Department of Housing and Urban Development, Office of Community Planning and Development, October 2014, https://www.hudexchange.info/resources/documents/2014-AHAR-Part1.pdf (accessed October 31, 2014)

69.3% of the total homeless population were counted in sheltered locations.

NCHE AND RELATED ESTIMATES. The NCHE collects estimates of homeless children from public school districts

FIGURE 5.8

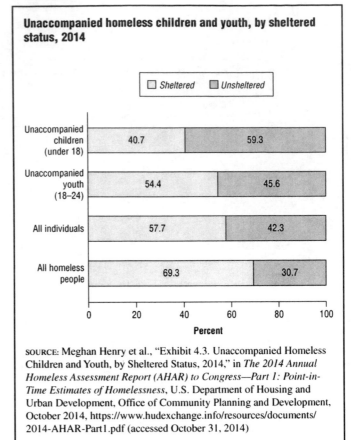

Unaccompanied homeless children and youth, by sheltered status, 2014

SOURCE: Meghan Henry et al., "Exhibit 4.3. Unaccompanied Homeless Children and Youth, by Sheltered Status, 2014," in *The 2014 Annual Homeless Assessment Report (AHAR) to Congress—Part 1: Point-in-Time Estimates of Homelessness*, U.S. Department of Housing and Urban Development, Office of Community Planning and Development, October 2014, https://www.hudexchange.info/resources/documents/2014-AHAR-Part1.pdf (accessed October 31, 2014)

and local education agencies. The data exclude infants as the HUD estimates do not, but the data include some children of preschool age. Also unlike HUD, the NCHE counts as homeless those students who are living doubled-up and in hotels and motels. Because it counts homeless students over the course of a school year and because it counts those who are doubled-up and living in hotels and motels, the NCHE arrives at a much larger estimate of the number of homeless children than do the HUD PIT counts. However, in "Record Number of Homeless Children Enrolled in US Public Schools" (CSMonitor.com, September 23, 2014), Amanda Paulson indicates that the NCHE data are widely believed to undercount the school-aged population of homeless children. Besides the likelihood that a sizable proportion of homeless children (especially teenagers) are not enrolled in school, it is also likely that some homeless children are not identified as such by school staff.

According to the NCHE, in *Education for Homeless Children and Youth: Consolidated State Performance Report Data, School Years 2010–11, 2011–12, and 2012–13* (September 2014, http://center.serve.org/nche/downloads/data-comp-1011-1213.pdf), nearly 1.3 million homeless children were enrolled in public schools during the 2012–13 school year. (See Table 5.2.) This total was up considerably from the previous school year, when the

NCHE counted fewer than 1.2 million homeless children in public schools, and it was nearly double the 679,724 homeless students during the 2006–07 school year, prior to the onset of the Great Recession, according to the NCHE in *Education for Homeless Children and Youth Program: Analysis of Data* (July 2008, http://center.serve .org/nche/downloads/data_comp_03-06.pdf).

In *America's Youngest Outcasts: A Report Card on Child Homelessness* (November 2014, http://new.home lesschildrenamerica.org/mediadocs/280.pdf), Ellen L. Bassuk et al. of the National Center on Family Homelessness supplement the 2012–13 NCHE data with an analysis of 2013 Census Bureau data to estimate the size of the child homeless population that is uncounted by the NCHE and to combine that with the NCHE counts. The researchers calculate that 2.5 million children, or one out of every 30 U.S. children, were homeless over the course of that year.

Doubled-up housing arrangements accounted for 75% (936,441) of total homelessness among public school students and another 6% (70,458) of homeless students lived in hotels or motels. (See Table 5.3.) Many advocates for homeless children argue that children who are doubled-up or living in hotels and motels experience all of the instability and emotional turmoil as those children that HUD classifies as homeless. According to this argument, these children are at a high risk of becoming homeless adults if they are not provided with assistance during their crucial childhood and adolescent years. Bipartisan legislation introduced in both houses of Congress in 2014 aimed to change the HUD definition of homelessness to include youth living in such circumstances. Rita Price reports in "Congress May Expand Who Counts as Homeless" (Dispatch.com, August 6, 2014) that such legislation was a longstanding priority of advocacy groups such as the National Association for the Education of Homeless Children and Youth. Critics of the proposed legislation included advocates for the homeless population as a whole, such as the NAEH, whose leadership felt the bill would expand the definition of homelessness to an impractical extent, given that the bill did not include any increased funding for the HUD programs that serve the homeless. The 113th Congress (2013 to 2015) took no action on the bill, and it was reintroduced during the 114th Congress (2015 to 2017) in January 2015.

Regardless of their shelter situation, homeless children have less than optimal conditions for educational achievement. According to Bassuk et al., studies suggest that homeless children are sick more frequently than other children and they experience significant mental distress as a result of worries about whether they will continue to have food to eat and shelter at night and what will happen to their family. As a result, such children are more likely to demonstrate developmental delays and mental health problems that require clinical intervention. They also miss school more frequently than other children, are more often required to repeat grades, and are more likely to drop out of school.

LESBIAN, GAY, BISEXUAL, AND TRANSGENDER TEENS. In "The Forsaken: A Rising Number of Homeless Gay Teens Are Being Cast out by Religious Families"

TABLE 5.2

Homeless students enrolled in public schools, by subgroup, school year 2012–13

Homeless students enrolled	All homeless students	Unaccompanied youth	Migratory children/ youths	Children with disabilities (IDEA)	LEP students
Number	1,258,182	75,940	16,490	200,950	179,249
Percent	100	6	1	16	14

Note: The Individuals with Disabilities Education Act is abbreviated as IDEA. Limited English proficient is abbreviated as LEP. Subgroup categories are not mutually exclusive. It is possible for homeless students to be counted in more than one subgroup; i.e., an unaccompanied homeless youth may simultaneously be a migrant, LEP student who receives special education services.

SOURCE: "Table 4. Subgroups of Homeless Students Enrolled in LEAs with and without McKinney-Vento Subgrants (1.9.1.3), Percent of Total Homeless Students Enrolled, SY 2012–13 (Initial Data Collection)," in *Education for Homeless Children and Youth: Consolidated State Performance Report Data, School Years 2010–11, 2011–12, and 2012–13*, National Center for Homeless Education, September 2014, http://center.serve.org/nche/downloads/data-comp-1011-1213.pdf (accessed October 31, 2014)

TABLE 5.3

Homeless student population, by primary nighttime residence, school years 2010–11, 2011–12, and 2012–13

Type of residence	School year 2010–11		School year 2011–12		School year 2012–13	
	Number of students	Percent of residence	Number of students	Percent of residence	Number of students	Percent of residence
Shelters	187,675	18	180,541	15	192,391	16
Doubled-up	767,968	72	879,390	75	936,441	75
Unsheltered	51,897	5	41,575	4	41,635	3
Hotels/motels	55,388	5	64,930	6	70,458	6
Total	**1,062,928**	**100**	**1,166,436**	**100**	**1,240,925**	**100**

SOURCE: "Table 3. Primary Nighttime Residence of Homeless Students Enrolled in LEAs with and without McKinney-Vento Subgrants (1.9.1.2)," in *Education for Homeless Children and Youth: Consolidated State Performance Report Data, School Years 2010–11, 2011–12, and 2012–13*, National Center for Homeless Education, September 2014, http://center.serve.org/nche/downloads/data-comp-1011-1213.pdf (accessed October 31, 2014)

(RollingStone.com, September 3, 2014), Alex Morris reports that lesbian, gay, bisexual, and transgender (LGBT) young people account for only about 5% of the youth population, but they make up an estimated 40% of the homeless youth population. Research suggests that the number of homeless LGBT teens is rising and that a primary factor driving the phenomenon is the rejection such teens face in religious families. Buoyed by broad societal acceptance of LGBT lifestyles and by the ability to connect to like-minded people online and through social media, LGBT teens are more likely than in the past to come out to their family and friends while still dependent on their parents for housing and financial support. However, in many cases the societal acceptance of LGBT people does not extend to the extremely religious, and religious parents often feel their beliefs require them to kick their children out of their home and to cut off financial support for them. Morris explains, "Tragically, every step forward for the gay-rights movement creates a false hope of acceptance for certain youth, and therefore a swelling of the homeless-youth population." Carl Siciliano, the founder of New York City's Ali Forney Center for homeless LGBT youth, told Morris that in the months after LGBT couples in New York won the right to marry, the number of homeless youth in need of shelter rose 40%.

Military Veterans

Homeless veterans are another subpopulation of particular concern to many Americans and policy makers. Many ordinary people and policy makers believe that some level of gratitude and support is owed to those who serve the country in wartime. Additionally, the trauma of combat and the difficulty of reintegrating into civilian life leave veterans at an increased risk of homelessness relative to the general population.

HUD and the VA work together to generate accurate estimates of the population of homeless veterans for each annual PIT count, and their estimates of veteran homelessness are believed to be among the most accurate estimates of any subpopulation in each *AHAR*. The homeless veteran population on a single night in January 2014 was an estimated 49,933 (11.3% of the adult homeless population). (See Table 5.4.) Veterans accounted for approximately the same proportion of both the sheltered and unsheltered adult population. Almost all homeless veterans experienced homelessness as individuals, and 90% of homeless veterans were men.

Combating both homelessness and chronic homelessness among veterans has been a concerted focus of HUD, the VA, and the other government agencies associated with the USICH. Homeless veterans, who have been disproportionately represented among the chronic homeless

TABLE 5.4

Proportion of homeless adults that are veterans, by sheltered status, 2014

	# of homeless veterans	# of homeless adults	% of homeless adults who are veterans
Total	49,933	442,723	11.3
Sheltered	32,048	281,760	11.4
Unsheltered	17,885	160,963	11.1

SOURCE: Meghan Henry et al., "Exhibit 5.2. Proportion of Homeless Adults That Are Veterans, by Sheltered Status, 2014," in *The 2014 Annual Homeless Assessment Report (AHAR) to Congress—Part 1: Point-in-Time Estimates of Homelessness*, U.S. Department of Housing and Urban Development, Office of Community Planning and Development, October 2014, https://www.hudexchange.info/resources/documents/2014-AHAR-Part1.pdf (accessed October 31, 2014)

in most 21st-century PIT counts, have been a primary target of the efforts to expand the availability of PSH and to reduce the waiting and red tape previously associated with subsidized temporary and permanent housing. As a result of this and other efforts by USICH agencies and numerous private nonprofit organizations, the population of homeless veterans has fallen dramatically since 2009.

In 2009, at the height of the Great Recession, there were an estimated 74,050 homeless veterans, and the following year saw a slight uptick in the population of homeless veterans, to 74,770. (See Figure 5.9.) Following the 2010 release of the USICH strategic plan, the numbers of homeless veterans declined steadily, to 65,645 in 2011, 60,769 in 2012, 55,779 in 2013, and 49,933 in 2014. Overall, the number of homeless veterans declined by 24,117 (32.6%) between 2009 and 2014. (See Table 5.5.) Initiatives to end veteran homelessness found particular success with unsheltered veterans, whose numbers decreased by 12,756 (41.6%) during this period.

Demographic Characteristics of the Sheltered Homeless

HUD's yearly PIT counts provide only limited insight into the demographic characteristics of the homeless population. The agency's HMIS data, which are presented in part 2 of each year's *AHAR*, offer the most reliable demographic information about the homeless population. However, as noted earlier, this information is at any given moment less up-to-date than PIT count data, and it only pertains to the sheltered homeless population.

GENDER. According to Solari, Cortes, and Brown, between 2007 and 2012 the sheltered homeless population was disproportionately male. As Figure 5.10 shows, 63.2% of the homeless adult population was male in 2012, whereas males accounted for 48.6% of the U.S. adult population. These numbers had varied only slightly since 2007. Solari, Cortes, and Brown note that this gender imbalance is particularly striking when considered

FIGURE 5.9

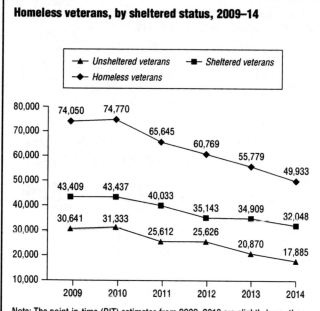

Homeless veterans, by sheltered status, 2009–14

Note: The point-in-time (PIT) estimates from 2009–2013 are slightly lower than estimates reported in past Annual Homeless Assessment Reports (AHARs). The reduction reflects an adjustment to the estimates of unsheltered homeless veterans submitted by the Los Angeles City and County CoC. The adjustment removed the following numbers of homeless veterans: 1,559 veterans in 2009 and 2010; 1,850 veterans in 2011 and 2012; and 2,241 veterans from 2013. Additionally, the Phoenix/Mesa/Maricopa County Regional CoC updated its 2013 sheltered count of homeless veterans from 174 to 388. These changes apply to all estimates in this section.

SOURCE: Meghan Henry et al., "Exhibit 5.1. Estimates of Homeless Veterans, by Sheltered Status, 2009–2014," in *The 2014 Annual Homeless Assessment Report (AHAR) to Congress—Part 1: Point-in-Time Estimates of Homelessness*, U.S. Department of Housing and Urban Development, Office of Community Planning and Development, October 2014, https://www.hudexchange.info/resources/documents/2014-AHAR-Part1.pdf (accessed October 31, 2014)

FIGURE 5.10

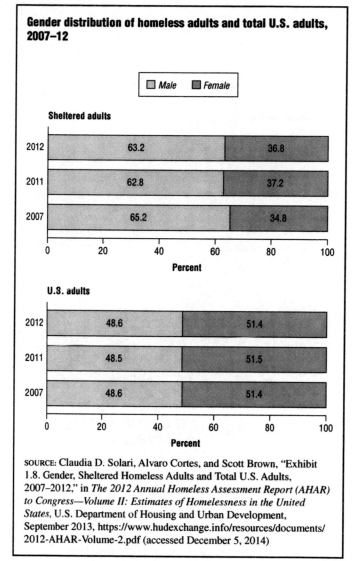

Gender distribution of homeless adults and total U.S. adults, 2007–12

SOURCE: Claudia D. Solari, Alvaro Cortes, and Scott Brown, "Exhibit 1.8. Gender, Sheltered Homeless Adults and Total U.S. Adults, 2007–2012," in *The 2012 Annual Homeless Assessment Report (AHAR) to Congress—Volume II: Estimates of Homelessness in the United States*, U.S. Department of Housing and Urban Development, September 2013, https://www.hudexchange.info/resources/documents/2012-AHAR-Volume-2.pdf (accessed December 5, 2014)

TABLE 5.5

Change in the numbers of homeless veterans, by sheltered status, 2009–14

	2013–2014		2009–2014	
	#	%	#	%
Homeless veterans	−5,846	−10.5	−24,117	−32.6
Sheltered	−2,861	−8.2	−11,361	−26.2
Unsheltered	−2,985	−14.3	−12,756	−41.6

SOURCE: Meghan Henry et al., "Exhibit 5.3. Change in the Number of Homeless Veterans, by Sheltered Status, 2009–2014," in *The 2014 Annual Homeless Assessment Report (AHAR) to Congress—Part 1: Point-in-Time Estimates of Homelessness*, U.S. Department of Housing and Urban Development, Office of Community Planning and Development, October 2014, https://www.hudexchange.info/resources/documents/2014-AHAR-Part1.pdf (accessed October 31, 2014)

in the context of the population that experiences poverty in a typical year. The population living below the poverty line in 2012 was 58% female.

The gender breakdown among the sheltered homeless varied dramatically among the homeless individual and family subpopulations, with men much more likely to be living as homeless individuals in 2012 and women much more likely to be living in homeless families. According to Solari, Cortes, and Brown, 72.3% of sheltered homeless individuals were male, whereas 77.9% of sheltered adults in homeless families were female.

AGE. In 2012 over one-third (35%) of sheltered homeless people were aged 31 to 50 years, 23.5% were aged 18 to 30 years, and 22.6% were children under the age of 18 years. (See Figure 5.11.) Adults aged 51 to 61 years accounted for 15.6% of the sheltered homeless population and adults aged 62 years and older accounted for a very small proportion of the sheltered homeless population, at 3.2%. Elderly adults' access to Social Security, Medicare, and other benefits was likely a key factor in the relative improbability of experiencing homelessness past the age of 62.

However, these proportions varied dramatically by subpopulation. Solari, Cortes, and Brown note that adults aged 31 to 50 years (45.2%) constituted the largest group

FIGURE 5.11

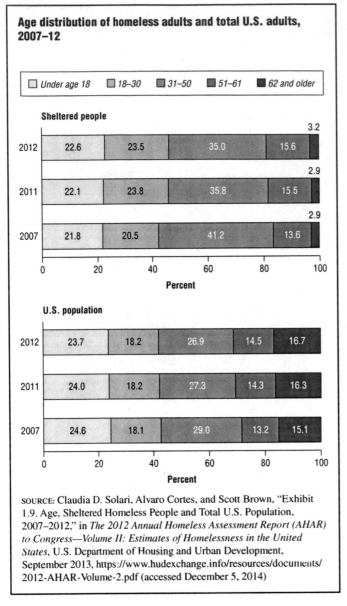

Age distribution of homeless adults and total U.S. adults, 2007–12

☐ Under age 18 ☐ 18–30 ☐ 31–50 ☐ 51–61 ■ 62 and older

Sheltered people

Year	Values
2012	22.6 / 23.5 / 35.0 / 15.6 / 3.2
2011	22.1 / 23.8 / 35.8 / 15.5 / 2.9
2007	21.8 / 20.5 / 41.2 / 13.6 / 2.9

U.S. population

Year	Values
2012	23.7 / 18.2 / 26.9 / 14.5 / 16.7
2011	24.0 / 18.2 / 27.3 / 14.3 / 16.3
2007	24.6 / 18.1 / 29.0 / 13.2 / 15.1

SOURCE: Claudia D. Solari, Alvaro Cortes, and Scott Brown, "Exhibit 1.9. Age, Sheltered Homeless People and Total U.S. Population, 2007–2012," in *The 2012 Annual Homeless Assessment Report (AHAR) to Congress—Volume II: Estimates of Homelessness in the United States*, U.S. Department of Housing and Urban Development, September 2013, https://www.hudexchange.info/resources/documents/2012-AHAR-Volume-2.pdf (accessed December 5, 2014)

FIGURE 5.12

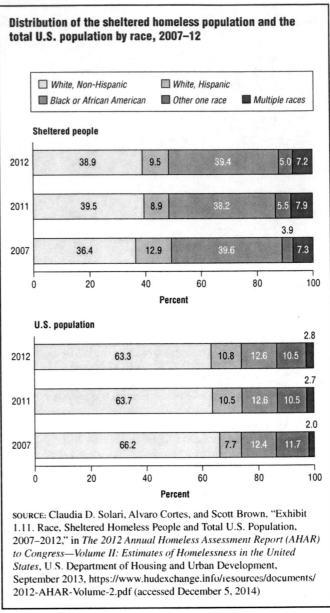

Distribution of the sheltered homeless population and the total U.S. population by race, 2007–12

☐ White, Non-Hispanic ☐ White, Hispanic
☐ Black or African American ☐ Other one race ■ Multiple races

Sheltered people

Year	Values
2012	38.9 / 9.5 / 39.4 / 5.0 / 7.2
2011	39.5 / 8.9 / 38.2 / 5.5 / 7.9
2007	36.4 / 12.9 / 39.6 / 3.9 / 7.3

U.S. population

Year	Values
2012	63.3 / 10.8 / 12.6 / 10.5 / 2.8
2011	63.7 / 10.5 / 12.6 / 10.5 / 2.7
2007	66.2 / 7.7 / 12.4 / 11.7 / 2.0

SOURCE: Claudia D. Solari, Alvaro Cortes, and Scott Brown, "Exhibit 1.11. Race, Sheltered Homeless People and Total U.S. Population, 2007–2012," in *The 2012 Annual Homeless Assessment Report (AHAR) to Congress—Volume II: Estimates of Homelessness in the United States*, U.S. Department of Housing and Urban Development, September 2013, https://www.hudexchange.info/resources/documents/2012-AHAR-Volume-2.pdf (accessed December 5, 2014)

of the sheltered individual population, followed by young adults aged 18 to 30 years (24.5%) and adults aged 51 to 61 years (23.7%), with children accounting for only 1.8% of the sheltered individual population. By contrast, children constituted 60.3% of the sheltered family population, adults aged 18 to 30 years constituted 21.9% of the sheltered family population, and adults aged 31 to 50 years constituted 16.6% of the sheltered family population. Only 1.1% of those living in sheltered families were over the age of 50 years.

RACE AND ETHNICITY. In 2012 the sheltered homeless population was disproportionately African American. As Figure 5.12 shows, African Americans accounted for 12.6% of the U.S. population that year and for 39.4% of the sheltered homeless population. Non-Hispanic whites accounted for an approximately equal share of the sheltered population, at 38.9% in 2012, while constituting

63.3% of the total U.S. population. The overrepresentation of African Americans in the sheltered homeless population was more pronounced among homeless families than among homeless individuals. Solari, Cortes, and Brown indicate that African Americans accounted for 45% of people in sheltered families and for 36.1% of sheltered individuals. There was no disproportion by Hispanic origin between the sheltered homeless population and the total U.S. population in 2012. (See Figure 5.13.) According to Solari, Cortes, and Brown, approximately 61% of the sheltered homeless population that year consisted of people who identified as part of a minority group. The largest minority subpopulations after African Americans were white Hispanics (9.5%), multiple races (7.2%), Native American or Alaskan Native (3.4%), Asian American (0.8%), and Native Hawaiian or other Pacific Islander (0.8%).

FIGURE 5.13

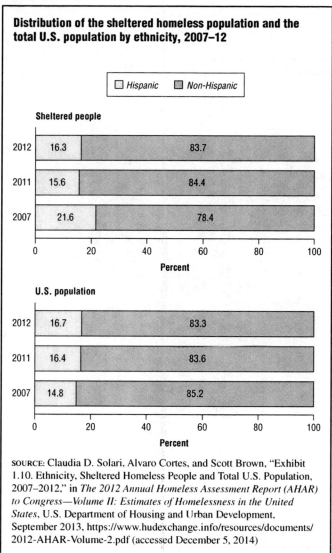

Distribution of the sheltered homeless population and the total U.S. population by ethnicity, 2007–12

☐ Hispanic ▨ Non-Hispanic

Sheltered people

Year	Hispanic	Non-Hispanic
2012	16.3	83.7
2011	15.6	84.4
2007	21.6	78.4

Percent (0 – 100)

U.S. population

Year	Hispanic	Non-Hispanic
2012	16.7	83.3
2011	16.4	83.6
2007	14.8	85.2

Percent (0 – 100)

SOURCE: Claudia D. Solari, Alvaro Cortes, and Scott Brown, "Exhibit 1.10. Ethnicity, Sheltered Homeless People and Total U.S. Population, 2007–2012," in *The 2012 Annual Homeless Assessment Report (AHAR) to Congress—Volume II: Estimates of Homelessness in the United States*, U.S. Department of Housing and Urban Development, September 2013, https://www.hudexchange.info/resources/documents/2012-AHAR-Volume-2.pdf (accessed December 5, 2014)

AGRM SURVEY. The AGRM's 2014 survey of 135 missions yielded demographic insights into the homeless population that broadly resembled those of HUD's 2012 HMIS data, while showing distinct differences. These differences were likely due to multiple factors, such as a portion of the AGRM client population was not homeless and the religious orientation of gospel missions may have appealed to some homeless people more than others. In 2014 the AGRM determined that its client population was 73% male and 27% female and that women with children constituted 54% of the subpopulation of those in family groups. (See Table 5.1.) Children (6%) accounted for a far smaller proportion of the 2014 AGRM population than HUD's 2012 HMIS population, and whites (49%) accounted for a significantly higher proportion of the AGRM population than the HUD HMIS population.

Geography of Homelessness

According to Henry et al., the January 2014 PIT count indicated that half of the U.S. homeless population

lived in five states: California, New York, Florida, Texas, and Massachusetts. (See Figure 5.14.) California alone had a homeless population of 113,952 people (20% of the national total). New York's homeless population was 80,590 (14% of the national total); Florida's, 41,542 (7%); Texas's, 28,495 (5%); and Massachusetts's, 21,237 (4%). Henry et al. note that the 25 states that each accounted for less than 1% of the national homeless population together accounted for only 12% of the national homeless population.

Homelessness in the popular imagination is primarily an urban phenomenon, and the data support this view to a significant extent. According to Solari, Cortes, and Brown, 70.2% of the sheltered homeless population lived in principal cities in 2012 and 29.8% were in suburban and rural areas. The U.S. population below the poverty line, perhaps surprisingly, was not concentrated in cities to the same extent. In fact, 65.2% of those living in poverty in 2012 were in suburban or rural areas. The concentration of homelessness in cities, then, may be driven as much by high housing-cost pressures as by the percentage of the population in poverty. Cities may also draw homeless people from rural and suburban areas due to the higher concentration of services and opportunities for work. However, this is not to suggest that rural homelessness is not a problem. In fact, according to Solari, Cortes, and Brown, 2007 to 2012 saw homelessness increase rapidly in suburban and rural areas (by 20.4%) while decreasing rapidly in cities (by 14.4%).

Rural homelessness can differ from urban homelessness in numerous important ways. Rural communities are often much less equipped to serve and assess their homeless populations. There are fewer official shelters, and the transportation infrastructure necessary for the homeless to access services is often lacking. There are also fewer public places (e.g., heating grates, subways, or train stations) where the homeless can find temporary shelter or relief from the elements. Therefore, the rural homeless are more likely to live in a car or camper or with relatives in overcrowded or rundown housing, than in shelters or typical unsheltered locations. As a result, finding the rural homeless is more difficult for investigators of the problem, so it is possible that they are typically undercounted in HUD and other surveys.

EMPLOYMENT AND THE HOMELESS

Barring significant assistance, finding a job is the only way for most people to escape homelessness. Unsympathetic views hold that people become homeless due to qualities such as laziness and an unwillingness to work. This belief is not supported by research. In "Employment, Day Labor, and Shadow Work among Homeless Assistance Clients in the United States" (*Journal of Poverty*, vol. 17, no. 3, 2013), Lei Lei of the

FIGURE 5.14

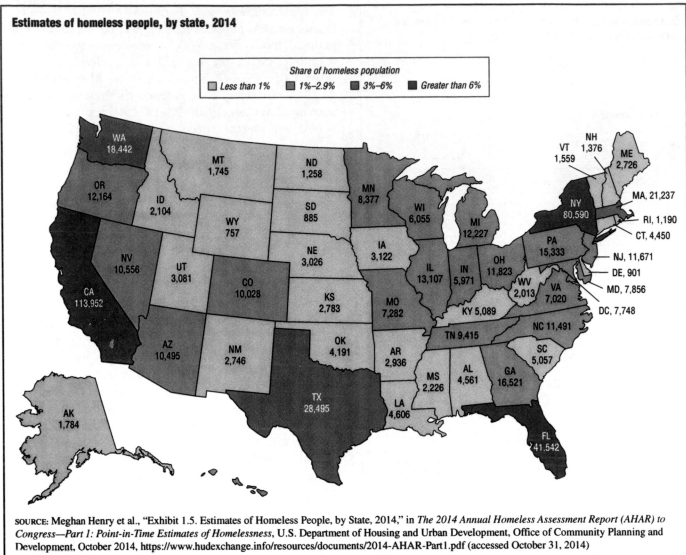

Estimates of homeless people, by state, 2014

Share of homeless population

☐ Less than 1%   ▨ 1%–2.9%   ▨ 3%–6%   ■ Greater than 6%

WA 18,442
OR 12,164
MT 1,745
ND 1,258
MN 8,377
VT 1,559
NH 1,376
ME 2,726
ID 2,104
WY 757
SD 885
WI 6,055
NY 80,590
MA, 21,237
RI, 1,190
CT, 4,450
NV 10,556
UT 3,081
NE 3,026
IA 3,122
MI 12,227
PA 15,333
NJ, 11,671
DE, 901
CA 113,952
CO 10,028
KS 2,783
IL 13,107
IN 5,971
OH 11,823
WV 2,013
VA 7,020
MD, 7,856
DC, 7,748
MO 7,282
KY 5,089
AZ 10,495
NM 2,746
OK 4,191
AR 2,936
TN 9,415
NC 11,491
SC 5,057
TX 28,495
LA 4,606
MS 2,226
AL 4,561
GA 16,521
AK 1,784
FL 41,542

SOURCE: Meghan Henry et al., "Exhibit 1.5. Estimates of Homeless People, by State, 2014," in *The 2014 Annual Homeless Assessment Report (AHAR) to Congress—Part 1: Point-in-Time Estimates of Homelessness*, U.S. Department of Housing and Urban Development, Office of Community Planning and Development, October 2014, https://www.hudexchange.info/resources/documents/2014-AHAR-Part1.pdf (accessed October 31, 2014)

University at Albany, State University of New York, notes that over 90% of homeless people express the desire to work and that approximately 80% have been found to be employed or looking for work. However, the homeless typically find it extremely difficult to find and keep good jobs.

The USICH notes in "How to Build Employment Programs That Prevent and End Homelessness" (2013, http://usich.gov) that the homeless and those at risk of becoming homeless must typically contend with numerous, sometimes overlapping barriers to finding work, including "low educational attainment levels, having young children and no access to child care, limited or no past work experience and few marketable job skills, mental health or substance abuse problems, chronic health problems or disability, no access to transportation, bad credit (which can make both finding a job and a house difficult as landlords and lower wage employers often run credit checks), and, for some, criminal histories." In the postrecession job market in 2010 to 2014, hundreds of thousands of workers without any of these problems found themselves unable to find employment. Especially for those homeless people with more than one of these problems, obtaining a job can often seem an impossible task.

In *Hunger and Homelessness Survey: A Status Report on Hunger and Homelessness in America's Cities, a 25-City Survey* (December 2014, http://www.usmayors.org/pressreleases/uploads/2014/1211-report-hh.pdf), the U.S. Conference of Mayors reports that between September 1, 2013, and August 31, 2014, 18% of homeless adults in its 25 survey cities were employed. This does not necessarily mean that all of these individuals were involved in regular work, which is characterized by a permanent and ongoing relationship between employer and employee. Regular work does not figure significantly in the lives and routines of most homeless people, as it is usually unavailable or inaccessible. Homelessness makes getting and keeping regular work difficult because of the lack of a fixed address, communication, and, in many cases, the inability to get a good night's sleep, clean up, and dress appropriately. Studies find that the longer a person is homeless, the less likely he or she is to pursue wage labor and the more likely he or she is to engage in some other form of work.

In the absence of regular employment, homeless people earn money in a number of different ways, although their earnings are usually not sufficient to lift them out of homelessness. Some of the most common income-generating activities the homeless engage in are day labor, shadow work, and the distribution of street newspapers. Lei notes that studies in different U.S. locations and at different dates ranging between 1992 and 2009 have found that between 20% and 50% of homeless people engage in either regular work, day labor, or other kinds of informal work. Many homeless people also attempt to produce and sell street newspapers as a way of earning income.

Day Labor

Day labor (wage labor secured on a day-to-day basis, typically at lower wages and changing locations) is somewhat easier for the homeless to secure than regular work. According to Lei, studies indicate that homeless people account for up to 50% of the day-labor workforce nationwide. Day labor is often accessed through hiring agencies or in informal ways usually occurring in public open-air contexts. Also, employers looking for day laborers frequently hire individuals at homeless shelters. Over 80% of homeless day laborers do light industrial or warehouse work. Property owners also hire a substantial portion of the homeless day-laboring population, often for the purpose of doing lawn care and other maintenance work. Besides being more accessible to the homeless than regular employment, day laboring often appeals to the homeless because it involves immediate payment after the day's work is finished, employers do not require references or work experience, and most of those who hire day laborers provide transportation to and from the worksite.

However, there are many disadvantages to day laboring beyond low pay and a lack of prospects for the future. Acquiring a day-laboring job usually involves arriving at an agency or open-air market extremely early in the morning and waiting for long periods to see whether any work will be available. There is no guarantee that such efforts will be rewarded with paying work, and those who do obtain work are often exploited by bosses who deduct money from paychecks for transportation and cashing checks. Moreover, because day laboring involves no contractual agreements beyond the day on which work is offered, such work opportunities are particularly susceptible to disappearing in challenging economic times. For example, Fernanda Santos reports in "In the Shadows, Day Laborers Left Homeless as Work Vanishes" (NYTimes.com, January 1, 2010) that during the Great Recession day-labor opportunities dried up considerably, leaving people who had depended on that work even more likely to become or remain homeless.

Shadow Work

Shadow work refers to income-earning opportunities that are outside the normal economy and distinct from ordinary wage-earning methods. Common forms of shadow work include peddling (selling various items), panhandling (asking passersby for money, food, or other goods without offering anything in return), prostitution, and stealing. Because the illegal forms of shadow work are difficult to research due to the obvious need for secrecy among its practitioners, most studies focus on peddling and panhandling. Lei notes that peddling practices vary depending on what individuals are able to acquire (often in the form of recycling, the receiving of gifts, and stealing) and that common items sold by the homeless include "clothing, shoes, watches, rings, calculators, cigarettes, and beer." Peddling typically brings in very low sums of money because the extreme levels of need among the homeless mean that they often must sell at any price and because they often sell to other homeless people who have little money.

According to Lei, different studies show that between 5% and 40% of homeless people engage in panhandling. Panhandling is widely regarded as degrading by both those who engage in the activity and those who are targeted, and panhandlers are routinely ignored by their targets, enhancing the level of degradation and making the activity an unreliable way of satisfying needs. Additionally, as Lei points out, since the 1970s many cities have passed ordinances restricting the legality of panhandling, in spite of the fact that the U.S. Supreme Court has ruled that it is protected by the First Amendment right to free speech. Thus, municipalities often pass laws that prohibit "aggressive panhandling," without defining what is meant by "aggressive." The effect is often to discourage even passive forms of panhandling, making the activity an even more difficult method of generating income than it has historically been.

Street Newspapers

In the United States, as well as in other countries, homeless people write, publish, and sell their own newspapers, which typically focus on poverty, homelessness, and related issues. Besides providing income for homeless individuals and funding for homeless shelters and assistance agencies, street newspapers attempt to educate the public about homelessness and poverty. Many street newspapers formerly belonged to the North American

Street Newspaper Association, which was organized in Chicago in 1996, but the organization was dissolved in 2013. Thereafter, street newspapers tended to be organized locally or regionally as part of nonprofit entities. For example, as of 2014 *Street Roots* (http://www.streetroots.org) of Portland, Oregon, produced and sold approximately 20,000 newspapers each month; and *Street Sense* (http://www.streetsense.org) of the District of Columbia sold approximately 16,000 papers every two weeks, with the average seller earning $45 per day. Danny Westneat explains in "Real Change Comes to Bellevue as Homeless Sell, Make News" (SeattleTimes.com, November 19, 2013) that one of the largest and most successful street newspapers is *Real Change* (http://www.realchangenews.org), a publication based in Seattle, Washington, that employed more than 300 homeless street vendors in the metropolitan area and sold 872,500 copies in 2012. According to Westneat, the paper's expansion during the 1990s and through the early 21st century was a boon to the homeless, but it was also a grim sign of the spread of homelessness and poverty in the area.

Although the income from selling street newspapers is unlikely, on its own, to provide a path back to permanent housing, it can provide people with crucial transitional funds as they prepare to embark on that path. Additionally, the activity of selling the newspapers can be a source of self-confidence, an aid in helping the homeless overcome the isolation they often feel, and a way to begin developing business skills. Many street newspapers accept submissions from the homeless themselves, including articles, letters, and artwork, offering an opportunity for self-expression that can further alleviate the feelings of marginalization common to many on the streets and in shelters. Finally, street newspapers dispel stereotypes about the homeless and offer a point of connection between them and the population at large.

However, not all municipalities welcome the vending of street newspapers. For example, in "Homeless Banned from Selling Newspapers on Major Roads?" (AlterNet.org, January 24, 2014), Tana Ganeva indicates that numerous cities in southern Florida have begun passing ordinances that prevent homeless-affiliated newspapers from being sold on major streets. These laws restrict the earning potential of many vendors for the Homeless Voice organization (http://www.homelessvoice.org), which operates numerous shelters in southern Florida and distributes street newspapers in Broward, Dade, and Palm Beach Counties.

CHAPTER 6
THE HOUSING PROBLEM

At one time a home was defined as a place where a family resided, but as American society changed, so did the definition of the term *home*. A home is now considered a place where one or more people live together, a private place to which they have legal right and where strangers may be excluded. It is the place where people keep their belongings and where they feel safe from the outside world. For housing to be considered a home, it should be permanent with an address. Furthermore, in the best of circumstances a home should not be substandard but should still be affordable. Many people would agree that a place to call home is a basic human right.

Those people who have no fixed address and no private space of their own are the homeless. The obvious solution to homelessness would be to find a home for everyone who needs one. There is enough housing available in the United States; as such, the problem lies in the affordability of that housing. Most of the housing in the United States costs far more than poor people can afford to rent or buy.

HIGH HOUSING COSTS AND HOMELESSNESS

Decades of research indicates that the primary cause of homelessness is the inability to pay for housing, which is itself caused by some combination of low income and high housing costs. Although many other factors may contribute to homelessness, such as a low level of educational achievement or mental illness, addressing such problems will seldom bring someone out of homelessness in the absence of attention to the problem of housing affordability.

Homeless people and homeless families are similar to other poor people. Given the disparity between incomes at the lowest strata of society and the costs of housing in the 21st century, most people living near or below the poverty line are at risk of becoming homeless at least periodically. Most of the homeless, in turn, do not

stay homeless for long periods. These families and individuals are often able to return to permanent housing when they solve their income problems, such as by finding a job, or when they receive government or other assistance with housing.

For the chronically homeless, or those who experience long-term or repeated homelessness, other problems must often be addressed at the same time as housing affordability. The chronically homeless have higher rates of chronic disabilities, substance abuse disorders, physical disabilities, human immunodeficiency virus, and acquired immunodeficiency syndrome (AIDS). Because of these disabilities and diseases, combating chronic homelessness requires providing permanent housing that is linked to other supportive services that address the wide array of medical and social problems with which this population struggles.

Although government and nonprofit efforts to reduce chronic homelessness between 2007 and 2014 were unambiguously successful, as discussed in Chapter 5, in the eyes of many experts the problem driving the majority of homelessness—a lack of affordable housing—was worsening rather than improving as of late 2014.

THE SCOPE OF THE HOUSING PROBLEM

The federal government establishes the official standard for low-income housing at 30% of a family's annual income. If a poor or near-poor household must spend more than 30% of its income on rent and utilities, its members risk being unable to afford other basic necessities. Low-income housing, then, is housing that is affordable to those in poverty based on this formula. In 2014 a family of two with an annual income of less than $15,730 was in poverty; a family of four was in poverty if its income was less than $23,850. (See Table 1.1 in Chapter 1.) Thus, in 2014 a single mother of one child generally qualified for low-income housing if her housing costs exceeded 30% of $15,730 annually, or more than $393.25 per month; a family of four qualified if its housing costs were more than 30% of $23,850 annually, or more than $596.25 per month.

However, qualifying for housing subsidies is much easier than obtaining them. Due to an insufficient supply of affordable housing as well as to limited government funding, many public housing programs have waiting lists on which applicants can expect to remain for years or even decades. Althea Arnold et al. of the National Low Income Housing Coalition estimate in *Out of Reach 2014: Twenty-Five Years Later, the Affordable Housing Crisis Continues* (2014, http://nlihc.org/sites/default/files/oor/2014OOR.pdf) that approximately three-quarters of extremely low income (ELI; those who make less than 30% of an area's median income [the middle value; half of all renters earn less and half earn more]) renters fail to obtain housing assistance.

In the absence of housing assistance, the majority of low-income individuals and families are forced to acquire housing at market rates. The price of rental units has been on the rise since 1980, at the same time that the real income of renters has been declining. In *The State of the Nation's Housing 2014* (June 2014, http://www.jchs.harvard.edu/sites/jchs.harvard.edu/files/sonhr14-color-full.pdf), the Joint Center for Housing Studies (JCHS) of Harvard University notes that the situation for renters in the United States is a "crisis of affordability." The share of renters considered cost-burdened (those who paid more than 30% of their income in rent) increased steadily between 2001 and 2011, to over 50% of the total. During that same period the share of renters considered severely cost-burdened (those who paid more than 50% of their income in rent) reached 28%. These percentages declined slightly in the following years, but they remained extremely high by historical standards, and there was significant variation from state to state. As Table 6.1 shows, 47.6% of renters in the United States were considered cost-burdened in 2013. The proportion was over 50% in seven states (California, Florida, Hawaii, New Jersey, New York, Oregon, and Vermont). It is no coincidence that the three states with the largest homeless populations (California, at 113,952; New York, at 80,590; and Florida, at 41,542) were among the states in which renters were most cost-burdened. (See Figure 5.14 in Chapter 5 for homeless population estimates by state.)

According to the U.S. Census Bureau, the median monthly gross rent for renter-occupied housing units was $905 in 2013. (See Table 6.2.) Although this represented a yearly rental expense of approximately 20.8% of the 2013 national median household income of $52,250, the median income for renters is far lower. (See Table 6.3.) The median income for renter households was $32,831.

TABLE 6.1

Percentage of renter-occupied units spending 30% or more of household income on rent and utilities, by state, 2013

Geographic area	Percent
United States	**47.6**
Alabama	43.6
Alaska	39.8
Arizona	45.8
Arkansas	42.2
California	54.1
Colorado	49.0
Connecticut	49.3
Delaware	46.7
District of Columbia	46.7
Florida	53.4
Georgia	47.8
Hawaii	50.8
Idaho	43.1
Illinois	45.8
Indiana	45.2
Iowa	39.6
Kansas	41.3
Kentucky	40.1
Louisiana	45.5
Maine	47.8
Maryland	48.4
Massachusetts	47.5
Michigan	48.2
Minnesota	44.8
Mississippi	43.5
Missouri	44.7
Montana	42.5
Nebraska	41.3
Nevada	46.7
New Hampshire	45.3
New Jersey	51.1
New Mexico	46.0
New York	50.8
North Carolina	45.1
North Dakota	38.6
Ohio	44.6
Oklahoma	40.4
Oregon	50.2
Pennsylvania	46.1
Rhode Island	49.3
South Carolina	45.2
South Dakota	36.4
Tennessee	44.6
Texas	44.2
Utah	43.6
Vermont	50.3
Virginia	45.6
Washington	48.0
West Virginia	38.4
Wisconsin	44.3
Wyoming	37.4
Puerto Rico	32.0

A household earning the median renter income and paying the median rent would thus need to spend 33.1% of its income on housing.

Table 6.4 breaks down renter households by income level and rental costs as a share of income. In 2013 nearly 19.8 million renter households, or 46.6% of the total 42.4 million renter households, had an annual income of less than $35,000. Among these 19.8 million households, 11.3 million had incomes of less than $20,000 per year and 8.5 million had incomes between $20,000 and $34,999. Roughly nine out of 10 (88.9%, or 10 million) renter households making less than $20,000 per year paid over

TABLE 6.1

Data are based on a sample and are subject to sampling variability. The degree of uncertainty for an estimate arising from sampling variability is represented through the use of a margin of error. The value shown here is the 90 percent margin of error. The margin of error can be interpreted roughly as providing a 90 percent probability that the interval defined by the estimate minus the margin of error and the estimate plus the margin of error (the lower and upper confidence bounds) contains the true value. In addition to sampling variability, the American Consumer Survey (ACS) estimates are subject to nonsampling error. The effect of nonsampling error is not represented in these tables. In data year 2013, there were a series of changes to data collection operations that could have affected some estimates. These changes include the addition of Internet as a mode of data collection, the end of the content portion of failed edit follow-u interviewing, and the loss of one monthly panel due to the federal government shut down in October 2013. Estimates of urban and rural population, housing units, and characteristics reflect boundaries of urban areas defined based on Census 2010 data. As a result, data for urban and rural areas from the ACS do not necessarily reflect the results of ongoing urbanization.

SOURCE: Adapted from "GCT2515. Percent of Renter-Occupied Units Spending 30 Percent or More of Household Income on Rent and Utilities—United States—States; and Puerto Rico," in *2013 American Community Survey 1-Year Estimates*, U.S. Census Bureau, 2014, http://factfinder2.census.gov/faces/tableservices/jsf/pages/productview.xhtml?pid=ACS_13_1YR_GCT2515.US01PR&prodType=table (accessed December 8, 2014)

30% of their annual income in rent, as did 72.7% (6.2 million) of renter households making between $20,000 and $34,999. Even at income levels placing all but the largest families well above the poverty line, those making $35,000 to $49,999, 39.8% (2.4 million) of households paid 30% or more of their annual income in rent.

Many households, especially those living in or near poverty, pay far more than 30% of their annual income in rent. As Table 6.5 shows, 3.4 million renter households living below the poverty line paid 100% or more of their income in rent, and 1.3 million renter households in poverty paid between 70% and 99% of their income in rent. Overall, approximately 6.3 million, or 56.1% of the 11.1 million renter families living in poverty, paid over half of their income in rent, and the median renter household in poverty paid 74% of its income in rent.

Arnold et al. introduce a metric called the "housing wage," which is the level of income needed to obtain adequate, affordable housing in the U.S. rental market. Using the 2014 fair market rent (FMR; the U.S. Department of Housing and Urban Development's [HUD] estimate of what a household seeking modest rental housing must expect to pay for rent and utilities) for a two-bedroom rental, the researchers determine that the hourly wage needed to pay for such an apartment while spending no more than 30% of one's income on rent was $18.92, more than 2.5 times the federal minimum wage of $7.25. Arnold et al. note that "in no state can a full-time minimum wage worker afford a one-bedroom or a two-bedroom rental unit at Fair Market Rent."

Since 1991 HUD has released biannual reports to Congress on those renters who have what the agency

TABLE 6.2

Median monthly housing costs for renter-occupied housing units, by state, 2013

Geographic area	Dollar
United States	**905**
Alabama	694
Alaska	1,117
Arizona	890
Arkansas	659
California	1,224
Colorado	971
Connecticut	1,040
Delaware	999
District of Columbia	1,307
Florida	972
Georgia	850
Hawaii	1,414
Idaho	725
Illinois	885
Indiana	730
Iowa	679
Kansas	745
Kentucky	668
Louisiana	763
Maine	760
Maryland	1,210
Massachusetts	1,077
Michigan	768
Minnesota	832
Mississippi	708
Missouri	734
Montana	690
Nebraska	714
Nevada	952
New Hampshire	995
New Jersey	1,171
New Mexico	772
New York	1,109
North Carolina	778
North Dakota	690
Ohio	709
Oklahoma	705
Oregon	887
Pennsylvania	828
Rhode Island	918
South Carolina	766
South Dakota	637
Tennessee	748
Texas	857
Utah	881
Vermont	865
Virginia	1,086
Washington	989
West Virginia	620
Wisconsin	758
Wyoming	780
Puerto Rico	448

Note: Data are based on a sample and are subject to sampling variability.

SOURCE: Adapted from "GCT2514. Median Monthly Housing Costs for Renter-Occupied Housing Units (Dollars)—United States—States; and Puerto Rico," in *2013 American Community Survey 1-Year Estimates*, U.S. Census Bureau, 2014, http://factfinder2.census.gov/faces/tableservices/jsf/pages/productview.xhtml?pid=ACS_13_1YR_GCT2514.US01PR&prodType=table (accessed October 31, 2014)

calls "worst-case housing needs." Renters with worst-case needs are, according to the HUD definition, those with incomes below 50% of the area median income (the median income in the locality in which the individual lives) who receive no housing assistance from the government and who pay more than half of their income for housing, live in substandard conditions, or experience

TABLE 6.3

TABLE 6.4

Median household income in the past 12 months, by housing type, 2013

	United States Estimate
Median household income in the past 12 months (in 2013 inflation-adjusted dollars)—	
Total	52,250
Owner occupied (dollars)	66,828
Renter occupied (dollars)	32,831

Note: Data are based on a sample and are subject to sampling variability.

SOURCE: Adapted from "B25119. Median Household Income in the Past 12 Months (in 2013 Inflation-Adjusted Dollars) by Tenure," in *2013 American Community Survey 1-Year Estimates*, U.S. Census Bureau, 2014, http://factfinder2.census.gov/faces/tableservices/jsf/pages/productview.xhtml?pid=ACS_13_1YR_B25119&prodType=table (accessed December 8, 2014)

Rent as a percentage of total household income, by income level of renter households, 2013

	United States Estimate
Total	116,291,033
Renter-occupied housing units	42,447,172
Less than $20,000	11,300,915
Less than 20 percent	288,159
20 to 29 percent	969,849
30 percent or more	10,042,907
$20,000 to $34,999	8,466,112
Less than 20 percent	515,931
20 to 29 percent	1,795,671
30 percent or more	6,154,510
$35,000 to $49,999	6,105,088
Less than 20 percent	1,132,572
20 to 29 percent	2,540,267
30 percent or more	2,432,249
$50,000 to $74,999	6,365,355
Less than 20 percent	2,606,052
20 to 29 percent	2,541,668
30 percent or more	1,217,635
$75,000 or more	7,004,569
Less than 20 percent	5,035,466
20 to 29 percent	1,595,212
30 percent or more	373,891
Zero or negative income	963,376
No cash rent	2,241,757

Note: Data are based on a sample and are subject to sampling variability.

SOURCE: Adapted from "B25106. Tenure by Housing Costs as a Percentage of Household Income in the Past 12 Months," in *2013 American Community Survey 1-Year Estimates*, U.S. Census Bureau, 2014, http://factfinder2.census.gov/faces/tableservices/jsf/pages/productview.xhtml?pid=ACS_13_1YR_B25106&prodType=table (accessed on December 8, 2014)

both of these housing problems. HUD's findings in "Worst Case Housing Needs 2011: Report to Congress, Summary" (February 2013, http://www.huduser.org/Publications/pdf/HUD-506_WorstCase2011.pdf) support the dire assessments of the National Low Income Housing Coalition and other organizations.

HUD notes that between 2009 and 2011 the overall economy was slowly recovering from the Great Recession (which officially lasted from December 2007 to June 2009), but that the benefits of recovery had not begun to reach low-income renters. In fact, there had been "dramatic increases in worst-case housing needs during the 2009–2011 period that cut across demographic groups, household types, and regions. This rise in hardship among renters is due to substantial increases in rental housing demand and weakening incomes that increase competition for already-scarce affordable units."

Between 2007 and 2011 the number of renters with worst-case needs grew by an unprecedented 43.5%, from 5.9 million to 8.5 million. (See Figure 6.1.) HUD indicates that only 3% of those designated as having worst-case needs qualified for the designation because of the inadequacy of their housing; 97% qualified because they were paying more than half of their income for rent. The increase in worst-case housing needs affected virtually all household types and demographic groups. Among those with worst-case needs in 2011, there were 3.2 million households with children, 1.5 million elderly households, and 3 million nonfamily households (households consisting of unrelated people). Approximately one out of six households with worst-case housing needs in 2011 included a nonelderly disabled member, and such cases were rising dramatically. Between 2009 and 2011 the number of households both including a disabled person and experiencing worst-case housing needs grew from 990,000 to 1.3 million.

FEDERALLY SUBSIDIZED HOUSING

The federal government, operating primarily through HUD, has a number of housing programs that help poor and low-income people. Subsidized housing, like other social welfare programs aimed specifically at low-income individuals and families, is means-tested, or based on income thresholds. The qualifying income level—much like the definition of poverty—changes over time. Beneficiaries of housing assistance never receive cash outright. The benefits are therefore labeled "means-tested noncash benefits." According to the Census Bureau (September 2014, http://www.census.gov/hhes/www/cpstables/032014/pov/pov26_001_1.xls), 11.7 million people, or 3.7% of the population, lived in subsidized housing in 2013.

HUD operates many different kinds of subsidized-housing programs, but there are two basic forms of subsidies: vouchers and public housing. There are also two main types of voucher programs: tenant based and project based. In tenant-based programs the voucher stays with the tenant when the tenant moves to another qualifying unit. In project-based programs the voucher is attached to a particular housing project and remains available for a new tenant when a unit is vacant. Families are directed to participating projects after they qualify. Tenants cannot

TABLE 6.5

Housing costs of renters, by selected characteristics, 2013

[Numbers in thousands, except as indicated. Weighting consistent with Census 2010. Geography = United States.]

Characteristics	Total renter-occupied units	Household characteristics			
		Black alone	Hispanic	Elderly (65 years and over)	Below poverty level
Total	40,218	8,542	7,783	5,151	11,140
Monthly housing costs as percent of current income[a]					
Less than 5 percent	278	32	47	35	21
5 to 9 percent	1,140	185	154	109	32
10 to 14 percent	2,312	402	332	183	79
15 to 19 percent	3,609	618	586	323	120
20 to 24 percent	4,319	814	719	363	298
25 to 29 percent	4,178	876	852	575	522
30 to 34 percent	3,324	765	634	418	470
35 to 39 percent	2,471	579	534	327	360
40 to 49 percent	3,848	826	865	484	772
50 to 59 percent	2,412	528	623	302	799
60 to 69 percent	1,749	350	450	234	737
70 to 99 percent	2,570	604	562	405	1,322
100 percent or more[b]	4,339	1,076	845	817	3,397
Zero or negative income	1,594	477	302	75	1,387
No cash rent	2,076	409	277	501	825
Median (excludes 2 previous lines)(percent)	33%	36%	37%	39%	74%

[a]This item uses current income in its calculation.
[b]May reflect a temporary situation, living off savings, or response error.
Note: Monthly costs are calculated from yearly estimates.

SOURCE: Adapted from "C-10-R0," in *2013 American Housing Survey*, U.S. Census Bureau, 2014, http://factfinder2.census.gov/faces/tableservices/jsf/pages/productview.xhtml?pid=AHS_2013_C10RO&prodType=table (accessed December 8, 2014)

FIGURE 6.1

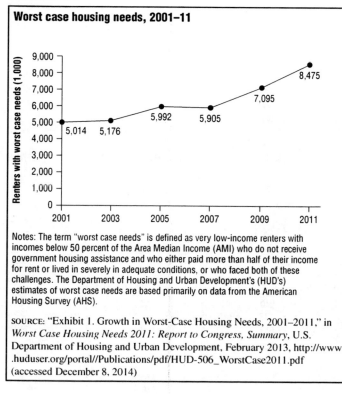

Worst case housing needs, 2001–11

Notes: The term "worst case needs" is defined as very low-income renters with incomes below 50 percent of the Area Median Income (AMI) who do not receive government housing assistance and who either paid more than half of their income for rent or lived in severely in adequate conditions, or who faced both of these challenges. The Department of Housing and Urban Development's (HUD's) estimates of worst case needs are based primarily on data from the American Housing Survey (AHS).

SOURCE: "Exhibit 1. Growth in Worst-Case Housing Needs, 2001–2011," in *Worst Case Housing Needs 2011: Report to Congress, Summary*, U.S. Department of Housing and Urban Development, February 2013, http://www.huduser.org/portal//Publications/pdf/HUD-506_WorstCase2011.pdf (accessed December 8, 2014)

vouchers have increasingly become the most common mechanism for delivering federal housing subsidies.

In its 2015 budget estimate, HUD noted its intention to allocate approximately $20 billion of its total spending of $38.1 billion to tenant-based rental assistance. (See Table 6.6.) Another $10.3 billion was earmarked for project-based rental assistance. The agency planned to spend approximately $6.7 billion on public housing, $2.2 billion of which would go to the public housing capital fund and $4.5 billion of which would go to the public housing operating fund.

Vouchers

Voucher programs, which make up the bulk of HUD's efforts to provide housing for low-income Americans, pay a portion of the rent for qualifying families. Only low-income families are eligible, specifically those with incomes lower than half of an area's median income. Under some circumstances, families with up to 80% of the local median income may also qualify; such cases may involve, for example, families that have been displaced by public housing demolition. The family pays 30% of its income toward the rent, and the voucher covers the remaining balance. Vouchers are issued by the local public housing agency (PHA), which executes assistance contracts with the landlord, who must also qualify.

automatically transfer their voucher from one project-based dwelling to another, but they may qualify for another tenant-based voucher after they move. Tenant-based

TABLE 6.6

U.S. Department of Housing and Urban Development (HUD), budget outlays by program, fiscal years 2013–15

[Dollars in millions]

	2013 Actual	2014 Enacted	2015 Estimate
Discretionary programs			
Public and Indian housing			
Housing Certificate Fund	$479	$326	$199
Tenant-based rental assistance	18,022	19,014	19,963
Family self-sufficiency	—	—	75
Public Housing Capital Fund	2,139	2,021	2,231
Revitalization of severely distressed public housing projects	159	130	110
Choice neighborhoods	1	36	63
Public Housing Operating Fund	4,068	4,224	4,462
Native American housing block grants	726	654	587
Indian Housing Loan Guarantee Fund	9	8	8
Native Hawaiian housing block grants	4	8	14
Subtotal, public and Indian housing	**25,607**	**26,421**	**27,712**
Community planning and development			
Community Development Fund	5,768	10,221	8,383
Community development loan guarantees	2	9	6
Self-Help Homeownership Opportunity/Habitat	67	74	67
Brownfields Redevelopment Program	5	5	5
HOME Investment Partnerships Program	1,420	1,406	1,239
Homeless assistance grants	1,735	2,036	1,992
Housing Opportunities for Persons with AIDS (HOPWA)	307	322	318
Permanent supportive housing	9	7	7
Rural housing and economic development	11	8	4
Subtotal, community planning and development	**9,324**	**14,088**	**12,021**
Housing programs			
Project-based rental assistance	$9,429	$9,860	$10,340
Energy Innovation Fund	6	19	9
Housing counseling assistance	44	62	54
Housing for the Elderly (Section 202)	855	673	763
Housing for Persons with Disabilities (Section 811)	218	218	175
Flexible subsidy	(41)	(44)	(44)
Federal Housing Administration (FHA) funds:			
Mutual Mortgage Ins. and Coop. Management Housing Ins. Funds:			
Program account	107	102	117
General Insurance and Special Risk Insurance Funds:			
Program account	—	5	—
Subtotal, FHA funds	**107**	**107**	**117**
Other assisted housing	391	372	300
Manufactured home inspection and monitoring	7	10	10
Payments to Manufactured Housing Fees Trust Fund	2	1	—
Subtotal, housing programs	**11,018**	**11,278**	**11,724**
Policy development and research			
Research and technology	54	53	53
Fair housing and equal opportunity			
Fair housing activities	73	71	72
Office of Lead Hazard Control and Healthy Homes			
Lead hazard reduction	125	128	129
Management and administration			
Salaries and expenses, HUD	$1,309	$1,347	$1,364
Salaries and expenses, Office of Inspector General (OIG)	127	119	130
Information technology fund	248	256	254
Gifts and bequests	(1)	(1)	—
Subtotal, management and administration	**1,683**	**1,721**	**1,748**
HUD transformation initiatives	107	102	88
Subtotal, HUD discretionary outlays (gross)	**47,991**	**53,862**	**53,547**
Deductions for offsetting receipts (discretionary)	(919)	(935)	(886)
Reclassification of Money Management International (MMI) receipts	(17,444)	(10,186)	(12,190)
Government National Mortgage Association (GNMA) program account	(119)	(55)	(66)
GNMA receipts	(1,068)	(542)	(832)
Total, HUD discretionary outlays (net)	**28,441**	**42,144**	**39,573**

TABLE 6.6

U.S. Department of Housing and Urban Development (HUD), budget outlays by program, fiscal years 2013–15 [CONTINUED]

[Dollars in millions]

	2013 Actual	2014 Enacted	2015 Estimate
Mandatory programs			
Indian Housing Loan Guarantee Fund	$8	$107	—
Native American housing block grants	2	—	—
Public Housing Capital Fund	43	—	—
Community development loan guarantees	8	2	—
Project rebuild	793	503	$168
Revolving fund	—	2	2
Housing trust fund	—	—	10
FHA MMI program account	27,673	5,769	—
FHA MMI liquidating	9	75	68
FHA MMI capital reserve account	(5,251)	(3,458)	(382)
FHA General and Special Risk Insurance Fund (GI/SRI) program	5,682	210	—
FHA GI/SRI Funds liquidating	(130)	(23)	20
Emergency Homeowners' Relief Fund	53	63	66
Rental Housing Assistance Fund	—	(3)	(3)
Home Ownership Preservation Equity Fund program account	(1)	—	—
Housing for the Elderly or Handicapped Fund liquidating account	(587)	(542)	(542)
Green Retrofit Program for Multifamily Housing, Recovery Act	1	—	—
Guarantees of mortgage-backed securities	102	40	—
Guarantees of mortgage-backed securities capital reserve account	—	(672)	(876)
Guarantees of mortgage-backed securities liquidating account	306	3	3
Gifts and bequests	1	3	—
Subtotal, HUD mandatory outlays (gross)	**28,712**	**2,079**	**(1,466)**
Deductions for offsetting receipts (mandatory)	(575)	(2,102)	(19)
Total, HUD mandatory outlays (net)	**28,137**	**(23)**	**(1,485)**
Total, HUD outlays	**56,578**	**42,121**	**38,088**

Note: Totals may differ from president's budget due to rounding. HUD = United States Department of Housing and Urban Development.

SOURCE: "Department of Housing and Urban Development Budget Outlays by Program: Comparative Summary, Fiscal Years 2013–2015," in *HUD's Proposed 2015 Budget: Congressional Justifications*, U.S. Department of Housing and Urban Development, March 4, 2014, http://portal.hud.gov/hudportal/documents/huddoc?id=fy15cj_bdgt_otly_tbl.pdf (accessed November 12, 2014)

Besides these two basic programs, HUD also has five other voucher programs. Conversion vouchers are used to help tenants relocate when public housing is demolished. Family unification vouchers are used to help families stay together. Homeownership vouchers assist families in purchasing a first home or another home if the family has not lived in a house in the past three years. Participants must be employed and have an income of at least minimum wage. Vouchers for people with disabilities and welfare-to-work vouchers assist the elderly or nonelderly disabled and families transitioning from welfare to work.

In all these programs the housing supplied is privately owned and operated, and the rents paid are at or below the FMR. HUD determines the FMR in every locality of the nation by an annual survey of new rental contracts that have been signed during the past 15 months. In most cities the FMR is set at the 40th percentile of rents paid, meaning that 40% of renters paid a lower rent and 60% paid a higher rent; in certain cities the FMR is calculated at the 50th percentile. HUD has chosen the 40th percentile to increase housing choices while keeping budgets at reasonable levels. Table 6.7 presents the FMRs that were used by HUD in a sample of small and large cities throughout the country in fiscal year 2015. Of the cities shown, San Francisco, California,

had the highest average FMR. Although Honolulu, Hawaii, had the country's highest FMR for a studio apartment ($1,260), FMRs were set higher for San Francisco's one-bedroom ($1,635), two-bedroom ($2,062), three-bedroom ($2,801), and four-bedroom ($3,386) apartments. At the other end of the scale, the Cincinnati, Ohio, metropolitan area and Bismarck, North Dakota, had FMR levels nearly three times lower than those of San Francisco and Honolulu.

According to HUD, in *Resident Characteristics Report* (November 30, 2014, https://pic.hud.gov/pic/RCRPublic/rcrmain.asp), 1.9 million households with 4.5 million individual members and an average annual income of $14,071 benefited from HUD's public housing between August 2013 and November 2014. Approximately 70% of voucher recipients were classified as extremely low income, with incomes below 30% of their area's median; 19% were classified as very low income, with incomes below 50% of their area's median; and 4% were classified as low income, with incomes below 80% of their area's median. Less than 1% were classified as above low income, with incomes above 81% of their area's median, and there were no income data in the report for 7% of voucher recipients.

TABLE 6.7

Fair market rental rates for selected metropolitan areas, fiscal year 2015

Area definition	0 bedroom	1 bedroom	2 bedroom	3 bedroom	4 bedroom
Bismarck, ND	$535	$607	$759	$1,076	$1,269
Cincinnati-Middletown, OH-KY-IN	$463	$579	$769	$1,065	$1,173
Lexington-Fayette, KY	$508	$593	$776	$1,105	$1,237
Kansas City, MO-KS	$559	$719	$891	$1,221	$1,360
Albuquerque, NM	$543	$682	$836	$1,210	$1,481
Salt Lake City, UT	$606	$727	$901	$1,285	$1,513
Memphis, TN-MS-AR	$614	$702	$832	$1,137	$1,267
Dallas, TX	$607	$728	$921	$1,229	$1,484
Minneapolis-St. Paul-Bloomington, MN-WI	$641	$796	$996	$1,403	$1,656
Charlotte-Gastonia-Rock Hill, NC-SC	$636	$701	$831	$1,120	$1,389
Ann Arbor, MI	$675	$813	$964	$1,318	$1,707
New Orleans-Metairie-Kenner, LA	$648	$767	$950	$1,192	$1,443
Atlanta-Sandy Springs-Marietta, GA	$708	$773	$916	$1,213	$1,474
Portland, ME	$730	$869	$1,074	$1,421	$1,492
Las Vegas-Paradise, NV	$630	$787	$969	$1,428	$1,695
Gulfport-Biloxi, MS	$653	$673	$808	$1,039	$1,107
Orlando-Kissimmee-Sanford, FL	$707	$836	$997	$1,330	$1,608
Chicago-Joliet-Naperville, IL	$812	$922	$1,093	$1,393	$1,624
Flagstaff, AZ	$710	$825	$1,033	$1,311	$1,671
Anchorage, AK	$809	$936	$1,199	$1,767	$2,124
Seattle-Bellevue, WA	$811	$959	$1,180	$1,739	$2,090
Philadelphia-Camden-Wilmington, PA-NJ-DE-MD	$814	$959	$1,156	$1,440	$1,546
Baltimore-Towson, MD	$833	$985	$1,232	$1,574	$1,713
Los Angeles-Long Beach, CA	$913	$1,103	$1,424	$1,926	$2,145
Boston-Cambridge-Quincy, MA-NH	$1,071	$1,196	$1,494	$1,861	$2,023
San Francisco, CA	$1,256	$1,635	$2,062	$2,801	$3,386
Washington-Arlington-Alexandria, DC-VA-MD	$1,167	$1,230	$1,458	$1,951	$2,451
New York, NY	$1,196	$1,249	$1,481	$1,904	$2,134
Honolulu, HI	$1,260	$1,374	$1,810	$2,667	$3,061

SOURCE: Adapted from *FY2015 Final Fair Market Rents Documentation System*, U.S. Department of Housing and Urban Development, 2015, http://www .huduser.org/portal/datasets/fmr/fmrs/FY2015_code/select_Geography.odn (accessed November 12, 2014)

During the first decade of the 21st century there was a pronounced shift of the subsidized population from public housing toward voucher housing. This represented a major change in the direction of federal policy, and in the view of many analysts, it foreshadows a continued shift toward increased privatization of housing subsidies. Among voucher types, tenant-based programs are least dependent on nonmarket forces; they do not require the participation of developers, many of whom complain that the construction and maintenance of low-income housing is less profitable than other types of construction. Tenant-based vouchers also give low-income people choices in housing, allowing poor families to be more flexible in the pursuit of job opportunities. Tenant-based voucher recipients can move to areas with better opportunities and transportation options, and in the aggregate this offers possibilities to avoid one of the unintended negative effects of public housing and some project-based subsidies: the concentration and entrenchment of poverty in certain urban areas.

Public Housing

Although much maligned due to perceived failures in planning and upkeep—and not considered as central to HUD's mission as in earlier decades—the agency's provision of public housing remained an important source of assistance to some of the poorest U.S. families and individuals as of 2014. According to the agency, in *Resident Characteristics Report*, 965,665 households with 2.1 million individual members and an average annual income of $14,071 benefited from HUD's public housing between August 2013 and November 2014. Approximately 66% of public housing recipients were classified as extremely low income, with incomes below 30% of their area's median; 20% were classified as very low income, with incomes below 50% of their area's median; 9% were classified as low income, with incomes below 80% of their area's median; and 3% were classified as above low income, with incomes above 81% of their area's median. (There were no income data in the report for 2% of those in public housing.)

The management of public housing is handled by PHAs that have been established by local governments to administer HUD housing programs. The U.S. Housing Act of 1937 required that PHAs submit annual plans to HUD and declared that it was the policy of the United States "to vest in public housing agencies that perform well, the maximum amount of responsibility and flexibility in program administration, with appropriate accountability to public housing residents, localities, and the general public."

Thus, PHAs operate under plans that are approved by HUD and under HUD supervision, and the HUD budget's allotment to public housing programs flows through these PHAs. However, the PHAs are also expected to operate with some independence and to be accountable to their residents, local (or state) governments, and the public.

Not all PHAs have performed well, and HUD has been accused of lax supervision. PHAs and public housing generally reflect the distressed economic conditions of the population living in government-owned housing. Many PHAs have been charged with neglecting maintenance, tolerating unsafe living conditions for tenants, and conducting fraudulent or careless financial practices. In an effort to improve its accountability for the conditions of low-income housing, HUD implemented the Public Housing Assessment System (PHAS) in January 2000. The PHAS is used to measure the performance of PHAs. The assessment system consists of four primary components:

- Ensure, through physical inspection, that PHAs meet the minimum standard of being decent, safe, sanitary, and in good repair

- Oversee the finances of PHAs

- Evaluate the effectiveness of the management of PHAs

- Receive feedback from PHA residents on housing conditions

In *PHAS Made Simple... in 0 to 2.6 Seconds* (June 2005, http://portal.hud.gov/hudportal/documents/huddoc?id=DOC_14721.pdf), HUD explains that individual PHAs are given a score for all four components. The first three components each account for 30% of the total score, and the fourth component (residents' feedback) accounts for 10%. The four component scores are combined for a total PHAS score, and the scores affect the PHAs' status with HUD. PHAs are classified as "high performers" when they score 90% or higher and score at least 60% in all four areas and as "standard performers" when they score between 60% and 90% and receive at least 60% on all but the residents' feedback. PHAs considered "substandard" receive 60% scores or higher on their overall PHAS but receive less than 60% on one of the subsections other than residents' feedback, and PHAs considered "troubled" receive less than 60% on their total PHAS score. Troubled PHAs are subject to increased HUD oversight and the possibility of being suspended or debarred if no improvement is made in two years.

PHAS scores are assembled and processed by HUD's Integrated Assessment Subsystem (NASS), a computer system that provides quality assurance, dissemination of scores to PHAs, and procedures for appeals and waiver requests. Because of the growing centrality of the NASS to the overall PHAS process, HUD increasingly refers to the assessment system as the NASS-PHAS.

Other Housing Assistance Programs

Besides its main voucher programs and public housing, HUD operates programs that offer subsidized housing for people living with AIDS, elderly people, Native Americans and Native Hawaiians, and people with disabilities. The Prisoner Reentry Initiative, begun in 2005, helps former prisoners find housing and receive job training and other services.

Other federal programs aim to increase privately owned low-income housing stock. HUD's Federal Housing Administration (FHA) offers mortgage insurance for multifamily projects, tax credits to housing developers who provide a portion of their projects at low rents, and a Community Development Block Grant program that is used to rehabilitate housing within urban communities that have people with low and moderate incomes.

HUD maintains demographic and income data only on participants in its major programs. For that reason, information on the characteristics of participants in many other HUD subsidy programs aimed at low-income people is unavailable.

Rural Housing Programs

The U.S. Department of Agriculture's (USDA) Rural Housing Service (RHS) administers a variety of rural housing programs. These programs make federal money available for housing in rural areas, which are considered places with populations of 50,000 or less. Eligibility for rural rental assistance is similar to that of subsidized urban programs. Other RHS programs include grants or low-interest loans to repair substandard housing, subsidized mortgages and down-payment assistance for low-income homeownership, and loans that help developers build multifamily housing for low-income residents. According to the USDA, in *USDA Rural Development 2013 Progress Report* (March 2014, http://www.rd.usda.gov/files/reports/RD_ProgressRpt2013.pdf), the RHS's multifamily housing programs served approximately 523,000 households in over 1,600 apartment developments in 2013. Among those served were 280,000 low-income rural residents who received rental assistance subsidies and 3,500 families who received rent subsidies in the form of vouchers.

Foreclosure Prevention Programs

With the collapse of the housing market during the Great Recession, millions of Americans saw the value of their homes drop below what they owed on their mortgages, leaving it difficult or impossible to refinance or sell their homes. Although the recession ended in mid-2009, many U.S. homeowners continued to struggle making their mortgage payments due to persistently high unemployment, and as a result foreclosure rates remained high for years afterward. The government responded by establishing a number of programs to help homeowners at risk of foreclosure.

The FHA put in place an early delinquency intervention program to help up to 400,000 homeowners avoid foreclosure. Through the agency, lenders could offer formal forbearance agreements (agreements that lending institutions will delay foreclosing on loans provided the borrowers perform certain agreed-on terms and conditions) to borrowers who were under 90 days in default of their loans. Loss mitigation (the process of attempting to collect past-due mortgage payments) programs were also created by the FHA to assist an additional 300,000 homeowners. Mortgage modifications, preforeclosure sales, and special forbearance agreements were also offered by the early delinquency intervention program.

A joint program offered by HUD and the U.S. Department of the Treasury, the Making Home Affordable (MHA) program, was aimed at helping homeowners refinance or modify mortgages to make them more affordable. Part of the program was designed to specifically assist borrowers who owed more on their mortgage than their home was worth. In addition, HUD reoriented its free counseling programs that had previously helped consumers make well-informed decisions about taking on mortgages. By fiscal year 2010 most counseling services were geared toward helping homeowners avoid foreclosure. In the press release "Obama Administration Extends Deadline for Making Home Affordable Program" (May 30, 2013, http://www.makinghomeafford able.gov), HUD and the Department of the Treasury note that approximately 1.3 million homeowners had received direct assistance through the program between March 2009 and May 2013 and that the median amount of savings these homeowners obtained was $546 per month. The MHA program was set to expire on December 31, 2013, but the continued difficulties faced by homeowners led the agencies to extend the program through December 31, 2015.

DIFFICULTIES IN MEETING HOUSING NEEDS

Arnold et al. note that, based on their analysis of 2012 census data, one out of four renter households was considered ELI and that 7.7 million of the total 10.2 million ELI households in the country spent 75% or more of their income on rent. Spending this amount of total household income on rent left ELI families incapable of meeting the remainder of their basic needs. For such households to have even a basic level of health and stability, they would need to pay no more than $493 per month in rent, and yet the national two-bedroom FMR stood at $984 in 2014.

Although households in such situations theoretically qualify for rent subsidies, obtaining housing assistance can in reality be very challenging. Arnold et al. explain that "housing assistance programs are oversubscribed and three-quarters of eligible households go unassisted. Low income households desperately in need of housing find themselves on years-long waiting lists, or find that waiting lists for affordable housing in their area are closed entirely. For example, in April 2013, the DC Housing Authority decided to close its waiting list of nearly 70,000 applicants when the average wait time for a studio apartment was 39 years and 28 years for a one-bedroom unit." The researchers further note that among those applicants for rental assistance who are waitlisted, 40% end up doubled up with family or friends and 23% become at least temporarily homeless.

The situation for applicants in the District of Columbia is not unique among large city housing agencies. For example, Lolly Bowean reports in "Chicago Housing Authority Opens Wait Lists for Public Housing, Vouchers" (ChicagoTribune.com, October 27, 2014) that in 2014 the Chicago Housing Authority (CHA) allowed the city's residents to enter into a lottery to be added to one of three waiting lists for public housing (one for public housing, one for vouchers, and one for privately owned subsidized housing). The waiting lists had been closed for more than four years, and the CHA expected more than 250,000 families to apply for spots on the waiting lists. Selection in the lottery did not mean a family would receive a voucher or apartment; it simply meant that the family would be added to a list on which it could expect to wait for years, at the end of which it would be screened for eligibility to receive vouchers or subsidized housing.

According to the New York City Housing Authority, in "About NYCHA: Fact Sheet" (April 1, 2014, http://www.nyc.gov/html/nycha/html/about/factsheet.shtml), on March 17, 2014, there were 247,262 families on the waiting list for public housing, 121,999 families on the waiting list for vouchers (or Section 8 housing, as the main HUD voucher program is often called, in reference to the relevant section of the Housing Act of 1937), and 21,663 families on both lists. At that time, there were 178,557 total apartments in the city's traditional public housing developments, nearly 70,000 fewer than the number of applicants, and the turnover rate in 2013 (the rate at which apartments became available to people on the waiting list) was 3.1%. Assuming that approximately 3.1% of apartments would become available in 2014, an estimated 5,535 of the families, or 2.2% of the families on the public housing waiting list, might be able to move into an apartment that year. At that rate it would take decades to exhaust the waiting list. The waiting list for Section 8 housing (121,999) exceeded the number of Section 8 apartments currently rented (91,103) by a similar proportion.

Reasons for the Shortage of Affordable Housing

In December 2000 Congress established the bipartisan Millennial Housing Commission to examine the role of the federal government in meeting the nation's housing needs. In *Meeting Our Nation's Housing Challenges* (May 30, 2002, http://permanent.access.gpo.gov/lps19766/www.mhc.gov/mhcfinal.pdf), the commission states that "there is simply not enough affordable housing. The inadequacy of supply increases dramatically as one moves down the ladder of family earnings. The challenge is most acute for rental housing in high-cost areas, and the most egregious problem is for the very poor."

In "Worst Case Housing Needs 2011," HUD indicates that the supply of affordable housing for those renters at the lowest end of the income scale had been decreasing since 2003. (See Figure 6.2.) In 2011 only 65 units of adequate and affordable rental housing were available for every 100 very low income renters, and only 36 such units were available for every 100 extremely low income renters. This scarcity was most extreme in central cities and suburbs. HUD notes that the major causes of the increases in worst-case needs among very low income renters were shrinking incomes due to unemployment, a growing lack of federal rental assistance, and competition for affordable units. HUD further observes that competition for rental units increased primarily due to the foreclosure crisis and the high rate of unemployment, both of which persisted well beyond the end of the Great Recession. Although most of those who lost their homes were not at the lowest end of the income scale, almost all of them subsequently entered the rental market, increasing the competition and, as a consequence, the prices for rental homes and apartments. Likewise, many of those who lost their job during the recession went from being a homeowner to being a renter.

Although real estate developers are constantly adding housing units to the nation's supply, it is almost always less profitable to build affordable housing for low-income families and individuals than to build housing for those at the middle and upper portions of the income scale. To provide incentives to developers, the 1986 Low-Income Housing Tax Credit (LIHTC) program gave the states $1.25 per capita (per person) in tax credits toward the private development of low-income housing. In "A New Era for Affordable Housing" (NREIOnline.com, March 1, 2003), H. Lee Murphy reports on data from the National Council of State Housing Agencies indicating that construction hit a high in 1994, when 117,100 apartment units were built with the credits. Skyrocketing construction costs brought a decline in new construction, which reached a low of 66,900 units in 2000. In 2001 Congress raised the per capita allotment to $1.75, and beginning in 2003 the allotment was adjusted each year

FIGURE 6.2

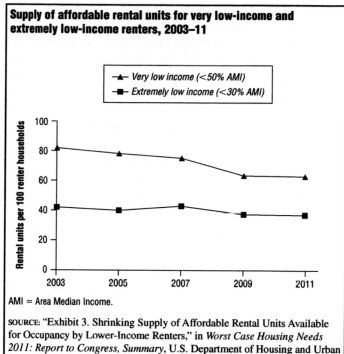

Supply of affordable rental units for very low-income and extremely low-income renters, 2003–11

AMI = Area Median Income.

SOURCE: "Exhibit 3. Shrinking Supply of Affordable Rental Units Available for Occupancy by Lower-Income Renters," in *Worst Case Housing Needs 2011: Report to Congress, Summary*, U.S. Department of Housing and Urban Development, February 2013, http://www.huduser.org/portal//Publications/pdf/HUD-506_WorstCase2011.pdf (accessed December 8, 2014)

to account for inflation. HUD reports in "Low-Income Housing Tax Credits" (2014, http://www.huduser.org/portal/datasets/lihtc.html) that between 1995 and 2012 an average of more than 1,400 projects and roughly 105,000 housing units per year were built because of the tax credit.

However, this rate of construction is not keeping pace with the demand for affordable housing. Besides the decay and demolition of older public housing units, a perpetual issue in maintaining the current stock of subsidized housing is the expiration of contracts between government agencies such as HUD and the private owners of buildings who offer voucher-based assistance. When such contracts expire, building owners are typically free to offer the apartments to renters on the open market, and many owners find it advantageous to remove their buildings from the subsidized marketplace, renovate them to suit the tastes of more affluent families, and either rent them on the open market or sell them as condominiums.

The JCHS notes in *State of the Nation's Housing 2014* that "contracts on an estimated 596,000 units in properties with project-based rental assistance—more than a quarter (28 percent) of the total—will come up for renewal by 2024." Additionally, the LIHTC's provision of tax credits to developers who build and preserve affordable housing are likewise in effect for finite periods. Once owners of these properties reach the end of their compliance periods, they are allowed to apply for tax credits again, continue to offer affordable housing without receiving subsidies in the form of tax credits, or convert their affordable housing to market-rate units. The JCHS indicates that although most LIHTC property owners elect to continue offering affordable housing after their compliance periods end, those owned by for-profit companies in high-cost housing markets are oftentimes converted to market-rate housing. Furthermore, LIHTC buildings that reach the end of their compliance period typically require substantial repairs and renovations before the owners can qualify for another round of tax credits. These extensive repairs provide a further incentive for owners to remove their buildings from the affordable housing stock when their local housing market is capable of supporting a profitable conversion to market-rate housing.

Besides these complex factors, a comparatively simple force often stands in the way of new construction of low-income housing: community resistance based on the stigma conventionally associated with the occupants of public and subsidized housing. Many middle- and upper-income people resist the introduction of low-income housing in their communities out of a traditional "not in my backyard" mentality, believing that such developments will bring rising crime, falling property values, and overcrowded classrooms, dragging down living standards for existing residents.

WHERE THE HOMELESS LIVE

When faced with high rents and low housing availability, many poor people become homeless. What happens to them? Where do they live? Research shows that after becoming homeless, many people move around, staying in one place for a while, then moving on to another place. Many homeless people take advantage of homeless shelters at some point. Such shelters may be funded by the federal government, by religious organizations, or by other private homeless advocates.

Emergency Shelters, Transitional Housing, and Permanent Supportive Housing

Typically, emergency shelters provide dormitory-style sleeping accommodations and bathing facilities, with varying services for laundry, telephone calls, and other needs. Residents are often limited in the length of their stay and must leave the shelters during the day under most circumstances. These shelters are often run by nonprofit groups. Some groups are local chapters of national organizations, such as the Salvation Army, whereas others are standalone local nonprofits that serve a single community. As noted in Chapter 5, shelters in many localities are operated by churches or Christian organizations affiliated with the Association of Gospel Rescue Missions (AGRM). The AGRM has over 300 missions that can be searched by region at the association's website (http://www.agrm.org/agrm/Locate_a_Mission.asp). For example, as of February 2015, the AGRM listed 34 shelters in its directory for the Pacific region, which included California, Nevada, and Hawaii. Most of these shelters were in California, which has the largest homeless population in the country.

By contrast, transitional housing is intended to bridge the gap between the shelter or street and permanent housing, with appropriate services to move the homeless into independent living. It may be a room in a hotel or motel, or it may be a subsidized apartment in a development where services are accessible onsite. Like emergency shelters, transitional housing typically depends on federal funding through HUD, which often takes the form of grants to developers who build or convert buildings into such housing and vouchers that provide rental subsidies to occupants. Although federal funding agencies have begun to shift resources from transitional housing to permanent supportive housing, numerous transitional housing programs continue to serve pressing needs, often when a specific homeless subpopulation's needs align more closely with long-term but temporary housing than with permanent housing. One example is the Transitional Housing Assistance Grants for Victims of Domestic Violence, Dating Violence, Stalking, or Sexual Assault Program, which is funded through the U.S. Department of Justice's Office on Violence against Women. In "Grant Programs" (July 24, 2014, http://www.justice.gov/ovw/grant-programs), the Department of Justice indicates that these grants are awarded to state and local governments as well as to organizations that have a proven ability to serve this specific subpopulation. Similarly, the Family and Youth Services Bureau (FYSB) of the U.S. Department of Health and Human Services funds transitional housing for homeless youth through its Transitional Living Program. The FYSB notes in "Transitional Living Program Fact Sheet" (November 5, 2014, http://www.acf.hhs.gov/programs/fysb/resource/tlp-fact-sheet) that in 2014 it awarded $43.7 million to state and local government agencies and nonprofit groups serving homeless youth aged 16 to 22 years with housing that was available for up to 21 months.

Permanent supportive housing is the emerging paradigm for housing the chronically homeless, as discussed at length in Chapters 5 and 7. Typically constructed or developed in the same way as transitional housing, with linked services and with federal funding, and operated by local nonprofit groups or public–private partnerships, there are no time limits on occupancy or service utilization. As Figure 5.1 in Chapter 5 shows, between 2007 and 2014 the number of emergency shelter beds increased significantly, from 211,451 to 249,497; the number of transitional housing beds decreased significantly, from 211,205 to 173,224; and the number of permanent supportive housing beds increased dramatically, from 188,636 to 300,282.

Illegal Occupancy

Poor neighborhoods are usually full of abandoned buildings. Often, falling real estate prices or the high costs of renovation leave landlords unable to maintain their properties without losing money, so they let their buildings deteriorate or simply walk away, leaving the fate of the building and its residents in the hands of the government. Despite overcrowding and unsafe conditions, many homeless people move into dilapidated buildings illegally, glad for what shelter they can find. Municipal governments, which are overwhelmed by long waiting lists for public housing, by a lack of funds and personnel, and by an inadequate supply of emergency shelter beds, are often unable or unwilling to strictly enforce housing laws, allowing the homeless to become squatters rather than forcing them into the streets. Some deliberately turn a blind eye to the problem, knowing they have no better solution for the homeless.

The result is a multitude of housing units with deplorable living conditions—tenants bedding down in illegal boiler basements, sharing beds with children or in-laws, or sharing bathrooms with strangers. The buildings may have leaks and rot, rusted fire escapes, and rat and roach infestations. Given the alternative, many homeless people feel lucky to be sheltered at all.

As a result of the housing crisis that began in 2008, some homeless people began turning to foreclosed homes in their search for shelter. According to the article "Some Homeless Turn to Foreclosed Homes" (Associated Press, February 17, 2008), many homeless began moving into these vacant homes and became squatters. The article notes that "foreclosed homes often have an advantage over boarded-up and dilapidated houses that have been abandoned because of rundown conditions: Sometimes the heat, lights and water are still working." The article "Activist Moves Homeless into Foreclosures" (Associated Press, December 1, 2008) explains that in 2008 homeless people were squatting in foreclosed homes in southern Florida with the help of the national organization Take Back the Land. This group finds empty foreclosed properties, arranges to have the utilities turned on, and becomes a pseudo landlord. Taryn Wobbema reports in "City Foreclosures Open Space for Squatters" (MNDaily .com, March 4, 2009) that in Minneapolis, Minnesota, the Poor People's Economic Human Rights Campaign places homeless people in empty homes illegally.

In "Homeless Squatting in Foreclosed City Homes" (13WHAM.com, December 20, 2010), Rachel Barnhart indicates that in 2010 homeless squatters were moving into some of the 3,000 empty houses in Rochester, New York. The squatters were helped by Take Back the Land.

Similar actions were taking place around the country. Take Back the Land explains in "US Senators Contact Take Back the Land–Rochester to Address the Housing Crisis" (http://www.takebacktheland.org) that in March 2011 it staged a two-week-long community eviction defense by physically blocking authorities from removing Catherine Lennon and 10 extended family members from her Rochester home, which had been foreclosed. Eventually, the police were ordered to forcibly evict Lennon and her family. Intense media scrutiny led Representative Louise McIntosh Slaughter (1929–; D-NY) to intervene and ask the federal authorities to negotiate with Lennon. Although Bank of America and the Federal National Mortgage Association, a federally subsidized mortgage-backed securities company, continued to press their foreclosure case, the negative publicity eventually led them to pursue a settlement that allowed Lennon and her family to stay in the home.

Tent Cities

The Great Recession also saw an increase in the number of homeless people living in "tent cities"—mass encampments that in many cases grew large enough to become communities in their own right. Although overall levels of homelessness declined between 2010 and 2014, according to HUD's annual point-in-time counts, the situation varied by state and locality. Many individual tent cities continued to grow larger during this time, and the phenomenon of tent cities attracted increased media attention. In *Welcome Home: The Rise of Tent Cities in the United States* (March 2014, http://nlchp.org/documents/WelcomeHome _TentCities), Julie Hunter et al. analyze local and national media accounts of tent cities across the United States between 2008 and 2013 and also convey the results of first-hand research that was conducted at select tent cities treated as "case studies." The researchers document the existence of over 100 tent communities in 46 states and the District of Columbia, and their interviews with tent city residents led them to isolate a number of factors that are believed to be driving the tent city trend:

- A general lack of availability of shelter space compared to the number of homeless individuals in need of shelter.

- Inadequacies with the shelter system in certain locations, including safety concerns, a lack of a sense of community or participation, and logistical problems that hamper homeless individuals' ability to seek employment or to carry out daily life activities.

- A pattern of criminalizing behaviors, such as public urination and sleeping in public, that homeless individuals engage in of necessity, because of their lack of access to shelter, with enforcement usually focused on driving homeless individuals out of the central city or other highly visible areas.

- An approach to the problem of homelessness focused not on solving the problem of homelessness but instead aimed largely at decreasing the visibility of homeless individuals and communities.

- A lack of attentiveness by service providers and state and local governments to the participation of homeless individuals in creating the solutions that are offered to them.

- A lack of political will to devote sufficient resources to addressing the problem in a long-term, sustainable manner, and a focus instead on short-term solutions that take homeless people off the streets but are not responsive to the needs of homeless people themselves or, indeed, to longer term community interests.

Like many media outlets reporting on the phenomenon, Hunter et al. note that tent cities offer homeless people an alternative to emergency shelters that in some cases provide for increased feelings of safety and a sense of belonging to a community. However, levels of comfort and functionality vary by location. According to Blake Ellis, in "America's Homeless: The Rise of Tent City, USA" (CNN.com, May 16, 2014), "Some have 'mayors' who determine the rules of the camp and who can and can't join, others are a free-for-all. Some are overflowing with trash, old food, human waste and drug paraphernalia, others are relatively clean and drug-free." Hunter et al. determine that of the 100 or so camps that existed between 2008 and 2013, eight were allowed to exist legally, 10 were not legally authorized but were allowed to go on existing while city or county authorities looked the other way, and most of the rest were dismantled and the occupants evicted.

CHAPTER 7
DEALING WITH THE PROBLEM OF HOMELESSNESS

THE CHANGING RESPONSE TO HOMELESSNESS

In "The New Approach: The Emergence of a Better Way to Address Homelessness" (November 18, 2014, http://b.3cdn.net/naeh/f022a3e40771e1eea8_6nm6iyueq.pdf), the National Alliance to End Homelessness (NAEH) notes that prior to the 1980s the phenomenon of mass homelessness during times when the economy was otherwise operating at or near capacity was unprecedented. After a period of high unemployment and inflation (the devaluation of a country's currency, which causes people to become poorer even when the amount of money they earn or possess remains the same) during the early 1980s, the U.S. economy rebounded strongly later in that decade, but the homeless population did not decline. Numerous government programs and nonprofit attempts to address the problem of homelessness emerged, many of which emphasized the construction of emergency shelters, transitional housing, and services intended to help the homeless until they were capable of becoming self-sufficient. The model for helping an individual escape homelessness typically involved a move from emergency housing to transitional housing, where one had to abide by rules meant to address addiction, promote mental health, develop productive routines, and build employment skills. Transitional housing often proved successful for those who were able to abide by the restrictions placed on them, but a large proportion of chronically homeless people left such programs before completion and returned to the streets.

The homeless population continued to grow through the late 1990s in spite of a growing economy and the many government and nonprofit efforts to address the population's needs. This situation led many advocates for the homeless to call for a shift in tactics. Rather than continue to support the homeless until they became self-sufficient, numerous advocacy groups and local governments began experimenting with programs to end homelessness first

and then consider the potential for individuals and families to become self-sufficient. Local governments and nonprofit agencies pioneered these types of programs between the late 1990s and the onset of the Great Recession (which officially lasted from December 2007 to June 2009).

Pioneering Change at the Local Level

Individual programs varied, but many of the most successful ones shared an emphasis on what is called "housing first," an approach that calls for providing the homeless with permanent housing as quickly as possible. Housing-first approaches represent an alternative to the other major programs that offer federally subsidized housing, which are discussed in Chapter 6. Whereas traditional subsidized housing, including temporary housing, is typically available on a first-come first-serve or lottery basis and often involves an extended waiting period before housing becomes available, housing-first programs seek to place the homeless in houses immediately, with a minimal application process and regardless of their eligibility for other government services. After housing is secured, these programs then address clients' needs for services.

The housing-first approach varies by type of homelessness. Those who are chronically homeless, often because of disabilities or conditions that prevent them from becoming self-sufficient, are best served by permanent supportive housing. Permanent supportive housing includes immediate placement in a permanent home as well as the provision of services that will allow clients to remain in their home permanently. There are no time limits on the assistance that the formerly homeless receive through permanent supportive housing.

For families and individuals who become homeless due to temporary crises, rapid rehousing represents a cost-effective intervention. Like permanent supportive housing, rapid rehousing involves quickly getting the homeless into a permanent home and supplying them with the services they need to remain housed. However, unlike permanent supportive housing, rapid rehousing does not involve permanent subsidies and services. Aimed at those who need temporary help to escape homelessness, the program seeks to return clients to self-sufficiency so that they can eventually pay rent and expenses on their own.

Other successful programs pioneered at the local level include efforts to prevent people from becoming homeless in the first place. Prevention programs are often geared toward families, whose homelessness is frequently a result of unforeseen crises, such as abrupt increases in household expenses, job loss, or illness. Prevention can take many forms, including cash assistance, housing subsidies, and other short-term services that allow families to weather periods of acute financial stress.

The NAEH notes in "Local Progress" (2015, http://www.endhomelessness.org/pages/local_progress) that Chicago, Illinois, used a housing-first approach to reduce homelessness by 12% between 2005 and 2007; Columbus, Ohio, reduced family homelessness by 46% between 1997 and 2004 as a result of prevention and other measures; and Denver, Colorado, reduced chronic homelessness by 36% between 2005 and 2007 as a result of an integrated approach that involved permanent housing creation and mental health services. Other local governments that pioneered efforts to end rather than manage homelessness include Hennepin County, Minnesota; New York, New York; Westchester County, New York; Norfolk, Virginia; the Fairfax–Falls Church area of Virginia; Portland, Oregon; Quincy, Massachusetts; San Francisco, California; and Wichita, Kansas.

Housing First at the National Level

The federal government, along with numerous nonprofit groups, attempted to adapt local successes on a national scale during the administrations of George W. Bush (1946–) and Barack Obama (1961–). Besides the demonstrated success of local programs, the housing-first approach found support at the national level because it did not involve an increase in government funding. Instead, the U.S. Department of Housing and Urban Development (HUD) reallocated funding from transitional housing and other programs and grants were increasingly awarded to local service providers based on their adoption of a housing-first approach.

These efforts gained momentum during the Great Recession, when homelessness became increasingly visible, as foreclosures, job losses, and other financial difficulties pushed large numbers of people into homelessness, including many whose earnings had previously been well above the poverty line. A key element in the federal push to expand housing-first programs was passage of the Homeless Emergency Assistance and Rapid Transition to Housing (HEARTH) Act of 2009, which altered the structure of HUD's main homeless assistance programs to focus on permanent supportive housing and rapid rehousing and which required the U.S. Interagency Council on Homelessness (USICH) to create a national strategic plan to end homelessness. That plan, *Opening Doors: Federal Strategic Plan to Prevent and End Homelessness* (June 2010, http://usich.gov/PDF/OpeningDoors_2010_FSPPreventEndHomeless.pdf), codified the housing-first approaches to chronic and veteran homelessness that were already under way and set a target for ending chronic homelessness by 2015.

The large-scale effort to implement housing-first policies was not, however, strictly a government endeavor. Housing-first programs, like most programs that serve the homeless, are typically operated locally, by government agencies and nonprofit organizations that receive grants from HUD, the U.S. Department of Veterans Affairs (VA), or other federal agencies. One of the leading forces in the effort to take the housing-first approach national was the nonprofit organization Community Solutions, which launched the "100,000 Homes" campaign (http://100khomes.org) in July 2010. As of July 2014, the campaign had united 186 communities to find permanent homes for 100,000 homeless people. Working through a wide range of local agencies and organizations, participating communities employed a methodology that involved getting to know every homeless person in a community by name and evaluating his or her individual needs. The resulting profiles of individual homeless people were then entered in a database that allowed the participating community organizations to prioritize housing for those who needed it most and to locate the available government subsidies that could be used to pay for housing. This proactive approach to screening and application allowed the organizations affiliated with 100,000 Homes to place the chronically homeless into homes much more rapidly than is typical of government assistance programs. The campaign exceeded its goal, successfully generating 105,000 homes for homeless people nationwide in the four years of its existence.

A housing-first approach is not only successful in reducing homelessness, it is also believed to offer substantial cost savings relative to a "management" approach to homelessness. According to Christina Scotti, in "How Housing for the Chronically Homeless May Save Taxpayers Money" (FOXBusiness.com, July 7, 2014), 100,000 Homes claims that its success at placing the chronically homeless in permanent housing saves taxpayers approximately $1.3 billion annually, or $13,000 annually per each chronically homeless person. Although the costs of subsidizing housing and services (which are typically paid by the federal government) rise in a housing-first approach, the costs to the many organizations and institutions that deal with the problems of the chronically homeless, including incarceration and treatment in emergency departments, fall precipitously.

Persistent Problems

The success of housing-first and other efforts was offset to a large degree by a worsening shortage of affordable housing during the first decade of the 21st century. In most major cities and suburbs real estate prices rose rapidly prior to the Great Recession, but wages, especially for those at the lower end of the income scale, did not rise comparably. Althea Arnold et al. of the National Low Income Housing Coalition note in *Out of Reach 2014: Twenty-Five Years Later, the Affordable Housing Crisis Continues* (2014, http://nlihc.org/sites/default/files/oor/2014OOR.pdf) that the national "housing wage" (the hourly wage a full-time worker would need to afford adequate two-bedroom housing, as established by HUD's fair market rents) was $18.92 in 2014, more than 2.5 times higher than the federal minimum wage of $7.25. Additionally, in *No Safe Place: The Criminalization of Homelessness in U.S. Cities* (2014, http://www.nlchp.org/documents/No_Safe_Place), the National Law Center on Homelessness and Poverty (NLCHP) observes that decreased funding for federal housing subsidies led to the loss of approximately 12.8% of the United States' overall supply of low-income housing between 2001 and 2014. The NLCHP estimates that three-quarters of those who qualify for federal housing subsidies fail to receive assistance due to the supply shortage. Many families and individuals remain on waiting lists for years or even decades before receiving housing assistance.

Thus, critics of housing first sometimes characterize the approach as a last resort generated in response to wider government failures. For example, Pat LaMarche quotes in "Housing First Doesn't Work: The Homeless Need Community Support" (HuffingtonPost.com, January 16, 2014) Ralph DaCosta Nunez, the president and chief executive officer of the Institute for Children, Poverty, and Homelessness, who described housing first as "all that's left after the other poverty fighting programs have been underfunded or eliminated." Nunez argued that housing first is a one-size-fits-all approach that addresses the need for housing but does not adequately address corresponding problems such as mental illness, domestic violence victimization, and a lack of education, all of which affect sizable proportions of the homeless population.

Although housing enjoys widespread support at the federal level and has been lauded in numerous national and local media stories, most homeless advocacy organizations stress the need to focus on numerous fronts in the attempt to end homelessness. In its "Five Fundamentals to Prevent and End Homelessness," which were issued in 2007, the National Coalition for the Homeless (NCH; January 25, 2012, http://www.nationalhomeless.org/publications/fivefundamentals/index.html) identified what it considered the keys to solving the problem. The first fundamental concerned the reauthorization of key federal funding under the McKinney-Vento Homeless Assistance Act, which was accomplished with the passage of the HEARTH Act in 2009. The other four fundamentals remain works in progress: a dramatic increase in the supply of affordable housing; access to health care, education, and social services for all who need them; a better match between personal incomes and living expenses; and ending discrimination against the homeless.

Similarly, the NAEH lists "Ten Essentials" (2015, http://www.endhomelessness.org/pages/ten-essentials) that communities must address if they are to find permanent solutions to homelessness. These 10 strategies for ending homelessness include not only permanent supportive housing and rapid rehousing but also the prevention of homelessness (both in emergency situations and in cases where individuals are transitioning out of institutions such as jails and the foster care system), systematic planning, data collection that allows full understanding of the problem, outreach to homeless families and individuals to guide them out of homelessness, an emphasis on shortening the period that any given person or family spends without a home, connecting the homeless with government services, and ensuring that people exiting homelessness have income.

FEDERAL PROGRAMS TO ASSIST THE HOMELESS

Since 1860 the federal government has been actively involved with the housing industry, specifically the low-income housing industry. In 1860 the government conducted the first partial census of housing—by counting slave dwellings. Twenty years later the U.S. census counted the living quarters of the rest of the population in its first full housing census. Prior to the rise of homelessness during the 1980s the federal government played an increasingly larger role in combating housing problems in the United States. Major expansions of federal authority over issues related to low-income housing include:

- 1937—the U.S. Housing Act established the Public Housing Administration (which was later merged into the Federal Housing Administration and HUD) to create low-rent housing programs across the country through the establishment of local public housing agencies.

- 1949—the Housing Act set the goals of "a decent home and a suitable environment" for every family and authorized an 810,000-unit public housing program over the next six years. Title I of the act created the Urban Renewal Program, and Title V created the basic rural housing program under the Federal Housing Administration, which put the federal government directly into the mortgage business.

- 1965—Congress established HUD. Its goal was to create a new rent supplement program for low-income households in private housing.

- 1974—the Housing and Community Development Act created a new leased-housing program that included a certificate (voucher) program, expanding housing choices for low-income tenants. The voucher program soon became known as Section 8, after the section of the act that established it.

The McKinney-Vento Homeless Assistance Act

Widespread public outcry over the plight of the homeless during the early 1980s prompted Congress to pass the Stewart B. McKinney Homeless Assistance Act of 1987. Congress renamed the act the McKinney-Vento Homeless Assistance Act in 2000 to honor Representative Bruce F. Vento's (1940–2000; D-MN) service to the homeless. The range and reach of the act has broadened over the years. Most of the money authorized by the act went, initially, toward the funding of emergency and transitional homeless shelters. Amendments to the act later enabled funding and other services to support permanent housing and other programs to help the homeless. Throughout the act's history, HUD has been the lead funding agency for homeless assistance.

In May 2009 President Obama signed the HEARTH Act, ushering in a new era of homeless assistance under McKinney-Vento. The act consolidated a number of HUD homeless assistance programs, expanded the definition of homelessness, added new funds in areas including emergency shelter needs and rural housing, and codified the shift toward a goal of ending rather than managing homelessness, as described earlier.

HUD Homeless Assistance Programs

By far the largest homeless assistance program among HUD's homeless assistance efforts is the Continuum of Care (CoC) Program. The CoC Program is competitively funded; that is, nonprofit groups, as well as state and local governments, apply for grants in competition with one another. HUD explains in "Continuum of Care (CoC) Program" (2014, https://www.hudexchange .info/coc) that the program is "designed to promote communitywide commitment to the goal of ending homelessness; provide funding for efforts by nonprofit providers, and State and local governments to quickly rehouse homeless individuals and families while minimizing the trauma and dislocation caused to homeless individuals, families, and communities by homelessness; promote

access to and effect utilization of mainstream programs by homeless individuals and families; and optimize self-sufficiency among individuals and families experiencing homelessness."

Originally the vehicle for providing much of the funding for emergency and transitional shelters, the CoC Program has increasingly emphasized housing-first efforts, in keeping with the trends described earlier. Also, the USICH notes in "Department of Housing and Urban Development" (2013, http://usich.gov/member_agency/ department_of_housing_and_urban_development) that the HEARTH Act consolidated three "legacy" programs for combating homelessness under the umbrella of the CoC Program:

- Supportive Housing Program—provides funding for the purchasing, renovation, leasing, and construction of housing for homeless people; for supportive services such as case management, outreach, and behavioral health care; for the development and maintenance of the Homeless Management Information Systems; and for administrative costs related to such projects.

- Shelter Plus Care Program—funds rent subsidies for permanent supportive housing aimed at homeless people with serious mental illness, chronic substance abuse problems, and diseases such as the human immunodeficiency virus or the acquired immunodeficiency syndrome.

- Section 8 Moderate Rehabilitation for Single Room Occupancy Dwellings—provides funding to public housing agencies and nonprofit groups that provide single room occupancy housing with supportive services for homeless individuals.

Table 7.1 outlines the categories of homeless people and services that qualify for funding under the CoC Program.

Another major component of HUD's homeless assistance efforts is the Emergency Solutions Grant (ESG) Program, which was established by the HEARTH Act as the successor of the Emergency Shelter Grants Program. In "Emergency Solutions Grants" (2013, http://usich.gov/ about_us/funding_programs/programs/emergency_solutions _grants), the USICH indicates that the ESG Program is aimed at promoting housing-first approaches as well as homelessness prevention and emergency shelters by providing funding to states, large cities, urban counties, and U.S. territories. These local and state governments do not compete for funding; rather, eligible governments apply for and receive funding based on formulas that calculate the funding levels necessary to meet the needs of their communities. These jurisdictions then distribute funds at their discretion to the local government agencies or nonprofit groups that are best positioned to provide

TABLE 7.1

Eligibility requirements for HUD Continuum of Care homeless assistance

Eligibility by component

Supportive services only

Individuals and families defined as homeless under the following categories are eligible for assistance in Supportive Services Only projects:
- Category 1—Literally homeless
- Category 2—Imminent risk of homeless
- Category 3*—Homeless under other federal statutes
- Category 4—Fleeing/attempting to flee domestic violence

Safe havens

Individuals defined as homeless under the following categories are eligible for assistance in Safe Havens projects:
- Category 1—Literally homeless

SH projects have the following additional Notice of Funding Availability (NOFA) limitations on eligibility within Category 1:
- Must serve individuals only
- Individual must have a severe mental illness
- Individual must be living on the streets and unwilling or unable to participate in supportive services

Transitional housing

Individuals and families defined as homeless under the following categories are eligible for assistance in Transitional Housing projects:
- Category 1—Literally homeless
- Category 2—Imminent risk of homeless
- Category 3*—Homeless under other federal statutes
- Category 4—Fleeing/attempting to flee domestic violence

Permanent supportive housing

Individuals and families defined as homeless under the following categories are eligible for assistance in Permanent Supportive Housing projects:
- Category 1—Literally homeless
- Category 4—Fleeing/attempting to flee domestic violence

Permanent Supportive Housing projects have the following additional NOFA limitations on eligibility within Category 1:
- Individuals and families coming from Transitional Housing must have originally come from the streets or emergency shelter
- Individuals and families must also have an individual family member with a disability

Projects that are dedicated chronically homeless projects, including those that were originally funded as Samaritan Bonus Initiative Projects must continue to serve chronically homeless persons exclusively.

*Projects must be located within a CoC that has received HUD approval to serve this category.
Notes: HUD = Department of Housing and Urban Development.

SOURCE: Adapted from "The Homeless Definition and Eligibility for SHP, SPC, and ESG," U.S. Department of Housing and Urban Development, May 2012, https://www.hudexchange.info/resources/documents/HomelessDefEligibility%20_SHP_SPC_ESG.pdf (accessed November 13, 2014)

assistance to the homeless population or to specific subpopulations, such as veterans, victims of domestic violence, unaccompanied youth, or families. HUD requires recipients of ESG funds to coordinate with the CoC Program in their area to determine optimal funding allocations. Table 7.2 outlines the categories of homeless people and services that qualify for funding under the ESG Program.

HUD manages two more homeless assistance programs in collaboration with other federal agencies. The HUD-VASH Program, which is administered in partnership with the VA, combines the targeting of tenant-based rental vouchers with supportive services for homeless veterans. The supportive services, including case management, medical services, and mental health care, are provided primarily through VA medical centers and clinics and their personnel. HUD also operates the Base Realignment and Closure Program, a partnership with the U.S. Department of Defense, which enables homeless assistance providers to house and serve the homeless in the buildings and on the grounds of decommissioned military bases.

In 2013 and 2014 HUD was operating in a very difficult budget environment due to intense political

pressures to curtail federal spending, which culminated in sequestration, a set of sweeping federal budget cuts triggered by the failure to resolve a fiscal standoff between Republicans in Congress and the Democratic Obama administration. As a result of the sequester, programs to combat homelessness were funded at lower levels in 2013 and 2014 than in previous years in spite of the high level of need and the agency's recent record of success at reducing the homeless population. In 2013 the agency spent $1.7 billion on homeless assistance programs. (See Table 6.6 in Chapter 6.) This amount increased to just over $2 billion in 2014, but it still remained below pre-sequestration levels. According to HUD, in "Notice of Funding Availability (NOFA) for the Fiscal Year (FY) 2014 Funds in the FY 2013–FY 2014 Continuum of Care Program Competition" (September 2014, https://www.hudexchange.info/resource/4032/nofa-for-fy2014-funds-in-the-fy2013-fy2014-coc-program-competition), approximately $1.8 billion of the agency's total fiscal year (FY) 2014 homeless assistance funding was dedicated to the CoC Program.

President Obama's 2015 budget proposal included a request to increase HUD's homeless assistance funding to $2.4 billion, a level that was considered necessary if the

TABLE 7.2

Eligibility requirements for HUD Emergency Solutions Grants homeless assistance

Eligibility by component

Street outreach

Individuals defined as homeless under the following categories are eligible for assistance in street outreach:
- Category 1—Literally homeless
- Category 4—Fleeing/attempting to flee domestic violence (where the individual or family also meets the criteria for Category 1)

Street outreach projects have the following additional limitations on eligibility within Category 1:
- Individuals and families must be living on the streets (or other places not meant for human habitation) and be unwilling or unable to access services in emergency shelter

Emergency shelter

Individuals and families defined as homeless under the following categories are eligible for assistance in emergency shelter projects:
- Category 1—Literally homeless
- Category 2—Imminent risk of homeless
- Category 3—Homeless under other federal statutes
- Category 4—Fleeing/attempting to flee domestic violence

Rapid re-housing

Individuals defined as homeless under the following categories are eligible for assistance in rapid re-housing projects:
- Category 1—Literally homeless
- Category 4—Fleeing/attempting to flee domestic violence (where the individual or family also meets the criteria for category 1)

Homelessness prevention

Individuals and families defined as homeless under the following categories are eligible for assistance in homelessness prevention projects:
- Category 2—Imminent risk of homeless
- Category 3—Homeless under other federal statutes
- Category 4—Fleeing/attempting to flee domestic violence

Individuals and families who are defined as at risk of homelessness are eligible for assistance in homelessness prevention projects.

Homelessness prevention projects have the following additional limitations on eligibility with homeless and at risk of homeless:
- Must only serve individuals and families that have an annual income below 30% of area median income

SOURCE: Adapted from "The Homeless Definition and Eligibility for SHP, SPC, and ESG," U.S. Department of Housing and Urban Development, May 2012, https://www.hudexchange.info/resources/documents/HomelessDefEligibility%20_SHP_SPC_ESG.pdf (accessed November 13, 2014)

agency was to complete its implementation of the HEARTH Act requirements, including the fulfillment of the goal of ending chronic homelessness. However, Alan Pyke reports in "8 Things to Know about the 'Cromnibus' Budget Deal Congress Just Unveiled" (ThinkProgress.org, December 10, 2014) that the congressional spending bill passed in December 2014 to fund the government through 2015 kept HUD's homeless assistance funding at around $2.1 billion, or slightly higher than the 2014 levels that were considered inadequate.

VA Homeless Assistance Programs

After HUD, the VA is the most important federal funder of assistance to the homeless. As noted in Chapter 5, U.S. military veterans have historically been disproportionately represented among the homeless. In the fact sheet "Supportive Services for Veteran Families (SSVF) Program" (November 23, 2010, http://www.va.gov/HOMELESS/docs/Prevention_Fact_Sheet_11-22-10.pdf), the VA notes that there were an estimated 313,000 homeless veterans on one night in 2003. In the years that followed, widespread public and bipartisan outrage at the fact of veteran homelessness led to an intense focus on this subpopulation. Since then veteran homelessness has been rapidly reduced. A result of the same trends that have led to rapid decreases in the chronic homeless population, the progress in ending veteran homelessness is attributable to a number of VA programs in addition to the HUD programs that fund local homeless assistance efforts. By

2014 the number of homeless veterans on one night in January had fallen to 49,933. (See Table 5.4 in Chapter 5.)

As noted earlier, homeless veterans often access permanent supportive housing through the HUD-VASH Program. HUD supplies the housing subsidies through its voucher programs, and the VA supplies supportive services. According to the USICH, in *Proposed Fiscal Year 2015 Budget Fact Sheet: Homelessness Assistance* (March 5, 2014, http://usich.gov/resources/uploads/asset_library/FY2015_Budget_Fact_Sheet_-_Homelessness_Programs.pdf), there are four main VA programs that provide support for homeless veterans:

- Supportive Services for Veteran Families—provides funding to nonprofit groups that focus on providing the supportive services that enable veterans and their families to make the transition to permanent housing

- Homeless Providers Grant and Per Diem Program—provides funding to community organizations that aid homeless veterans through transitional housing and related services

- Domiciliary Care for Homeless Veterans Program—provides around-the-clock in-home rehabilitation and treatment to homeless veterans with severe health problems

- Healthcare for Homeless Veterans Program—funds outreach to homeless veterans undertaken by VA social workers and clinicians, with the goal of helping veterans access the health care services they need to escape homelessness, and additionally funds in-home treatment and long-term case management

According to the USICH, the VA requested $1.6 billion for its four homeless assistance programs in FY 2015. Approximately $500 million of this total was earmarked for Supportive Services for Veteran Families, $253 million for the Homeless Providers Grant and Per Diem Program, $219 million for the Domiciliary Care for Homeless Veterans Program, and $155 million for the Healthcare for Homeless Veterans Program.

Programs Administered by Other Government Agencies

A number of other federal agencies also provide services to the homeless. Many of these programs dovetail with the HUD and VA efforts described in this chapter, whereas others are attempts to address individual issues or subpopulations, in keeping with the given agency's mandate.

U.S. DEPARTMENT OF EDUCATION. At the time of the original McKinney Homeless Assistance Act's passage in 1987, only an estimated 57% of homeless children were enrolled in school. The act thus included an Education for Homeless Children and Youth Program, which is overseen by the U.S. Department of Education under the terms of the updated McKinney-Vento Act. The program ensures that homeless children and youth have equal access to the same free, appropriate education that is provided to other children. School systems are run by the individual states, so the Education for Homeless Children and Youth Program provides funding to states to maintain an office to coordinate homeless education, to develop and execute a state plan for educating homeless children, and to make subgrants to individual school districts that serve homeless students. The USICH notes in *Proposed Fiscal Year 2015 Budget Fact Sheet* that the Department of Education requested $65 million for the program in FY 2015—a level of funding that was unchanged since FY 2010 (with the exception of the sequester year of FY 2013, when the agency received only $62 million).

As discussed in Chapter 5, the National Center for Homeless Education (NCHE), which assists the Department of Education in data collection mandated under the Education for Homeless Children and Youth Program, employs a broader definition of homelessness than that used by HUD. Taking into account those students who are doubled-up and living in temporary quarters such as motels and hotels, the NCHE finds that homelessness among children has been increasing steadily since the Great Recession. The NCHE notes in *Education for Homeless Children and Youth Program: Analysis of Data* (July 2008, http://center.serve.org/nche/downloads/data_comp_03-06.pdf) that there were 679,724 homeless

students during the 2006–07 school. By 2012–13 this number had increased to nearly 1.3 million. (See Table 5.2 in Chapter 5.) This trend was cause for alarm among many homeless advocates, and it sized up the challenge faced by states and school districts that had seen their funding for homeless education remain flat during these years.

U.S. DEPARTMENT OF HEALTH AND HUMAN SERVICES. In *Proposed Fiscal Year 2015 Budget Fact Sheet*, the USICH indicates that the U.S. Department of Health and Human Services (HHS) manages five main programs for assisting the homeless. The Health Care for the Homeless Program, provisionally budgeted at $323 million for FY 2015, delivers a range of health care and related services to the homeless, including primary care, substance abuse treatment, emergency care, referrals for in-patient hospital and other care, outreach, and help determining eligibility for government benefits and housing. The agency's Runaway and Homeless Youth Program, budgeted at $116 million in FY 2015, funds over 740 local government, nonprofit, and faith-based organizations that serve runaway children and homeless youth. HHS's Projects for Assistance in Transition from Homelessness, budgeted at a proposed $65 million in FY 2015, funds state programs that serve homeless people with mental illness or co-occurring mental illness and substance abuse. Grants for the Benefit of Homeless Individuals, a program budgeted at $41 million in FY 2015 and administered by the Substance Abuse and Mental Health Services Administration (SAMHSA), funds local public and nonprofit entities that serve homeless people with mental illness or co-occurring mental illness and substance abuse. SAMHSA's Services in Supportive Housing Grants Program, budgeted at $33 million in FY 2015, supplies funding to individuals and families that need mental health and addiction treatment to escape homelessness.

According to the USICH, the U.S. Departments of Justice and Labor also manage programs that serve the homeless. The Department of Justice funds local programs that help people who have become homeless as a result of sexual assault, domestic violence, dating violence, and stalking; and the Department of Labor awards competitive grants to organizations that assist homeless veterans who want to reintegrate into the labor force.

The Role of Private Nonprofit Groups

As outlined earlier, the majority of all federal funding to combat homelessness is channeled into local government agencies and nonprofit groups that serve the homeless populations and subpopulations in their communities. Nonprofit groups in particular often have the flexibility to undertake projects that are tailored to their individual communities and to experiment with new methods for serving the homeless. Indeed, the housing-first approach that has become the preferred federal approach to homelessness has its roots in the work of one local nonprofit group. Deborah K. Padgett notes in "Choices, Consequences and Context: Housing First and Its Critics" (*European Journal of Homelessness*, vol. 7, no. 2, December 2013) that one of the most influential models for the housing-first approach was the work of the "tiny upstart" group Pathways to Housing, which began operating in New York City in 1992 with a philosophy that housing is a fundamental human right. Ignoring then-prevailing notions that substance abuse and mental health treatment should precede the effort to find housing for the homeless, Sam Tsemberis, the founder of Pathways, conducted rigorous studies that demonstrated the effectiveness of a housing-first approach relative to the existing models, and by around 2005 his work was beginning to transform opinions at the highest levels of government in the United States, Canada, and elsewhere.

In "Housing First" (2013, http://usich.gov/usich_re sources/solutions/explore/housing_first), the USICH singles out the work of another nonprofit pioneer: the Downtown Emergency Service Center (DESC) of Seattle, Washington. The DESC's permanent supportive housing program, 1811 Eastlake, targets homeless people with chronic alcoholism, a group known to impose enormous costs on the public in the form of jail time, hospital visits, publicly funded alcohol treatment, and Medicaid usage. In "Health Care and Public Service Use and Costs before and after Provision of Housing for Chronically Homeless Persons with Severe Alcohol Problems" (*Journal of the American Medical Association*, vol. 301, no. 13, April 1, 2009), Mary E. Larmer et al. report on a study that compared the homeless people served by 1811 Eastlake's housing-first approach with a comparable group of homeless people who were waitlisted for temporary housing. The study showed that 1811 Eastlake participants on average cost the public $2,449 less per person per month, excluding the costs of housing.

Besides deriving their funding from federal agencies, nonprofit organizations also frequently collaborate with local government agencies. For example, the USICH notes in "Columbus Coordinated Entry System: YWCA Family Center and Coordinated Point of Access" (2013, http:// usich.gov/usich_resources/solutions/explore/columbus_ coordinated_entry_system_ywca_family_center_and_co ordinated_point) that the Community Shelter Board (CSB), a public–private organization (a group that includes both government and private nonprofit involvement), partnered with the local YWCA in Columbus, Ohio, to coordinate emergency shelter access community-wide. Prior to 1999, families that needed housing had to contact numerous shelters to determine which one(s) had vacancies, and they frequently had to move from shelter to shelter. By establishing the YWCA as a central access point for all homeless families, the CSB was able to

reduce the volatility of the experience of family homelessness and to provide a means of accessing a range of homeless assistance. Families that obtained shelter through the YWCA were also provided information about how to access transitional and permanent housing and services. Eventually, the CSB established a parallel system for homeless individuals, and it transitioned to a phone-based central access point through which individuals and families could enter the homeless assistance system. This program has since become a model for homeless assistance at the national level.

There are thousands of similar nonprofit groups and initiatives intent on transforming the experience of homelessness in the United States. Any community that has a sizable homeless population is likely to have nonprofit organizations devoted to serving the homeless. No successful effort to combat homelessness in the United States is conceivable without the involvement of these groups.

THE CRIMINALIZATION OF HOMELESSNESS

Although local governments often lead the fight to combat homelessness in their communities, they are also subject to pressures from the nonhomeless population, many of whom feel threatened by the sight of impoverished people going about their lives in public spaces. Many people believe that providing space for the homeless to sleep, eat, or even sit will attract more homeless people, straining the capacity of public resources and leading to a deterioration of the quality of life in the area. Furthermore, the influential "broken windows" theory of the criminologists James Q. Wilson (1931–2012) and George L. Kelling (1935–), as detailed in "Broken Windows" (Atlantic.com, March 1982), is used to support homeless criminalization efforts. Wilson and Kelling argue that allowing indications of disorder, such as a broken window or street people, to remain unaddressed shows a loss of public order and control, as well as apathy in a neighborhood, which breeds more serious criminal activity. Therefore, keeping a city neat and orderly should help prevent crime.

Motivated by such rationales, city and county governments in the 21st century have increasingly passed laws that make it a crime to engage in many of the daily activities associated with homelessness. Advocates for the homeless contend that these laws deny the homeless their most basic human, legal, and political rights. Furthermore, most experts argue that the criminalization of homelessness defers and even exacerbates the problem rather than solving it.

In *No Safe Place*, the NLCHP finds that although few cities had sufficient affordable housing and shelter space for their homeless populations in 2014, 34% of cities imposed citywide bans on public camping and 57%

imposed camping bans in certain locations. The NLCHP notes that laws prohibiting camping are typically written broadly and are used to prohibit all outdoor sleeping. Many cities also had laws that specifically outlawed outdoor sleeping. Nearly one out of five (18%) of the surveyed cities imposed citywide bans on sleeping in public and over a quarter (27%) imposed sleeping bans in certain locations. In 43% of cities the homeless were prohibited from sleeping in their own vehicle.

Likewise, one of the homeless population's only means of deriving income, begging or panhandling, was prohibited citywide in 24% of municipalities in 2014; and 76% of cities prohibited the activity in certain locations. Even being present in a public place, which is a necessity for homeless people who by definition have no private place to go, is frequently illegal—33% of surveyed cities had laws prohibiting loitering in public anywhere in the city and 65% prohibited loitering in certain locations. Similarly, sitting or lying down in certain public locations was prohibited in 53% of cities.

Numerous media reports in 2013 and 2014 pointed out a new development in the trend toward criminalizing homelessness: the criminalization of attempts to feed the homeless in public places where they are known to gather, such as parks and streets. The NCH reports in *Share No More: The Criminalization of Efforts to Feed People in Need* (http://nationalhomeless.org/wp-content/uploads/2014/10/Food-Sharing2014.pdf) that as of October 2014, 57 U.S. cities had passed legislation that outlawed the practice of sharing food with the homeless. The NCH further observes that 21 of these restrictive ordinances had been introduced since January 2013, suggesting that this trend is gaining momentum. Those who attempt to feed the homeless, often members of small faith-based or nonprofit organizations, are subject to citations and arrest under these ordinances. According to the NCH, serving food to the homeless in the locations where they are present is often the only way of ensuring that those with disabilities and a lack of transportation can meet their basic survival needs.

The NCH explains that cities outlaw the feeding of the homeless through multiple methods. The most common methods are restrictions on the use of public property that mandate permits, often limited in number, for which fees sometimes totaling hundreds of dollars must be paid. These costs can be prohibitive for many of the small organizations that engage in attempts to feed the homeless. Furthermore, permits to feed the homeless often include detailed guidelines, the violation of which can be used as grounds for revocation of the right to engage in the activity. Other cities have outlawed food-sharing by subjecting the activity to food-service regulations such as those that apply to restaurants, which are frequently difficult, if not impossible, to satisfy in the outdoor settings where food-sharing often takes place.

Violating Rights

In *No Safe Place*, the NLCHP notes that many laws criminalizing the activities of the homeless have been found to violate First Amendment rights to freedom of speech and assembly, Eighth Amendment rights to freedom from cruel and unusual punishment, and 14th Amendment rights to due process. According to the United Nations Human Rights Committee, laws criminalizing homelessness also violate international human rights treaties that the U.S. government has signed, including the International Covenant on Civil and Political Rights.

The USICH, speaking on behalf of the federal government, has made public its opposition to the criminalization of homelessness. In "We STILL Believe in Human Rights" (December 10, 2014, http://usich.gov/blog/we-still-believe-in-human-rights-1), Maria Foscarinis and Laura Green Zeilinger report that since 2010 the USICH has been advising the Department of Justice to take a human rights approach to the issue of criminalizing homeless behavior and that it is involved in ongoing efforts to persuade local and state governments, as well as other federal agencies, to adopt alternatives to criminalization.

Increasing Costs and Inefficiencies

The NLCHP maintains in *No Safe Place* that "criminalization is the most expensive and least effective way of addressing homelessness." The center points to numerous research studies that compare the cost of a "management" approach to homelessness that includes criminalization with the cost of a housing-first approach. For example, in 2013 the Utah Housing and Community Development Division found that the average homeless person in the state of Utah cost taxpayers $16,670 annually in hospital bills and jail expenses, compared with an average annual cost of $11,000 for providing a homeless person with an apartment and a social worker. Similarly, the University of New Mexico's Institute for Social Research found that a housing-first program in Albuquerque cut jail expenses related to the homeless by 64%.

Exacerbating the Problem

In *No Safe Place*, the NLCHP states that criminalizing homelessness fails to address the root causes of homelessness, such as a lack of affordable housing and job availability, and instead exacerbates the problem by burdening homeless individuals and families. Those who are arrested for going about the daily activities associated with being homeless typically spend a short amount of time in jail and then return to the streets; their preexisting burdens are amplified by the disruption and the inability to pay the fines and court fees they have often incurred in the process. Additionally, the criminal records that homeless people accumulate as a result of restrictive ordinances sometimes ruin their prospects for housing, employment, and government aid programs. Thus, criminalization can have the perverse effect of guaranteeing that the homeless will remain homeless.

Alternatives to Criminalization

The USICH and HUD suggest in "Human Rights and Alternatives to Criminalization" (2013, http://usich.gov/issue/human-rights) three key strategies to replace efforts at criminalization:

- The creation of comprehensive and seamless systems of care—in an effort to address gaps in service delivery, supported by communitywide planning, many local organizations partner to coordinate housing and services, creating systems of care. These systems of care enable long-term reductions in street homelessness and connect individuals with benefits and services that improve housing stability.

- Collaboration between law enforcement, behavioral health, and social service providers—collaboration between service providers and law enforcement regarding outreach to individuals and specialized crisis intervention training can limit the number of arrests for non-violent offenses. This partnership can also help link individuals experiencing homelessness with the system of care and permanent, supportive housing.

- Alternative justice system strategies—strategies that provide alternatives to prosecution and incarceration and offer reentry planning for individuals show an increase in the likelihood that people will connect to permanent housing and employment. This solution includes the use of specialty courts, citation dismissal programs, holistic public defenders offices, and reentry programs.

RAISING AWARENESS

The 1980s and 1990s saw a number of mainstream media events designed to raise awareness of homelessness as a national problem as well as to raise money to aid in the fight against homelessness. The Hands across America fund-raiser, held in 1986, involved approximately 6.5 million people who locked hands to form a 4,150-mile (6,680 km) human chain across the country. That same year the comedians Robin Williams (1951–2014), Whoopi Goldberg (1955–), and Billy Crystal (1948–) hosted the HBO comedy special *Comic Relief* to help raise money for the homeless. The show was a success and became an annual event through 1996.

New installments of *Comic Relief* appeared sporadically through the late 1990s and the early 2000s, but the prominence of later iterations faded. No comparable high-profile events have emerged to supplant the show, but numerous small organizations and individuals continue to experiment with ways of making the problem of homelessness matter to ordinary Americans. One prominent example is Street Soccer USA (http://streetsoccerusa.org), a group that organizes soccer practices and games among the homeless in urban areas nationwide. As of 2015, there were Street Soccer USA programs in 16 U.S. cities, including men's and women's teams as well as programs for homeless youth. Each year the organization selects national men's, women's, boys', and girls' teams from the rosters of the local teams. The adult teams travel to the annual Homeless World Cup (held in a different international city each year since 2003), where they represent the United States in competition against other countries' national homeless teams. The youth teams represent the United States in the Street Child World Cup, which is held in advance of each quadrennial Fédération Internationale de Football Association World Cup.

Another innovative approach to raise awareness about homelessness was established in 2014 by NearShot (http://www.nearshot.com), a digital media company in San Francisco, whose first project was called Homeless GoPro. In an attempt to help homeless people tell their own stories and build emotional connections with people in their communities, NearShot equips homeless San Franciscans with GoPro wearable digital video cameras, which are small devices that can be affixed to the body or head and that are typically used by adventure-sports enthusiasts to document their activities as they experience them. The homeless people wear the cameras and document daily life as they live it. The videos are then edited into short films and posted online. In "Homeless GoPro Offers 1st-Hand Look on S.F. Homeless" (SFGate.com, April 15, 2014), Kevin Fagan quotes Kevin Adler, a sociologist and founder of the project, who said, "This project is about building empathy. We walk by the homeless every day, and sometimes we smile, sometimes we give a dollar, sometimes we do nothing. But what do most people really know about those they are walking by?"

CHAPTER 8
HEALTH CARE

HEALTH OF POOR PEOPLE

Connection between Poor Health and Poverty

Adults in poverty are more likely than other adults to have health problems and to be uninsured, and on average they have shorter life spans than the nonpoor. Likewise, children in poverty have elevated risks for poor health and teen pregnancy and are more likely than nonpoor children to be uninsured.

Although the correlation between poverty and health problems is well established, less consensus exists about the specific nature of the cause and effect relationship. Low levels of education, low income, marginal employment status, and poor health reinforce one another in numerous ways. Those with low levels of education are more likely to have low-paying and low-status jobs or to be unemployed. Low-paying and low-status jobs can pose health risks that higher-status jobs do not, and because they are less likely to provide health insurance benefits, they correlate with lower access to preventive health care, including vaccinations. Additionally, low levels of education, which are common among the impoverished, can result in a lack of awareness about the health effects of certain lifestyle choices. These characteristics, which are often discussed together as measures of socioeconomic status (SES), correlate with behaviors that adversely affect health, including tobacco use and physical inactivity, and low-SES children and adults often live in low-income neighborhoods that are lacking in resources for promoting healthy lifestyles. Both the poor and the near-poor (those whose incomes are below 200% of the poverty level) are more likely to be uninsured than those in higher economic brackets, and therefore they often seek medical care only when health issues have reached a crisis stage. Low-SES women are less likely to use contraception to prevent pregnancy than are high-SES women, and when pregnant, they are less likely to receive satisfactory prenatal care.

ADULTS. In *Health, United States, 2013* (May 14, 2014, http://www.cdc.gov/nchs/data/hus/hus13.pdf), the National Center for Health Statistics (NCHS), a department within the Centers for Disease Control and Prevention, highlights some specific health challenges common among low-income adults. As Table 8.1 shows, the likelihood that an adult will have a disability increases as income decreases. In 2012, 38.4% of adults with incomes below the federal poverty threshold ($23,492 for a family of four) and 37% of adults whose incomes ranged from 100% to 199% of the poverty line had at least one difficulty that affected such basic actions as movement, sensory functioning (e.g., hearing or vision), emotions, or cognition. By comparison, 30.2% of adults at whose incomes ranged from 200% to 399% of poverty, and 21.7% of adults at 400% of poverty or more, had difficulties that affected their basic actions. The pattern held among working-age adults as well as among adults aged 65 years and older. Similarly, low-income adults were more likely than higher-income adults to suffer from one or more limitations that affected their ability to perform complex actions such as self-care or daily living activities, social interactions, or work.

The poor and the near-poor are similarly more likely than higher-income adults to experience mental health difficulties categorized by the NCHS as "serious psychological distress." For *Health, United States, 2013*, the agency determined levels of psychological distress by studying the frequency with which survey respondents felt "so sad that nothing could cheer you up," "nervous," "restless or fidgety," "hopeless," "that everything was an effort," or "worthless." In 2011–12 adults living below the poverty line were nearly eight times more likely (8.2%) to be living with serious psychological distress than adults living at 400% or more of poverty (1.1%). (See Table 8.2.) Although adults living at 100% to 199% of poverty (4.9%) were less likely than adults in poverty to describe experiencing serious psychological

TABLE 8.1

Percentage of adults with at least one disability, by poverty level, selected years 1997–2012

[Data are based on household interviews of a sample of the civilian noninstitutionalized population]

Characteristic	18 years and over				18–64 years				65 years and over			
	1997	2000	2010[a]	2012[a]	1997	2000	2010[a]	2012[a]	1997	2000	2010[a]	2012[a]
	At least one basic actions difficulty[a]											
Percent of poverty level[b]					Number, in millions							
Below 100%	41.9	38.4	40.6	38.4	36.2	31.9	36.3	34.5	74.1	71.6	72.7	70.4
100%–199%	38.2	37.1	38.7	37.0	29.2	26.5	30.5	29.2	66.6	69.4	69.5	67.1
200%–399%	28.4	28.2	31.1	30.2	22.0	22.1	24.1	23.3	56.1	53.9	58.9	57.1
400% or more	21.0	19.4	23.0	21.7	18.2	16.8	19.3	17.6	45.5	44.7	47.0	43.5
	At least one complex activity limitation[c]											
Percent of poverty level[b]					Percent							
Below 100%	30.0	26.0	27.5	27.7	25.2	22.0	24.0	24.8	56.9	46.7	54.5	51.7
100%–199%	23.3	22.0	23.7	23.7	16.7	15.1	18.4	18.8	43.9	42.8	43.7	42.7
200%–399%	13.3	12.8	14.5	14.7	9.3	9.2	10.8	10.5	30.6	27.5	29.3	31.0
400% or more	7.3	6.4	7.7	8.1	5.8	5.0	5.8	6.0	20.2	19.6	19.8	19.5

[a]A basic actions difficulty is defined as having one or more of the following difficulties: movement, emotional, sensory (seeing or hearing), or cognitive. Starting with 2007 data, the hearing question, a component of the basic actions difficulty measure, was revised. Consequently, data for basic actions difficulty prior 2007 are not comparable with 2007 data and beyond.
[b]Percent of poverty level is based on family income and family size and composition using U.S. Census Bureau poverty thresholds. Missing family income data were imputed for 1997 and beyond.
[c]A complex activity limitation is defined as having one or more of the following limitations: self-care (activities of daily living or instrumental activities of daily living), social, or work.

SOURCE: Adapted from "Table 49. Disability Measures among Adults Aged 18 and over, by Selected Characteristics: United States, Selected Years 1997–2012," in *Health, United States, 2013: With Special Feature on Prescription Drugs*, Centers for Disease Control and Prevention, National Center for Health Statistics, May 14, 2014, http://www.cdc.gov/nchs/data/hus/hus13.pdf (accessed November 13, 2014)

TABLE 8.2

Percentage of adults with serious psychological distress in the past 30 days, by poverty level, selected years 1997–2012

[Data are based on household interviews of a sample of the civilian noninstitutionalized population]

Characteristic	1997–1998	1999–2000	2001–2002	2004–2005	2009–2010	2011–2012
Percent of poverty level[b, c]	Percent of adults with serious psychological distress[a]					
Below 100%	9.1	6.8	8.4	8.6	8.4	8.2
100%–199%	5.0	4.4	5.2	5.0	4.8	4.9
200%–399%	2.5	2.3	2.8	2.5	2.8	2.6
400% or more	1.3	1.2	1.3	1.1	1.2	1.1

[a]Serious psychological distress is measured by a six-question scale that asks respondents how often they experienced each of six symptoms of psychological distress in the past 30 days.
[b]Estimates are age-adjusted to the year 2000 standard population using five age groups: 18–44 years, 45–54 years, 55–64 years, 65–74 years, and 75 years and over.
[c]Percent of poverty level is based on family income and family size and composition using U.S. Census Bureau poverty thresholds. Missing family income data were imputed for 1997 and beyond.

SOURCE: Adapted from "Table 55. Serious Psychological Distress in the Past 30 Days among Adults Aged 18 and over, by Selected Characteristics: United States, Average Annual, Selected Years 1997–1998 through 2011–2012," in *Health, United States, 2013: With Special Feature on Prescription Drugs*, Centers for Disease Control and Prevention, National Center for Health Statistics, May 14, 2014, http://www.cdc.gov/nchs/data/hus/hus13.pdf (accessed November 13, 2014)

distress, they were almost five times more likely to do so than adults at with incomes equaling 400% or more of poverty. These percentages had changed only slightly since 1997–98.

The relationship between income and the prevalence of chronic health conditions (arthritis, asthma, cancer, diabetes, heart disease, hepatitis, hypertension, obstructive pulmonary disease, stroke, weak or failing kidneys) was similar. The likelihood that an adult had no chronic health conditions or one chronic health condition increased in direct proportion to income in 2012 as in prior years, and the likelihood that an adult had two to three chronic health conditions or four or more chronic

health conditions increased as income fell. (See Table 8.3.) People with more than one chronic condition present particular complications to health care professionals, increasing both the amount of treatment typically required and the expense of that treatment. The correlation between income and the likelihood that an adult would have one of the deadliest of chronic health conditions (heart disease, cancer, or stroke) varied slightly by condition. (See Table 8.4.) The poor and near-poor are more likely than higher earners to have heart disease and stroke, whereas the percentage of adults with cancer does not meaningfully vary by income. This may reflect the fact that heart disease and stroke are linked not only to genetics but to environmental and

TABLE 8.3

Number of chronic conditions among adults, by poverty level, selected years 2002–12

[Data are based on household interviews of a sample of the civilian noninstitutionalized population]

	Number of respondent-reported chronic conditions from 10 selected conditions[a]											
	0–1 chronic conditions				2–3 chronic conditions				4 or more chronic conditions			
Characteristic	2002	2005	2011	2012	2002	2005	2011	2012	2002	2005	2011	2012
Percent of poverty level[b, c]					Percent distribution							
Below 100%	71.9	71.1	69.5	68.4	21.3	21.8	22.0	23.4	6.8	7.1	8.5	8.2
100%–199%	76.4	74.5	72.8	73.5	18.6	19.9	21.1	20.3	5.0	5.5	6.1	6.2
200%–399%	77.8	77.0	75.6	77.0	18.9	19.4	19.8	19.0	3.3	3.6	4.6	4.0
400% or more	81.2	80.3	79.0	80.0	15.9	16.9	18.0	17.3	2.8	2.8	3.0	2.7

[a]Adults were categorized as having 0 to 1, 2 to 3, or 4 or more of the following chronic conditions: hypertension, coronary heart disease, stroke, diabetes, cancer, arthritis, hepatitis, weak or failing kidneys, chronic obstructive pulmonary disease, or current asthma. Data from the National Health Interview Survey capture 10 of 20 chronic conditions used in a standardized approach for defining chronic conditions in the United States. Thus, these estimates are conservative in nature.
[b]Estimates are age-adjusted to the year 2000 standard population using five age groups: 18–44 years, 45–54 years, 55–64 years, 65–74 years, and 75 years and over.
[c]Percent of poverty level is based on family income and family size and composition using U.S. Census Bureau poverty thresholds. Missing family income data were imputed.
Notes: In 1997, the National Health Interview Survey questionnaire was redesigned.

SOURCE: Adapted from "Table 45. Number of Respondent-Reported Chronic Conditions from 10 Selected Conditions among Adults Aged 18 and over, by Selected Characteristics: United States, Selected Years 2002–2012," in *Health, United States, 2013: With Special Feature on Prescription Drugs*, Centers for Disease Control and Prevention, National Center for Health Statistics, May 14, 2014, http://www.cdc.gov/nchs/data/hus/hus13.pdf (accessed November 13, 2014)

TABLE 8.4

Percentage of adults with heart disease, cancer, and stroke, by poverty level, selected years 1997–2012

[Data are based on household interviews of a sample of the civilian noninstitutionalized population]

	Heart disease[a]				Cancer[b]				Stroke[c]			
Characteristic	1997–1998	2001–2002	2009–2010	2011–2012	1997–1998	2001–2002	2009–2010	2011–2012	1997–1998	2001–2002	2009–2010	2011–2012
Percent of poverty level[d, e]					Percent of adults							
Below 100%	15.3	14.4	14.5	13.3	4.9	5.4	5.4	5.8	4.3	3.7	4.4	4.6
100%–199%	13.2	12.4	12.8	11.9	4.8	5.0	6.1	5.3	3.1	3.3	3.5	3.6
200%–399%	11.5	11.3	11.3	10.7	4.9	5.6	5.9	5.9	2.1	2.4	2.6	2.4
400% or more	11.0	10.9	10.0	9.5	5.2	5.2	6.3	6.2	1.6	1.9	1.7	1.5

[a]Heart disease is based on self-reported responses to questions about whether respondents had ever been told by a doctor or other health professional that they had coronary heart disease, angina (angina pectoris), a heart attack (myocardial infarction), or any other kind of heart disease or heart condition.
[b]Cancer is based on self-reported responses to a question about whether respondents had ever been told by a doctor or other health professional that they had cancer or a malignancy of any kind. Excludes squamous cell and basal cell carcinomas.
[c]Stroke is based on self-reported responses to a question about whether respondents had ever been told by a doctor or other health professional that they had a stroke.
[d]Estimates are age-adjusted to the year 2000 standard population using five age groups: 18–44 years, 45–54 years, 55–64 years, 65–74 years, and 75 years and over. Age-adjusted estimates in this table may differ from other age-adjusted estimates based on the same data and presented elsewhere if different age groups are used in the adjustment procedure.
[e]Percent of poverty level is based on family income and family size and composition using U.S. Census Bureau poverty thresholds. Missing family income data were imputed for 1997–1998 and beyond.

SOURCE: Adapted from "Table 44. Respondent-Reported Prevalence of Heart Disease, Cancer, and Stroke among Adults Aged 18 and over, by Selected Characteristics: United States, Average Annual, Selected Years 1997–1998 through 2011–2012," in *Health, United States, 2013: With Special Feature on Prescription Drugs*, Centers for Disease Control and Prevention, National Center for Health Statistics, May 14, 2014, http://www.cdc.gov/nchs/data/hus/hus13.pdf (accessed November 13, 2014)

lifestyle factors (such as diet, smoking, alcohol and drug use, and stress levels), whereas cancer is less strongly linked to such factors.

CHILDREN. NCHS data also show that children in low-income households fare consistently worse on measures of health and well-being than children in higher-income households. Rates of current asthma as well as the prevalence of asthma attacks over the preceding year were noticeably higher among children living in poverty, and rates of attention-deficit/hyperactivity disorder (ADHD) and serious emotional or behavioral difficulties were dramatically higher for children in poverty than for children in higher income brackets. (See Table 8.5.) For example, in the period 2010 to 2012, 13.1% of poor children had been diagnosed with ADHD, compared with 9.1% of children in families having an income of 400% of poverty or more. In addition, 8.8% of poor children had serious emotional or behavioral difficulties, more than double the rate (4.2%) for children in homes with incomes at 400% or more of poverty.

Poverty and Access to Health Care

One of the major factors in low-income adults' negative health outcomes relative to higher-income adults is

TABLE 8.5

Health conditions among children, by percentage of poverty level, selected years 1997–2012

[Data are based on household interviews of a sample of the civilian noninstitutionalized population]

Characteristic	Current asthma[a]				Asthma attack in the past 12 months[b]			
	1997–1999	2000–2002	2003–2005	2010–2012	1997–1999	2000–2002	2003–2005	2010–2012
Percent of poverty level[c]					Percent of children			
Below 100%	—	—	10.4	12.5	6.1	7.1	6.5	7.5
100%–199%	—	—	8.6	9.9	5.3	5.4	5.2	6.0
200%–399%	—	—	8.3	8.7	5.0	5.3	5.2	4.7
400% or more	—	—	7.9	7.0	5.2	5.5	4.9	4.4

Characteristic	Attention deficit hyperactivity disorder[d]				Serious emotional or behavioral difficulties[e]			
Percent of poverty level[c]	1997–1999	2000–2002	2003–2005	2010–2012	1997–1999	2000–2002	2003–2005	2010–2012
Below 100%	7.2	8.2	8.4	13.1	—	—	7.4	8.8
100%–199%	6.7	7.5	7.8	9.2	—	—	5.4	5.9
200%–399%	6.2	7.7	7.8	8.9	—	—	4.9	5.0
400% or more	6.1	7.1	6.9	9.1	—	—	3.7	4.2

—Data not available.

[a]Based on parent or knowledgeable adult responding to both questions, "Has a doctor or other health professional ever told you that your child had asthma?" and "Does your child still have asthma?"

[b]Based on parent or knowledgeable adult responding to both questions, "Has a doctor or other health professional ever told you that your child had asthma?" and "During the past 12 months, did your child have an episode of asthma or an asthma attack?"

[c]Percent of poverty level is based on family income and family size and composition using U.S. Census Bureau poverty thresholds. Missing family income data were imputed for 1997 and beyond.

[d]Based on parent or knowledgeable adult responding to the question, "Has a doctor or health professional ever told you that your child had attention deficit hyperactivity disorder (ADHD) or attention deficit disorder (ADD)?"

[e]Based on parent or knowledgeable adult responding to the question, "Overall, do you think that [child] has difficulties in any of the following areas: emotions, concentration, behavior, or being able to get along with other people?"

SOURCE: Adapted from "Table 41. Health Conditions among Children under Age 18, by Selected Characteristics: United States, Average Annual, Selected Years 1997–1999 through 2010–2012," in *Health, United States, 2013: With Special Feature on Prescription Drugs*, Centers for Disease Control and Prevention, National Center for Health Statistics, May 14, 2014, http://www.cdc.gov/nchs/data/hus/hus13.pdf (accessed November 13, 2014)

their inability to afford medical care. As Figure 8.1 shows, the likelihood that an adult had to delay or forgo necessary medical treatment due to cost was directly correlated with income levels in 2002 through 2012, and among all income groups, the likelihood of delays or nonreceipt of care rose during this period. In 2012 as in prior years, the percentage of those living in poverty that had to delay or forgo care (22.4%) was almost identical to the percentage living at 100% to 199% who had to delay or forgo care (22.3%). A substantial portion of those living at 200% to 399% of poverty (13.2%) also had to delay or forgo care in 2012, a fact that underscores how expensive comprehensive health care was during this period. By comparison, 5.3% of those living at 400% of poverty or greater delayed or did not receive needed treatment during these years.

Oral health is strongly linked to overall health, as the Mayo Clinic reports in "Oral Health: A Window to Your Overall Health" (2013, http://www.mayoclinic.org/healthy-living/adult-health/in-depth/dental/art-20047475). Research suggests that oral health issues can affect, be caused by, or contribute to a number of diseases and conditions, including endocarditis (an infection in the heart), cardiovascular disease, premature birth and low birth weight, diabetes, human immunodeficiency virus (HIV)/acquired immune deficiency syndrome (AIDS), osteoporosis, and Alzheimer's disease, among other conditions. Good oral hygiene and regular dental care are accordingly considered important components of overall health, but low-income adults are much more likely than other adults to be unable to afford dental care. Over a quarter of those living in poverty (26.9%) and at 100% to 199% of poverty (25.3%) had to forgo dental care in 2012 because of cost, compared with 13.8% of those whose incomes reached 200% to 399% of poverty and 5.5% of those at 400% or more of poverty. (See Figure 8.1.)

Disparities in access to health care were less dramatic among children during this period, in large part due to Medicaid (a health care coverage program for which all children in poverty are eligible) and the Children's Health Insurance Program (CHIP), for which many low-income children who are above the poverty level are eligible. In 1993–94, 7.7% of children had no usual source of health care, and by 2011–12 the percentage of children with no regular source of care had fallen to 4.1%. (See Table 8.6.) Nevertheless, children in low-income households remained more likely than those in higher-income households to have no usual source of care. In 2011–12, 5.7% of children living in poverty and 5.7% of those at 100% to 199% of poverty had no usual source of care, compared with 3.6% of children in households with incomes at 200% to 399% of poverty and 1.6% of those at 400% or more of poverty.

FIGURE 8.1

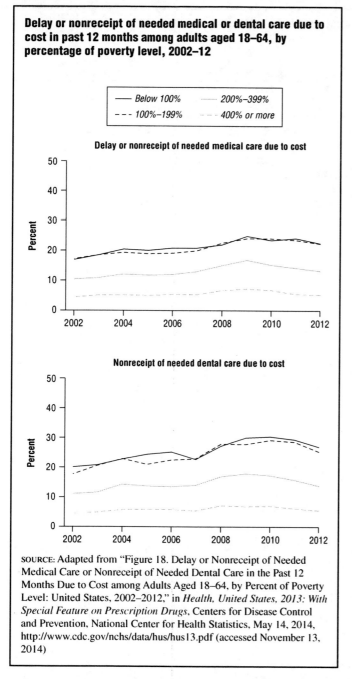

Delay or nonreceipt of needed medical or dental care due to cost in past 12 months among adults aged 18–64, by percentage of poverty level, 2002–12

— Below 100%   ⋯⋯ 200%–399%
--- 100%–199%   ⋯⋯ 400% or more

Delay or nonreceipt of needed medical care due to cost

Nonreceipt of needed dental care due to cost

SOURCE: Adapted from "Figure 18. Delay or Nonreceipt of Needed Medical Care or Nonreceipt of Needed Dental Care in the Past 12 Months Due to Cost among Adults Aged 18–64, by Percent of Poverty Level: United States, 2002–2012," in *Health, United States, 2013: With Special Feature on Prescription Drugs,* Centers for Disease Control and Prevention, National Center for Health Statistics, May 14, 2014, http://www.cdc.gov/nchs/data/hus/hus13.pdf (accessed November 13, 2014)

The percentage of children who made no health care visits to an office or clinic in the course of a given year declined significantly during this period, as well. As Table 8.7 shows, in 1997–98, 12.8% of all children made no office or clinic visits, and in 2011–12, 8.9% of children made no office or clinic visits. The percentage of children in families with incomes below 200% of poverty who made no office or clinic visits (10.7% of children below poverty, and 11% of children at 100% to 199% of poverty) was approximately twice the percentage of children at 400% or more of poverty who made no office or clinic visits. Children aged six to 17 years were more likely than children under the age of six years to make no office or clinic visits in all years and at all income levels.

Children in poor or near-poor families were roughly twice as likely to make no office or clinic visits than children in families that made 400% or more of poverty, and children in households at 200% to 399% of poverty were significantly more likely to make no office or clinic visits than those in households with higher incomes.

HEALTH INSURANCE AND HEALTH CARE REFORM
An Overview of the Health Insurance Landscape

U.S. health care is extremely expensive by world standards and in relation to American incomes, and few people can afford to pay for care at retail prices. Health insurance policies allow individuals and families to obtain care at reduced prices because insurance companies share the cost of treatments, drugs, and other services. Thus, the health of most Americans depends to a large extent on their ability to obtain and keep insurance coverage.

The overwhelming majority of U.S. residents obtain health insurance either through their employers or through the federal and state governments. In the Census Bureau's survey of health care coverage among U.S. residents, *Health Insurance Coverage in the United States: 2013* (September 2014, http://www.census.gov/content/dam/Census/library/publications/2014/demo/p60-250.pdf), Jessica C. Smith and Carla Medalia report that in 2013, 271.4 million Americans, or 86.6% of the total U.S. population, had health insurance. (See Figure 8.2.) Among insured people, 201.1 million people (64.2%) had private insurance policies, and 107.6 million (34.3%) had coverage through the government. Approximately 42 million people, who constituted 13.4% of the total U.S. population, were uninsured in 2013.

Most people who go without insurance typically do so for one or more of the following reasons: their employers do not offer coverage, they do not qualify for government-funded insurance, and/or they cannot afford to purchase individual policies directly from companies. Those who obtain employment-based insurance typically share the expense of their coverage with their employers, and their employers can, additionally, secure better pricing from insurance companies for group coverage (coverage offered to an entire employee pool) than can be secured for individual coverage (coverage purchased directly from insurance companies by individuals). Employment-based insurance is typically a perk available to salaried workers in middle- and upper-income jobs. As Figure 8.2 shows, 169 million people, or 53.9% of the U.S. population, had employment-based insurance in 2013.

Most low-income workers, including those who do hourly work for large corporations, those who work for very small businesses, and those who are self-employed, do not have access to employer-based coverage. To

TABLE 8.6

Percentage of children with no usual source of health care, by selected characteristics, selected years 1993–2012

[Data are based on household interviews of a sample of the civilian noninstitutionalized population]

Characteristic	Under 18 years			Under 6 years			6–17 years		
	1993–1994[a]	1999–2000	2011–2012	1993–1994[a]	1999–2000	2011–2012	1993–1994[a]	1999–2000	2011–2012
	Percent of children without a usual source of health care[b]								
All children[c]	7.7	6.9	4.1	5.2	4.6	2.5	9.0	8.0	4.9
Sex									
Male	8.1	6.7	4.0	5.3	4.5	2.4	9.6	7.8	4.8
Female	7.3	7.1	4.1	5.0	4.7	2.5	8.5	8.2	5.0
Race[d]									
White only	7.0	6.3	3.9	4.7	4.4	2.3	8.3	7.2	4.7
Black or African American only	10.3	7.7	4.4	7.6	4.4	3.2	11.9	9.1	4.9
American Indian or Alaska Native only	9.3*	9.4*	4.7*	*	*	*	8.7*	9.4*	6.6*
Asian only	9.7	10.0	5.6	3.4*	5.8*	*	13.5	12.2	7.6
Native Hawaiian or other Pacific Islander only	—	*	*	—	*	*	—	*	*
2 or more races	—	4.9*	3.9	—	*	3.0*	—	7.2*	4.4
Hispanic origin and race[d]									
Hispanic or Latino	14.3	14.2	6.2	9.3	9.0	2.9	17.7	17.2	8.1
Not Hispanic or Latino	6.7	5.5	3.4	4.4	3.6	2.3	7.8	6.3	3.9
White only	5.7	4.7	2.9	3.7	3.3	2.0	6.7	5.4	3.3
Black or African American only	10.2	7.6	4.5	7.7	4.5	3.4	11.6	9.0	5.1
Percent of poverty level[e]									
Below 100%	13.9	13.1	5.7	9.4	7.6	3.4	16.8	16.2	7.2
100%–199%	9.8	10.6	5.7	6.7	7.5	3.2	11.6	12.2	6.9
200%–399%	3.7	4.8	3.6	1.9	3.2	2.2	4.5	5.6	4.4
400% or more	3.7	2.6	1.6	1.6*	1.5	0.9*	5.0	3.0	1.9
Hispanic origin and race and percent of poverty level[d, e]									
Hispanic or Latino:									
Below 100%	19.6	19.4	7.0	12.7	11.6	3.0	24.8	24.5	9.7
100%–199%	15.3	17.1	6.9	9.9	11.3	3.6	18.9	20.4	8.7
200%–399%	5.2	8.3	5.4	*	5.0*	2.6*	6.7	10.1	7.1
400% or more	*	3.8*	2.6*	*	*	*	*	5.0*	*
Not Hispanic or Latino:									
White only:									
Below 100%	10.2	10.7	4.7	6.5	6.3*	*	12.7	13.1	5.5
100%–199%	8.7	7.8	4.3	6.3	5.7	*	10.1	8.8	5.0
200%–399%	3.3	4.0	3.0	1.6	2.7	1.9*	4.0	4.6	3.5
400% or more	4.0	2.3	1.4	1.7*	1.5*	*	5.4	2.6	1.6
Black or African American only:									
Below 100%	13.7	9.4	4.9	10.9	4.7*	3.9*	15.5	11.8	5.6
100%–199%	9.1	9.7	6.1	6.0*	6.4*	*	10.8	11.2	7.0
200%–399%	5.0	5.0	3.3*	*	*	*	6.2	5.7	3.7*
400% or more	*	3.5*	*	*	*	*	*	4.0*	*
Health insurance status at the time of interview[f]									
Insured	5.0	3.9	2.3	3.3	2.6	1.5	5.9	4.5	2.7
Private	3.8	3.4	1.7	1.9	2.2	1.0	4.6	3.9	2.1
Medicaid	8.9	5.3	3.1	6.4	3.5	2.1	11.3	6.7	3.7
Uninsured	23.5	29.3	28.4	18.0	20.8	20.1	26.0	32.9	31.0
Health insurance status prior to interview[f]									
Insured continuously all 12 months	4.6	3.6	2.2	3.1	2.3	1.4	5.5	4.2	2.5
Uninsured for any period up to 12 months	15.3	15.0	12.5	10.9	12.5	8.5	18.1	16.4	14.5
Uninsured more than 12 months	27.6	35.8	35.5	21.4	26.8	28.7	30.0	39.1	36.9

obtain private insurance coverage, such people must purchase policies directly from companies. These policies have historically been unaffordable for low- and even middle-income workers. Only 34.5 million people, or 11% of the population, had direct-purchase insurance in 2013; and as Smith and Medalia point out, a majority of these people (61.4%) had some other type of health insurance, which indicates that such plans may more often be purchased to supplement other plan types (such as Medicare or employer-provided coverage) than to serve the full range of a policyholder's health needs.

In 2013 many adults and all children living below the poverty level were eligible for Medicaid, a form of free

TABLE 8.6

Percentage of children with no usual source of health care, by selected characteristics, selected years 1993–2012 [CONTINUED]

[Data are based on household interviews of a sample of the civilian noninstitutionalized population]

	Under 18 years			Under 6 years			6–17 years		
Characteristic	1993–1994[a]	1999–2000	2011–2012	1993–1994[a]	1999–2000	2011–2012	1993–1994[a]	1999–2000	2011–2012
Percent of poverty level and health insurance status prior to interview[e, f]	Percent of children without a usual source of health care[b]								
Below 100%:									
Insured continuously all 12 months	8.6	5.7	3.2	5.8	2.7*	2.4	10.7	7.5	3.7
Uninsured for any period up to 12 months	21.7	19.8	13.4	18.0	16.0*	9.5*	23.7	21.9	15.5
Uninsured more than 12 months	31.2	42.7	43.2	25.5	31.0	*	33.4	47.1	44.9
100%–199%:									
Insured continuously all 12 months	5.6	5.2	2.4	3.7	3.7	1.6*	6.7	6.0	2.9
Uninsured for any period up to 12 months	14.5	15.4	13.4	9.7*	14.4*	7.9*	18.0	15.9	16.0
Uninsured more than 12 months	27.6	34.4	35.4	21.4	26.4	29.4*	30.2	37.4	36.6
200%–399%:									
Insured continuously all 12 months	2.8	3.2	2.0	1.5	2.1	1.2*	3.4	3.7	2.5
Uninsured for any period up to 12 months	9.1	11.1	13.0	*	8.4*	9.7*	11.6	12.7	14.7
Uninsured more than 12 months	18.2	27.1	28.7	9.7*	20.3*	*	21.0	29.4	29.8
400% or more:									
Insured continuously all 12 months	3.1	2.0	1.2	*	1.2*	*	4.3	2.4	1.5
Uninsured for any period up to 12 months	*	10.3*	*	*	*	*	*	*	*
Uninsured more than 12 months	*	30.0*	29.2*	*	*	*	*	33.3*	29.7*
Geographic region									
Northeast	4.1	2.8	1.9	2.9	2.3	1.5*	4.8	3.0	2.0
Midwest	5.2	5.3	3.5	4.1	3.7	2.1*	5.9	6.0	4.2
South	10.9	8.5	4.7	7.3	5.8	3.1	12.7	9.8	5.5
West	8.6	9.7	5.1	5.3	5.7	2.5	10.6	11.7	6.5
Location of residence									
Within MSA[g]	7.7	6.8	4.2	5.0	4.7	2.5	9.2	7.8	5.0
Outside MSA[g]	7.8	7.4	3.5	6.0	4.2	2.5*	8.7	8.7	4.0

*Estimates are considered unreliable.
—Data not available.
[a]Data prior to 1997 are not strictly comparable with data for later years due to the 1997 questionnaire redesign.
[b]Persons who report the emergency department as their usual source of care are defined as having no usual source of care.
[c]Includes all other races not shown separately and unknown health insurance status.
[d]The race groups, white, black, American Indian or Alaska Native, Asian, Native Hawaiian or other Pacific Islander, and 2 or more races, include persons of Hispanic and non-Hispanic origin. Persons of Hispanic origin may be of any race. Starting with 1999 data, race-specific estimates are tabulated according to the 1997 *Revisions to the Standards for the Classification of Federal Data on Race and Ethnicity* and are not strictly comparable with estimates for earlier years. The five single-race categories plus multiple-race categories shown in the table conform to the 1997 standards. Starting with 1999 data, race-specific estimates are for persons who reported only one racial group; the category 2 or more races includes persons who reported more than one racial group. Prior to 1999, data were tabulated according to the 1977 standards with four racial groups, and the Asian only category included Native Hawaiian or other Pacific Islander. Estimates for single-race categories prior to 1999 included persons who reported one race or, if they reported more than one race, identified one race as best representing their race. Starting with 2003 data, race responses of other race and unspecified multiple race were treated as missing, and then race was imputed if these were the only race responses. Almost all persons with a race response of other race were of Hispanic origin.
[e]Percent of poverty level is based on family income and family size and composition using U.S. Census Bureau poverty thresholds. Missing family income data were imputed starting in 1993.
[f]Health insurance categories are mutually exclusive. Persons who reported both Medicaid and private coverage are classified as having private coverage. Medicaid includes other public assistance through 1996. Starting with 1997 data, state-sponsored health plan coverage is included as Medicaid coverage. Starting with 1999 data, coverage by the Children's Health Insurance Program (CHIP) is included with Medicaid coverage. In addition to private and Medicaid, the insured category also includes military, other government, and Medicare coverage. Persons not covered by private insurance, Medicaid, CHIP, public assistance (through 1996), state-sponsored or other government-sponsored health plans (starting in 1997), Medicare, or military plans are considered to have no health insurance coverage. Persons with only Indian Health Service coverage are considered to have no health insurance coverage. Health insurance status was unknown for 8%–9% of children in 1993–1996 and about 1% in 1997–2012.
[g]MSA is metropolitan statistical area. Starting with 2005–2006 data, MSA status is determined using 2000 census data and the 2000 standards for defining MSAs.

SOURCE: "Table 72. No Usual Source of Health Care among Children under Age 18, by Selected Characteristics: United States, Average Annual, Selected Years 1993–1994 through 2011–2012," in *Health, United States, 2013: With Special Feature on Prescription Drugs*, Centers for Disease Control and Prevention, National Center for Health Statistics, May 14, 2014, http://www.cdc.gov/nchs/data/hus/hus13.pdf (accessed November 13, 2014)

---

health insurance coverage funded by the federal and state governments; and many children above the poverty level were eligible for either Medicaid or the Children's Health Insurance Program (CHIP), which offers free or reduced-price coverage to families whose incomes are too high to qualify for Medicaid but too low to enable the purchase of insurance. Elderly Americans are eligible for subsidized health insurance coverage under the federally funded Medicare program. As Figure 8.2 shows, 54.1 million people, or 17.3% of the population, obtained health care coverage through Medicaid in 2013; and 49 million, or 15.6% of the population, obtained coverage through Medicare.

The Uninsured

Figure 8.3 shows fluctuations in the uninsured rate from 2008 to 2013. This figure is based on information from the Census Bureau's American Community Survey (ACS). It

TABLE 8.7

Percentage of children who made no health care visits to an office or clinic within the past 12 months, by selected characteristics, selected years 1997–2012

[Data are based on household interviews of a sample of the civilian noninstitutionalized population]

Characteristic	Under 18 years			Under 6 years			6–17 years		
	1997–1998	2001–2002	2011–2012	1997–1998	2001–2002	2011–2012	1997–1998	2001–2002	2011–2012
	Percent of children without a health care visit[a]								
All children[b]	12.8	12.1	8.9	5.7	6.3	4.9	16.3	14.9	11.0
Sex									
Male	12.9	12.3	8.9	4.9	6.4	5.0	16.8	15.1	10.8
Female	12.7	11.9	8.9	6.5	6.1	4.8	15.8	14.6	11.1
Race[c]									
White only	12.2	11.5	8.8	5.5	6.4	4.7	15.5	13.9	10.9
Black or African American only	14.3	13.3	8.3	6.5	5.9	5.2	18.1	16.8	9.9
American Indian or Alaska Native only	13.8	18.6*	10.9	*	*	*	17.6*	23.0*	12.2*
Asian only	16.3	15.6	11.9	5.6*	6.8*	6.8*	22.1	20.5	14.5
Native Hawaiian or other Pacific Islander only	—	*	*	—	*	*	—	*	*
2 or more races	—	8.3	8.8	—	3.3*	4.6*	—	12.4	11.4
Hispanic origin and race[c]									
Hispanic or Latino	19.3	18.8	12.0	9.7	9.6	6.0	25.3	24.0	15.5
Not Hispanic or Latino	11.6	10.6	8.0	4.8	5.4	4.5	14.9	13.0	9.6
White only	10.7	9.7	7.5	4.3	5.3	4.2	13.7	11.7	9.0
Black or African American only	14.5	13.4	8.1	6.5	6.0	4.6	18.3	16.8	9.9
Percent of poverty level[d]									
Below 100%	17.6	17.3	10.7	8.1	9.1	5.8	23.6	21.8	13.9
100%–199%	16.2	14.8	11.0	7.2	7.4	5.7	20.8	18.7	13.6
200%–399%	11.7	11.2	8.9	4.9	5.4	5.1	14.8	13.8	10.8
400% or more	7.4	7.7	5.5	3.0	4.1	2.6	9.5	9.3	6.7
Hispanic origin and race and percent of poverty level[c, d]									
Hispanic or Latino:									
Below 100%	23.2	22.1	13.8	11.7	10.4	7.4	31.1	29.4	18.2
100%–199%	20.9	21.3	12.9	9.7	12.3	5.8	28.1	26.2	16.7
200%–399%	15.7	15.5	10.2	8.0	7.3*	4.3*	19.7	20.0	13.6
400% or more	7.8	9.7	6.7	*	*	*	9.3	12.5	7.6
Not Hispanic or Latino:									
White only:									
Below 100%	14.0	13.2	9.1	5.6*	8.6*	4.9*	19.7	15.6	11.8
100%–199%	14.1	11.8	10.1	6.0	6.0*	5.9	18.0	14.8	12.2
200%–399%	10.9	10.2	8.0	4.3	4.8	4.9	13.9	12.5	9.5
400% or more	7.2	7.4	4.9	2.8*	4.2	2.1*	9.1	8.6	6.1
Black or African American only:									
Below 100%	15.8	16.1	8.1	7.6	7.8*	4.7*	20.5	20.3	10.5
100%–199%	16.4	13.3	7.6	7.7*	4.4*	*	20.4	17.5	9.0
200%–399%	13.3	12.2	9.1	4.9*	6.5*	*	16.7	14.6	10.9
400% or more	8.3	8.9	7.4*	*	*	*	10.7	11.5	8.5*
Health insurance status at the time of interview[e]									
Insured	10.4	9.8	7.6	4.5	4.7	4.4	13.4	12.3	9.3
Private	10.4	9.5	7.1	4.3	4.3	3.5	13.1	11.8	8.7
Medicaid	10.1	10.3	8.1	5.0	5.5	5.2	14.4	13.3	10.2
Uninsured	28.8	31.9	27.6	14.6	21.0	15.3	34.9	36.3	31.3
Health insurance status prior to interview[e]									
Insured continuously all 12 months	10.3	9.5	7.5	4.4	4.6	4.3	13.2	12.0	9.1
Uninsured for any period up to 12 months	15.9	17.7	13.3	7.7	10.3	7.2	20.9	21.9	16.4
Uninsured more than 12 months	34.9	41.4	36.4	19.9	30.2	22.8*	40.2	45.3	39.2

provides a slightly different, although consistent, picture of the uninsured than do other tables and figures in this chapter (including Figure 8.2) that are based on data from the Census Bureau's Current Population Survey (CPS). (When not otherwise noted, Census Bureau data in this chapter are derived from the CPS.) Based on ACS data, the percentage of the population that was uninsured rose from 14.6% in 2008 to 15.5% in 2010, before falling again, to 14.5%, in 2013. The spike in the uninsured rate was likely caused by the Great Recession of 2007 to 2009, during which millions of people lost their jobs and, in many cases, lost the health insurance benefits that were tied to those jobs.

TABLE 8.7

Percentage of children who made no health care visits to an office or clinic within the past 12 months, by selected characteristics, selected years 1997–2012 [CONTINUED]

[Data are based on household interviews of a sample of the civilian noninstitutionalized population]

Characteristic	Under 18 years			Under 6 years			6–17 years		
	1997–1998	2001–2002	2011–2012	1997–1998	2001–2002	2011–2012	1997–1998	2001–2002	2011–2012
Percent of poverty level and health insurance status prior to interview[d, e]	Percent of children without a health care visit[a]								
Below 100%:									
Insured continuously all 12 months	12.6	11.7	8.9	5.7	6.1	5.4	17.6	14.9	11.4
Uninsured for any period up to 12 months	19.9	21.8	12.7	9.9*	14.4*	*	26.1	26.6	15.5
Uninsured more than 12 months	39.9	48.2	43.0	24.9	28.0*	*	45.2	55.7	46.3
100%–199%:									
Insured continuously all 12 months	12.6	10.9	8.3	4.8	4.2	4.7	16.7	14.5	10.2
Uninsured for any period up to 12 months	15.6	18.9	15.7	8.7*	10.7*	*	20.2	23.2	20.2
Uninsured more than 12 months	33.7	41.3	37.8	21.3	35.4	*	37.9	43.6	40.3
200%–399%:									
Insured continuously all 12 months	10.5	10.0	7.9	4.5	4.6	4.7	13.2	12.4	9.5
Uninsured for any period up to 12 months	12.8	14.5	11.3	*	7.1*	*	17.2	18.7	14.3
Uninsured more than 12 months	29.9	30.8	28.9	11.8*	24.2*	*	36.5	32.9	30.2
400% or more:									
Insured continuously all 12 months	7.0	7.2	5.1	2.9	3.9	2.3	8.8	8.7	6.3
Uninsured for any period up to 12 months	10.8*	11.4*	12.0*	*	*	*	15.1*	14.1*	*
Uninsured more than 12 months	28.8*	38.4*	27.9*	*	*	*	37.7*	40.3*	37.6*
Geographic region									
Northeast	7.0	6.0	5.9	3.1	3.9	5.2	8.9	6.9	6.2
Midwest	12.2	10.3	8.2	5.9	5.1	3.5	15.3	12.8	10.6
South	14.3	14.0	8.9	5.6	7.0	4.8	18.5	17.4	11.1
West	16.3	16.0	11.7	7.9	8.1	6.2	20.7	20.0	14.5
Location of residence									
Within MSA[f]	12.3	11.7	8.7	5.4	6.1	4.9	15.9	14.5	10.7
Outside MSA[f]	14.6	13.5	9.9	6.9	6.9	5.0	17.9	16.3	12.4

*Estimates are considered unreliable.
—Data not available.
[a]Respondents were asked how many times a doctor or other health care professional was seen in the past 12 months at a doctor's office, clinic, or some other place. Excluded are visits to emergency rooms, hospitalizations, home visits, and telephone calls. Starting with 2000 data, dental visits were also excluded.
[b]Includes all other races not shown separately and unknown health insurance status.
[c]The race groups, white, black, American Indian or Alaska Native, Asian, Native Hawaiian or other Pacific Islander, and 2 or more races, include persons of Hispanic and non-Hispanic origin. Persons of Hispanic origin may be of any race. Starting with 1999 data, race-specific estimates are tabulated according to the 1997 *Revisions to the Standards for the Classification of Federal Data on Race and Ethnicity* and are not strictly comparable with estimates for earlier years. The five single-race categories plus multiple-race categories shown in the table conform to the 1997 standards. Starting with 1999 data, race-specific estimates are for persons who reported only one racial group; the category 2 or more races includes persons who reported more than one racial group. Prior to 1999, data were tabulated according to the 1977 standards with four racial groups, and the Asian only category included Native Hawaiian or other Pacific Islander. Estimates for single-race categories prior to 1999 included persons who reported one race or, if they reported more than one race, identified one race as best representing their race. Starting with 2003 data, race responses of other race and unspecified multiple race were treated as missing, and then race was imputed if these were the only race responses. Almost all persons with a race response of other race were of Hispanic origin.
[d]Percent of poverty level is based on family income and family size and composition using U.S. Census Bureau poverty thresholds. Missing family income data were imputed starting in 1997.
[e]Health insurance categories are mutually exclusive. Persons who reported both Medicaid and private coverage are classified as having private coverage. Starting with 1997 data, state-sponsored health plan coverage is included as Medicaid coverage. Starting with 1999 data, coverage by the Children's Health Insurance Program (CHIP) is included with Medicaid coverage. In addition to private and Medicaid, the insured category also includes military, other government, and Medicare coverage. Persons not covered by private insurance, Medicaid, CHIP, state-sponsored or other government-sponsored health plans (starting in 1997), Medicare, or military plans are considered to have no health insurance coverage. Persons with only Indian Health Service coverage are considered to have no health insurance coverage.
[f]MSA is metropolitan statistical area. Starting with 2005–2006 data, MSA status is determined using 2000 census data and the 2000 standards for defining MSAs.
Note: In 1997, the National Health Interview Survey questionnaire was redesigned.

SOURCE: "Table 77. No Health Care Visits to an Office or Clinic within the Past 12 Months among Children under Age 18, by Selected Characteristics: United States, Average Annual, Selected Years 1997–1998 through 2011–2012," in *Health, United States, 2013: With Special Feature on Prescription Drugs*, Centers for Disease Control and Prevention, National Center for Health Statistics, May 14, 2014, http://www.cdc.gov/nchs/data/hus/hus13.pdf (accessed November 13, 2014)

Although the percentage of people nationwide who had no health insurance was 13.4% in 2013 according to the CPS and 14.5% according to the ACS, the percentage varied significantly by state. Some of the states with the highest uninsured rates also had very large populations, as Figure 8.4 (based on data from the ACS) shows. In 2013 approximately one-fifth or more of the populations of Florida (the nation's fourth-largest state by population), Nevada, and Texas (the second-largest state) were uninsured; and in 13 other states (Alaska, Arizona, Arkansas, California [the largest state], Georgia, Idaho, Louisiana, Mississippi, Montana, New Mexico, North Carolina, Oklahoma, and South Carolina) the uninsured accounted for between 15.1% and 19% of the total population.

FIGURE 8.2

Number and percentage of people, by health insurance status, 2013

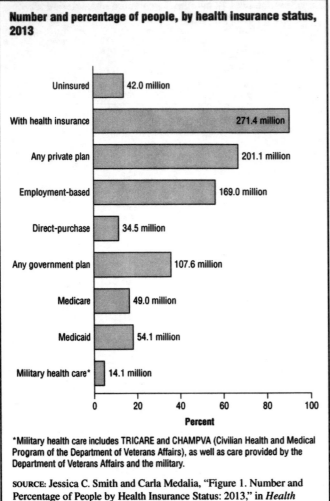

*Military health care includes TRICARE and CHAMPVA (Civilian Health and Medical Program of the Department of Veterans Affairs), as well as care provided by the Department of Veterans Affairs and the military.

SOURCE: Jessica C. Smith and Carla Medalia, "Figure 1. Number and Percentage of People by Health Insurance Status: 2013," in *Health Insurance Coverage in the United States: 2013*, U.S. Census Bureau, September 2014, http://www.census.gov/content/dam/Census/library/publications/2014/demo/p60-250.pdf (accessed November 13, 2014)

FIGURE 8.3

Percentage of people without health insurance, 2008–13

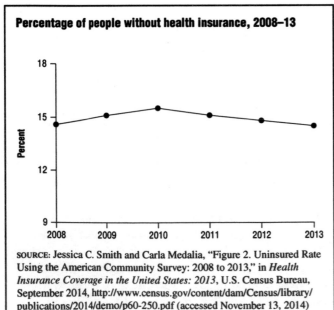

SOURCE: Jessica C. Smith and Carla Medalia, "Figure 2. Uninsured Rate Using the American Community Survey: 2008 to 2013," in *Health Insurance Coverage in the United States: 2013*, U.S. Census Bureau, September 2014, http://www.census.gov/content/dam/Census/library/publications/2014/demo/p60-250.pdf (accessed November 13, 2014)

Table 8.8, also based on ACS data, shows that 6.5 million people in California, 5.7 million people in Texas, 3.9 million people in Florida, and 2.1 million people in New York were without health insurance coverage in 2013. Other states with more than 1 million uninsured people were Arizona, Georgia, Illinois, Michigan, New Jersey, North Carolina, Ohio, and Pennsylvania.

Because most low- and middle-income children were eligible for health insurance through Medicaid or CHIP in 2013, and because all people aged 65 years and older were eligible for health insurance through Medicare, the uninsured population at that time primarily consisted of those between the ages of 19 and 64 years old. (See Figure 8.5.) The percentage of the population without insurance climbed between the ages of 19 and 22, peaked through age 28, and then fell through age 64. This is consistent with overall career patterns: as people move through their prime working years, they tend to advance in both pay and benefit levels, making it more likely that they will have access to employer-based insurance or the employer-based insurance of a spouse or partner. As Table 8.9 shows, in 2013 people became steadily more likely to have private insurance the older they were. Six out of 10 of those under the age of 18 years were covered by private insurance, and four out of 10 were covered by government-funded insurance. The private insurance rate rose only slightly for those between the ages of 19 and 25 (62.5%) and for those between ages 26 and 34 (62.9%), the years that people are most likely to be uninsured. Past age 35 people were significantly more likely than younger adults to have private insurance. Almost all of those aged 65 years and older had government health insurance through Medicare. However, 54% of those aged 65 years and older retained private insurance, usually in addition to Medicare.

Unsurprisingly, the likelihood that an individual will be uninsured or receive insurance through the government is directly proportional to household income levels. As Table 8.10 shows, those living in households making less than $25,000 in 2013 were the most likely group, by income, to receive insurance through the government (62.5% did so), but they were also the group most likely to be uninsured (21.6%). Both the percentage of those with government health insurance (45.9%) and with no insurance (18.7%) were slightly lower for individuals in households making between $25,000 and $49,999; and these percentages were lower again in households making $50,000 to $74,999 (30.8% and 13.1%), $75,000 to $99,999 (21.5% and 9.7%), $100,000 to $149,999 (17.3% and 6.3%), and over $150,000 (14.1% and 5.3%).

The likelihood that one will be uninsured varies significantly by other demographic characteristics, as well. By race and Hispanic origin, non-Hispanic whites were less likely to be uninsured than other groups. (See

FIGURE 8.4

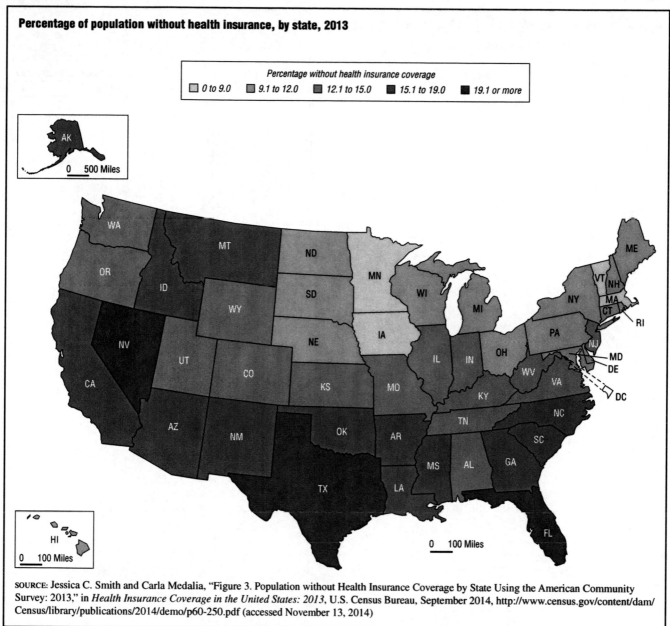

Percentage of population without health insurance, by state, 2013

Percentage without health insurance coverage

☐ 0 to 9.0   ☐ 9.1 to 12.0   ☐ 12.1 to 15.0   ■ 15.1 to 19.0   ■ 19.1 or more

SOURCE: Jessica C. Smith and Carla Medalia, "Figure 3. Population without Health Insurance Coverage by State Using the American Community Survey: 2013," in *Health Insurance Coverage in the United States: 2013*, U.S. Census Bureau, September 2014, http://www.census.gov/content/dam/Census/library/publications/2014/demo/p60-250.pdf (accessed November 13, 2014)

Figure 8.6.) A dramatically higher percentage of the adult Hispanic population, and a significantly higher percentage of the child Hispanic population, were uninsured than were adults and children of other racial and ethnic groups. This might be because many Hispanics in the United States are not citizens, and more than 40% of noncitizens were uninsured in 2013.

The Patient Protection and Affordable Care Act

The health care reform effort spearheaded by the administration of President Barack Obama (1961–) took the form of the Patient Protection and Affordable Care Act (typically referred to as the Affordable Care Act [ACA], or Obamacare). The ACA, which was signed into law in 2010 and fully implemented over the next four years, sought to make insurance more affordable for low- and middle-income workers who did not receive coverage through their employers. It also sought to expand the number of low-income people who receive coverage through Medicaid. This was accomplished by extending to most households making less than 400% of poverty the subsidies that could be used to purchase individual insurance through websites run by either state governments or the federal government. The ACA's expansion of Medicaid involved raising the income thresholds used to determine eligibility so that coverage would be available to all adults living below 138% of poverty, whereas Medicaid in most states had previously covered only certain adults with dependent children. Between the provision of subsidies to those purchasing individual policies and the expansion of Medicaid, near-universal health care coverage was considered an attainable eventuality.

TABLE 8.8

Number and percentage of population without health insurance, by state, 2013

[Numbers in thousands. Civilian noninstitutionalized population.]

State	2013 uninsured		2012 uninsured		Difference in uninsured	
	Number	Percent	Number	Percent	Number	Percent
United States	**45,181**	**14.5**	**45,615**	**14.8**	**−434**	**−0.2**
Alabama	645	13.6	632	13.3	13	0.2
Alaska	132	18.5	145	20.5	−13	−2.0
Arizona	1,118	17.1	1,131	17.6	−13	−0.4
Arkansas	465	16.0	476	16.4	−11	−0.5
California	6,500	17.2	6,710	17.9	−209	−0.7
Colorado	729	14.1	751	14.7	−22	−0.7
Connecticut	333	9.4	322	9.1	11	0.3
Delaware	83	9.1	80	8.8	3	0.3
District of Columbia	42	6.7	37	5.9	5	0.7
Florida	3,853	20.0	3,816	20.1	37	−0.1
Georgia	1,846	18.8	1,792	18.4	54	0.4
Hawaii	91	6.7	92	6.9	−2	−0.1
Idaho	257	16.2	255	16.2	3	*
Illinois	1,618	12.7	1,622	12.8	−4	*
Indiana	903	14.0	920	14.3	−17	−0.3
Iowa	248	8.1	254	8.4	−7	−0.3
Kansas	348	12.3	356	12.6	−7	−0.3
Kentucky	616	14.3	595	13.9	21	0.4
Louisiana	751	16.6	760	16.9	−8	−0.3
Maine	147	11.2	135	10.2	12	0.9
Maryland	593	10.2	598	10.3	−4	−0.2
Massachusetts	247	3.7	254	3.9	−8	−0.1
Michigan	1,072	11.0	1,114	11.4	−43	−0.5
Minnesota	440	8.2	425	8.0	15	0.2
Mississippi	500	17.1	498	17.0	2	*
Missouri	773	13.0	801	13.6	−29	−0.5
Montana	165	16.5	178	18.0	−14	−1.6
Nebraska	209	11.3	206	11.3	3	0.1
Nevada	570	20.7	603	22.2	−33	−1.5
New Hampshire	140	10.7	139	10.6	1	0.1
New Jersey	1,160	13.2	1,113	12.7	47	0.5
New Mexico	382	18.6	378	18.4	4	0.2
New York	2,070	10.7	2,103	10.9	−33	−0.2
North Carolina	1,509	15.6	1,582	16.6	−73	−0.9
North Dakota	73	10.4	69	10.0	5	0.3
Ohio	1,258	11.0	1,304	11.5	−47	−0.4
Oklahoma	666	17.7	685	18.4	−19	−0.7
Oregon	571	14.7	576	14.9	−5	−0.3
Pennsylvania	1,222	9.7	1,225	9.8	−2	*
Rhode Island	120	11.6	115	11.1	6	0.5
South Carolina	739	15.8	778	16.8	−39	−1.0
South Dakota	93	11.3	94	11.5	−1	−0.2
Tennessee	887	13.9	882	13.9	5	*
Texas	5,748	22.1	5,762	22.5	−14	−0.4
Utah	402	14.0	409	14.5	−7	−0.5
Vermont	45	7.2	40	6.5	5	0.8
Virginia	991	12.3	1,000	12.5	−9	−0.2
Washington	960	14.0	945	13.9	15	0.1
West Virginia	255	14.0	264	14.4	−9	−0.5
Wisconsin	518	9.1	506	9.0	12	0.2
Wyoming	77	13.4	87	15.4	−10	−1.9

*Represents or rounds to zero.
Note: Differences are calculated with unrounded numbers, which may produce different results from using the rounded values in the table.

SOURCE: Adapted from Jessica C. Smith and Carla Medalia, "Table A-1. Population without Health Insurance Coverage by State: 2013," in *Health Insurance Coverage in the United States: 2013*, U.S. Census Bureau, September 2014, http://www.census.gov/content/dam/Census/library/publications/2014/demo/p60250.pdf (accessed November 13, 2014)

Opponents of the ACA, however, mounted a two-part legal challenge to the law's constitutionality, and their case was eventually heard by the U.S. Supreme Court in *National Federation of Independent Business v. Sebelius* (567 U.S.___ [2012]). The Henry J. Kaiser Family Foundation (KFF) explains in "A Guide to the Supreme Court's Affordable Care Act Decision" (July 2012, http://kaiserfamilyfoundation.files.wordpress.com/2013/01/ 8332.pdf) that the plaintiffs in the case were in reality a combined set of plaintiffs from two separate lawsuits originally filed in Florida immediately after the law's passage. One group consisted of the state of Florida and 25 other states whose attorneys general opposed the law, and the other group consisted of the National Federation of Independent Business (a conservative lobbying group that advances the interests of small business owners), along with

FIGURE 8.5

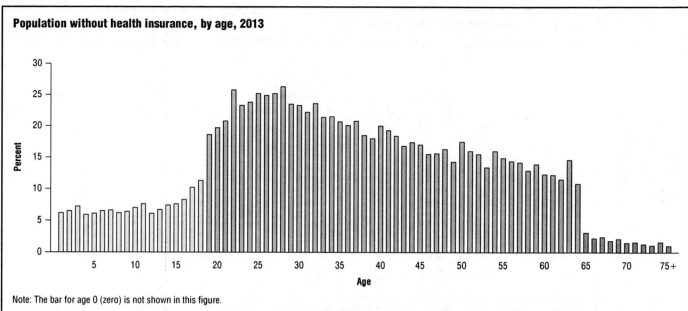

Population without health insurance, by age, 2013

Note: The bar for age 0 (zero) is not shown in this figure.

SOURCE: Jessica C. Smith and Carla Medalia, "Figure 4. Population without Health Insurance Coverage by Single Year of Age: 2013," in *Health Insurance Coverage in the United States: 2013*, U.S. Census Bureau, September 2014, http://www.census.gov/content/dam/Census/library/publications/2014/demo/p60-250.pdf (accessed November 13, 2014)

TABLE 8.9

Type of health insurance, by age, 2013

[Data are based on the CPS ASEC (Current Population Survey, Annual Social and Economic Supplement) sample of 68,000 addresses. Population as of March of the following year.]

Characteristic	Total	Any health insurance		Private health insurance[a]		Government health insurance[b]		Uninsured[c]	
		Number	Percent	Number	Percent	Number	Percent	Number	Percent
Total	313,395	271,442	86.6	201,064	64.2	107,581	34.3	41,953	13.4
Age									
Under age 65	268,888	227,627	84.7	177,026	65.8	65,913	24.5	41,260	15.3
Under age 18	74,055	68,613	92.7	44,429	60.0	30,410	41.1	5,441	7.3
Under age 19[d]	78,170	72,264	92.4	47,213	60.4	31,557	40.4	5,907	7.6
Aged 19 to 25[e]	30,384	23,520	77.4	18,976	62.5	6,033	19.9	6,864	22.6
Aged 26 to 34	38,020	29,072	76.5	23,922	62.9	6,601	17.4	8,948	23.5
Aged 35 to 44	39,789	32,233	81.0	27,661	69.5	6,214	15.6	7,556	19.0
Aged 45 to 64	82,524	70,539	85.5	59,254	71.8	15,507	18.8	11,985	14.5
Aged 65 and older	44,508	43,815	90.4	24,039	54.0	41,668	93.6	693	1.6

[a]Private health insurance includes coverage provided through an employer or union, or coverage purchased directly by an individual from an insurance company.
[b]Government health insurance coverage includes Medicaid, Medicare, TRICARE, CHAMPVA (Civilian Health and Medical Program of the Department of Veterans Affairs) and care provided by the Department of Veterans Affairs and the military.
[c]Individuals are considered to be uninsured if they do not have health insurance coverage for the entire calendar year.
[d]Children under the age of 19 are eligible for Medicaid/CHIP.
[e]This age group is of special interest because of the Affordable Care Act's dependent coverage provision. Individuals aged 19 to 25 years may be eligible to be a dependent on a parent's health insurance plan.
Note: The 2014 CPS ASEC included redesigned questions for income and health insurance coverage. All of the approximately 98,000 addresses were eligible to receive the redesigned set of health insurance coverage questions. The redesigned income questions were implemented to a subsample of these 98,000 addresses using a probability split panel design. Approximately 68,000 addresses were eligible to receive a set of income questions similar to those used in the 2013 CPS ASEC and the remaining 30,000 addresses were eligible to receive the redesigned income questions. The source of data for this table is the portion of the CPS ASEC sample which received the income questions consistent with the 2013 CPS ASEC, approximately 68,000 addresses.
The estimates by type of coverage are *not* mutually exclusive; people can be covered by more than one type of health insurance during the year.

SOURCE: Adapted from Jessica C. Smith and Carla Medalia, "Table 2. Type of Health Insurance Coverage by Age: 2013," in *Health Insurance Coverage in the United States: 2013*, U.S. Census Bureau, September 2014, http://www.census.gov/content/dam/Census/library/publications/2014/demo/p60-250.pdf (accessed November 13, 2014)

individuals who did not have insurance coverage. Both groups named Kathleen Sebelius (1948–), the secretary of the U.S. Department of Health and Human Services (the federal agency responsible for implementing the ACA), as the defendant in their cases. The U.S. Supreme Court heard both cases together and issued its ruling in June 2012.

TABLE 8.10

Type of health insurance, by household income and poverty level, 2013

[Data are based on the CPS ASEC (Current Population Survey, Annual Social and Economic Supplement) sample of 68,000 addresses. Numbers in thousands. Population as of March of the following year.]

Characteristic	Total	Any health insurance		Private health insurance[a]		Government health insurance[b]		Uninsured[c]	
		Number	Percent	Number	Percent	Number	Percent	Number	Percent
Total	313,395	271,442	86.6	201,064	64.2	107,581	34.3	41,953	13.4
Household income									
Less than $25,000	55,692	43,640	78.4	14,882	26.7	34,796	62.5	12,052	21.6
$25,000 to $49,999	70,057	56,932	81.3	35,260	50.3	32,132	45.9	13,125	18.7
$50,000 to $74,999	57,090	49,610	86.9	39,804	69.7	17,564	30.8	7,480	13.1
$75,000 to $99,999	42,650	38,497	90.3	33,939	79.6	9,161	21.5	4,153	9.7
$100,000 to $149,999	47,681	44,661	93.7	41,060	86.1	8,246	17.3	3,020	6.3
$150,000 or more	40,225	38,102	94.7	36,120	89.8	5,682	14.1	2,123	5.3
Income-to-poverty ratio									
Below 100 percent of poverty	45,318	34,042	75.1	10,317	22.8	26,565	58.6	11,276	24.9
Between 100 and 199 percent of poverty	60,706	48,031	79.1	25,894	42.7	29,645	48.8	12,675	20.9
Between 200 and 249 percent of poverty	26,958	22,580	83.8	16,645	61.7	9,738	36.1	4,377	16.2
At or above 250 percent of poverty	179,984	166,395	92.5	148,086	82.3	41,323	23.0	13,589	7.5

[a]Private health insurance includes coverage provided through an employer or union, or coverage purchased directly by an individual from an insurance company.
[b]Government health insurance coverage includes Medicaid, Medicare, TRICARE, CHAMPVA (Civilian Health and Medical Program of the Department of Veterans Affairs) and care provided by the Department of Veterans Affairs and the military.
[c]Individuals are considered to be uninsured if they do not have health insurance coverage for the entire calendar year.
Note: The 2014 CPS ASEC (Current Population Survey, Annual Social and Economic Supplement) included redesigned questions for income and health insurance coverage. All of the approximately 98,000 addresses were eligible to receive the redesigned set of health insurance coverage questions. The redesigned income questions were implemented to a subsample of these 98,000 addresses using a probability split panel design. Approximately 68,000 addresses were eligible to receive a set of income questions similar to those used in the 2013 CPS ASEC and the remaining 30,000 addresses were eligible to receive the redesigned income questions. The source of data for this table is the portion of the CPS ASEC sample which received the income questions consistent with the 2013 CPS ASEC, approximately 68,000 addresses. The estimates by type of coverage are not mutually exclusive; people can be covered by more than one type of health insurance during the year.

SOURCE: Adapted from Jessica C. Smith and Carla Medalia, "Table 4. Type of Health Insurance Coverage by Household Income and Income-to-Poverty Ratio: 2013," in *Health Insurance Coverage in the United States: 2013*, U.S. Census Bureau, September 2014, http://www.census.gov/content/dam/Census/library/publications/2014/demo/p60-250.pdf (accessed November 13, 2014)

One legal challenge to the ACA centered on the so-called individual mandate, a law requiring all U.S. residents who did not receive health insurance through their employers or through public programs to purchase an individual policy or pay a fine. The purpose of the individual mandate was to add young and healthy people to the pool of individuals who bought their coverage directly from insurers, a necessary development if the individual insurance market was to become affordable enough for a majority of potential purchasers.

Prior to the ACA's implementation, the market for individual coverage included a disproportionate number of older people and those with existing health problems. Such policies have historically been costly because insurers raise premiums (the monthly amount paid by the customer to obtain coverage) to account for the high costs of insuring those who need extensive medical care. An influx of young and healthy policyholders would, according to the ACA's architects, balance out the overall pool of individual policyholders, allowing insurance companies to lower rates to an entire state's pool of individual applicants regardless of their individual health status.

The logic of the individual mandate mirrored the logic of group coverage offered by businesses, which similarly spreads risk (the risk that any one individual will need high-cost medical treatment) among a group of people. Companies offer coverage to the whole group at rates lower than would be obtainable by the sickest members of the group if they were purchasing it on their own. In many cases the healthiest members of a group pay more than they might if coverage were based on their level of health. However, because all people will experience worsening health over time, everyone eventually benefits from the spreading of risk. The individual mandate extended this concept to the state level.

The second key challenge to the ACA in *National Federation of Independent Business v. Sebelius* centered on the Medicaid expansion. Medicaid is a joint federal-state program, whereby the federal and state governments share costs and the states oversee administration. Prior to the ACA, Medicaid eligibility varied by state, with eligibility standards set in relation to the federal poverty level. Some states offered coverage to adults at or even above the poverty line, but many states restricted eligibility to adults with dependent children in households making half or less of poverty. By expanding eligibility to almost all Americans under the age of 65 years whose incomes were below 138% of poverty, the ACA was expected to result in the extension of health coverage to approximately 17 million low-income people.

FIGURE 8.6

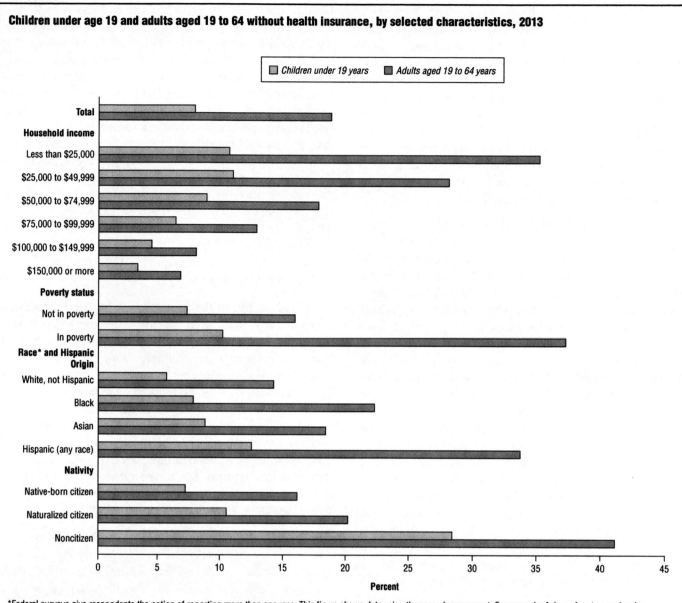

Children under age 19 and adults aged 19 to 64 without health insurance, by selected characteristics, 2013

*Federal surveys give respondents the option of reporting more than one race. This figure shows data using the race-alone concept. For example, Asian refers to people who reported Asian and no other race.

SOURCE: Jessica C. Smith and Carla Medalia, "Figure 6. Children under 19 Years of Age and Adults Aged 19 to 64 Years without Health Insurance Coverage by Selected Characteristics: 2013," in *Health Insurance Coverage in the United States: 2013*, U.S. Census Bureau, September 2014, http://www.census .gov/content/dam/Census/library/publications/2014/demo/p60-250.pdf (accessed November 13, 2014)

National Federation of Independent Business v. Sebelius challenged both the individual mandate and the Medicaid expansion on constitutional grounds. The plaintiffs argued that the government had no authority to force individuals to purchase a product or service from a company, and that the federal government's insistence that states expand their Medicaid coverage (which would ultimately create new costs and administrative responsibilities for the states, although the federal government would initially pay for 100% of the costs of expansion) represented an unconstitutionally coercive act by the federal government.

As the KFF notes, in a 5–4 decision written by Chief Justice John Roberts (1955–), the Supreme Court upheld the constitutionality of the individual mandate, ruling that the fines imposed on those who refused to purchase insurance represented an acceptable form of taxation. By a 7–2 majority, the court ruled that the Medicaid expansion was, as the plaintiffs had argued, an unconstitutionally coercive act by the federal government. However, the same 5–4 majority that upheld the individual mandate ruled that the coercive nature of the Medicaid expansion could be remedied by allowing the states to decide for themselves whether or not to participate. The implementation of the ACA thus proceeded over the following year and a half, taking full effect in 2014.

Medicaid

Medicaid, which is authorized under Title XIX of the Social Security Act, is a federal-state program that provides free medical insurance for low-income people. Within federal guidelines, each state designs and administers its own program. For this reason, there may be considerable differences from state to state as to who is covered, what type of coverage is provided, and how much is paid for medical services. As noted earlier, some states have historically gone beyond the minimum eligibility requirements established by the federal government, and some continue to extend eligibility above the income threshold of 138% established by the ACA.

As a result of the Medicaid portion of the Supreme Court's ACA ruling, a number of states chose not to participate in the Medicaid expansion. According to the KFF, in "Status of State Action on the Medicaid Expansion Decision" (December 17, 2014, http://kff.org/health-reform/state-indicator/state-activity-around-expanding-medicaid-under-the-affordable-care-act), as of year-end 2014, the District of Columbia and 27 states had adopted the Medicaid expansion: Arizona, Arkansas, California, Colorado, Connecticut, Delaware, Hawaii, Illinois, Iowa, Kentucky, Maryland, Massachusetts, Michigan, Minnesota, Nevada, New Hampshire, New Jersey, New Mexico, New York, North Dakota, Ohio, Oregon, Pennsylvania, Rhode Island, Vermont, Washington, and West Virginia. Of the 23 states that had not chosen to expand Medicaid as of that time, the Medicaid expansion was under discussion (that is, governors had announced plans to expand Medicaid, or variations on the proposed expansion had been announced) in Alaska, Indiana, Montana, Tennessee, Utah, Virginia, and Wyoming. There was no time limit for opting into the Medicaid expansion, so states that had thus far abstained from doing so may reverse course in the future.

Mandatory federal guidelines on eligibility for children and pregnant women apply even in states that have opted not to expand Medicaid under the ACA. The Center on Budget and Policy Priorities points out in "What Is Medicaid?" (May 8, 2013, http://www.cbpp.org/files/policybasics-medicaid.pdf), to receive federal funding, states are required to cover all children under the age of six years in families whose incomes fall below 133% of poverty, all children aged six to 18 years in families below the poverty line, and all pregnant women whose incomes are below 133% of poverty. Additionally, states are required to cover most of those disabled and elderly people who receive benefits under the Supplemental Security Income program.

However, in many of the states that have thus far chosen not to expand Medicaid, very few adults are eligible for coverage, no matter how poor they are. Typically these states provide no Medicaid coverage at all for adults without children, and they set eligibility for parents of dependent children at a threshold well below the poverty level. For example, the KFF notes in "Medicaid Income Eligibility Limits for Adults as a Percent of the Federal Poverty Level" (February 1, 2015, http://kff.org/health-reform/state-indicator/medicaid-income-eligibility-limits-for-adults-as-a-percent-of-the-federal-poverty-level) that Alabama provided Medicaid only to parents of dependent children making 18% of poverty or less. Other states that provided no coverage for adults without children and that set exceptionally low income thresholds for adults were Florida, which limited eligibility to parents of dependent children in households with incomes of 34% of the federal poverty level, Georgia (38%), Idaho (27%), Kansas (38%), Louisiana (24%), Mississippi (28%), Missouri (23%), Montana (51%), Nebraska (55%), North Carolina (45%), Oklahoma (46%), South Carolina (67%), South Dakota (53%), Texas (19%), Utah (46%), Virginia (45%), and Wyoming (58%).

Additionally, in those states that have not expanded Medicaid, low-income adults (those making 138% or less of poverty) are not eligible for the subsidized private insurance plans that are available to middle-income individuals in all states. Since the Supreme Court upheld the constitutionality of the individual mandate (the mechanism that underpins the marketplace for subsidized individual policies), all states provide subsidized insurance policies for people making between 138% and 399% of poverty. In those states that have not expanded Medicaid, therefore, the poorest adults are typically ineligible for government-funded health insurance, while comparatively wealthier adults are eligible for assistance.

As the Center on Budget and Policy Priorities notes in "Federal Government Will Pick Up Nearly All Costs of Health Reform's Medicaid Expansion" (March 28, 2012, http://www.cbpp.org/files/4-20-10health2.pdf), since the inception of Medicaid, the federal government has paid, on average, 57% of the costs of the program, with states contributing the remainder. Under the ACA, the federal government agreed to pay 100% of the costs of covering newly eligible Medicaid enrollees for the first three years of the expansion (2014–16), and then the federal share of the expansion costs was scheduled to fall slightly. By 2020 the federal government would pay 90% of the costs of all newly eligible individuals, and it would continue to pay this share of the expansion costs indefinitely.

In "Number of Uninsured Eligible for Medicaid under the ACA" (February 2015, http://kff.org/health-reform/state-indicator/number-of-uninsured-eligible-for-medicaid-under-the-aca), the KFF estimated that in the ACA's second year of full implementation, approximately 8.3 million low-income adults and 3.9 million low-income children remained uninsured but eligible for Medicaid under the terms of the ACA. These included people who were eligible under the ACA but whose states had chosen not to adopt the expansion, as well as people who were eligible for Medicaid (either in states that had expanded eligibility or in states that had not expanded eligibility) but who had not enrolled.

Children's Health Insurance Program

The Children's Health Insurance Program (CHIP) was introduced in 1997 in an effort to provide health coverage to uninsured children in families with incomes too high to qualify for Medicaid but too low to afford private health insurance. Authorized under Title XXI of the Social Security Act, CHIP is structured like Medicaid, as a joint federal-state program. The federal government contributes a majority of funding, and the states provide the remainder of funding as well as administration. The federal share of costs typically exceeds that of Medicaid by approximately 15 percentage points. Thus, in a state where the federal government pays the national average of 57% of Medicaid costs, the federal government typically pays 72% of CHIP costs. States may use this money to expand their Medicaid programs, design new child health insurance programs, or create a combination of the two. According to the Centers for Medicare and Medicaid Services (CMS), in "Children's Health Insurance Program (CHIP)" (http://www.medicaid.gov/chip/chip-program-information.html), as of 2014 seven states and the District of Columbia had opted to expand Medicaid, 17 states had set up separate CHIP programs, and 26 states had created a combination of the two programs.

The Children's Health Insurance Program Reauthorization Act (CHIPRA) was signed into law by President Obama in February 2009, extending and expanding CHIP. The ACA maintained current levels of CHIP funding through October 1, 2015, after which point the federal share of CHIP funding was scheduled to increase dramatically, to an average of 93% of total costs in each state.

As with Medicaid, states have the ability to set their own eligibility standards for CHIP. However, states must enroll children who meet Medicaid's eligibility requirements in Medicaid rather than in CHIP. Thus, CHIP eligibility typically picks up at the income thresholds where Medicaid cuts off, and it rises above 300% of poverty in some states. According to the KFF, in "Where Are States Today? Medicaid and CHIP Eligibility Levels for Adults, Children, and Pregnant Women as of January 2015" (http://kff.org/medicaid/fact-sheet/where-are-states-today-medicaid-and-chip), 23 states had income cutoffs ranging from 175% to 249% of the federal poverty level; nine states had income limits between 250% and 300% of poverty; and the District of Columbia and 18 states set income requirements greater than 300% of the federal poverty level. States have the option to determine how much, if any, costs are shared by applicant families.

Generally, cost-sharing requirements cannot rise above 5% of a family's annual income, and cost-sharing is prohibited for certain services, such as well-baby and well-child visits, which are free to all families enrolled in the program.

Early ACA Enrollment Statistics

As of late 2014 there were indications that the ACA had succeeded in substantially reducing the uninsured population, in keeping with its design and in spite of the limitations placed on it by those states that had opted not to expand Medicaid. However, the best available data at that time were preliminary, suitable for drawing conclusions about the reform effort's broad outlines but not about more specific concerns.

As Sharon K. Long et al. of the Urban Institute report in "Taking Stock: Health Insurance Coverage under the ACA as of September 2014" (December 3, 2014, http://hrms.urban.org/briefs/Health-Insurance-Coverage-under-the-ACA-as-of-September-2014.html), between September 2013 and September 2014 the uninsured population fell by 10.6 million, a one-year decline of 30.1%. Most of those gaining coverage were the low- and middle-income adults who were the target of either the Medicaid expansion or the provisions for subsidizing private individual policies. Among those adults with household incomes of 138% or less of poverty (the target of the Medicaid expansion), there was a 12 percentage-point increase in the insured portion of the population; and among those with incomes between 138% and 399% of poverty (the target of the measures introducing subsidized private plans), there was a 5.2 percentage-point increase.

There was a large disparity in changes to the uninsured rate in states that expanded Medicaid versus those that did not implement the Medicaid expansion. The uninsured rate fell by 36.3% in states that expanded Medicaid and by 23.9% in states that did not. There was little difference in the coverage gains through the private insurance subsidies between expansion and non-expansion states, according to the Urban Institute. Thus, the disparity in the overall rate of insured vs. uninsured was almost entirely attributable to the non-expansion states' refusal to provide government-funded coverage to low-income adults. Over half (54.7%) of those nonelderly adults who remained uninsured as of 2014 were in the states that had opted not to expand Medicaid.

HEALTH OF THE HOMELESS

The rates of both chronic (long-term) and acute (severe or intense) health problems are disproportionately high among the homeless population. Except for obesity, strokes, and cancer, homeless people are more likely than housed people to suffer from every category of chronic health problems. Other serious illnesses, such as tuberculosis (TB), are almost exclusively associated with the unhealthy living conditions brought on by poverty, and homeless people are especially vulnerable to them. In general, experts agree that homeless individuals suffer from more types of illnesses, for longer periods, and with more harmful consequences than housed people. Meanwhile, delivery of health care is complicated by a patient's homeless status, making management of chronic diseases such as diabetes, HIV, and hypertension more difficult.

Street living comes with a set of health conditions that living in a home does not. Homeless people fall prey to parasites, frostbite, leg ulcers, and infections. They are also at greater risk of physical and psychological trauma resulting from muggings, beatings, and rape. With no safe place to store belongings, the proper storage or administration of medications becomes difficult. In addition, some homeless people with mental disorders may use drugs or alcohol to self-medicate, and those with addictive disorders are more susceptible to HIV and other communicable diseases.

Homeless people may also lack the ability to access some of the basic rituals of self-care: bed rest, adequate nutrition, and good personal hygiene. Infections that are easy to prevent among those able to clean themselves thoroughly and frequently can pose persistent threats to the homeless. Additionally, the ability to rest and recuperate, which is often essential for the recovery process, is almost impossible for homeless people. Not only must they spend time locating places to sleep and food to eat, in many cities it is illegal for them to rest in public, as discussed in Chapter 7.

In "Homelessness as an Independent Risk Factor for Mortality: Results from a Retrospective Cohort Study" (*International Journal of Epidemiology*, March 21, 2009), David S. Morrison of the University of Glasgow concludes that homelessness itself is an independent risk factor for death; it appears to substantially increase mortality risk from specific causes. In "Programmatic Impact of 5 Years of Mortality Surveillance of New York City Homeless Populations" (*American Journal of Public Health*, supplement 2, vol. 103, no. S2, 2013), Melissa Gambatese et al. note that homeless individuals' risk of death ranges from 1.5 to 11.5 times greater than that of the population at large. Gambatese et al. further report on a study of the causes of death among New York City's homeless population in 2005 through 2010 and find that the leading causes of death were heart disease, drug overdoses, accidents, alcohol abuse, and assault/homicide. Heart disease is the leading cause of death for the U.S. population at large, but New York City's homeless population, like homeless people generally, appear much more likely than the general population to die from alcohol and drug-related causes as well as from violence and other external factors.

In "Psychiatric Disorders and Mortality among People in Homeless Shelters in Denmark: A Nationwide Register-Based Cohort Study" (*Lancet*, June 2011), a Danish study of 32,711 homeless people over the course of a decade (1999 to 2009), S. F. Nielsen et al. assessed the degree to which homeless health outcomes differ from those of the general population, particularly in relation to mental health and substance abuse issues. The researchers found that 62.4% of homeless men and 58.2% of homeless women had psychiatric disorders, and they found that 49% of homeless men and 36.9% of homeless women had substance abuse diagnoses. During the 10 years of research, 16.7% of the male study cohort and 9.8% of the female cohort died, and external causes accounted for 27.9% of the deaths for which a cause could be established. The researchers found that for homeless men between the ages of 15 and 24, life expectancy was 21.6 years lower than that of the corresponding age group in the population at large; and for homeless women between the ages of 15 and 24, life expectancy was 17.4 years lower than that of the corresponding age group in the population at large.

Many studies have focused on the rates of prevalence of specific diseases among the homeless. Bonnie D. Kerker et al. find in "A Population-Based Assessment of the Health of Homeless Families in New York City" (*American Journal of Public Health*, vol. 101, no. 3, March 2011) that rates of TB infection among homeless families were three times higher than among housed low-income families. In "Prevalence, Distribution, and Correlates of Hepatitis C Virus Infection among Homeless Adults in Los Angeles" (*Public Health Reporter*, vol. 127, no. 4, July–August 2012), Lillian Gelberg et al. find that 26.7% of homeless people sampled in Los Angeles, California, tested positive for hepatitis C. The study authors note that the most recent national data at the time of publication indicated a prevalence rate of 1.6% among the population at large. They also note that despite the extremely high rate of infection among the homeless population, approximately half of the cases were unknown, and almost all were untreated.

In "Housing Status and the Health of People Living with HIV/AIDS" (*Current HIV/AIDS Report*, vol. 9, no. 4, December 2012), Michael-John Milloy et al. conduct an exhaustive analysis of major academic studies on the subject of HIV/AIDS as it relates to housing status. They note that studies of people living with HIV/AIDS (PLWHA) find that a substantial portion are homeless or living in marginal housing situations such as shelters or hotel rooms. For example, a study of PLWHA in New York City found that 33% were homeless or marginally housed and that during the study 70% of study participants reported housing needs ranging from homelessness to eviction threats to fears of physical violence. A study of

PLWHA in Los Angeles found that 13% were homeless or living in marginal housing. The survey of research on the subject also finds that homeless individuals living with HIV/AIDS consistently receive suboptimal treatment for the disease, which is typically highly treatable through antiretroviral therapy. A study of patients in a public health clinic in Florida found that homeless HIV/AIDS patients were nearly 10 times more likely to die from the disease than HIV/AIDS patients who were housed. A study of 1,661 PLWHA in New York City isolated housing need as a reliable predictor of patients' likelihood of receiving appropriate HIV treatment or any medical care at all. A study conducted in Los Angeles also found that homelessness was the strongest factor predicting whether or not a PLWHA had unmet treatment needs.

Ulla Beijer, Achim Wolf, and Seena Fazel similarly reviewed published research on the correlation of homelessness and disease in "Prevalence of Tuberculosis, Hepatitis C Virus, and HIV in Homeless People: A Systematic Review and Meta-Analysis" (*Lancet Infectious Diseases*, vol. 12, no. 11, November 2012). In 43 studies that together surveyed a total homeless population of 63,812, the prevalence rates for TB ranged from 0.2% to 7.7%, the prevalence rates for hepatitis C ranged from 3.9% to 36.2%, and the prevalence rates for HIV infection ranged from 0.3% to 21.1%. The homeless were thus 34 to 452 times more likely than the general population to have TB, four to 70 times more likely to have hepatitis C, and one to 77 times more likely to be infected with HIV.

Mental Illness and Substance Abuse

Before the 1960s people with chronic mental illness were often committed involuntarily to state psychiatric hospitals. The development of medications that could control the symptoms of mental illness coincided with a growing belief that involuntary hospitalization was warranted only when a mentally ill person posed a threat to him- or herself or to others. Gradually, large numbers of mentally ill people were discharged from hospitals and other treatment facilities. Because the community-based treatment centers that were supposed to take the place of state hospitals were often either inadequate or nonexistent, many of these people ended up living on the streets.

Experts debate the rate of mental disorders among homeless populations, but they generally agree that it is greater among the homeless than the general population. In "The Prevalence of Mental Disorders among the Homeless in Western Countries: Systematic Review and Meta-Regression Analysis" (*PLoS Medline*, vol. 5, no. 12, December 2, 2008), Seena Fazel et al. analyze data from 29 surveys of the homeless in Western countries to find the prevalence of mental disorders in this population. The researchers find that the most common mental disorders were alcohol and drug dependence. The prevalence rates

of psychosis and depression ranged from 2.8% to 42.3%. Fazel et al. conclude that the prevalence of substance abuse disorder, psychotic disorders, and depression are higher among the homeless population than among the general population.

Mentally ill homeless people present special problems for health care workers. They may not be as cooperative and motivated as other patients. Because of their limited resources, they may have difficulty getting transportation to treatment centers. They frequently forget to show up for appointments or to take medications. The addition of substance abuse can make them unruly or unresponsive. Among people with severe mental disorders, those at greatest risk of homelessness are both the most severely ill and the most difficult to help.

The National Alliance on Mental Illness states in "Dual Diagnosis: Substance Abuse and Mental Illness" (January 2013, http://www.nami.org/Template.cfm?Section=By_Illness&Template=/TaggedPage/TaggedPage Display.cfm&TPLID=54&ContentID=23049) that mental illness and substance abuse frequently occur together; clinicians call this dual diagnosis. The National Alliance on Mental Illness notes that certain groups, including men, individuals of low SES, military veterans, and people who are frequently ill, are more likely than the general population to abuse drugs and/or alcohol. Each of these groups overlaps considerably with the homeless population.

Traumatic Stress

The National Center on Family Homelessness (NCFH) notes in "Trauma-Informed Care" (2015, http://www.familyhomelessness.org/tic_resources.php?p=ss) that the prevalence of traumatic stress (negative psychological states brought about by having witnessed or been the victim of violence or loss) is "extraordinarily high" among the homeless. Traumatic stress is particularly damaging for children, whose early exposure to trauma is one of the most influential links to difficulties in later life. Sarah L. Cristofaro et al. observe in "Measuring Trauma and Stressful Events in Childhood and Adolescence among Patients with First-Episode Psychosis: Initial Factor Structure, Reliability, and Validity of the Trauma Experiences Checklist" (*Psychiatry Research*, vol. 210, no. 2, December 15, 2013) that exposure to traumatic stress has been firmly linked to a multitude of poor mental-health and other outcomes, including homelessness and many mental-health conditions prevalent among the homeless. Additionally, homelessness itself raises the likelihood that one will experience or witness traumatic incidents.

Violence

VIOLENCE TOWARD HOMELESS WOMEN. In "Correlates of Adult Assault among Homeless Women" (*Journal* of *Health Care for the Poor and Underserved,* vol. 21, no. 4, November 2010), Angela L. Hudson et al. find that some homeless women are more likely than others to experience violence. Noting that "homeless women are highly susceptible to victimization," the authors cite research that finds that a third of homeless women reported experiencing sexual assault within the past year and another third reported being physically assaulted within the past year. Hudson et al. studied homeless women in Los Angeles, California, to uncover relationships among homeless women's psychological functioning, past victimization, and the likelihood of adult victimization. They determine that mental illness and low self-esteem were important risk factors for physical and sexual victimization among the homeless women in their study. Physical victimization was also associated with a history of physical abuse as a child, and sexual victimization was associated with a history of sexual abuse as a child. Current and previous substance abuse as well as involvement in the sex trade placed homeless women at great risk for physical and sexual victimization.

Suzanne L. Wenzel et al. find in "Sexual Risk among Impoverished Women: Understanding the Role of Housing Status" (*AIDS and Behavior,* vol. 11, supplement 6, November 2007) that impoverished women who are homeless or who have been recently victimized are also more likely to engage in risky sexual behavior that can lead to HIV infection. The researchers indicate that homeless African American and Hispanic women had from two to five times greater odds of engaging in risky sexual behavior than women who were housed.

HATE CRIMES. In *Vulnerable to Hate: A Survey of Hate Crimes & Violence Committed against Homeless People in 2013* (June 2014, http://nationalhomeless.org/wp-content/uploads/2014/06/Hate-Crimes-2013-FINAL.pdf), the National Coalition for the Homeless notes that between 1999 and 2013, 1,437 acts of violence against the homeless were reported and that 375 victims of such violence died. Hate crimes against the homeless tend to be committed by males under the age of 30 years, and the targets are also typically male. In 2013, 85% of all homeless hate-crime perpetrators were under 30 years old, and 93% were male, whereas 65% of victims were aged 40 years and older, and 90% were male. Of the 109 reported hate crimes against homeless people in 2013, 18 resulted in the victim's death.

The Health of Homeless Children

The NCFH reports in "Children" (2014, http://www.familyhomelessness.org/children.php?p=ts) that homeless children "are sick four times more often than other children," with four times the respiratory infections of other children, twice the ear infections, five times the number of gastrointestinal illnesses. They are four times

more likely to have asthma, more likely to be obese, and twice as likely to go hungry than housed children. They also have three times more emotional and behavioral problems than housed children and are disproportionately likely to have been exposed to violence. The NCFH estimates that 1.6 million children in the United States experience homelessness each year.

HEALTH CARE FOR THE HOMELESS

The homeless share the same barriers to health care that low-income housed people do, with the added constraints that come with the instability of life on the streets or in shelters. Prior to the implementation of the ACA, homeless children and some homeless adults had access to health care through Medicaid, and homeless veterans had access to care through the U.S. Department of Veterans Affairs. By attempting to expand Medicaid eligibility to all adults making less than 138% of poverty, the ACA offered the chance to improve health outcomes for the homeless dramatically. This opportunity was limited by the refusal of many states to expand Medicaid, but preliminary data indicate that in states that expanded the program, the homeless were already receiving significantly improved care as of late 2014.

In "Early Impacts of the Medicaid Expansion for the Homeless Population" (November 13, 2014, http://kff.org/uninsured/issue-brief/early-impacts-of-the-medicaid-expansion-for-the-homeless-population), Barbara DiPietro, Samantha Artiga, and Alexandra Gates of the KFF report on the findings of focus groups conducted with administrators, providers, and those helping to enroll the homeless in Medicaid at five homeless-serving organizations across the country. Four of these organizations were located in cities whose state governments had gone forward with the Medicaid expansion (Albuquerque, New Mexico; Baltimore, Maryland; Chicago, Illinois; and Portland, Oregon), and one was located in a city whose state government had not (Jacksonville, Florida). The KFF authors note that the Albuquerque, Baltimore, and Portland organizations reported dramatic increases in the percentage of their homeless clients who had health coverage, whereas the Chicago organization reported significant but less dramatic coverage gains, and the Jacksonville organization reported no change in the number of homeless people covered.

The four homeless health care providers in Medicaid expansion states also reported that the acquisition of coverage allowed patients to access "life-saving or life-changing surgeries or treatments," including health interventions that allowed individuals to work and remain housed following their receipt of care. Providers reported that the Medicaid expansion allowed them to practice medicine more effectively, as well, since the funding of care gave them increased options for treatment, whereas prior to the expansion they had to decide on treatment based on what could be done for free (based on resources provided through charity efforts) or at discounted prices. Increased funding of these homeless health care services allowed providers to increase staff size and better allocate resources. The Jacksonville provider of health care to the homeless reported no change in the quality of coverage that they were able to provide. That site was facing increasing financial challenges given the absence of Medicaid funding and a decline in funding from other sources.

Beyond providing care to the homeless through Medicaid and the Department of Veterans Affairs (which funds health care for all veterans, including those who are homeless), the federal government funds homeless health efforts by providing assistance to local organizations under the Health Care for the Homeless (HCH) program, authorized under Title VI of the McKinney-Vento Homeless Assistance Act, which was signed into law in 1987. In 2013 the U.S. Department of Health and Human Services funded 250 programs serving 851,641 homeless people under the program, according to "Homeless Program Grantee Data" (2014, http://bphc .hrsa.gov/uds/datacenter.aspx?fd=ho&year=2013). The goal of the HCH programs is to improve the health of homeless individuals and families by improving access to primary health care and substance abuse services. The HCH programs provide outreach, counseling to clients explaining available services, case management, and referrals to services such as mental health treatment, housing, benefits, and other critical supports. Access to around-the-clock emergency services is available, as is help in establishing eligibility for assistance and obtaining services under entitlement programs.

IMPORTANT NAMES
AND ADDRESSES

Association of Gospel Rescue Missions
7222 Commerce Center Dr., Ste. 120
Colorado Springs, CO 80919
(719) 266-8300
1-800-473-7283
FAX: (719) 266-8600
E-mail: info@agrm.org
URL: http://www.agrm.org/

**Center on Budget and Policy
Priorities**
820 First St. NE, Ste. 510
Washington, DC 20002
(202) 408-1080
FAX: (202) 408-1056
E-mail: center@cbpp.org
URL: http://www.cbpp.org/

Child Care Aware of America
1515 N. Courthouse Rd., 11th Floor
Arlington, VA 22201
1-800-424-2246
FAX: (703) 341-4101
URL: http://www.childcareaware.org/

Children's Defense Fund
25 E St. NW
Washington, DC 20001
1-800-233-1200
E-mail: cdfinfo@childrensdefense.org
URL: http://www.childrensdefense.org/

Community Solutions
125 Maiden Ln., Ste. 16C
New York, NY 10038
(646) 797-4370
URL: http://www.cmtysolutions.org/

**Innocenti Research Centre
United Nations Children's Fund**
Piazza SS. Annunziata, 12
Florence, 50122 Italy
(011-39-055) 20330
FAX: (011-39-055) 2033220
URL: http://www.unicef-irc.org/

**Joint Center for Housing Studies
Harvard University**
1033 Massachusetts Ave., Fifth Floor
Cambridge, MA 02138
(617) 495-7908
FAX: (617) 496-9957
URL: http://www.jchs.harvard.edu/

Kaiser Family Foundation
2400 Sand Hill Rd.
Menlo Park, CA 94025
(650) 854-9400
FAX: (650) 854-4800
URL: http://www.kff.org/

**National Alliance on Mental
Illness**
3803 N. Fairfax Dr., Ste. 100
Arlington, VA 22203
(703) 524-7600
FAX: (703) 524-9094
URL: http://www.nami.org/

National Alliance to End Homelessness
1518 K St. NW, Second Floor
Washington, DC 20005
(202) 638-1526
FAX: (202) 638-4664
E-mail: naeh@naeh.org
URL: http://www.endhomelessness.org/

**National Center for Children in Poverty
Columbia University**
215 W. 125th St., Third Floor
New York, NY 10027
(646) 284-9600
FAX: (646) 284-9623
E-mail: info@nccp.org
URL: http://www.nccp.org/

**National Center for Homeless Education
SERVE**
Gateway University Research Park
Dixon Bldg.
5900 Summit Ave.
Browns Summit, NC 27214

1-800-308-2145
FAX: (336) 315-7457
E-mail: homeless@serve.org
URL: http://center.serve.org/nche/

**National Center on Family
Homelessness
American Institutes for
Research**
201 Jones Rd., Ste. 1
Waltham, MA 02451
(781) 373-7080
FAX: (781) 899-3287
E-mail: info@familyhomelessness.org
URL: http://www.familyhomelessness.org/

**National Coalition for the
Homeless**
2201 P St. NW
Washington, DC 20037
(202) 462-4822
E-mail: info@nationalhomeless.org
URL: http://www.nationalhomeless.org/

**National Law Center on Homelessness
and Poverty**
2000 M St. NW, Ste. 210
Washington, DC 20036
(202) 638-2535
FAX: (202) 628-2737
URL: http://www.nlchp.org/

**National Low Income Housing
Coalition**
727 15th St. NW, Sixth Floor
Washington, DC 20005
(202) 662-1530
FAX: (202) 393-1973
URL: http://www.nlihc.org/

**Organisation for Economic Co-operation
and Development**
2 rue André Pascal
Paris, 75775 France

(011-33-1) 45-24-82-00
FAX: (011-33-1) 45-24-85-00
URL: http://www.oecd.org/

Southern Education Foundation
135 Auburn Ave. NE, Second Floor
Atlanta, GA 30303
(404) 523-0001

FAX: (404) 523-6904
URL: http://www.southerneducation.org/

Urban Institute
2100 M St. NW
Washington, DC 20037
(202) 833-7200
URL: http://www.urban.org/

U.S. Conference of Mayors
1620 Eye St. NW
Washington, DC 20006
(202) 293-7330
FAX: (202) 293-2352
E-mail: info@usmayors.org
URL: http://www.usmayors.org/

RESOURCES

The federal government is the premier source of facts on many issues related to social welfare, including poverty, employment, the welfare system, housing, and homelessness. A variety of government agencies and departments provide detailed data related to these issues in the form of reports, websites, and searchable databases.

Data gathered by the U.S. Census Bureau was central to compiling this book. The Census Bureau's searchable web portal *American FactFinder* was particularly helpful, as were the following reports: *Custodial Mothers and Fathers and Their Child Support: 2011* (Timothy Grall, October 2013), *Dynamics of Economic Well-Being: Poverty, 2009–2011* (Ashley N. Edwards, January 2014), *Health Insurance Coverage in the United States: 2013* (Jessica C. Smith and Carla Medalia, September 2014), *Income and Poverty in the United States: 2013* (Carmen DeNavas-Walt and Bernadette D. Proctor, September 2014), and *The Supplemental Poverty Measure: 2013* (Kathleen Short, October 2014).

The U.S. Department of Labor's Bureau of Labor Statistics (BLS) provides valuable data on wages and work patterns in its searchable web portal *Databases, Tables & Calculators by Subject* and its *Labor Force Statistics from the Current Population Survey*, on which it collaborates with the Census Bureau. The BLS also offers details about low-income workers in *A Profile of the Working Poor, 2012* (March 2014) and about minimum-wage workers in *Characteristics of Minimum Wage Workers, 2013* (March 2014). The Department of Labor's Employment and Training Administration offers data on unemployment compensation claims in *Unemployment Insurance Data Summary* (2014) and detailed historical data pertaining to the recipients of unemployment compensation in *UI Benefits Study: Recent Changes in the Characteristics of Unemployed Workers* (Marios Michaelides, August 2009).

The U.S. Department of Housing and Urban Development (HUD) is the source for much valuable data on homelessness, housing affordability, and subsidized housing programs. Among the HUD publications used in this book are *The 2014 Annual Homeless Assessment Report (AHAR) to Congress—Part 1: Point-in-Time Estimates of Homelessness* (Meghan Henry et al., October 2014), *The 2012 Annual Homeless Assessment Report (AHAR) to Congress—Volume II: Estimates of Homelessness in the United States* (Claudia D. Solari, Alvaro Cortes, and Scott Brown, September 2013), *HUD's Proposed 2015 Budget: Congressional Justifications* (March 2014), and *Worst Case Housing Needs 2011: Report to Congress, Summary* (February 2013).

Important data on federal nutrition programs came from the U.S. Department of Agriculture's (USDA) Food and Nutrition Service, which provides detailed tables about the National School Lunch Program, the School Breakfast Program, the Supplemental Nutrition Assistance Program, and the Special Supplemental Food Program for Women, Infants, and Children. Additionally, the USDA's Economic Research Service provides data on those Americans whose food needs either go unmet or are in danger of going unmet in *Household Food Security in the United States in 2013* (Alisha Coleman-Jensen, Christian Gregory, and Anita Singh, September 2014).

Other valuable data came from the U.S. Department of Health and Human Services' (HHS) Office of Family Assistance, in particular the report *Temporary Assistance for Needy Families Program (TANF): Tenth Report to Congress* (December 2013). The Centers for Disease Control and Prevention (CDC), which is also a part of HHS, was a valuable source of data on health care and illness. The CDC's National Center for Health Statistics report *Health, United States, 2013* (May 2014) offers particularly useful insights into the connections between poverty and health.

Many different organizations study the poor and homeless. Notable among them for their many studies on poverty and homelessness are the Urban Institute (UI) and the Center on Budget and Policy Priorities (CBPP). UI publications used in preparing this volume include *How Has the TANF Caseload Changed over Time?* (Pamela J. Loprest, March 2012), *SNAP's Role in the Great Recession and Beyond* (Sheila Zedlewski, Elaine Waxman, and Craig Gundersen, July 2012), and *Welfare Rules Databook: State TANF Policies as of July 2013* (Erika Huber, David Kassabian, and Elissa Cohen, September 2014). CBPP publications that were useful in compiling this book include *Chart Book: TANF at 18* (August 2014) and *Contrary to "Entitlement Society" Rhetoric, over Nine-Tenths of Entitlement Benefits Go to Elderly, Disabled, or Working Households* (Arloc

Sherman, Robert Greenstein, and Kathy Ruffing, February 2012) and the "Policy Basics" features on its website that provide up-to-date overviews of all major federal public assistance programs.

Additional information on poverty, homelessness, and related issues came from a variety of organizations, including the Association of Gospel Rescue Missions, the National Center for Homeless Education, the National Alliance to End Homelessness, the National Coalition for the Homeless, the National Law Center on Homelessness and Poverty, the U.S. Conference of Mayors, the Joint Center for Housing Studies of Harvard University, the Henry J. Kaiser Family Foundation, and the Innocenti Research Centre of the United Nations Children's Fund.

INDEX